Representation in Western Music

Representation in Western Music offers a comprehensive study of the roles of representation in the composition, performance, and reception of Western music. In recent years, there has been increasing academic interest in questions of musical interpretation and meaning and in music's interactions with other artistic media, and yet no book has dealt extensively with representation's important role in these processes. This volume presents new research about musical representation, with particular focus on Western art and popular music from the nineteenth century to the present day. It assembles essays by an international assortment of leading scholars on a range of subjects including instrumental music, opera, popular song, dance, cinema, and the music video. Individual sections address representation, interpretation, and musical meaning; music's relationships with visual modes of representation; musical representation in dramatic forms; and the functions of music in the representation of identity.

JOSHUA S. WALDEN is Andrew W. Mellon Postdoctoral Fellow at Johns Hopkins University and Peabody Conservatory. After earning his PhD at Columbia University, he held a Junior Research Fellowship at Merton College, University of Oxford. His articles appear in the *Journal of the American Musicological Society*; *Musical Quarterly*; *Journal of Musicological Research*; *Journal of the Society for American Music*; and elsewhere. His primary area of research considers the intersecting influences of nationalism, modernism, and technological innovation on representations of ethnic and national identities in twentieth-century art music. He has also published essays on film music, eighteenth-century music, and intersections between music and the visual arts. He has taught at Johns Hopkins, Oxford, Columbia, and the University of California, Davis.

Representation in Western Music

Edited by JOSHUA S. WALDEN

CAMBRIDGE
UNIVERSITY PRESS

CAMBRIDGE
UNIVERSITY PRESS

University Printing House, Cambridge CB2 8BS, United Kingdom

Cambridge University Press is part of the University of Cambridge.

It furthers the University's mission by disseminating knowledge in the pursuit of education, learning and research at the highest international levels of excellence.

www.cambridge.org
Information on this title: www.cambridge.org/9781107021570

© Cambridge University Press 2013

This publication is in copyright. Subject to statutory exception and to the provisions of relevant collective licensing agreements, no reproduction of any part may take place without the written permission of Cambridge University Press.

First published 2013

A catalogue record for this publication is available from the British Library

Library of Congress Cataloguing in Publication data

Representation in western music / edited by Joshua S. Walden.
    p. cm.
Includes bibliographical references and index.
ISBN 978-1-107-02157-0 (Hardback)
    1. Music–Philosophy and aesthetics.   2. Music–Social aspects.   3. Mental representation.
I. Walden, Joshua S.
ML3800.R37 2013
781.1–dc23

    2012029087

ISBN 978-1-107-02157-0 Hardback

Cambridge University Press has no responsibility for the persistence or accuracy of URLs for external or third-party internet websites referred to in this publication, and does not guarantee that any content on such websites is, or will remain, accurate or appropriate.

For Susanna, Danny, and my parents

Contents

List of illustrations [*page* ix]
Notes on contributors [xi]
Acknowledgements [xv]

Introduction [1]
JOSHUA S. WALDEN

PART I REPRESENTATION AND THE INTERPRETATION
OF MUSICAL MEANING [11]

1 Layers of representation in nineteenth-century genres:
  the case of one Brahms *ballade* [13]
  MATTHEW GELBART

2 'As a stranger give it welcome': musical meanings in 1830s
  London [33]
  ROGER PARKER

3 'Music is obscure': textless Soviet works and their phantom
  programmes [47]
  MARINA FROLOVA-WALKER

4 Representing Arlen [64]
  WALTER FRISCH

5 Video cultures: 'Bohemian Rhapsody', *Wayne's World*,
  and beyond [79]
  NICHOLAS COOK

PART II SOUND AND VISUAL REPRESENTATIONS:
MUSIC, PAINTING, AND DANCE [101]

6 'On wings of song': representing music as agency in
  nineteenth-century culture [103]
  THOMAS GREY

7 Representation and musical portraiture in the twentieth century [127]
JOSHUA S. WALDEN

8 Representational conundrums: music and early modern dance [144]
DAVINIA CADDY

PART III MUSICAL REPRESENTATIONS IN OPERA AND CINEMA [165]

9 Allusive representations: homoerotics in Wagner's *Tristan* [167]
LAURENCE DREYFUS

10 *Der Dichter spricht*: self-representation in *Parsifal* [182]
KAROL BERGER

11 Memory and the leitmotif in cinema [203]
GIORGIO BIANCOROSSO

12 Self-representation in music: the case of Hindemith's meta-opera *Cardillac* [224]
HERMANN DANUSER, TRANSLATED BY J. BRADFORD ROBINSON

PART IV MUSIC, REPRESENTATION, AND THE CONCEPTS OF EAST AND WEST [247]

13 Doing more than representing western music [249]
RACHEL BECKLES WILLSON

14 The persistence of Orientalism in the postmodern operas of Adams and Sellars [267]
W. ANTHONY SHEPPARD

Afterword: what else? [287]
RICHARD TARUSKIN

Index [310]

Illustrations

0.1 Max Klinger, *Accorde* from *Brahms-Phantasie*, c.1894. Courtesy Davison Art Center, Wesleyan University. Photo Credit: John Wareham. [2]

1.1 Diagram showing the genre *ballade* within some broader genre groupings. [17]

6.1 Benedetto Montagna, 'Orpheus', 1500–20. 26 × 19.6 cm. © Trustees of the British Museum. [105]

6.2 Marcantonio Raimondi (after Raphael), 'St Cecilia', c.1480–c.1534. 25.4 × 16 cm. Image © Sterling and Francine Clark Art Institute, Williamstown, Massachusetts, USA (photo by Michael Agee). [106]

7.1 Chuck Close, b.1940, *Phil*, 1969. Synthetic polymer on canvas, 108¼ × 84 × 2¾in. (275 × 213.4 × 7 cm). Whitney Museum of American Art, New York; purchase, with funds from Mrs Robert M. Benjamin 69.102. © Chuck Close, courtesy The Pace Gallery. [131]

8.1 R. Moreau, *Loïe Fuller dansant* (à la Carrière), c.1904. Calotype, 15.5 × 11.4 cm. Courtesy of the Musée Rodin, Paris (Ph 1674). [153]

8.2 Gino Baldo, study of a metachoric figure, 1914. Lithograph of pen and ink drawing. Courtesy of the Jerome Robbins Dance Division, The New York Public Library for the Performing Arts, Astor, Lenox, and Tilden Foundations. [155]

8.3 Gino Baldo, drawing of Saint-Point, 1914. Lithograph of pen and ink drawing. Courtesy of the Jerome Robbins Dance Division, The New York Public Library for the Performing Arts, Astor, Lenox, and Tilden Foundations. [157]

10.1 Richard Wagner, *Parsifal*, director Hans Jürgen Syberberg, Act III, at 39:45. [183]

11.1–11.2 Evelyn Mulwray rescues J.J. 'Jake' Gittes, *Chinatown* (dir. by Roman Polanski, 1974). [204]

12.1 Paul Hindemith, note on the sequence of numbers in the plan for Lully's opera *Phaëton* in Act III of *Cardillac* (1952). Source: Hindemith Institute, Frankfurt am Main. [231]

13.1 Front cover of *The School Song Collection*, ed. Khalil Totah (Jerusalem, 1921).   [258]
13.2 'The Song of the Institute for Teacher Training', from *The School Song Collection*, ed. Khalil Totah (Jerusalem, 1921).   [260]

Contributors

KAROL BERGER teaches musicology as the Osgood Hooker Professor in Fine Arts at Stanford University. His books include *Musica Ficta* (Cambridge University Press, 1987), which won the Otto Kinkeldey Award of the American Musicological Society; *A Theory of Art* (Oxford University Press, 2000); and *Bach's Cycle, Mozart's Arrow* (University of California Press, 2007), which won the Marjorie Weston Emerson Award of the Mozart Society of America.

GIORGIO BIANCOROSSO is Associate Professor in Music at the University of Hong Kong. He has published in the areas of musical aesthetics, film music, Hong Kong cinema, and the psychology of music in *ECHO, SHIMA, Music and the Moving Image, Music and Letters*, and *Music Analysis*. He has contributed chapters, most recently, to *The Routledge Companion to Film and Philosophy* and *Wagner and Cinema*. He is completing a book entitled *Musical Aesthetics Through Cinema* for Oxford University Press. Biancorosso is active as a curator and programmer and is a member of the Programme Committee of the Hong Kong Arts Festival.

DAVINIA CADDY is Senior Lecturer at the School of Music, University of Auckland. She completed a doctorate at Cambridge University and a Junior Research Fellowship at The Queen's College, Oxford. Her research interests include French music, culture, and criticism during the *belle époque*, with special focus on ballet, opera, singing, and gesture. Her first book, *The Ballets Russes and Beyond: Music and Dance in Belle-Époque Paris,* was published by Cambridge University Press in 2012. She is currently working on an edited volume provisionally entitled *Towards a Musicology of Dance*.

NICHOLAS COOK is 1684 Professor of Music at the University of Cambridge. From 2004 to 2009 he directed the AHRC Research Centre for the History and Analysis of Recorded Music (CHARM). He is the author of nine books on topics from Beethoven to multimedia; the most recent, *The Schenker Project: Culture, Race, and Music Theory in Fin-de-siècle Vienna* (2007), won the 2010 Wallace Berry Award of the

Society for Music Theory. His *Music: A Very Short Introduction* has appeared in fourteen different languages. He was elected Fellow of the British Academy in 2001.

HERMANN DANUSER is Professor of Historical Musicology at the Humboldt University in Berlin. He coordinates the research of the Paul Sacher Foundation in Basel and is a member of the Berlin-Brandenburg *Akademie der Wissenschaften*. In 2005, Royal Holloway, University of London, bestowed upon him an honorary doctorate. His research interests include music history and historiography since the eighteenth century, aesthetics, music theory, analysis, and interpretative practices. His book *Weltanschauungsmusik* was published by Edition Argus in 2009. He is currently writing a monograph on metamusic.

LAURENCE DREYFUS, Professor of Music at the University of Oxford and a Fellow of Magdalen College, has written two books on J.S. Bach, *Bach's Continuo Group* and *Bach and the Patterns of Invention*. His book *Wagner and the Erotic Impulse* was published by Harvard University Press in 2010. He leads the viol consort Phantasm and was elected a Fellow of the British Academy in 2002.

WALTER FRISCH is H. Harold Gumm/Harry and Albert von Tilzer Professor of Music at Columbia University. He has written widely about music from the Austro-German sphere in the nineteenth and twentieth centuries, and about the history of early modernism. He serves as general editor of a new series from W.W. Norton, *Western Music in Context*, for which he has written *Music in the Nineteenth Century*, to appear in late 2012. He is planning a book-length study of the music and career of Harold Arlen.

MARINA FROLOVA-WALKER is Reader in Music History at the Faculty of Music, University of Cambridge, and Fellow of Clare College. She received her PhD from Moscow Conservatoire before moving to the UK. She is the author of *Russian Music and Nationalism from Glinka to Stalin* (Yale University Press, 2007) and co-author of *Music and Soviet Power, 1917–32* (with Jonathan Walker; Boydell and Brewer, 2012), and has written numerous scholarly articles and popular essays on Russian and Soviet music and culture.

MATTHEW GELBART is Assistant Professor in the Department of Art History and Music at Fordham University. He is the author of *The Invention of 'Folk Music' and 'Art Music': Emerging Categories from Ossian to*

Wagner (Cambridge University Press, 2007) and has published articles in several journals. He is currently working on a new book project on musical genre and romantic ideologies.

THOMAS GREY, Professor of Music at Stanford University, is the author of books and essays on Richard Wagner, opera, nineteenth-century music and aesthetics, and music and visual culture. He is editor of *Richard Wagner: Der fliegende Holländer* (Cambridge University Press, 2000), *The Cambridge Companion to Wagner* (Cambridge University Press, 2008), and *Richard Wagner and His World* (Princeton University Press, 2009).

ROGER PARKER teaches at King's College London. He is general editor (with Gabriele Dotto) of the Donizetti critical edition. His most recent book, written jointly with Carolyn Abbate, is *A History of Opera*, due out with Penguin in November 2012. He is now working on a study of music in London in the 1830s.

W. ANTHONY SHEPPARD is Professor of Music at Williams College. His first book, *Revealing Masks: Exotic Influences and Ritualized Performance in Modernist Music Theater* (University of California Press, 2001), received the Kurt Weill Prize, his article on *Madama Butterfly* and film earned the ASCAP Deems Taylor Award, and his article on anti-Japanese World War II film music received the Alfred Einstein Award from the American Musicological Society. He has been supported by grants from the Institute for Advanced Study, the National Endowment for the Humanities, and the American Philosophical Society, and is currently completing a book entitled *Extreme Exoticism: Japan in the American Musical Imagination*.

RICHARD TARUSKIN is Class of 1955 Professor of Music at the University of California at Berkeley. He is the author of *Stravinsky and the Russian Traditions, Defining Russia Musically,* and the *Oxford History of Western Music*. His essays appear in the recent collections *On Russian Music* and *The Danger of Music and Other Anti-Utopian Essays* (University of California Press, 2008).

JOSHUA S. WALDEN is Andrew W. Mellon Postdoctoral Fellow at Johns Hopkins University and Peabody Conservatory. He has held a Junior Research Fellowship at Merton College, University of Oxford and an Edison Fellowship from the British Library Sound Archive. His articles appear in journals including the *Journal of the American Musicological Society, Musical Quarterly,* and the *Journal of Musicological Research*. He is editor of the *Cambridge Companion to Jewish Music,* currently in progress.

RACHEL BECKLES WILLSON is Reader in the Music Department at Royal Holloway, University of London. Her research into the music politics of Eastern Europe and Palestine has been published in two monographs and over twenty book chapters and journal articles. Her most recent book was *Ligeti, Kurtág, and Hungarian Music during the Cold War* (Cambridge University Press, 2007). While based at the Humboldt University in Berlin, funded by a Fellowship for Experienced Researchers from the Alexander von Humboldt Foundation, she wrote her monograph *Orientalism and Musical Mission: Palestine and the West* (Cambridge University Press, forthcoming 2013). She is now studying Arabic and Turkish *ouds* and their associated repertories, supported by the Leverhulme Trust.

Acknowledgements

This volume originated in a conference on 'Music and Representation' that took place at Merton College, University of Oxford, 26–28 March 2010. For their sponsorship of this event, I wish to acknowledge the John Fell OUP Research Fund, the Institute of Musical Research, the Royal Musical Association, the Music and Letters Trust, the British Society of Aesthetics, and the Oxford faculties of Music and Philosophy. I am thankful to Douglas Bamber, Anna Maria Busse Berger, Andy Byford, Suzannah Clark, Eric Clarke, Christopher Doll, Peter Franklin, Walter Frisch, Daniel Grimley, Nicolette Makovicky, Caroline Massey, Anthony Newcomb, Hollis Robbins, Elaine Sisman, Gabrielle Spiegel, Elizabeth Tolbert, Julia Walworth, Clifford Webb, and Susan Weiss for their help and advice at various stages of the conference organization and the creation of this book. I undertook this project as a Junior Research Fellow at Merton College and an Andrew W. Mellon Postdoctoral Fellow at Johns Hopkins University, and I am grateful to these institutions for their support. Tremendous thanks are due to Victoria Cooper, Teresa Royle, Rebecca Taylor, and Fleur Jones at Cambridge University Press for their invaluable advice throughout the process of creating this volume.

I would like to express my appreciation to Wye J. (Wendy) Allanbrook, my mentor during my undergraduate studies at the University of California, Berkeley, for providing support as I embarked on this project in 2009. Since I enrolled in her seminar on Mozart many years ago, I have always been inspired by Wendy's path-breaking writings on *topoi* in eighteenth-century music, and her work as well as her kindness have often been in my mind as I have edited this volume. She is deeply missed.

Finally, I am immensely thankful, as ever, to Susanna Berger, Daniel Walden, and my parents, Michael Walden and Judith Schelly, for their love, kindness, and endless good ideas.

∽ Introduction

JOSHUA S. WALDEN

On the first of January 1894, the artist Max Klinger presented Johannes Brahms with a publication titled *Brahms-Fantasie*, Opus XII, which contained a collection of the composer's scores printed alongside images depicting mythic figures and dramatic landscapes inspired by the music.[1] Klinger insisted that these were not 'illustrations', but something more introspective and interpretive; he explained, 'I wanted to move outward from the judgments into which we are led – led blindly – by poetry and above all music.'[2] The first image in the score, *Accorde* (Chords), depicts a fantastical scene illustrating music's power to transport the listener and performer (Figure 0.1). On the right edge of the print, in the corner of a bourgeois parlour, Klinger himself sits in profile, playing the piano. To his left, the room's walls have disappeared and a curtain has been pulled back, revealing a stormy seascape and craggy island terrain. In the way it emerges behind the domestic interior as though from the back of the pianist's mind, this dramatic space appears to be a depiction of the mental representation conjured in Klinger's imagination by Brahms's music. At the right edge of the water and below Klinger's parlour floor, a nereid plays the harp – a reminder, perhaps, of Orpheus's lyre, a common allegory of music in the visual arts – as a triton holds firmly to the body of the instrument. On the treacherous waters, a small, vulnerable ship sails towards the island, approaching a cove set amid the rocks. The boat appears to stand in for the listener, navigating across the virtual musical landscape.

Brahms was fascinated by Klinger's score, and approved of the artist's renderings of the mythical figures and landscapes that the music inspired in his imagination. Brahms wrote to Klinger that when he looked through the book:

> I see the music, together with the nice words – and then your splendid engravings carry me away unawares. Beholding them, it is as if the music resounds farther into the infinite and everything expresses what I wanted to say more clearly than would be possible in music, and yet still in a manner full of mystery and foreboding ... I must conclude that all art is the same and speaks the same language.[3]

In Brahms's description, his music and Klinger's prints evoke the same ideas, though the images do so with more precision than the sounds; visual and musical arts speak the same 'language', but the former with greater clarity than the latter.

Figure 0.1 Max Klinger, *Accorde* from *Brahms-Phantasie*, c.1894. Courtesy Davison Art Center, Wesleyan University. Photo Credit: John Wareham.

Klinger's score and Brahms's enthusiastic response bring to the fore a number of important questions about the nature of musical representation. How does music convey meaning, and in what ways are its processes of doing so different from and similar to those of other art forms? How can music be conceived of as a language, and why might this language be less clear than literature or visual representation? How, as listeners and performers, do we interpret music, forming mental representations of what we hear and play, and what is the relationship between our impressions and the composer's own ideas of what he or she aimed to evoke in the music? The question at the centre of this volume is how music operates as a representational art. The concept of representation in the study of music refers to the relationship between musical sounds and the meanings that listeners derive from them. The term 'representation' is typically understood in three principal ways in discussions of music. First, and most simply, it has been used to denote mimesis, the process by which a composer creates the resemblance of recognizable sounds in a work of music – musical references to birdsong and flowing water, or quotations of pre-existing melodies, might be examples of this sort of representation. Second, it is often employed to explain the manifestations of music in performances and texts. For example, 'representation' is sometimes invoked to explain the relationship of a performance to the sheet music;

of a musical score to the composer's ideas; of a transcription to a performance; or of critical, scholarly, and literary discussions of music to the sounds they describe. And third, it is used in a broader sense to characterize the ways listeners interpret more abstract meanings from music, such as emotion, narrative, values, place, and identity. These uses of the term 'representation' are also the subject of debate, as a number of the chapters in this book will show.

Perhaps not surprisingly, scholars have addressed the concept of representation more frequently in connection with literature and the visual arts than with music, because questions of resemblance and meaning have seemed more straightforward in these art forms. In the nineteenth century, the concept of instrumental music as an 'absolute' art form made the notion of music's representational capacities a subject of contention among some musicians and commentators. Such an understanding of music's autonomy, of its abstraction from the social worlds of its listeners, has by today lost most of its adherents; composing and performing music and attending concerts are commonly understood to be social activities in which people communicate through and interpret music, respond to it emotionally, or contemplate it in relation to other works of music.[4] In recent years, there has been increasing academic interest in these modes of interpretation and the ways music conveys meaning, subjects explored in studies of music's reception, interactions between music and other art forms, music's social and cultural functions, and the uses of music in identity construction and political movements.

These trends underscore the importance of the study of representation in music. This book shows how representation can be understood to operate in musical composition, performance, and listening from the early nineteenth century to the present, and identifies the key terms in the debate over the concept in the field of musicology. Some chapters approach elements of music commonly associated with representation – for example, the leitmotif, the programme, or the semiotic properties of musical topics (gestures, figures, and styles considered to signify particular references or characteristics) – to explore new ways of understanding how these systems operate. Among other important issues that arise in a number of the book's chapters is the question of authorial intention, and how it should enter into discussions of how and what music represents. A few chapters also challenge the notion of representation, searching for other explanations of musical meaning.

The five chapters in Part I address topics related to 'Representation and the interpretation of musical meaning'. Interpretation can involve listening, performance, analysis, and other forms of activity, and, of course, these modes of interpretation often overlap with one another. These chapters ask what roles representation plays when we interpret music and derive meanings and expression from its structures and sounds. Matthew Gelbart's chapter opens Part I with a consideration of one of the fundamental ways by which musicians and listeners interpret compositions: through the expectations and meanings associated with musical genres. Gelbart argues that in the nineteenth century, the larger generic categories of art, folk, and popular music, as well as lower-level genres such as those defined by instrumentation, form, or programme, were increasingly thought to represent their intended audiences, by revealing characteristics about the values and tastes of groups of people differentiated by nationality, social class, and other attributes. In an investigation of the genre of the *ballade*, and in particular of Johannes Brahms's 1856 *Ballade* Op. 10, no. 1, Gelbart shows that contemporary listeners interpreted the work to convey meanings not simply through the mimetic effects of its implied programme, but by virtue of the more complex representational conventions of the relatively new genre of the *ballade* and the broader overarching genres of which it was a component, including art music.

In the following chapter, Roger Parker pursues another association between representation and interpretation in the nineteenth century that is similarly linked to issues of audience and genre, in a study of writings about musical aesthetics and meaning in journalism and criticism. Parker explores documents from the early decades of the century to view what they reveal about the burgeoning of concert life and developments in audiences' musical tastes in London in the 1830s. Parker tracks the ways cultural commentators described the emergence of an 'elite' musical audience, the expansion of interest in new concert repertoire, and the growth of middle-class music-making in the home, particularly with the increasing availability of the domestic piano. The chapter views how these journalistic voices interpreted the meanings and values they saw represented in these changes. Parker also addresses a related anxiety of the age that resulted from the association of musical genres and their audiences (as described in Gelbart's chapter): some audiences expressed a growing sense of alarm about the new popularity of instrumental music among the lower social classes, because of the difficulty of controlling and censoring music lacking in text and, thus, in clear meanings. This concern led many to attempt to further stratify musical participation by reserving vocal music for the working classes and instrumental music only for the 'elite'.

The third chapter similarly addresses anxiety over what instrumental music represents to its listeners and how external control can be exerted over its reception, here in the context of musical sponsorship, censorship, and aesthetics in the Soviet Union. Marina Frolova-Walker considers instances of the Soviet government's attachment of particular interpretations to instrumental works, often without regard for the intentions of their composers. State officials developed what Frolova-Walker calls 'phantom programmes' for textless compositions, publicizing these interpretations by printing them in journalistic reviews and deliberately spreading rumours about the works' putative nicknames, sources, and subject matter. The attribution of meaning to instrumental works often involved the retroactive identification in their scores of musical topics – gestures, figures, and styles considered to signify particular meanings or characteristics – that were typically nationalist in nature and often related to the theme of war. Frolova-Walker considers music criticism and minutes from official meetings to examine the history of this interpretive practice.

The final two chapters of Part I turn from the question of meaning in instrumental music to consider the role of representation in interpretations of twentieth-century popular song in performances, recordings, film, and video. In Chapter 4, Walter Frisch examines the contribution of Harold Arlen during the period known as the Golden Age of American popular song, to address how Arlen and the singers with whom he worked, particularly Judy Garland and Barbra Streisand, represented his music in their performances and recordings through the nuanced interpretation of his scores. Frisch analyses what Alec Wilder has called Arlen's 'thoroughness' – his unique ability to write out his songs and accompaniments in full detail without the help of an arranger – by examining 'The Man That Got Away' and 'A Sleepin' Bee' from their initial conception, through their notation, and finally to their performance. By exploring the history and content of these songs, Frisch shows how Arlen's repertoire can be understood to represent Arlen himself, by containing in their intricate formal structures evidence of the 'thoroughness' of his activity as a collaborator, composer, and performer.

The chapter that follows also investigates the roles of representation in the field of popular song: focusing on Queen's 'Bohemian Rhapsody', Nicholas Cook considers how the iconic status of the original music video has influenced the subsequent interpretation of the song. Cook approaches the question of representation from multiple perspectives. He first examines how the video's visual component operates as an extension of the music, blurring the distinction between presentation and representation. From here, he asks how the song is visualized in the film *Wayne's World*, in a passage in which the music retains a dominant position over the filmic accompaniment, becoming a representation of the values of the protagonists. Finally, he asks what this case study can tell us about how musicologists represent their subject matter.

He sorts through the numerous video remakes of the song, both professional and amateur, that can be found on the internet, viewing how the music has inspired a participatory culture in which fans produce their own personal multimedia interpretations, sharing them with others in order to carve a role for themselves in the song's history. Cook concludes by asking how musicology, a discipline that has traditionally privileged original, canonical works, might be expanded to account for such instances of the reception, interpretation, and appropriation of music.

In Part II, 'Sound and visual representation: music, painting, and dance', three chapters address overlaps and interactions between aural and visual modes of artistic representation. Thomas Grey investigates nineteenth-century conceptions of the medium of music, looking at representations of music in painting, poetry, and, finally, music itself. Grey employs the term 'representation' to refer to the concept of 'mental representations', imagined perceptions of objects in the mind. He argues that whereas before the nineteenth century music was typically represented through allegory – for example, in the figure of Orpheus or St Cecilia – during the period he considers there was a move away from allegory towards imagining music's effects on listeners, its agency. Representations of music during this time invoked a trope of song as transcendent, capable of disembodying, lifting, and transporting immaterial objects such as feelings, prayers, or souls. Grey examines scenes representing this sort of musical apotheosis in theatrical works including Wagner's *Tristan* and late nineteenth-century productions of Goethe's *Faust*. Finally, he examines instances of the merging of these standard modes of representing music – through musical allegory and the evocation of music's agency – in multiple works of visual art as well as in the third movement of Robert Schumann's Fantasy Op. 17. Grey explains how Schumann composes figures in his Fantasy that aim self-reflexively to represent the medium of music, signifying harmony, melody, and its other attributes.

In my chapter, I consider the ways in which music can represent itself and other art forms to be a question of central importance to the investigation of recent works of musical portraiture. My chapter explores compositions in this genre that represent contemporary artists and musicians, including Philip Glass's 'A Musical Portrait of Chuck Close' and György Ligeti's 'Selbstportrait mit Reich und Riley (und Chopin ist auch dabei)'. These works represent their subjects not only by capturing aspects of their characters and biographies, but more importantly by evoking their artistic styles and techniques. The titles of these works indicate that the music represents aspects of particular individuals, and invite listeners to consider the portraits' subjects, imagining aspects of their identities and artistry as depicted in musical notes. In keeping with the convention in portrait painting of depicting artists with the tools of their trade – such as brushes, paints, and easels – these musical portraits evoke the materials and styles their subjects employ in creating their art. In the case of Glass's portrait, brief melodic building blocks that form the work imitate the repeating patterns of Close's large-scale portraits; and in Ligeti's work, compositional techniques associated with all four composers are combined in a group portrait that reflects the oeuvres and techniques of each musician.

The final chapter in Part II addresses the question of music's relation to another form of visual art, one that incorporates music's temporal element: dance. Davinia Caddy explores contrasting ways three dancers and choreographers at the turn of the twentieth century – Jean d'Udine, Loie Fuller, and Valentine de Saint-Point – conceived of how their art should respond to, reflect, or contradict the sounds and structures of music. These three choreographers found innovative ways to engage with the compositions to which they designed their dances, exploring contrasting modes of the physical and visual representation of music. They also represented their conceptions of the association between dance and music in their aesthetic writings. By mining this textual legacy, Caddy investigates how these artists articulated their views of the rich and nuanced interrelation between music and dance. In her chapter, she reveals what they contributed to early twentieth-century notions of musical representation, and extends the discussion begun in the previous two chapters about artistic modes of representing music, here through the movement of the dancing body.

Part III explores the subject of musical representation in opera and cinema. The first three chapters address questions of musical meaning in leitmotif and orchestration, and the fourth turns to address an example of reflexive musical self-representation in the genre of meta-opera. In the opening chapter, a study of homoerotic friendship in Richard Wagner's *Tristan*, Laurence Dreyfus offers an opportunity to question how music produces meaning in dramatic forms. Dreyfus contends that the complex relationship between music and meaning is better served by the notion of musical metaphor than by representation, which he considers too narrowly associated with the simple processes of mimesis. Dreyfus shows how Brangäne's declaration of her affection for her mistress Isolde and King Marke's and Kurwenal's expressions of devotion to Tristan allude to a form of homoerotic love that reflects Wagner's own support of the concept of *Freundesliebe*, or romantic friendship, and his close relationship with his male followers. Through analyses of two leitmotifs he calls the *Freundesliebe* and Silken Longing motifs, Dreyfus argues that these gestures act as musical metaphors, as allusions to homoerotic love that enable the listener to achieve a richer understanding and experience of the music.

In the chapter that follows, Karol Berger further pursues questions of operatic meaning, returning to the concept of representation to contemplate the role of the orchestra in Wagner's music. Berger explores how we might understand the orchestra's music as another voice in the opera's texture. He asks whose voice it is – in other words, whose point of view is being represented through the orchestral writing and leitmotifs? To pursue this question, Berger turns to *Parsifal*. Berger concludes that orchestral leitmotifs can generally be heard as representations of the 'inner world', the conscious and unconscious thoughts and subjectivities, of the characters onstage. In some rare instances such as the 'Good Friday Spell' in Act III, however, the orchestra's music can be attributed to an invisible narrator, the composer himself. Through an intricate analysis of this scene and its place in the opera, Berger shows why the extended orchestral melody represents a narrator's voice, not the characters' inner thoughts, emerging from the orchestra pit as Wagner's gloss on the dramatic action. And like Dreyfus, Berger shows how an understanding of Wagner's values and beliefs, as revealed in his writings, letters, and earlier works, can inspire the listener's interpretation of the meanings conveyed by his orchestral leitmotifs.

The subsequent chapter further pursues the question of how leitmotifs work, in this case in the context of the cinematic soundtrack. Giorgio Biancorosso reconsiders prevalent explanations of the ways leitmotifs come to identify particular characters and ideas in film scores, seeking to move beyond the understanding of leitmotifs as musical signifiers of fixed meaning. With particular attention to Jerry Goldsmith's music for Roman Polanski's film *Chinatown*, Biancorosso examines the complex processes by which leitmotifs are introduced, and seeks to show how their meanings can change over the course of a film. Rather than being associated with meanings in a process akin to the way people acquire proper names, cinematic leitmotifs come to represent characters, ideas, places, or events through a dynamic process in which memory plays a crucial role. Biancorosso explains that the representational function of a leitmotif depends on the listener's recognition of the gesture's earlier iterations in the soundtrack, including its first appearances, before its referent could be recognized. The leitmotif, he shows, typically achieves meaning in retrospect, and through experience and recollection.

The final chapter in Part III turns from leitmotif and orchestration to the question of musical self-representation in opera, in an investigation of operatic borrowing in meta-opera. Hermann Danuser opens his chapter with a discussion of musical representation that addresses the four media in which music can be represented: sound, notation, words, and images. In addition to representing music, these media can also represent one another, or stand for music 'as a whole' (a phenomenon explored in the chapters in Part II). All four of these media are present in opera, and their combination is particularly visible in meta-opera – operatic works in which multiple levels of narrative weave together in a way that reflexively foregrounds the genre of opera. Danuser illustrates his arguments about musical self-representation and meta-opera with a study of the revised version of Paul Hindemith's *Cardillac*. When he returned to the opera almost three decades after he first composed it, Hindemith incorporated a scene of *mise en abyme* in which the characters perform passages of Jean-Baptiste Lully's opera *Phaëton*, whose narrative and music intertwine in complex ways with those of Hindemith's work.

The final section of the book in Part IV addresses representation's roles in the construction of concepts of East and West through music. In a chapter about historical writings on music in Ottoman and British Mandate Palestine, Rachel Beckles Willson describes the problematic nature of the term 'western', and the role that the traditional understanding of representation has played in the development of the opposing notions of 'westernness' and 'non-westernness' in music. Seeking to find a remedy to the one-dimensionality that can result from traditional readings of music as representational, Beckles Willson follows Hayden Lorimer in adopting the understanding of historical sources as 'more-than-representational', allowing her to address the roles of representation while looking beyond them for a richer understanding of history. By focusing on Palestine, Beckles Willson can re-examine European visitors' written descriptions of music-making in the Middle East and also explore how the category of 'western music' was conceived of in colonized communities, with the ultimate goal of breaking from a notional rigid binary of the 'west' and its others, through an expanded understanding of representation.

In the final chapter, W. Anthony Sheppard further pursues the roles of representation in the construction of 'western' and 'eastern' identities and cultures and the displacement of 'others' in music through an examination of exoticist representation in recent works of opera. Although some composers and musicologists alike have described the end of operatic exoticism in the postmodern era, Sheppard argues, the style is still in common use to mark characters, places, and on-stage musical performances occurring within the narrative as different and separate from the world of the spectator. Sheppard looks particularly at four works by John Adams and Peter Sellars – *Nixon in China, A Flowering Tree, The Death of Klinghoffer*, and *Doctor Atomic* – to identify examples of the persistence of older musical techniques of exoticism. He contrasts Adams and Sellars's statements about contemporary multiculturalism and their belief that they have transcended exoticizing representation with examples of traditional techniques for marking ethnic 'others' in their music, librettos, and staging.

In his Afterword, Richard Taruskin recalls scholarship on musical representation from recent decades, to map out new strategies for understanding the roles representation plays in musical composition, performance, listening, and historiography. Taruskin examines a wide variety of forms of musical representation, surveying issues from mimetic tone painting in the choral works of J.S. Bach and Handel and the signification of topics in eighteenth-century composition to the uses of music to represent identities in the contexts of nationalism and political organizations. Finally, Taruskin suggests an understanding of artistic representation in music that depends on the concept of affordance as described by philosopher and musician Charles O. Nussbaum. When we listen to music, we form an internal mental representation of virtual musical space through which we move, as we interpret meanings and experience emotional responses. Different musical passages afford different sorts of actions within this imagined space: we move quickly through some and step back in others. This is a description of how we understand music through representation that perhaps returns us to Max Klinger's depictions of the experience of listening to Brahms. Through the study of affordance and representation, writes Taruskin, we can better understand how we are moved by music, and are inspired to move along with it, as we negotiate our way across these virtual musical landscapes.

Notes

1 For a detailed study of Klinger's *Brahms-Fantasie*, see Walter Frisch, *German Modernism: Music and the Arts* (Berkeley and Los Angeles: University of California Press, 2005), 93–106. See also Leon Botstein, 'Brahms and Nineteenth-Century Painting', *19th-Century Music*, 14.2 (Autumn 1990), 154–68 (166–8). The full document, with high-resolution images of each page, can be viewed at www.wesleyan.edu/dac/view/brahmsphantasie/index.html (accessed 2 May 2012).
2 Frisch, *German Modernism*, 95.
3 *Ibid.*, 96.
4 On the history of philosophies of musical meaning and contemporary notions of musical meaning in social and cultural contexts, see Ian Cross and Elizabeth Tolbert, 'Music and Meaning' in Susan Hallam, Ian Cross, and Michael Thaut (eds.), *Oxford Handbook of Music Psychology* (Oxford University Press, 2011). On musical representation in relation to cultural and social contexts, particularly as understood in the field of ethnomusicology, see Philip V. Bohlman, 'Music as Representation', *Journal of Musicological Research*, 24.3–4 (2005), 205–26.

PART I

Representation and the interpretation of musical meaning

1 | Layers of representation in nineteenth-century genres: the case of one Brahms *ballade*

MATTHEW GELBART

'It takes all sorts to make a world; and each sort must have its music', wrote George Bernard Shaw in 1890. He continued, 'There is the stupid sort, for instance: the people who cannot follow the thread of any connected entertainment; whose attention cannot stand a ten minutes' strain.' When Shaw saw a concert entitled 'the unique and incomparable Bohee operatic minstrels' at the Café Monaco, he 'took the title as a guarantee that the audience would be tolerably simple folk'; so he went along to see that this gullible audience would not be unduly fleeced.[1]

A clear subtext of Shaw's quips is the entrenchment in the late nineteenth century of the split between so-called art music and popular music, groupings that map loosely onto several related binary oppositions.[2] This type of musical ordering indicates a growing correlation of genre labels with specific audience groups, and if we look deeper into blatant statements such as Shaw's, we will also find that such correlation occurs not only at the level of the broadest categories such as popular, art, and folk music, but also for many narrower categories as well. In this chapter, I want to expose and explore this phenomenon.

Before the nineteenth century, taxonomies of genre (and its related variables, mode and style) dealt with the representation of character; however, the emphasis was more on the character depicted in the music rather than on the character of the creators and audiences. From Tinctoris to Mattheson to Koch and beyond, we have orderings of musical genres tied to appropriate affects, mapping onto expression of high, middle, and low character[3] – but these generally sidestepped the question of *who* made or listened to the music. Increasingly in the nineteenth century, genres came to 'represent', as cultural capital, their makers and audiences as well.

I would not want to overplay this paradigm shift too heavily, for genre labels large and small had always carried hints of social identity within them. Whether it was an early eighteenth-century English public divided over whether or not to embrace the foreign style of Italian opera, or a recognition of the difference between *Kenner* and *Liebhaber* well before romantic ideologies set in, there was never a time when it was possible for social animals such as humans to ignore the question of who made and who responded to different types of music. Similarly, on the other side of the coin, new nineteenth-century typologies of genre did not ignore criteria of character *depicted* and methods for such depiction. Rather than a clean break from earlier ways of thinking about music, the nineteenth century presents a period during which assertions and assumptions of special affinities between different social groups and different types of music came starkly centre stage in musical discourse despite the fact, or probably largely because of the fact, that more traditional ways of considering genre in music were partially breaking down.[4]

When they began to enter formal taxonomies of musical types, criteria focusing on social identity were sometimes grafted irregularly onto more established systems. An example is Johann Nikolaus Forkel's discussion of genre from the ending years of the eighteenth century. Along traditional lines, Forkel treats genre under the umbrella of musical rhetoric and relates it to apposite styles for expressing different moods, or for effect in different settings. But in his discussion of fugue and counterpoint, he also introduces the idea that homophony represents individuals, whereas polyphony represents an entire people, and he not only dismisses those who fail to appreciate counterpoint along these lines as wrong, but implicitly also sorts them into a social 'sort' that cannot grasp great music: they are branded as lacking understanding of the complexity of human emotions and society.[5] Although Forkel's specific ideas are personal and idiosyncratic, they also demonstrate a new direction.[6]

Over the course of the nineteenth century, links between genres and audience types moved from quirky asides within function-based typologies such as Forkel's into the centre of the discourse. Indeed, they progressively came to dominate discussions of musical type. By the time Shaw wrote about the Bohee minstrels in 1890, what *communities* were 'represented' as both music-makers and audiences had become one of the primary factors in parsing music – with the assumption that music, musicians, and audiences would gravitate towards each other if they matched in attributes, like pet-owners and their pets. Whether those communities were national groups, social classes, or more amorphous collectives shaped by personality type, Shaw's quip that 'each sort must have its music' actually summarized and crystallized a great deal of musical and aesthetic argument from the later nineteenth century.

I want here to consider some possible relationships between representations of audience and other elements channelled through genre labels. I suggest that the increasing trend for audiences to identify with larger genre categories, to see them as representing themselves and their values, can situate a genre label to a large extent – and by so doing, determine and shape some of the most essential elements of musical experience. This assertion runs against many twentieth-century studies of musical genre after 1800. Generally, these studies continued to be governed by the romantic ideologies they supposedly dissected. An example is Dahlhaus's extensive writing on genre, which embraced and even treated as axiomatic the romantic claim that genre more or less lost meaning when composers become truly original. In this narrative, which prioritizes the claims and actions of composers themselves, the force of genre begins to ebb in the early nineteenth century, and by the late twentieth, genre practically ceases to be an important concept in musical communication.[7] Thus, on one level, my approach aims to present a corrective to such accounts. Not only are reception and listener response in general vital aspects of musical communication, alongside composers' claims, but I also believe that the increasing correlation across the nineteenth century of audience values to genre labels (through self-identity or through the stereotypes of others) in fact means that reception-driven generic concerns must become *more* central to understanding how musical communication was shaped in this period, rather than less. Indeed, social connotations governed and determined many apparently 'free' creative choices by composers rather than vice versa.

Nevertheless, the extent to which the full symbolic 'meaning' of a genre label can be isolated through a social-group-based reception approach is still limited. If romantic composers were relatively constrained by the social implications of large categories (what I have elsewhere called 'meta-genres' and 'governing genres'), when it came to the smallest sub-genres, the audience groups were not differentiated, and listener expectations in general were more flexible. At this level, a social framework generally fails to distinguish sub-genres from each other. Where specified labels for narrow sub-genres are not roughly synonymous or interchangeable, then other factors must come into play to distinguish between them. Form, subject matter, and other aspects of 'character' (now the emotion in the music, separated from the general character of its audience) can all isolate individual sub-genres. But in many cases, we must also turn to conjecture about the creative process of genre creation and inflection, grounding a winnowed understanding of how a specific label works in more speculative and old-fashioned discussion of composerly concerns. This is especially true when we think about relatively new labels, as opposed to more established ones such as symphony or concerto. Even here, however, considerations of authorial intention and conjecture about the creative process must remain balanced by and often subjugated to the social concerns discussed above if they are to present a full picture of how a genre articulates meaning. Otherwise, we fall back into the trap of imagining musical meaning entirely as intention, and miss both the importance and the complexity of genre as a mediator of music's significance and effects.

As an example, I will focus here on one genre, the piano *ballade*, and in fact, on one piece: Brahms's *Ballade* Op. 10, no. 1, in D minor, published in 1856. Since the *ballade* genre was so new in the middle of the nineteenth century, it presents a case that exaggerates the truism that genre labels are in constant flux. Chopin more or less created the label as a name for an instrumental piece, and those composers who applied it later, as James Parakilas has studied,[8] took very different approaches, so that an audience's expectations for a piece called a *ballade* would have been defined (again, as with any genre tag, but more so) by their expectations about the composer as well as about audience values. This exaggerated version of a generalized situation thus highlights the creative and receptive aspects of genre formation or inflection – both separately and in mutual interaction and influence.

Op. 10, no. 1 was the first piece to which the young Brahms applied the label *ballade*, and he would use it for only four more pieces afterwards, three published with this one. At a time when some avant-garde composers consciously sought to apply new names to many of their pieces (and sometimes denied that such names constituted genres at all, although they did, of course),[9] Brahms was a composer who was particularly sensitive to older ideas about genre. He had a great respect for established genre labels at a narrow level and fastidiously considered 'appropriate' archetypal models in each genre when he first explored it. He modelled his sonatas on Beethoven and Schumann, his early chamber music on Schubert, his concertos on Mozart and Beethoven, and so forth.[10] Such a clear vision of generic propriety, however, poses new challenges in understanding those cases where Brahms applied a title that was *not* a time-honoured tradition, such as here. Particularly striking is the fact that Brahms chose to depart rather blatantly from Chopin's approach to the *ballade*, rather than treating this one established set of models for the label as normative. The question at hand, then, is: in light of Brahms's sensitivity to minute aspects of genre history, his sense of propriety in what constituted acceptable innovation in each type of composition, what might have inspired the use of a relatively new label, in a completely new sense, and how did such a decision fit into the socially determined constraints of writing music in the 1850s in Germany?

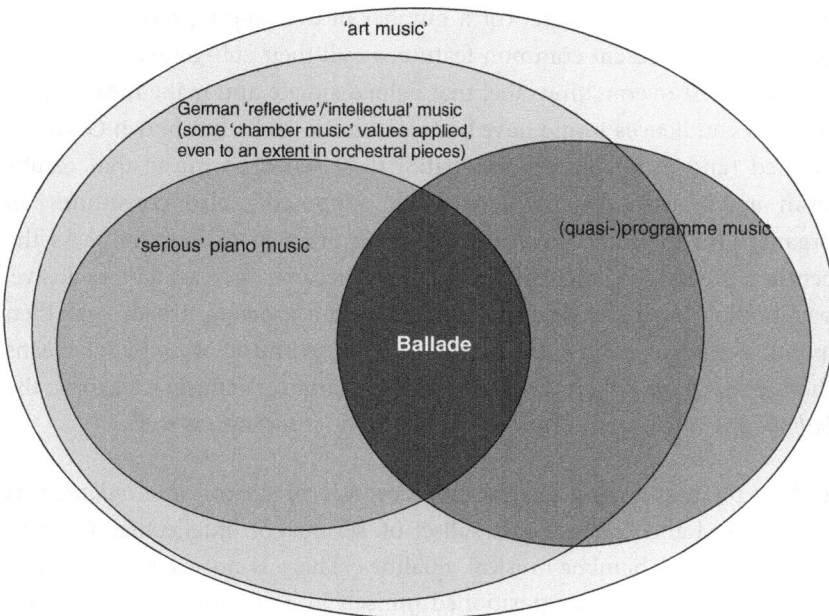

Figure 1.1 *Ballade* within some broader genre groupings.

A note before continuing: it should be obvious that I am using the word 'genre' to cover a wide array of different musical labels, from what Hermann Danuser has called musical *Oberbegriffe* down to the smallest sub-genres, and in between.[11] I begin from the position that these levels cannot be separated cleanly – that overarching groupings such as 'classical', 'folk', and 'popular' music, by virtue of being mutually dependent for their own definitions, came to determine important elements of the categories that formed discursively below them. At the same time, very specific labels such as *ballade* had repercussions on all broader groupings discursively above them. Here I will refer to all of these different divisions of music with the term 'genre' without further discussion – because the word has, historically, been used in ideologically charged ways at all these levels – and I will look at a small example of how meta-genres, genres, and small sub-genres might interact to create meaning through different types of representation.

First, let us consider the 'horizon of expectations' that an audience would have held when first encountering a *ballade* by Brahms in the 1850s in Germany,[12] paying particular attention to the reflection of audience values in different categories. As Figure 1.1 makes clear, the *ballade*, like any genre label, fits within a set (or a number of overlapping sets) of broader genres, which present common features in all their sub-genres.

The largest overarching label that helped situate and make meaning for Brahms's audiences would have been 'art music' in its full-blown German-defined (and generally German-nationalist) sense, as music that results from assiduous individual labour yet supposedly also constitutes an organic growth from a national collective or mass of humanity. As the century progressed, the 'art music' label became increasingly exclusive, partitioning out more and more music into a growing 'trivial' and then 'popular' category. But meta-genres such as 'art music' were by no means themselves monolithic. Thus, within the large art music category, the *ballade* fits into various smaller, overlapping groupings as well.

1 As a piece appealing to Brahms's devotees in general, the *ballade* was conceived and received as a subset of 'serious' or 'intellectual' German music, with 'chamber-musical' qualities. There is no need to review in full here how Brahms positioned himself in a community that, contra Wagner and his camp, stressed established contrapuntal and formal techniques, and was seen to be driven by many of the 'reflective' values associated with chamber music. (It is thus that Wagner and Wagnerian critics, for example, objected to Brahms's alleged importation of such intellectual 'chamber music' qualities even to his symphonic music, which they felt should be more accessible and anthemic.) Yet it is worth reaffirming that the use of certain generic labels, small and large, was part of what established such camps. These labels (symphony versus tone poem, etc.) were politically loaded.[13] Furthermore, such aesthetic camps show how a composer's name could itself become almost a generic category in reception, through close association with a particular approach to music, and thus a particular public. The name 'Brahms', for instance, especially after Schumann's 'Neue Bahnen' article in the *Neue Zeitschrift für Musik*, became closely linked with an intellectual, politically liberal population that valued gravitas and respect for artistic tradition. Indeed, Shaw himself had almost as little patience for Brahmsians as for the audience of the Bohee minstrels, suggesting in several quips that the primary public for Brahms was people who simply thought anything staid, studied, and pious must be good music.[14]
2 A *ballade* was also a subset of 'serious' music specifically written for one instrument: the piano. Instrumentation played an important role in the growing association of genre labels with audience communities too, partly because of the centrality of public concerts and related institutions

to romantic musical community-building. William Weber has recently charted how, in the mid-nineteenth century, concert programmes became more varied in one way, by presenting music from more historical periods, while at the same time they became much more uniform in terms of performing forces (i.e., instrumentation) and in terms of 'levels of taste'.[15] That is, pieces that shared a concert (and hence a conceptual grouping) were increasingly judged using the same values and criteria. A review in the *Allgemeine musikalische Zeitung* of an 1872 piano concert given in Vienna by Hans von Bülow shows the application of a common yardstick to various piano pieces from several eras. The reviewer discussed the placement of the Brahms *Ballades* along with the composer's Handel Variations and Scherzo Op. 4 on the programme, where it followed Bach's Chromatic Fantasy and Fugue, more Bach, and Mozart's Sonata in F major, K. 533. The reviewer is full of praise for the Brahms works as a whole, using terms such as 'high artistic value' and 'brimming with life'. He also finds that Bülow's decision to follow the Brahms with an E minor suite by Joachim Raff, a composer championed by the pianist, only made Raff's music look less masterful in comparison.[16] In sum: a Brahms *ballade* was expected to appeal to the same audiences as Brahms's other finely wrought intimate music, and to be judged – often in shared concert programmes – in comparison to other keyboard music, from across several eras, that was conceived (or re-conceived) as 'serious' piano music.

3 Additionally, the *ballade* was part of a subset of genres that implied a programme. In fact, in a collection on 'representation in Western music', programmatic concerns might have seemed the obvious place to begin to look at such a piece. However, to consider narrative and mimetic representation meaningfully from the perspective of genre, programmatic elements must be considered in the context of other factors. In Op. 10, no. 1, the programme is specific. The printed music bears the inscription 'after the Scottish Ballad, Edward, in Herders's *Voices of the Folk* collection'. The ballad text unveils piece by piece a dialogue between the eponymous character and his mother, in which she questions why his sword drips with blood. Edward is at first evasive, though he later reveals not only that he has killed his father, but also, in the final climactic moment, that he did so on his mother's counsel – and he curses her to hell. In context, what is most striking about the programme of this piece is that it is somewhat of an anomaly. Most piano *ballades* (including the others by Brahms) imply a narrative by the very use of the *ballade* title, but do not reveal their stories explicitly. Thus, what seems at stake in understanding *ballade* as a genre is not a particular programme, but what *ballades* share or do not

share with other programmatic genres appreciated by the same audiences. In the case of this piece, we should ask how the uncharacteristically specific programme dovetails into these broader concerns.

At times narrative representation (i.e., a programme) and representation through self-image (i.e., the sense of communal identity in the music that I have been emphasizing) may be related by homology. Karol Berger has argued of Chopin's *Ballade* Op. 23 that the aspirations and the narratives of selfhood treasured by exiled Polish émigré audiences for the *Ballade* in Paris might be conflated with imagined eschatological narrative strategies in the piece.[17] And these parallels are not inconsistent with various attempts to find more specific programmes in Chopin's *Ballades*, such as in Jonathan Bellman's recent book on Op. 38.[18] In the Brahms work at hand, however, the difference between a communal identity and the narrative development may seem more resistant to immediate conflation: a tale of bloody patricide executed on a mother's advice does not easily sit with the self-images of Brahms's target audience. We should remember, however, that the resonance between audience identity and implied narrative in music (for instance in Berger's analysis of the Chopin *Ballade*) is not the actual story, but the way it is presented. This abstract reverberation remains crucial in Brahms's case. Early reviews of the Brahms Op. 10 *Ballades* focused on the fact that the narrative is suggested in a manner consistent with the values that Brahms's devotees sought in *all* music, and/or all piano music.

A reviewer in the *Signale für die musikalische Welt* wrote when Op. 10 was first published: 'One will be particularly moved by the *original* harmonies, which erupt with a certain natural force ... In these pieces, you hear "Edward, Edward" and the tragic "Oh" better than any narrator could express it. The rhythm and harmony have a stark, acerbic quality, a defiant attitude, then a half-woolly melancholy ... it is all chilling.'[19] Some terms of praise here, such as 'defiant' and 'melancholy', suggest the particular character of this *ballade*, but they are couched in plaudits such as 'natural' and 'original' – which are the same qualities that bind the critical framework for the larger German art-music domain discussed above. Similarly, when the reviewer criticizes Brahms, bemoaning the composer's apparent penchant for occasionally slipping into harmonic and formal chaos, he stresses that this is a general flaw in the composer's style, rather than a trait unique to this opus, or caused by programmatic striving. Another example comes in an 1882 article by Gustav Doempke on Brahms's piano music in the 'family'-oriented *Musik-Welt*. Though ostensibly an admirer of the composer, Doempke used the article to attack Brahms's apparent lack of self-regulation in juxtaposing elements the critic found incompatible. The article spends some time on the Op. 10 *ballades*, and while it hints that in the *ballades* some 'quirks' were possibly 'dramatic' in motivation, Doempke's criticism clearly and explicitly extends to Brahms's style in general, especially other early works such as the Sonata in F sharp minor. His objections are evidently not to any programmatic nature of the *ballades* in particular, but once again to what they represent as part of a larger body of 'serious' piano music.[20] The gory story of Edward is thus accepted (or rejected) by an audience community insofar as it fits with a vision of what 'serious' piano music should be, and what art music should be in general.[21]

So far we have situated the Brahmsian *ballade* in a complex of other genres. But it is more than a subset of larger categories; it is also a specific, chosen designation. Neither its programmatic aspects nor its 'serious' nature separate it very far from several other labels used by the composer, or other composers for that matter. Given the nineteenth-century penchant for reading implied narratives into *many* pieces, the borders of the programmatic are nebulous and vague. To isolate the *ballade* further, we might start by noting the label's unique connotations. Audiences might have expected to find in any piano *ballade* archaizing and folk-like elements in the music (modal implications, etc.) and in the stories they were encouraged to imagine. Yet even the presence of apparent 'folk' elements cannot single out the *ballade*, since the romantics conceived of 'folk music' as an organic source for all the best art music.[22] Recall that Schumann even discussed Zuccalmaglio's suggestion to rename the symphony genre the 'bardiet' – indicating Germanic and ancient bardic origins.[23] So what then *is* left to define the *ballade* more specifically, in isolation or at least nearer isolation? To consider this, I will move the focus here somewhat away from audiences and onto speculation about Brahms's ideas – while trying to keep in sight the connections between these two focal points.

We can ask two particularly helpful questions. First: how did Brahms initially come to apply the label *ballade* to a piano piece? And second: once he chose to apply the label more times, what common features bind together the works he so designated?

Since the piece at hand is Brahms's first *ballade*, we stand at a moment when a key decision was made about genre by the composer. Paul Mies suggested in 1920 that the composition began as a vocal melody, inspired by the final stanza of Herder's text, but was then turned into a piano

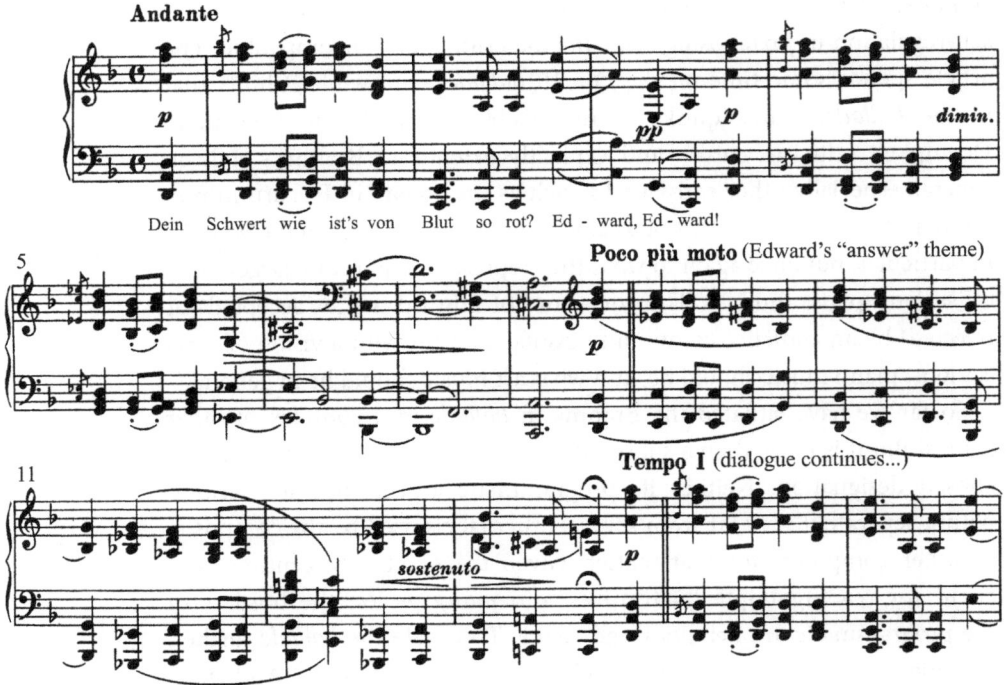

Example 1.1 Brahms, *Ballade* Op. 10, no. 1, opening, with Herder's opening text underlaid.

piece.[24] This makes logical sense, and Brahms's friend and biographer Max Kalbeck had noted already before Mies that the opening of Op. 10, no. 1 lines up exactly with the words of Herder's version of 'Edward' – it could be sung to them. Furthermore, with two alternating themes at the beginning, Op. 10, no. 1 is presented as a dialogue, just like the poem, featuring one melody that aligns with the mother's questioning, and a second melody that seems to align with Edward's answers (Example 1.1). It appears that what suggested the title *ballade* to the composer was not the model of Chopin's *ballades* but the fact that this work was inspired by a specific text ballad. And rather than starting from the notion of shaping the *ballade* narrative mimetically, as Chopin seems to have done, Brahms apparently initially sought to reflect the text's *poetic* form, in this case a dialogue form. However, as Parakilas has pointed out, one cannot use strophic repetition to pattern an entire textless *ballade*, and the strophic dialogue mould here must soon break to present a more traditionally mimetic rendering of the action.[25] Brahms's piece thus turns into an ABA form and works within that form towards a cataclysmic climax suggesting Edward's last response in the poem, and using his initial 'answer' theme (from m. 44, Example 1.2).

However, for my purposes, what ends up being most striking in this *ballade* is not the climax itself, but what happens afterwards. While the poem ends with the cataclysm, expressed as a curse in first person, Brahms's climax peters out and, after a pause, the *ballade* then offers a bleak, stammering denouement based on the mother's theme (from m. 60, Example 1.2) – and lasting roughly a third of the whole performance time.

Kalbeck saw the Op. 10 ballades as 'continuations or analogues' of the middle movements from Brahms's early piano sonatas.[26] This rings true, as those movements, featuring poetic mottos and references to vocal song, also seem to experiment with how to mirror and eventually move away from a direct reflection of poetic structure (strophic and otherwise), in a patently instrumental setting.[27] John Rink's observation that the long and irregular coda to the slow movement of the Op. 5 sonata invokes a 'sudden, unforeseen abandonment of a vocal idiom' and an 'instrumental commentary' on what has been a shadow-vocal number goes to the heart of the matter.[28] In fact, I find that Rink's characterization applies even more to the *ballade* at hand than to Op. 5. In the Op. 5 movement, there are several moments of disjuncture towards the end of the piece, each potentially offering another layer of commentary.[29] However, in Op. 10, no. 1 there is but one crucial moment, where despite the appearance of a vocal theme transformed, the poetic text contraindicates the presence of any further human 'voice'. Rather, a new non-singing 'voice' emerges at this break, precisely what Carolyn Abbate has explored in those special moments when musical rupture seems to create a 'past tense' – to shove the mimetic action we have followed into a separate time frame from the present and to comment on it.[30]

In Rink's discussion of the earlier Op. 5 sonata movement coda, he also mentions possible predecessors: the piano postludes to Beethoven's *Ferne Geliebte* and especially Schumann's *Dichterliebe*. Again, this is an extremely compelling comparison, and again the idea of these pieces as models seems at least or even more fitting here with Op. 10. The piano postludes to those song cycles are key loci where the idea was inscribed of romantic instrumental music attaining its own voice, a poetic voice with the power to create a synthetic, organic whole and to take over where the poetic protagonist does not, in fact cannot, finish the story.[31] Indeed, to those examples might be added the end of *Frauenliebe und Leben*, and on a smaller scale many individual Schumann Lieder.[32] Thus, while in genres with strong precedents Brahms was very dependent on models from the

Example 1.2 Brahms, *Ballade* Op. 10, no. 1, conclusion.

same genre, in the case of the *ballade* (or even with individual middle movements in the early sonatas), he appears to have felt that the field was open enough to take inspiration from a genre that was further removed at least in terms of performing forces: vocal Lieder.

Of course, the transfer and abstraction of the vocal to the instrumental had precedents itself – most notably and explicitly in Mendelssohn's *Lieder ohne Worte*. But Brahms seems to have emphasized different elements from Mendelssohn, who had organized his pieces around lyricism and the suggestion that instrumental music could be more accurately descriptive than words.[33] The distinguishing quality of Brahms's transfers of vocal-type pieces to piano solos is the distancing frame, characteristic of many Schumann Lieder.[34] In fact, it is narrower than this. The distancing that emerges in Brahms's *ballades* (not just the first, as we shall see) is different from the bardic 'strumming' frames in some nineteenth-century works (even including some Schumann Lieder). That strumming implies a narrator as human character, and one who is probably historically distant from us as well, himself a relic of the past. In Brahms's *ballades*, however, I would argue that the framing device reinscribes the *modern* and the instrumental, creating discursive distance from the action by drawing attention to the power of organic, romantic piano music itself – and by extension flattering and representing the values of the modern community of listeners who could appreciate it.

We are beginning to come full circle, back to the issue of audience values. Kalbeck devoted a substantial passage in his biography to discussing the power of Brahms's coda in Op. 10, no. 1:

The musician's bleak coda achieves for the poet's ballad an epilogue of tragic proportion and weight. The composer in no way here oversteps the boundaries set forth for a musical narrator – but he may also, as a painter of the soul, like Beethoven in his great Leonora overture, unite the [roles of] Lyricist and Dramatist with [that of] the epic poet.[35]

Here Kalbeck's Brahms, like Beethoven at his best, moves beyond narration to create a modern 'synthetic' genre in the Schlegelian sense. Kalbeck invokes the romantic cliché of fusing Goethe's 'natural' poetic forms (lyric, epic, and dramatic).[36] The biographer's emphasis is in no way on the ability of music to represent by indicating or imitating specific extra-musical ideas, but rather on the power of modern instrumental music to achieve its own potent voice beyond such miming. Similarly, that power is vested not in a virtuoso performer, but supposedly in 'the music' at a more cerebral level.[37] In sum, the *ballade* for Brahms comes into being as an assertion of the discursive authority of instrumental music to frame implied song, drawing on Brahms's great mentor, Schumann, for inspiration – but transferring the Schumannian disjunctive, commenting coda from actual song to a purely instrumental genre. And it is this assertion of the ability of modern instrumental music to speak and frame *independently* of either a text or a specified programme that helped Brahms's audiences see themselves represented and reflected in the music – and thus set themselves apart from devotees of the New German School.

The four other piano pieces that Brahms called *ballade* share a common feature: they too all end quietly, dissolving or transforming material from earlier in the piece, implying a postlude to the action. For example, in the coda of Op. 10, no. 4, from the *poco a poco riten. e dim.* at m. 140, echoes of the *two* main melodic figures in the piece alternate and peter out (Example 1.3).[38] After Op. 10, Brahms used the *ballade* title once more, near the end of his life, for Op. 118, no. 3. This piece begins by storming in, *in medias res*. This is another ABA form, but after the build-up to the climactic reprise of A (at m. 105), it is the transformed, pensive, and interrupted head of the B section theme that returns *una corda* in the last four measures and dies out (Example 1.4). The dissolving, fractured epilogue becomes the defining feature of the Brahmsian *ballade* generic label.[39]

We will never actually get to the point where we can isolate the characteristics of one genre label from all others at all times, certainly not through one single feature. It would of course be silly to try to do so, since once a label comes into being, it is immediately in a constant state of transformation, affected by each new piece that earns the label, and indeed each hearing of the same piece by new ears in new contexts.[40] But by considering the process through which the label was first applied by Brahms, we can get closer to understanding how a free creative choice – the adaptation and inflection of a new genre by a specific composer – works within a broader framework of 'generic contracts' and audience values.

Chopin's *ballades* mainly end with the climax itself – a feature that certainly does not disqualify them from potentially being music for the 'serious' German, liberal, *bildungsbürgerlich* 'sort', in Shaw's terms. Indeed, Brahms's own *capriccios* for instance tend to end the same way, in climactic action. Nevertheless, the epilogue feature that perhaps most specifically demarcates the Brahmsian *ballade* also helps it work in a framework of broader genres that 'represent' its ideal audience, affirming their understanding of modern instrumental music as a powerfully synthetic, poetic, commenting 'voice' in the absence of grand programmatic claims or of singing.

Example 1.3 Brahms, *Ballade*, Op. 10, no. 4, conclusion.

Example 1.4 Brahms, *Ballade*, Op. 118, no. 3, conclusion.

Notes

1 George Bernard Shaw, *Shaw's Music: The Complete Musical Criticism in Three Volumes*, ed. Dan H. Laurence (New York: Dodd, Mead, 1981), vol. I, 955–6 (14 March 1890).

2 Schumann's metaphorical *Davidsbündler* battling the Philistines already adumbrated such a dichotomy. However, over the years between the writings of Schumann and Shaw, the urbanization of Europe and a series of other social and economic changes helped add, to the difference in *Bildung* implied in Schumann's division, further criteria for differentiating serious and popular music types: most notably social class, national identity, and, later, racial overtones. All these can be found echoing around in Shaw's dismissal of the Bohee minstrels and their audiences.

3 Examples and quick outlines of several of these groupings can be found in Hermann Danuser's article on 'Gattung' in Ludwig Finscher (ed.), *Die Musik in Geschichte und Gegenwart*, Sachteil, 2nd edn, 10 vols. (Kassel: Bärenreiter, 1995), vol. III, 1046–51.

4 By shunning the most rigid definitions of genre's functions from earlier periods, the nineteenth century left barer (and hence more glaring) one core of the functional aspect of genre: community-building.

5 Johann Nikolaus Forkel, *Allgemeine Geschichte der Musik*, 2 vols. (Leipzig: Schwickert, 1788), vol. I, 43–9, esp. 47–8.

6 It is thus no coincidence that Forkel's description of fugue and counterpoint – its organic mediation between the individual and the *Volk*, and its need for an understanding audience – in fact anticipates the conception of the more general meta-genre of 'art music' that would emerge in the next generation.

7 See, for example, Carl Dahlhaus, 'Zur Problematik der musikalischen Gattungen im 19. Jahrhundert' in Wulf Arlt, Ernst Lichtenhahn, and Hans Oesch (eds.), *Gattungen der Musik in Einzeldarstellungen: Gedenkschrift Leo Schrade* (Bern: Francke, 1973), 840–95; *Foundations of Music History*, trans. J.B. Robinson (Cambridge University Press, 1983), passim; *Esthetics of Music*, trans. William W. Austin (Cambridge University Press, 1982), esp. 14–15; and 'New Music and the Problem of Musical Genre' in *Schoenberg and the New Music*, trans. Derrick Puffett and Alfred Clayton (Cambridge University Press, 1987), 32–44. Claims such as Friedrich Schlegel's that 'of the modern genres there exists only one or infinitely many. Every poem is a genre unto itself' seem to underpin Dahlhaus's narrative (cited in Hans Eichner (ed.), *Literary Notebooks, 1797–1801* (University of Toronto Press, 1957), 116).

8 James Parakilas, *Ballads without Words: Chopin and the Tradition of the Instrumental* Ballade (Portland, OR: Amadeus Press, 1992).

9 Not only do new labels to a certain extent inherently establish new genres, whether or not they are conceived that way, but, more importantly, they also undeniably fit into systems and frameworks of genres that need to be considered together. I argue elsewhere that as avant-garde composers claimed to dispense with genre, they were largely arguing about sub-genres, while their claims left mid-level 'governing' genres such as 'chamber music' intact, and in fact strengthened and formed 'meta-genres' such as 'art music'. See Matthew Gelbart, 'Speaking of Music in the Romantic Era: Dynamic and Resistant Aspects of Musical Genre' in Keith Chapin and Andrew Clark (eds.), *Speaking of Music* (New York: Fordham University Press, forthcoming).

10 See, for example, Charles Rosen, 'Influence: Plagiarism and Inspiration', *19th-Century Music*, 4.2 (1980), 87–100; and James Webster, 'Schubert's Sonata Form and Brahms's First Maturity', *19th-Century Music*, 2.1 (1978), 18–35, and 3.1 (1979), 52–71.

11 Danuser, 'Gattung', 1042–3.

12 On the horizon of expectations, see Hans Robert Jauss, *Towards an Aesthetic of Reception* (Minneapolis: University of Minnesota Press, 1982), esp. 22–4 and 39–44.

13 As Michael Vaillancourt put it recently in an article on Brahms's use of the label *Serenade*: 'Many contemporary critics understood genre as a coded collection of stylistic features that could be employed by a composer to assert allegiance to an aesthetic position.' Vaillancourt, 'Brahms's "Sinfonie-Serenade" and the Politics of Genre', *Journal of Musicology*, 26 (2009), 379–403 (380).

14 'Academic gentlemen' and 'those who, having found by experience that good music bores them, have rashly concluded that all music that bores them must be good' (*Shaw's Music*, vol. II, 376–7). He mocks English audiences in general for

appreciating Brahms just because he keeps a severe countenance, and for listening with their 'in-churchiest expression' (II, 93). Shaw's opinion of Brahms was at best ambivalent. It was most particularly derived from the critic's famous backhanded reaction to Brahms's *German Requiem*. ('You feel at once that it can only have come from the establishment of a first-class undertaker' (II, 67).)

15 William Weber, *The Great Transformation of Musical Taste: Concert Programming from Haydn to Brahms* (Cambridge University Press, 2008).
16 'Berichte. Nachrichten und Bemerkungen, Wien', *Allegemeine musikalische Zeitung*, 47 (1872), 755–7.
17 Karol Berger, 'Chopin's Ballade Op. 23 and the Revolution of the Intellectuals' in John Rink and Jim Samson (eds.), *Chopin Studies 2* (Cambridge University Press, 1994), 272–83.
18 Jonathan Bellman, *Chopin's Polish Ballade: Opus 38 as Narrative of National Martyrdom* (Oxford University Press, 2010).
19 *Signale für die musikalische Welt*, 14.18 (1856), 201–2.
20 In fact, a recurring element in Doempke's article is the common objection that Brahms's music is *too* 'serious', too overlaboured. Thus, Doempke openly touches on genre by asserting that Brahms's *capriccios* are not light enough for the label, and that his piano music suffers from the apparent contradiction that it requires a virtuoso to play (and a man, as a woman's hands generally are not large enough), but is not aimed towards a large audience – rather at a small intellectual gathering, or at the performer himself (Gustav Doempke, 'Aus der Correspondenz eines jungen Brahms-Verehrers an einem alten', *Musik-Welt: Musikalische Wochenschrift für die Familie und den Musiker*, 2 (1882), 43–5 and 51–3).
21 A couple of generations later, the English organist Edwin Evans went even further, in his *Handbook to the Pianoforte Works of Johannes Brahms* (London: William Reeves, 1936). Evans asserted that the programmes in Brahms's *ballades* were presented successfully since 'A constant feature of Brahms' [sic] melodies is that they are always manly' (even when expressing feminine sentiment), because there is no 'Southern' brooding submission to fate here (110–12).
22 It is a question of degree, since German 'art-music' was basically defined around the idea that it grew organically from a folk element. See Matthew Gelbart, *The Invention of 'Folk Music' and 'Art Music': Emerging Categories from Ossian to Wagner* (Cambridge University Press, 2007).
23 Robert Schumann, *On Music and Musicians*, ed. Konrad Wolff, trans. Rosenfeld (New York: Pantheon, 1946), 48.
24 Paul Mies, 'Herders Edward-Ballade bei Joh. Brahms', *Zeitschrift für Musikwissenschaft*, 2.4 (1920), 225–32, esp. 229. Mies also sees the basis of Op. 10, no. 1 as variation form (231).
25 Parakilas, *Ballads without Words*, 141. And Kalbeck had already noted that the text lines up with music as though it could be sung at the start, and, as he sees it, then breaks away almost immediately (Max Kalbeck, *Johannes Brahms*

(Vienna and Leipzig: Wiener Verlag, 1904), vol. I, 197). Mies makes a similar analysis ('Herder's Edward-Ballade', 232-3).

26 Kalbeck, *Brahms*, vol. I, 196. Kalbeck in fact sees these as middle movements to uncomposed sonatas.

27 The variations in Op. 1 might be considered as reflective of a strophic setting.

28 John Rink, 'Opposition and Integration in the Piano Music' in Michael Musgrave (ed.), *The Cambridge Companion to Brahms* (Cambridge University Press, 1999), 79–97 (82 and 85).

29 And indeed the entire 'intermezzo (Rückblick)' fourth movement might be seen as further such commentary.

30 Carolyn Abbate, *Unsung Voices: Opera and Musical Narrative in the Nineteenth Century* (Princeton University Press, 1991), 55–60.

31 John Rink, 'Opposition and Integration', 82. (Rink thus also cogently relates these moments to the end of *Kinderszenen*, 'Der Dichter spricht'.)

32 For example, 'Wehmut' from the Eichendorff *Liederkreis*.

33 Recall his famous quote that 'A piece of music that I love expresses thoughts to me that are not too *imprecise* to be framed in words, but too *precise*' (cited in Peter Le Huray and James Day (eds.), *Music and Aesthetics in the Eighteenth and Early Nineteenth Centuries* (Cambridge University Press, 1981), 457).

34 It should be noted that a possible precedent within the piano *ballade* genre was Kullak's 1853 *ballade* 'Lenore', available in James Parakilas, *The Nineteenth-Century Piano Ballade: An Anthology* (Madison, WI: A-R Editions, 1990).

35 Kalbeck sees the final broken return of the opening as the 'babblings and stammerings of insanity', then: 'und die düstere Coda des Musikers verhilft der Ballade des Dichters zu einem Epiloge von tragischer Grösse und Weihe. Niemals überschreitet dabei der Komponist die ihm vorgesteckten Grenzen des musikalischen Erzählers, ob er auch als Seelenmaler, wie Beethoven in seiner grossen Leonoren-Ouvertüre, den Lyriker und Dramatiker mit dem epischen Dichter vereinigt' (*Brahms*, vol. I, 198). Note here that the combination of epic/lyric/dramatic as a modern whole is a romantic cliché (see John Daverio, *Nineteenth Century Music and the German Romantic Ideology* (New York: Schirmer Books, 1993), esp. 143–4). Mies sees the ending as following the impulse of instrumental music to round itself off, and he thus claims it is not 'programme music' in one sense. He compares it to the endings of Brahms's 'Song of Destiny' (Schicksalslied) Op. 54, and 'Song of the Fates' (Gesang der Parzen), Op. 89 (Mies, 'Herders Edward-Ballad', 232).

36 See Goethe, *West-östlicher Divan*, Johann Wolfgang Goethe Sämtliche Werke, Abt. I, vol. III/i, ed. Hendrik Birus (Frankfurt: Deutscher Klassiker Verlag, 1994), 206–8. Nineteenth-century literary and musical theorists often outlined teleological visions of how different genres might synthesize these basic forms into a modern or romantic whole. Kalbeck's description should be seen in this light.

37 Evans, writing around the same time as Kalbeck, claimed that, unlike in Chopin, in Brahms's *ballades* the pianist is 'not a person to be even thought of', and that Op. 10, no. 4 was the least successful because the figurations make the performer 'intrude', where the other three were based on the facts of the narrative (Evans, *Pianoforte Works of Johannes Brahms*, 118).

38 Meanwhile, in Op. 10, no. 3, when the A section returns (m. 93) it is *pianissimo* instead of *forte*, and it reaches its triple-piano ending without ever regaining its energy from its first presentation. The entire reprise thus seems like a spectral transformation of the dramatic opening, a postlude to the implied action. Op. 10, no. 2 has the least sense of a disjunctive postlude of all the ballads. But it too ends quietly, and by virtue of having its climax in the extended middle section, the entire return of the A section (from m. 118) again to an extent (if less than in Op. 10, no. 3) acts as an ethereal commentary on the climax, and the coda dissolves the music further to end *pianissimo*.

39 And it is notable that Schumann focused on the end of two in a letter to Clara when he first examined the music in 1855.

40 Brahms's *Romanze*, Op. 118, no. 5, shares many elements with his *ballades*, though here the epilogue, while quiet, is neither extended nor stressed. In some ways, the closest piece he wrote later and did not call a *ballade* is the *Intermezzo*, Op. 118, no. 6, with its climactic apotheosis of the main theme followed by a return of the quiet pensive version.

2 | 'As a stranger give it welcome': musical meanings in 1830s London

ROGER PARKER

> Horatio:
> O day and night, but this is wondrous strange!
> Hamlet:
> And therefore as a stranger give it welcome.
> There are more things in heaven and earth, Horatio,
> Than are dreamt of in your philosophy.
>
> *Hamlet*, Act I, scene 5

London has long been a musicologically peripheral nineteenth-century place: inevitably so, perhaps, given its paucity of indigenous composers of international standing (a situation endlessly lamented at the time); also given musicology's determined love-affair with the 'supply-side' of its subject. If your business was The Music Itself, then early nineteenth-century London did not detain you long, despite its otherwise robust claims to be (*pace* Walter Benjamin) the Capital of the Nineteenth Century. However, with changing times and mores, it might be that a nineteenth-century London musicological renaissance is now on the horizon, one whose chronological purview predates by a good half century that routinely celebrated national musical reawakening associated with Elgar and Vaughan Williams. These positive prospects partly have to do with the rapidly changing pragmatics of current research. A huge proportion of the printed matter that emerged from nineteenth-century London, whether in books, journals, or newspapers, is now online and text searchable, thus forming – for this as for many other disciplines – an archive of reception and social activity unparalleled anywhere else in the world. As the immensity of this archive suggests (no other city has remotely the volume of print that England's capital generated at this time), London boasted the largest musical public in Europe – which meant in the world – during most of the century, and its pre-eminence in the 1830s was especially pronounced. Famously, this was the result of its burgeoning middle class and 'their' burgeoning concert culture, although operatic life in the capital was also an industry of great vigour and prestige, superseded in splendour and budget only by Paris.

A brace of general ruminations can precede my main topic. One is broadly political. A concentration on the 1830s might seem inevitably to advance claims for that decade as an important moment of change – to dally once more with a weather-beaten old metaphor, as a 'watershed' in London's musical history. Such claims would almost inevitably start with reference to the most celebrated event in the 1830s British political calendar: the Reform Act of 1832, commonly seen as a vital step in the diffusion of political power, in particular in its gradual transfer to the middle classes from the aristocracy. However, as modern historians have repeatedly shown, the effect of the Act (as opposed to the rhetoric that often surrounded it) hardly weakened the power of the landed interest in the short term; indeed, in some ways it served to strengthen it.[1] The debates themselves were accompanied by alarming slippery-slope arguments among Ultra Tory opponents of the Act: if, they thundered, the so-called 'rotten' boroughs and their aristocratic privilege were taken away by parliament, then the royal family, the Church of England, the peerage, the Bank of England and the East India Company would in time disappear into the abyss.[2] Only the last of these august institutions eventually succumbed; the rest have survived – albeit in varying states of good health and good cheer – to the present day. However, it is now generally agreed that the Reform Act was important in a broader sense: one that proved, in the longest run, critical. It created a more secure self-awareness on the part of the middle classes, fractured and politically weak though that class remained: it generated a new self-confidence that slowly led to significant political changes – ones that might well have manifested themselves in cultural matters, musical activities among them.

My second general point concerns the wider cultural context. Here I want to suggest that, when considering music and urban culture, we might take more heed of what could broadly be called a history of sensibilities. As Alain Corbin has stated with Gallic polemical force in a number of publications, 'It would be futile to analyse social tensions and conflicts without accounting for the different kinds of sensibilities that decisively influence them.'[3] The challenge here is to find ways in which familiar kinds of political history, such as that sketched a moment ago, might productively be brought into dialogue with such 'other' histories. Apart from pioneering work by Richard Sennett and a few others, such questions have of late been most thoroughly examined from the point of view of visual culture.[4] There is nevertheless a consensus that this period – characterized by virtually uncontrolled urban expansion – was one in which the metropolis was increasingly associated with damaged (or at least compromised) sensibilities of many kinds. London was, for example, regularly accused of bombarding the senses of its inhabitants, depriving them of or flooding them with light, assailing them with unwanted noise (musical or otherwise), nauseating them with foul bodily odours. And, as so often, this assault was intimately associated with (or, perhaps better, was dragooned into articulating) class divisions within society, those divisions indeed being illustrated by the presumed existence of startlingly different sensibilities. Most obviously this occurred in the case of the poor, who were characterized by their social superiors as noisy, smelly, in the worst cases doing little more than groping in the dark of their homes; they were, in a word, seen as desensitized, with their consumption of alcohol a formidable accomplice, and an obvious case for the application of reforming zeal. As we shall see later, music was also thought of as a key element in this reforming process.

Whatever the connections between political, social, and musical activity, there is little doubt that cultural commentators of the time, overwhelmingly based in the capital and perhaps caught up in its pervading political rhetoric, were prone to see their milieu in terms of reform, perhaps especially when it came to musical developments. In that sphere, reform has – as hinted earlier – usually been charted through the decisive emergence and growing self-confidence of a realigned audience for symphonic and other types of German instrumental music, a movement whose trajectory clearly encouraged the long-lived English enthusiasm for rabid, xenophobic polemics against opera, in particular Italian opera. The decade also saw an accompanying celebration, sometimes verging on idolatry, of the talisman of German instrumental music, Ludwig van Beethoven. This story – the rise of a newly configured 'elite' audience in London, together with different kinds of concert, fresh repertoire, and adjusted behaviour both in listening to and in discourse about music – has of course often been told.[5] Its attractions, even in our present beleaguered times for 'classical' music, are obvious: in many ways, the London sea-changes seemed to herald a kind of musical world we still tenuously inhabit, or at least like to idealize. The capital's musical realignments around the 1830s could, in other words, be thought to put in place, and just as Queen Victoria began her long tenure, yet another example of what has recently been called 'the spectral presence of the Victorian past ... all around us'.[6] That presence is obvious enough in the persistence to the present day of the nineteenth-century fabric of our cities; less often remarked, though, is the surprising longevity of the cultural practices those cities did so much to enable and then foster. It is, then, with an awareness of the potential seductions of this sense of historical kinship and closeness – of the puissant sway that spectral presences can have over us, not least when gazed at nostalgically from supposedly bleaker times – that we might examine afresh some fault lines which accompanied the musical 1830s in London, some new tensions that seemed to accompany the locomotive cultural energies of the age.

An immediately arresting aspect of this period is that music in general was commonly regarded as an art form in the ascendant. Some critics, particularly those in the musical press, were indeed triumphant. A correspondent of the aptly, imperialistically entitled new journal *The Musical World*, writing in 1838, used language similar to that applied to the burgeoning railway network now spreading around London's periphery and even penetrating the city itself: 'The nineteenth century seems peculiarly to belong to musical art ... The history of the arts affords no example of a development of genius at once so powerful and rapid.'[7] However, this metropolitan expansion (which was a pan-European phenomenon, but with London, the world's largest and most developed metropolis, in the vanguard) could also be seen in terms of the darker side of urban expansion, the side that brought poverty, overcrowding, pollution, and disease, and the side leading to those damaged sensibilities mentioned earlier. At around the same time that *The Musical World* was celebrating 'powerful and rapid' musical expansion, the French journalist Albert Cler described Paris as in the grip of 'so-called amateur concerts, which have lately increased and multiplied in a most fearful manner, and which now constitute a perfect pest, which we might term the musica-morbus. All these frightful abuses are caused by the mania which has seized the Dilettanti of the middle-classes.'[8] This negative image – of music-making as dangerously porous, spreading through the population, oblivious of class structures, just like the cholera epidemics that periodically ravaged so many nineteenth-century cities – is echoed surprisingly often in the English press. Here is one commentator, writing as early as 1823:

England, more than any nation in the world, is governed by fashion. In other countries, she may be powerful, but here she is omnipotent. She controls our opinions, our manners, our habits of social intercourse, our tastes; reconciling us to error in our judgments, discomfort in our lives, and barbarism in the fine arts. Music is a fashion at present, and therefore everyone is musical ... Its influence is almost as extensive as that of the blessed sun himself, cheering and animating all nature ... But we abuse this ... by sacrificing the genuine delights which we could derive from music suited to our different degrees of taste and education, to a vain and heartless affectation and parade of technical learning and skill.[9]

There are strands to this commentary that we must revisit later, in particular the idea that music should be calibrated 'to our different degrees of taste and education'; but for the moment we can follow the broader argument a little further. It becomes clear that this writer's discontent focused principally (as it did for Albert Cler) on one instrument: the domestic piano. What had gone wrong? After all, the technological developments of the instrument – owing (it was routinely claimed) in no small part to triumphs of British engineering – were significant, and in step with the progress of the age. But this writer declared that,

> while the powers of this noble instrument are daily extended by our manufacturers, those powers are every day more and more abused by our performers. What is the use of the mechanism by which our Clementis and Broadwoods have given it the mellowness of voice, and almost the *sostenuto* of the violin, if it is to be used to exercise the two hands in galloping and clattering from one end of its keys to the other?[10]

What he called this 'general contagion' could be easily summed up. As he put it, 'the established forms of the concerto and the sonata are thrown aside; and all instrumental compositions, for public or private performance, consist of *fantasias, capriccios, pot-pourris* – any thing, in short, that releases the author from the fetters of art, and enables him to string together as many flourishing vagaries as he may think proper'.[11] Among composers, bewigged, ever-young Mozart remained untouchable, a paragon of high-mindedness and classical spirit; but even the sublime Beethoven, 'in his grand and expressive compositions for the piano-forte, introduced passages similar to those of which the music of Czerny, Herz, Pixis, &c. is almost entirely made up'.[12] In other words, music was multiplying dangerously: its new cascades of notes and proliferating harmonies, now unfettered by formal constraints and causing agonized distortions in the performing body, were spreading through the urban population, unheeding of divisions between public and private space, and even of the class divisions that urban proximity had made so newly fraught.

Considerations such as these might bring us somewhere within hail of the present book's topic. Amid the journalistic polemics just discussed are strewn a gathering mass of what might broadly be called music aesthetics. What's more, much of this writing concerns musical meaning, sometimes even musical 'representation'. However, my source material is noticeably devoid of the lofty intentions, still less the intellectual reach, that we modern musicologists are wont to find in this branch of discourse. There is, for one thing, an inescapable impression that London's home-grown mass of aesthetical forays are for the most part disconcertingly secondary or, perhaps better, disconcertingly reactive. Rather than boldly setting forth an agenda, marching in step with the most progressive composers of the age, my self-made London philosophers seem rather to be responding to, or just trying to make sense of, the rapidly changing times. What is more, they are thus stimulated not so much by changes in musical language as by changes in musical *practice*, by the new ways urban music was being consumed, and – in particular – by the new strata of society that were consuming it.

More of that in a moment; but first, and to do further duty to the book's overarching theme, I should add that the word *representation* did not – so far as I can tell – have much echo in 1830s London, at least in a musical context. Perhaps significantly, references to 'musical representation' in the more modern, philosophical sense mostly seem derived from German contexts.[13] This is probably because the word already had an uncomplicated musical usage in English – to witness a *representation* of a piece of music or a drama, rather than, as we would say, a *performance* of it, was after all why you donned your striped trousers and walked abroad on a nightly basis.

However, the broader issue of musical meaning was extensively aired, with a variation of approach that we today could find surprising, and with definite resonances for my topic in hand. As one might expect in the wake of the Beethoven-fuelled concert-culture expansion, many writers betrayed the influence of aesthetic positions available elsewhere on the continent: ones that roundly declared instrumental music's newfound superiority. This typical journalistic foray bears an unmistakeable closeness to E.T.A. Hoffmann's milieu:

Words, the language of thoughts, are too definite, and clip the wings and clog the graceful movements of this unresting spirit [i.e., music]: she chants forgetfulness of limits, and charms us along with her to the Infinite; she loves to wander through the vague immense, and seems everywhere at once; then only is she beautiful. With the growth of musical taste, therefore, one acquires a more and more decided preference for instrumental music rather than song; music *pure*, rather than music wedded with another art, which never can be quite congenial. We prefer a Beethoven's [sic] Symphony to anything ever sung.[14]

One might expect sentiments such as these to have become something like an orthodoxy by the 1830s, particularly as the critical establishment from which aesthetic discourse mostly emerged was for the most part staunchly pro-concert culture. But in fact this was far from the case. Indeed, the majority of writers, even when they openly declared the superiority of Beethoven and the wretchedness of most operatic music, still seemed liable to drift into aesthetic positions reminiscent of a much more venerable tradition. The article I just quoted gives a hint of the compromises required. That final sentence, 'We prefer a Beethoven's Symphony to anything ever sung', might seem uncomplicated; but it is less so when we read its continuation: 'We prefer a Beethoven's Symphony to anything ever sung, with the single exception of Handel's *Messiah*.' This eminently Anglo-Saxon caveat then entailed, as one might imagine, energetic aesthetic justifications, ones needed for assimilation into the newer regime: '[in *Messiah*] the words seem one with the music, – as eternal, as sublime, as universal and impersonal. They set no limit to the music, but contain in themselves seeds of inexhaustible harmonies and melodies. We could not spare a word, or suffer any change. "The Messiah" always must have meaning to all men, it is so impersonal.'[15]

It is clear that many who sailed close to these more old-fashioned positions were in part reacting to Albert Cler's musica-morbus: to the alarming spread of virtuosity in instrumental music, both in the concert hall and, more worrying still, in middle-class domestic spaces.[16] Sometimes the demand for simplicity and directness of expression, when it veered into aesthetic territory, came down to simple equations that privileged melody over harmony. One correspondent in *The Harmonicon* in 1833 summed up this position with disarming directness:

The object and end of all music is the expression and excitement of passion, of which the notes are signs ... We know that two passions cannot coexist in the mind, except at the expense of their respective continuity, depth, and intensity ... Melody consists of a succession of simple sounds, and harmony of coexistent and related or concordant sounds. It is obvious therefore that melody is alone adapted to the expression of passion – that is to musical expression.[17]

The seeming logic of this position quickly developed into alarming historical–racial generalities: 'The practice of harmony has, indeed, been borrowed by us from the boors of Russia, Bohemia, and Swabia, whose broad and flat configuration of head seems to be as much connected with this practice as their coldness and apathy are utterly opposed to musical *feeling*, which has no existence independent of passion.'[18] As before, Beethovenian pre-eminence is still insisted on, but is incorporated into the new world-view with palpable strain:

It is evident, too, that, in descriptive or epic music, harmony may form the background of the picture – the accompaniment of the narration – in the front of which some kind of melody appears; and of this the most admirable examples are to be found in the works of Beethoven, the most profound and philosophical of composers. But whoever mistakes this for the highest species of music is not in a condition to understand the present paper.[19]

The question immediately arises: what is behind these strange prevarications, this uncomfortable retreat into an aesthetic position that then required such elaborate justification? To answer at least a part of this, I need to return to one of my earlier quotations, about the new *fashion* for music that to some seemed so disquieting. As that earlier quotation put it: 'We abuse this [the beneficial influence of music] ... by sacrificing the genuine delights which we could derive from music suited to our different degrees of taste and education.'[20] One important element of the spread and democratization of musical culture was, as mentioned earlier, the fact that it had become diffused more widely across class boundaries, barriers policed with unusual severity (at least in comparison to the continent) in Britain at the time. The same author continued, making explicit his worries about new instrumental music in the home:

Were it from a genuine love of the art that music is so much cultivated by the public, ... music only would be sought ... which is truly calculated to give pleasure ... There ... would no longer be an indiscriminate study of the same kind of music among all classes and degrees of society. Were music cultivated for its own sake, its higher and more difficult branches would form the pursuit of those who, from station in society and education, possessed the means of studying it successfully.[21]

Language such as this, extremely common in the period, reveals a new angle on the whole debate, one often ignored in current music histories and a side of the 'spectral presence' of Victoriana we prefer to leave aside. The spectacular success of instrumental music among the middle classes, both in concert and in the home, had newly alerted writers to one of music's oldest dangers, what I called earlier its porosity. In this respect, instrumental music's spread was particularly alarming, chiefly because its lack of words made it almost impossible to police or censor by the usual means. Part of the reaction to this state of affairs then came in the form of renewed attempts to *stratify* music, thus containing its least controllable aspects. For the most elevated taste, instrumental genres were a fine and noble thing; but the lower such genres descended among the social ranks, the less desirable they became, and the more they should be replaced with vocal music (recall that mention of Handel's *Messiah*), whose piety of sentiment could be readily assured and judiciously rationed. As the same writer continued:

There is much good music suited to the opportunities and capacities of persons in every class. Then, certainly, the general diffusion of music would not only advance the progress of art, but would have a beneficial effect on the manners of the age, by adding to the amount of pure and innocent enjoyment.[22]

It is in this context hardly coincidental that the 1830s saw two other powerful reform movements in the musical sphere. The first, on which I can spend little time here, was the gathering obsession with legal control of what became known as 'street music', in particular with more rigorous policing of a branch of instrumental music that had devolved into the hands of the lower classes and whose sounds were penetrating the walls and windows of middle- and upper-class homes. As one passionate reformer observed: 'We have of late repeatedly heard the juvenile unwashed, whistling airs learned from these instruments, which, however humble, thus appear to influence the taste of the poorer classes.'[23] The resonances here with those damaged sensibilities mentioned earlier are again palpable. Small wonder in this context that the issue of street music brought out a particularly violent strain of the anti-music rhetoric, encouraging a tone that allowed English xenophobia and class anxiety (always willing bedfellows) to join forces. The keeper of prints at the British Museum, John Thomas Smith, writing in 1839, described indigent Italian musicians roaming London, many of them children, as 'infesting our streets with their learned mice and chattering monkeys'.[24]

The second reform movement was related to the same problem – the eternal nineteenth-century issue of unstable class distinctions – but took a positive route: it saw the passionate advocacy of and dramatic increase in choral societies and other singing groups in industrial centres. As its great champion, John Hullah, wrote in 1841: 'Among the lower portions of the middle classes, the formation and rapid success of choral and harmonic societies is one of the most pleasing characteristics of the recent improvement of the class of apprentices, foremen and attendants in shops, who were a century ago (especially in the metropolis) privileged outlaws in society.'[25] George Hogarth, one of the most influential writers of the decade, put it tellingly near the end of his *magnum opus* on music history, first published in 1835:

In the densely peopled manufacturing districts of Yorkshire, Lancashire, and Derbyshire, music is cultivated among the working classes to an extent unparalleled in any other part of the kingdom. Every town has its choral society, supported by amateurs of the place and its neighbourhood, where the sacred works of Handel, and the more modern masters, are performed with precision and effect, by a vocal and instrumental orchestra consisting of mechanics and work people ... Hence the practice of this music is an ordinary domestic and social recreation among the working classes of these districts; and its influence is of the most salutary kind. The people, in their manners and usages, retain much of the simplicity of 'the olden time'; the spirit of industrious independence maintains its ground among them, and they preserve much of their religious feeling and domestic affections, in spite of the demoralizing effects of a crowded population, fluctuating employment, and pauperism.[26]

What is more, there is little doubt that this *sending down* of vocal music, this controlled dissemination, became a powerful propaganda tool, a story to counter those writers impertinent enough to broadcast the squalid conditions in which manufacturing workers were constrained to live. An editorial in *The Musical World* was vehement about the matter. London had become musically pre-eminent, and of course 'possesses orchestras and concerts which no provincial town can rival'. But that was not the whole story of music's triumphant march:

In spite of the alleged mental corruption produced by the factory system, we find in Lancashire and Yorkshire a more insatiable thirst for, and greater patience in the practice of, classical music than in any other part of the kingdom; – in spite of the alleged physical imbecility produced by 'heated rooms, long working-hours, and inhuman treatment', we find in these two counties the finest voices in the world. Next to a specific contravertion of the falsehoods set on foot by the ignorance and quackery of the Trollope-school, we know no better refutation of such absurdities than the facts here mentioned; – among a people really demoralized music would long since have vanished in the pursuit of grosser pleasures – among a people physically emaciated sonorousness of voice would be the first corporeal quality to disappear.[27]

Passages offering similar sentiments are commonplace in the most 'advanced' musical journals: so long as the workers can sing, and so long as their words are controlled, we at the centre of the metropolis can be assured of their contentedness and of our own humanity; and we can also, of course, enjoy with an easy conscience the more refined musical pleasures that befit our education and station in life.

Conclusions beckon and, as always, there are several on offer. An obvious one would be to weave all these threads together, as they undoubtedly could be, under the sign of industrialization and its anxieties. We might even want to talk about an always-uneasy industrialization of musical experience: of music in this period and place being thought of as both newly 'fashionable' and newly 'mechanical'. This notion might justify the emerging idea of music as in fresh need of calibration according to social class, with 'pure' meaning (that deriving from The Music Itself) reserved for the elite, while those at the coalface, less sensitive by far, could sing away innocently, by this means somehow being returned to a comforting, pre-industrial past. These notions would, what is more, mesh productively with distinctions emerging elsewhere between the 'useful arts' on the one hand and the 'fine arts' on the other.[28]

However, I prefer to end by returning to my title and to earlier gestures to the idea of spectral presence. As a venerable author put it, near to the end of his long life, 'A masked and muffled figure loiters persistently at the back of every room as if waiting for a word at the most tactful moment; a presence more easily discernible than heretofore that exudes undoubted menace yet also extends persuasive charm of an enigmatic kind.'[29] Some of our continuing fascination with nineteenth-century London is with its prodigious energies: energies that seemed to put in place so much of what we now live in and live by. Our great cities, their musical institutions, even their musical practices; we live with their remnants and their revenants. Small surprise then that in these dystopian times for concert music, the spectral presence does indeed extend pervasive charm. It tells us of the rise of the middle classes, and with them the rise of the instrumental concert and of a newfound, self-defining 'elite': of the rise, if you will, of The Music Itself; but also, and quite simply, the rise of music, its diffusion into middle class homes, where armies of obedient daughters were disciplined by means of musical exercise. But at the same time, and surely connected, are the fault lines. These very developments brought with them anxieties, reanimating old fears about music and its subterranean powers of communication, its ability to cross boundaries that helped protect cherished identities and their accompanying privileges. It is as well periodically to remind ourselves of this other story; to remind ourselves that, perhaps in common with those of all human artefacts, music's meanings are not always benign; that its proliferation could, and in some senses still can, exude menace as well as enigmatic charm.

Notes

1 The literature on this topic is of course immense. For an able recent summing-up, with some basic bibliography, see Boyd Hilton, *A Mad, Bad, and Dangerous People? England 1783–1846* (Oxford University Press, 2006), 429–37.

2 The vogue for all things apocalyptic, brought to one visual climax in the work of painter John Martin (1789–1854), was frequently aired in the various Reform debates. One Ultra Tory started his speech in the Commons thus: 'I approach the discussion of this question with a sensation of awe at the contemplation of the abyss, on the brink of which we stand, and into which the noble lord will, if successful, hurl us.' Quoted in Edward Pearce, *Reform! The Fight for the 1832 Reform Act* (London: Jonathan Cape, 2003), 78.

3 Alain Corbin, *The Foul and Fragrant*; quoted in Chris Otter, *The Victorian Eye: A Political History of Light and Vision in Britain, 1800–1910* (University of Chicago Press, 2008), 54. Another obvious port-of-call in this sub-field would be Jacques Rancière, in particular his notion of 'the distribution of the sensible' (*le partage du sensible*); see Rancière, *The Politics of Aesthetics: The Distribution of the Sensible*, trans. Gabriel Rockhill (New York: Continuum, 2004).

4 Richard Sennett's many publications in this area are headed by the still-influential *The Fall of Public Man* (New York: W.W. Norton, 1974). More recently, Jonathan Crary has specifically identified this period, in the early to mid-nineteenth century, as the one in which a new ocular regime came into force: a regime in which visuality came to be thought of as more firmly grounded in the body and its unreliable and idiosyncratic mechanisms. Aspects of Crary's work, almost inevitably given its celebrity, have of late been called into question (see, for example, Otter, *The Victorian Eye*). We might also note a distinction in Crary between 'perception' (what he calls a psychological process) and 'sensation' (a physiological process); see Crary, *Suspensions of Perception: Attention, Spectacle, and Modern Culture* (Boston: MIT Press, 1999).

5 Retellings include William Weber, *Music and the Middle Class: The Social Structure of Concert Life in London, Paris and Vienna between 1830 and 1848* (London: Croom Helm, 1975; republished with a new introduction, Aldershot and Burlington, VT: Ashgate, 2004); and Ruth Solie, *Music in Other Words: Victorian Conversations* (Berkeley and Los Angeles: University of California Press, 2004). For a more recent examination, see Roger Parker, 'Two Styles in 1830s London: "The Form and Order of a Perspicuous Unity"' in Nicholas Mathew and Benjamin Walton (eds.), *Beethoven and Rossini* (Cambridge University Press, forthcoming).

6 Rosario Arias and Patricia Pulham, 'Introduction' in *Haunting and Spectrality in Neo-Victorian Fiction* (London: Palgrave Macmillan, 2009), xi.

7 *The Musical World* (17 May 1838), 47.

8 Albert Cler, 'The Dilettante' in *Pictures of the French: A Series of Literary and Graphic Delineations of French Character by Jules Janin, Balzac, Cormenin [...]* (London: Wm S. Orr and Co., 1840), 153–60. For further information about Cler and his attachment to the satirical magazine *Le Charivari*, see David S. Kerr, *Caricature and French Political Culture 1830–1848* (Oxford University Press, 2000), 31.

9 'Fashion in Music', *Metropolitan: Monthly Journal of Literature, Science, and the Fine Arts*, 1 (May 1823), 23.

10 *Ibid.*, 23–4.

11 *Ibid.*, 24.

12 *Ibid.*, 23.

13 A good example is a notice, in *The Quarterly Review*, 66 (June–September 1840), 503–15, of Prince George of Hanover's *Ideen und Betrachtungen über*

die Eigenschaften der Musik (Hanover, 1839), which claimed the author (then second in line to the English throne) as 'the most accomplished amongst contemporary scions of royalty' (503), and which ended: 'The work before us shows that, weighed in the strictest scales of reason or philosophy – and connoisseurship, enthusiasm, or partiality apart – it merits far higher praise; for it has not only been cultivated without debasement by the great, and enjoyed without depravation by the good, but it has been made the means, under Providence, of developing intellectual resources in which the fate of one of the most cultivated divisions of the great German nation is involved' (515).

14 'Concerts of the Past Winter', *The Dial: Magazine for Literature, Philosophy and Religion*, 1 (July 1840), 124–34 (126–7).

15 *Ibid.*, 127. The word 'impersonal' here (tellingly repeated) is I assume being used in the manner of 'universal' elsewhere: as a way of commandeering music as national while simultaneously furthering the claims of the nation in question to supranational dominance.

16 The critic quoted immediately above is a good example. Later in the same review he welcomed the appearance of various lions of the keyboard and their repertoire of Thalberg, Döhler, Chopin, Henselt, and Liszt, but nevertheless admitted that 'we should have been much more pleased to have heard the Sonatas of Beethoven … and such true classic works, not written for the sake of displaying the Piano Forte, but for the sake of the music'. *Ibid.*, 130.

17 Donald Walker, 'Melody and Harmony', *The Harmonicon*, 1 (1833), 145–6 (145).

18 *Ibid.*, 145–6.

19 *Ibid.*, 146.

20 'Fashion in Music', 23.

21 *Ibid.*, 26.

22 *Ibid.*, 26.

23 'English Music and English Musicians', *Blackwood's Edinburgh Magazine*, 4 (July 1843), 23–41 (33). For more on this subject, see in particular Peter Bailey, *Popular Culture and Performance in the Victorian City* (Cambridge University Press, 1998); and John M. Picker, *Victorian Soundscapes* (Oxford University Press, 2003).

24 John Thomas Smith, *The Cries of London* (London: J.B. Nichols, 1839), 50–2; quoted in Jerry White, *London in the Nineteenth Century: A Human Awful Wonder of God* (London: Vintage Books, 2008), 140.

25 John Hullah, 'Wilhelm's Method of Teaching Singing', *The Saturday Magazine* (supplement to June 1841), n.p. For more on Hullah and the tonic sol-fa movement, see Charles Edward McGuire, *Music and Victorian Philanthropy: The Tonic Sol-fa Movement* (Cambridge University Press, 2009).

26 George Hogarth, *Musical History, Biography and Criticism: Being a General Survey of Music, from the Earliest to the Present Time* (London: John W. Parker, 1835), 430–1.

27 Editorial, *The Musical World* (17 December 1840), 381. The reference to 'Trollope-school' is to the writings of Frances Trollope (the mother of Anthony Trollope), possibly to her industrial novel *Michael Armstrong: Factory Boy*, which first appeared in 1840.
28 My thanks, for this insight as for several others in these closing paragraphs, to Flora Willson. See in particular her 'Classic Staging: Pauline Viardot and the 1859 *Orphée* Revival', *Cambridge Opera Journal*, 22.3 (2010), 301–26 (318, n. 61).
29 Anthony Powell, *The Strangers All Are Gone* (London: Heinemann, 1982), 194.

3 | 'Music is obscure': textless Soviet works and their phantom programmes

MARINA FROLOVA-WALKER

This chapter is deeply influenced by my own experience of Soviet music as it was taught to me in Soviet institutions.[1] In particular, I focus here on the tendency of Soviet musicologists and critics to follow music topic by topic, finding a 'theme of the Motherland' here, and a 'theme of heroic struggle' there. Such labels were not just the stuff of musicological discourse, but were also publicly known and used. While a certain embarrassment came to surround such listening habits after the collapse of the Soviet Union, it would be unfortunate if such feelings were allowed to outweigh the consideration that not only the reception but also the production of Soviet music was shaped by the cultivation of topics. What I want to look at here is the origins of this informal but pervasive system of topic labelling, based on public and semi-public strands of the Soviet music discourse, such as press reviews and minutes of official meetings. The aim of this archaeological expedition is to show how the system of topics effectively saved instrumental music from marginalization or even extinction in Stalin's Soviet Union.[2]

Since the aesthetic of Socialist Realism required artworks of all kinds to display 'socialist content', music with appropriate texts clearly fitted the bill, as did music for films on appropriate subject matter. Instrumental works with a publicized programme could also justify themselves; even a suggestive dedication could suffice, as with Shostakovich's Seventh Symphony, which was 'dedicated to the city of Leningrad'. But what of symphonies that were presented simply as symphonies on concert posters and in scores, with a number and key, but nothing more? And likewise for piano sonatas, string quartets, and so on? At first sight, it would be hard to see how such works could still be produced under Socialist Realism, but in fact they flourished. Many, indeed, proved to be of lasting value, and still appear frequently in concert programmes today. For this, we should give some thanks to our own predecessors: Soviet musicologists, who took it upon themselves to provide an exegesis for important works, not merely according to whim or inspiration, but carefully tuned to the needs of the day. This unwritten part of their job description made them powerful agents in the Soviet musical landscape. Composers also participated in this pursuit, from the laconic to the gushing.

The initial success of the enterprise created a feedback loop, in which topics established themselves and multiplied in the public mind, while compositions became saturated with them in such a way as to suggest further plausible narratives to the critics. I propose to call the products of this self-conscious game 'phantom programmes'.

I The origins of the Soviet phantom programme

It was one of those tedious meetings Soviet composers had to sit through, long, but requiring little attention. Nikolai Myaskovsky was passed a piece of paper on which he found a note from Marian Koval, one of his Conservatoire students:

N.Ya. [Myaskovsky's initials], what would you think of a topic like this for your symphony?

Sowing the seed.

The new people come out to fight nature, not just as individuals, but now as a collective, and their attitude to nature is also different. You could build a symphony on this: from the sufferings of endless toil through to joyful and inspired collective construction. In my view, this is a great topic.[3]

This casual incident at a meeting in the summer of 1931 was eventually to acquire a pivotal significance in the course of Soviet music. Here we have Myaskovsky, a distinguished symphonist of international renown, who for many years had played a leading role in ASM, the Association for Contemporary Music. And beside him, we have Koval, the writer of the note, a mere student composer who had become a leading light in RAPM, the Russian Association of Proletarian Musicians. Now this unlikely pair would join forces to produce a new symphony on a truly Soviet scenario. Even a few months earlier, the very notion would have been utterly implausible: RAPM despised traditional concert-hall genres, promoting instead the revolutionary mass song. Conversely, Myaskovsky had nothing but contempt for RAPM, and had suffered considerable demoralization at its hands. Now the rules of the game had changed. RAPM had to modify its tactics under growing pressure from above: it was required to abandon its blinkered commitment to mass song, and instead needed to look outwards and harness the talents and expertise of fellow travellers like Myaskovsky.

We can well guess at Myaskovsky's opinion on the matter, but Koval, through his RAPM connections, had power and influence. Myaskovsky decided to heed his student's advice and duly sat down to work on a new symphony, the Twelfth, attempting to forge a new style appropriate to the new times. He even sought further advice from Koval. Evidently relishing his new role as Myaskovsky's unofficial political commissar, Koval replied with a very detailed letter full of worthy ideological guidance. He advised Myaskovsky to read the works of Lenin and Stalin, and quoted appositely from a speech by another Bolshevik, Mikhail Pokrovsky, on the desirability of clear language. Addressing the matter at hand directly, he sketched out the potential traps; Myaskovsky was to avoid both a 'light' approach (quoting from revolutionary songs or appropriate folksongs) and an individualistic 'heavy' approach, which his teacher had been known for.[4] In conclusion, Koval suggested that it would be impossible for Myaskovsky to manage without a text. He proposed a lonely solo at the start to represent the suffering people and a rousing chorus at the end, directing Myaskovsky to the poetry of Demyan Bedny for the purpose.[5] As it happened, Myaskovsky had worked with such speed that the symphony was near completion when Koval's letter arrived on 6 December 1931. Myaskovsky finished the piano score of the symphony only six days later, with no texts to be sung, or even a programmatic title.[6]

Eventually Myaskovsky sent a report to Koval explaining the discrepancy. Although RAPM's star was now clearly on the wane, the composer's letter to his student is still remarkably deferential. Apologizing for not following Koval's advice, he nevertheless was not prepared to alter his conception of the piece:

I understand the idea of the work in exactly the same way as you, namely that the centre of gravity must be in the October Revolution, i.e. in that historical moment that must transform the 'idiocy of village life' into something else, from whence an entirely new historical epoch will begin; moreover, I think that in the collectivist transformation of the countryside into a truly socialist sector we inaugurate a new *era* of life for the whole world. Unfortunately, this theme proved to be beyond my powers, and, without feeling that I am a vocal composer, I did not, and could not think organically except through instrumental music. This was my original conception: an impetus that led me to express the theme through purely instrumental means. And I did not seek out any texts ... I wrote three separate chapters with a gradual brightening-up towards the end, along these lines, roughly: the old – the struggle for the new – the new.[7]

The premiere of the symphony took place on 1 June 1932. Amusingly, this was after RAPM had been forced to disband in accordance with a Party Resolution of April 1932. The symphony was now officially presented as the embodiment of the new, post-RAPM era of Soviet music, the fruits of the April Resolution. With hindsight, we can easily hear the Twelfth as a

Socialist Realist symphony *avant la lettre*, since it became an important model for the development of Socialist Realism in music. In this chapter, I will concentrate on just one aspect that proved forward looking – the relationship of the symphony to its purported programme.

This relationship was clouded from the outset. Dmitry Kabalevsky, another of Myaskovsky's ideologically aware students, tried to clarify matters in the post-premiere review.[8] He admitted that exceptional interest in the symphony had been stirred up in advance by various printed statements and by word of mouth, all leading the public to expect 'Kolkhoznaya', or Collective-Farm Symphony. Yet the concert booklet left the symphony untitled and gave no hint at a programme for the symphony. Although Kabalevsky, in his review, explained various representational aspects of the symphony in detail, he did so entirely in his own words, not in the composer's. The symphony's collective-farm programme was never canonized in the printed score even though it was otherwise endorsed by the composer. It became a 'phantom programme'.

By happy chance, Myaskovsky's dithering over the status of the programme solved one of the major conundrums of Soviet music culture; namely, the need to justify the creation of purely instrumental music in the Soviet Union. Even before official demands were circulated for 'realist' musical content, whatever that might be, the number of textless and programme-less symphonies had dwindled dramatically (Table 3.1). At this juncture, only Myaskovsky and his former student Shebalin still dared to produce them (Shostakovich's Second and Third both featured revolutionary texts). In Leningrad, there was also Gavriil Popov, who wrote a symphony of major stature in 1931–4, but this suffered a troubled history leading to an outright ban in 1935.

In increasing numbers, composers now embraced Soviet themes, creating symphonies that shouted out their loyalty. The press openly discussed the impending demise of pure instrumental music. But once RAPM had been removed from the scene, there were no longer any significant calls to ban it outright, and critics now strove to show that it had a legitimate place within the Soviet arts. This was particularly in evidence at the 1935 discussion of Soviet symphonism, where at least three important speakers converged on what was essentially the same concept. Alexander Ostretsov called for '*fabula* symphonism', while Iosif Rïzhkin called for '*sujet*-logical symphonism'.[9] While fabula and *sujet* were opposites in their original literary context,[10] for music they meant the same thing. The intention of both speakers was to find a middle ground for symphonies and other purely instrumental works: while composers should not follow a purely abstract musical logic,

Table 3.1 Soviet symphonies, 1927–34, with textual component indicated

Shostakovich	Second	1927	Title ('Dedication to October'), sung poetic text
Shostakovich	Third	1930	Subtitle ('The First of May'), sung text
Shebalin	'dramatic symphony'	1931	Title ('Lenin'), sung and recited text
Shaporin	Symphony	1932	Poetic epigraph and titles of movements
Myaskovsky	Twelfth	1932	
Myaskovsky	Thirteenth	1933	
Shteynberg	Fourth	1933	Title ('Turksib'), poetic epigraphs, titles of movements
Knipper	Third	1933	Title ('The Far Eastern'), sung text
Korchmaryov	Second	1933	Title ('October'), sung text
Korchmaryov	Fourth	1934	Title ('Holland'), sung text
Knipper	Fourth	1934	Title (The poem of a Komsomol Fighter), sung text
Popov	First	1934	
Shebalin	Third	1934	

nor should they simply abandon musical form to any extra-musical programme. Instead, the work should follow its course with reference to a generalized narrative, where form and content could balance each other. The prime example of such a work was Beethoven's Fifth Symphony, which, as it happens, boasts one of the most celebrated phantom programmes. A third speaker, Georgy Khubov, emphasized that 'the concrete link with reality need not be expressed through words', and called on composers to re-visit the Lisztian principle of 'philosophical generalization' as opposed to Berlioz's works driven by literary considerations – in effect, he found historical precedents to flesh out the ideas of the other two speakers.[11]

A pattern soon emerged: with the appearance of each new instrumental work of importance, critics would invent a plausible programme, and these would often be endorsed by the composers. But as with Myaskovsky's Twelfth, when the scores of these works were published, they usually contained nothing but the notes. One of the most celebrated cases in the following years was the phantom programme that attached itself to Shostakovich's Fifth Symphony: *'stanovleniye lichnosti'*, the construction of character, or the building of a personality (the phrase was coined by Alexei Tolstoy).[12] While this has been much discussed, I would like to point out some ironies here.[13] Shostakovich's own earliest remarks on this symphony were guarded and vague: he mentioned 'tragic conflicts' and 'inner struggle' that were later resolved, leading to an optimistic close; he did not say himself that the work had an autobiographical dimension, but hinted as much by citing comments made by his Leningrad colleagues.[14] In this form, Shostakovich's own intimation of the content is not at odds with the symphony's most recent outing as a searing poem of love directed at Shostakovich's object of passion at the time, his mistress Elena Karmén.[15] Shot through with multiple quotations from Bizet's *Carmen* (as a reference to her surname) and also from *Tristan*, the score offers a good deal of support for this latest phantom programme – although these things can sometimes be taken too far. Back in the 1930s, however, Shostakovich's original comments were somehow turned into the famed '*stanovleniye lichnosti*' programme. Shostakovich then retrospectively endorsed the programme, together with the suggestion in circulation that the symphony was his 'reply to just criticism' – this story has been eloquently told by Richard Taruskin.[16] Even at this point, however, he insisted that the symphony was 'lyrical from beginning to end'.[17] What was initially lyrical and quite possibly private became a part of Shostakovich's public life, and took on heroic associations. In Genrich Orlov's formulation, the 'hero' of the symphony is the coryphée of the masses, the carrier of the civic idea. His feat is to overcome the 'Hamlet-like' emotions that had plagued him. Orlov even goes as far as to see here the life journey of a born leader of the masses where others had seen the plight of a weak and doubting *intelligent* who undergoes a reformation (whether convincingly or unconvincingly is another matter).[18]

It goes without saying that the malleability of phantom programmes proved to be of great use to both composers and critics. Tolstoy's capacious '*stanovleniye lichnosti*' was in fact one of the more concrete formulations, as the tendency to make the phantoms as general as possible was clearly on the increase. In essence, every Soviet work of pure instrumental music could be described as reflecting the 'thoughts and feelings of the Soviet people' (the 'thoughts and feelings' coupling, '*mïsli i chuvstva*', was still one of the most intractable clichés of my student years). Here is an example of the self-conscious application of this approach to quartets rather than symphonies:

Not only the genres that have long been considered fitting for our composers (opera, symphony, song), but also a genre such as the quartet, considered suspect since the times of Stasov and Musorgsky, are today used for pieces that portray the mode of feelings and thoughts of the new man.[19]

Two sub-groups of instrumental pieces apparently justified themselves and thus did not require a phantom programme. One group consisted of works that featured material drawn from folk music sources, since the connection to the people was self-evident, and the material was considered inherently realist. The other group, less predictably, was the concerto: the presence of the soloist and the virtuosity of the writing removed the genre from the domain of the abstract. Concertos appeared to be readily accepted by the Soviet public, unlike the more suspect genres of the symphony and the string quartet, and the soloist's evident industriousness and technical skill also fitted the concerto neatly into various favoured themes in Soviet discourse. Accordingly, hostile criticism was easily deflected. One critic, for example, reproached Khachaturian's Violin Concerto for being 'problem-free', by which he meant roughly that it was devoid of content. This was easily deflected:

The life-affirming fullness and power, the full-blooded joy that literally overflows in this Concerto, and its wonderful optimism – don't these qualities constitute an essential part of our philosophy? Don't they express a truth about our times?[20]

II The licence of war: representation in Soviet music, 1941–1948

And when the war broke out, its real horrors, its real dangers, its menace of real death, were a blessing compared with the inhuman power of the lie, a relief because it broke the spell of the dead letter. (Pasternak, *Doctor Zhivago*)

This view of the war period is common to the thinking of many Soviet memoirists, who recalled the early 1940s as the 'best' of times, even a 'blessed' time. Strange as such ideas may seem, they are familiar to all working in Soviet studies today. The memoirs refer to a wartime sense of freedom, fearlessness, and authentic and sincere patriotism. For the intelligentsia in particular, it was a time when the split between public and private domains of thought was eliminated, a time when they could identify wholeheartedly with their country and the war it was fighting. In the first year of war especially, the press reflected a great empowerment of the individual, celebrating acts of individual heroism and initiative. Literature and film were able to supply further insight, not only describing the heroic deeds of individuals, but also providing the complex psychology that lay behind them. Tragedy was not only an inescapable part of Soviet life now, but it could also be discussed, since its source was external. These circumstances posed a strong challenge to the one-dimensional rosy-optimistic narratives of the 1930s, which now seemed inappropriate to the times. Soviet art was being humanized and psychologized by the day, and though these developments would eventually be curbed, this 'breath of freedom' would be of lasting significance for those who experienced it.

The coming of war provided Soviet composers and critics with a catch-all phantom programme: the magnitude of the event was such that every work written during the war and shortly afterwards was expected to reflect it in some way. A typical description would proceed like this:

> There can be absolutely no doubts about the content of the first movement, even though the composer does not decode the music in the form of a programme here. This is a tale of the war we have lived through. The composer has embodied his thoughts in artistic form, and they have acquired all the significance of a document of our era, which is moving and comprehensible, and close to the needs of our listeners.
> (G. Kreytner on Balanchivadze's First Symphony)[21]

More cautiously, critics sometimes located the war programme in the listeners' perceptions rather than in the details of the score:

> This quartet is not a programmatic work and is not immediately related to the theme of war. But this does not hamper our perceptions as we draw a connection between the music of the quartet and the war years.
> (A. Ikonnikov on Myaskovsky's Ninth Quartet)[22]

And indeed the expectations of listeners, their automatic presumption of a connection with the war, greatly assisted the official elevation of such unlikely pieces as Prokofiev's Seventh Sonata. Conceived in 1939 and completed in 1942, this turbulent sonata was premiered by Svyatoslav Richter, who describes it in accordance with the terms of the war programme: the first movement presents 'murderous forces', the second offers 'human emotions', while the unstoppable finale represents 'the will to victory'.[23]

Such an interpretation allowed the members of the Stalin Prize Committee to award the work a Stalin Prize. Prokofiev was taken by surprise, since two years earlier, even his much less demanding film score for *Alexander Nevsky* had been turned down by the same body. As he said:

> Why would they give [the prize] to such a convoluted piece when it had been denied to pieces that were simpler and more transparent?[24]

At the same time, however, the Sonata could be described in very different terms. Grigory Shneyerson, a critic writing for Western readers in the English-language *Moscow News*, invoked a very different set of associations: he mentioned both primitivism and the complexities of modern metropolitan life, and emphasized the connection with Prokofiev's earlier style, pointing back to the *Sarcasms* and the Scythian Suite.[25] Indeed, the syncopated dissonances could even invite comparison with Stravinsky's *Piano-Rag-Music*, pointing the listener towards an urban jazz club in Paris or New York, rather than war-ravaged Russia.

Nevertheless, the wartime phantom programmes were also attractive in the West, which had its own need for morale-raising music, and so the Seventh was there nicknamed the 'Stalingrad Sonata' (as a companion to Shostakovich's 'Leningrad Symphony'). Back in the Soviet Union, the assumption of the war programme was extended to the Sixth and Eighth Sonatas, even though the Sixth had been completed in 1940, the year before Hitler's invasion had forced the Soviet Union to enter the war. The wartime Eighth, however, placed even higher demands on the listener than the Seventh, but it, too, received a Stalin Prize three years later. The critic Izrail Nestyev, who was later to become Prokofiev's biographer, could not help but notice that Prokofiev's characteristic grotesque manner had now found its way into the repertoire of gestures that were acceptable in Socialist Realist music. Nestyev labels this the *guignol* style, connecting Prokofiev's grotesqueries with the French *Grand Guignol* tradition of puppet horror shows. The *guignol* elements in the finales of Prokofiev's 'war sonatas' were, according to Nestyev, associated with mockery of the hated Nazi invaders.[26]

Nestyev was thus one of the first critics to point out how the expressive and stylistic remit of musical Socialist Realism had broadened enormously through the harnessing of war imagery. This development was by no means unique to music, and all the arts were drawn into this expansion of the means of expression. In writing, it was journalism that led the way, bringing the horrors of war to all Soviet citizens before most had begun to experience it at first hand. In the early phase of the war, when the situation on the fronts was beyond desperate, the vigorous encouragement of public hatred towards the Nazi invaders was approved policy, and the newspapers were filled with prints from the cameras of snap-happy Nazi officers who had proudly documented their own atrocities, such as the massacre in the city of Kerch. The shock at a moment-by-moment photo report on the hanging of a seventeen-year-old girl, Zoya Kosmodemyanskaya, must have been unprecedented: my own grandmother, for example, kept a crumbling copy of this newspaper for fifty years. It was this environment that produced the lines such as the following from a poem by Konstantin Simonov, simply entitled 'Kill him!':

So kill the German yourself then,
Hurry up, kill him right now,
As many times as you see him,
Kill him that many times.

Portrayals of unspeakable horrors and inhuman suffering and bloodthirsty calls for revenge opened up new depths in the flat, cardboard landscape of Socialist Realism. A number of films such as *Rainbow*, *Zoya*, and *She Defends the Motherland* contained graphic depictions of Nazi atrocities. It was this new context that allowed audiences to appreciate and identify with Shostakovich's Seventh and Eighth Symphonies. Note that even the celebrated Seventh bore no title or programme, only the dedication 'to the city of Leningrad'. And it was within this context that the critic Lev Danilevich placed Shostakovich's Eighth in 1946, with a description which is very much of its time:

> Seven thousand executed in a ditch near Kerch, corpses on the streets of Leningrad, the black skeleton of Chernigov, the plumes of smoke over Auschwitz – all of this lives on in our memory. It is the duty of the artist to speak about the suffering of the people.[27]

And it was precisely the Eighth Symphony that proved to be the test case for the system's new-found tolerance. It was nominated for the Stalin Prize twice. On the first occasion, in 1944, a fierce debate broke out over the symphony's ideological suitability: the extreme nature of its expression and the lack of a final apotheosis were set against the general agreement that it was a great work on a grand scale that simply could not be ignored. As an uncomfortable compromise, the vote proposed the Symphony for a second-degree prize in the end, but in the event, Stalin cancelled the awards for that year. In 1945, the prize selection process had to start again from scratch, and the Symphony was again the cause of bitter controversy between its supporters and detractors, indicating that nothing less than the definition of musical Socialist Realism was at stake here. This time, however, there were alternative offerings from Shostakovich – his Second Quartet and his Second Piano Trio, which were also both perceived to be war pieces (the Trio's Jewish theme brought associations with the revelation of Nazi atrocities in Majdanek, which was much discussed at the time). At this point, the normally civil procedure of the Stalin Prize Committee plenary session was interrupted by a heated outburst from Arkady Mordvinov, an architect and himself a laureate:

> I must raise an issue of principle here. The Stalin Prize Committee has a certain criterion of evaluation. It approaches every work from the point of view of Socialist Realism. If we were offered some kind of futurist smear as a painting, we would not even look at it ... So why in music do we have to listen to these formalist scams?

At this point the superannuated actor Ivan Moskvin interjected from the floor: 'Music is the most obscure business.' Picking up on this, Mordvinov suggested in no uncertain terms that Shostakovich's reputation depended upon the prestige and tolerance the war narrative brought him, and questioned the validity of the narrative itself:

When the Eighth Symphony is performed, there is a lot of cacophony there, but people hear something in it that reminds them of the cannons firing and the *Katyusha* rocket launchers squealing, but in the Quartet and the Trio this justification is not present.[28]

In the end, the Eighth Symphony was dropped from the prize list in exchange for the more populist and less controversial Trio, but the debate about the validity of war programmes was to continue in other arenas.

It is difficult to pin down a moment when the freedom that Soviet people had enjoyed at the start of the war started to ebb. Some point to August of 1942 when Stalin passed the momentous decree 'not a step backwards', ruling all unsanctioned retreat to be treason punishable by death. Others point to 1943 and the turning point of Stalingrad – from around that time the raw truth of war reporting was progressively exchanged for more easily digestible screeds on generalized accounts of heroism, stoicism, and triumph. The individual small stories of ordinary people were replaced by dutiful reminders of how the wisdom of the great Leader was directing the nation to victory. After the war, the archives remained closed, disabled war veterans were moved off the streets of central Moscow and out of sight, and as early as 1947, even Victory Day was demoted to an ordinary working day. Stalin did not wish the memory of war to persist – neither the painful scars nor the dangerous liberties of individualism and internationalism. Despite this, the licence of war still worked for a time in literature, when the writers, having in 1944 made a conscious resolution to become the healers of war wounds, produced a spate of poignant novels featuring the difficult re-integration of physically and psychologically damaged soldiers into peacetime life, among them Wanda Wasilewska's *Simply Love*, another Stalin Prize winner.

Critics who summed up the developments of art music during the war often converged on the same idea: the experience of war found its most faithful reflection not in operas or oratorios, but in textless and programme-less symphonies: Shostakovich 7 and 8, Prokofiev 5, Khachaturian 2, Popov 2, Muradeli 2, and Myaskovsky 22 and 24. Discussing this phenomenon, Dmitry Kabalevsky notably tried to ward off accusations that the 'war programme' might be nothing more than an invention of the critics:

We can boldly say that during the war years a new and special type of symphony emerged in our music, one that is connected to images born from contemporary Soviet life. [This shared content of ideas, images and emotions] explains the fact that in many critical articles about works that are sometimes very diverse (but of this same type!) one finds similar characteristics and descriptions. It is wrong to blame critics for what seems to be a unified approach to [what are superficially] very different creative phenomena.[29]

Writing these lines early in 1947, Kabalevsky had evidently noticed that the war-related justifications of textless music appeared increasingly threadbare under sustained criticism. At the 1946 Plenum of the Composers' Union, the preoccupation with 'pure' instrumental genres was seen as nothing less than 'a weakening of interest in Soviet contemporary life'.[30] Echoing Mordvinov's earlier concerns, the musicologist Kremlyov wrote:

It is easy to point out the unnaturalness of a square physiognomy or a pyramid-shaped nose. It is much more difficult to establish the unnaturalness of intonations in the unstable [*zïbkiy*] sound world of music. But it is only a matter of time.[31]

III The game exposed

That time came in 1948, when Andrei Zhdanov's assault on the Soviet musical elite demonstrated that the fears of Kremlyov and Kabalevsky were well grounded. Several composers were invited to the January meeting of the Central Committee, where Zhdanov made it clear to them that the game was up:

It is patently obvious that the proportion of programme music has decreased almost to nothing. It has come to the point when the content of musical work has to be explained after it has already been published. A whole new profession has emerged – the interpreters [*istolkovateli*] of musical works who hail from the milieu of friendly critics, who try by subjective and retrospective guesswork to decipher the content of already published musical works, the obscure meaning of which, as they say, is sometimes not quite clear even to their composers.[32]

Tikhon Khrennikov, who was appointed to do Zhdanov's bidding, elaborated on the notion of this 'obscure meaning':

The coded, abstract character of the musical language often concealed images and emotions that were alien to Soviet realist art: expressionist Angst [*vzvinchennost'*], neurosis, and [generally,] the world of ugly, repulsive, and pathological phenomena.[33]

What, then, were the works in which all these dreadful things lay beneath the surface? Khrennikov names Shostakovich's Eighth and Ninth

Symphonies, and Prokofiev's piano sonatas – that is, precisely the works that had benefited from the licence of war. Another composer, Mikhail Glukh, was eager to jump on the bandwagon, adding further fuel to the accusations; in his view, Shostakovich's Eighth does not present the collective suffering of the Soviet people, but something else entirely:

> Isn't Shostakovich Eight a symphonic expression of the pathological neurosis that is typical of the so-called 'atomic age', while it lacks any positive programme? In a number of musical works, we hear a shriek or cry of the soul that expresses the contradictions of the last stage of capitalism, but if the optimistic, constructive element is completely absent, then there is no sense of the future.[34]

Two months later, at the Congress of the Composers' Union, Khrennikov was bolder still, not only denouncing the Eighth, but casting a shadow over the celebrated Seventh:

> Shostakovich's Seventh Symphony proved that his musical thinking was more effective in expressing sinister images of fascism and the world of subjective reflection, rather than it was in embodying any positive heroic images of our land in the present. The abstract nature of his intonations, the cosmopolitanism of his musical language … served as an obstacle to the symphony's popularity in the long run for the Soviet people.
>
> The Eighth Symphony was blatantly symptomatic of the composer's deep crisis, how blinded he was by formalism, and how much he was divorced from the reality around him.[35]

This reinterpretation of the Eighth, formerly a reflection of painful wartime truths, but now a portrayal of Shostakovich's own diseased soul, makes a near traitor of the composer, as if he was to be lumped with those who were said to have 'surrendered into captivity' or who collaborated with the Nazis. Strikingly, this fundamental reinterpretation was performed openly and insolently, without any prior attempt to erase the memory of the war programme that had originally been found universally persuasive. Thus, polemicizing with a 1942 positive review of Shostakovich's Seventh by the critic Zaslavsky, Koval wrote:

> The listener of that time heard in the Seventh Symphony something beyond what was there, while the listener of today hears only what it actually contains.[36]

Shostakovich was not alone, and most of the symphonies I listed earlier were dethroned and sometimes denounced. As the whipping of the composers in 1948 flowed into the anti-Semitic campaign of 1949, which encompassed musicologists, those who had supplied the original phantom programmes were now also picked out for castigation. Here is Tamara Livanova's brutal assessment of her colleague Nestyev's writings on Prokofiev:

> While Nestyev claimed that Prokofiev's expressive tendencies towards *guignol* became stronger during the war, he maintained that they acquired 'more concrete' forms of expression such as 'a feeling of uncompromising hatred towards killers and destroyers, towards enemies of culture'. But Nestyev confuses things that must not be confused. There is no way Prokofiev's '*guignol*' tendencies could possibly reflect the sufferings of our people.[37]

What, then, was the point of Soviet phantom programmes? One possible explanation is that this was simply a consensus-based wall of pretence erected to protect a large group of composers and musicologists from official interference. Around 1944, the consensus within this group is lost, largely through the extraordinary elevation of Shostakovich and his disciples under the aegis of the 'war programme'. As a result, one faction stops participating in the pretence and punctures it to hurt the other. In a broader context, upholding similar pretences on many levels was typical of Soviet culture; Andrey Sinyavsky marvelled at the extent to which 'the whole iron structure of the Soviet state rests on language, on trite bureaucratic phrases'.[38] Those 'trite bureaucratic phrases', written in a kind of Newspeak, created a pacifyingly smooth surface for Soviet musical culture, an anodyne for everyone, an atmosphere of bored placidity. The extreme experiences of the war disrupted the system and sent waves across the surface: the proverbial 'thoughts and feelings' of the New Soviet Man were certainly not the thoughts and feelings conveyed through expressionist shrieks or grotesque clowning. The obscurity of the music suddenly became threatening and the interpretative space had to be eliminated.

But while this explanation is fine as far as it goes, the phantom programmes served another function: they offered a crutch to the arts bureaucrats who may have had expertise in other, representational arts, but found music hermetic and inscrutable. Shostakovich's deliberately misleading use of the dedication 'to the victims of fascism and war' in his Eighth Quartet (1960) comes to mind here. By resuscitating the 'war programme' which had served him so well in the past, Shostakovich provided a sop for the bureaucrats, concealing behind this a very different, autobiographical story. Although a reluctant entrant to the phantom-programme game, Shostakovich had become a truly expert player. However, together with the officials, he misled everyone else: a couple of generations of his listeners, both East and West, heard 'cannon fire' and missed the DSCH

(Shostakovich's musical signature) references. The fact that both the 'war' and the DSCH programme work equally well (and moreover, the quartet works very well without either of them) points at the heart of the phantom programme game.

What are we supposed to do now: discard the 'war programme' as false and the DSCH as authentic and binding on our interpretation of the quartet? Or can we use both at once (as some have done), or switch between them, or even reject both? Perhaps the conclusion should be twofold. Within a culture where people are versed in attaching such floating meanings to music, phantom programmes like either of these assume a kind of real existence, they matter, they influence not just the reception of music, but its production, too. However, any attempt to establish one programme as the last, authoritative word, is doomed to fail. The DSCH programme, like the war programme, is in the end another crutch. It is very telling that Shostakovich, in the personal letter in which he discusses the quartet as his own requiem, treats this programme with a degree of embarrassment and distances himself from it in jocular terms; but in the same letter, he discusses details of the quartet's construction with unalloyed enthusiasm.[39] In this spirit, let us discuss the programmatic elements of music by all means, but critically, as any other part of cultural history, not as a search for an illusory final truth.

Notes

1 This chapter draws together the material of two papers: one given at the conference 'Music and Representation', convened by Joshua Walden in Oxford (March 2010), the other at the symposium 'Music in World War II', convened by Annegret Fauser in Berlin (June 2009).
2 Textless music came under fire in the early 1930s (from the Russian Association of Proletarian Musicians), and in the wake of the anti-formalist Resolution of 1948.
3 Note from Koval to Myaskovsky (undated), RGALI, fund 2040 (Myaskovsky), list 2, folder 161, 2.
4 Letter from Koval to Myaskovsky, 6 December 1931, *ibid.*, 3–4.
5 Demyan Bedny (Yefim Alekseyevich Pridvorov, 1883–1945), Soviet poet. The son of a peasant, and a Party member since 1912, Bedny was ideally placed to become the Soviet poet laureate. He was close to Lenin, had his topical satirical verses published in *Pravda*, and was even allocated an apartment within the Kremlin.
6 He notes this date in his diary: see O.P. Lamm, *Stranitsï tvorcheskoy biografii Myaskovskogo* (Moscow: Sovetskiy kompozitor, 1989), 210.

7 Myaskovsky's letter to Koval of 16 January 1932, repr. in G. Polyanovskiy, *Marian Koval'* (Moscow: Muzïka, 1968), 14–15. I thank Patrick Zuk for providing me with this source.
8 D. Kabalevskiy, 'Simfoniya bor'bï: o 12-y simfonii N.Ya. Myaskovskogo', *Sovetskoye iskusstvo*, 27 (15 June 1932), 3.
9 A. Ostretsov, 'Sovetskoye simfonicheskoye tvorchestvo', *Sovetskaya muzïka* (1935), no. 4, 3–21; I. Rïzhkin, 'Zadachi sovetskogo simfonizma', *Sovetskaya muzïka* (1935), no. 6, 3–22.
10 The terms were used as opposites by Russian formalists: the fabula is the material of the story, the chronological succession of events, while the *sujet* is the literary organization of this material.
11 'Diskussiya o sovetskom simfonizme: vïstupleniye G. Khubova', *Sovetskaya muzïka* (1935), no. 6, 33–6.
12 A. Tolstoy, 'Pyataya simfoniya Shostakovicha', *Izvestiya* (28 January 1937), 5.
13 Richard Taruskin, *Defining Russia Musically: Historical and Hermeneutical Essays* (Princeton University Press, 1997), 521–4.
14 'Pyataya simfoniya Shostakovicha', *Literaturnaya gazeta* (12 January 1938), 5.
15 A.S. Benditskiy, *O pyatoy simfonii Shostakovicha* (Nizhny Novgorod: Nizhegorodskaya gosudarstvennaya konservatoriya im. M.I. Glinki, 2000).
16 Taruskin, *Defining Russia Musically*, 521–4.
17 D. Shostakovich, 'Moy tvorcheskiy otvet', *Vechernyaya Moskva* (25 January 1938), 8.
18 G. Orlov, *Russkiy sovetskiy simfonizm* (Moscow: Muzïka, 1966), 128.
19 A. Rabinovich, 'Zametki o novïkh kvartetakh', *Sovetskaya muzïka* (1935), no. 11, 47–51 (47).
20 D. Rabinovich, 'Tvorchestvo i kritika', *Sovetskaya muzïka* (1941), no. 2, 42–7 (45).
21 G. Kreytner, 'Pervaya simfoniya A. Balanchivadze', *Sovetskaya muzïka* (1946), nos. 2–3, 43–57 (46).
22 A. Ikonnikov, 'Tri kvarteta Myaskovskogo', *Sovetskaya muzïka* (1946), no. 12, 37–46 (41).
23 Sviatoslav Richter, *Notebooks and Conversations*, ed. Bruno Monsaingeon, trans. Stuart Spencer (London: Faber and Faber, 2001), 79–81, quoted in Nathan Seinen, *The Spoils of War: Prokofiev's Seventh Piano Sonata from Composition to Reception* (MPhil dissertation, University of Cambridge, 2003), 45.
24 Letter to Myaskovsky, 4 April 1943, in S.S. Prokofiev and N.Ya. Myaskovsky, *Perepiska* (Moscow: Sovetskiy kompozitor, 1977), 466. Quoted in Seinen, *The Spoils of War*, 22.
25 Grigoriy Shneyerson, 'The Week in Music', *Moscow News* (27 January 1943), 4. Quoted in Seinen, *The Spoils of War*, 46.
26 I. Nest'yev, 'O stile S. Prokof'yeva', *Sovetskaya muzïka* (1946), no. 4, 10–26 (12).
27 L. Danilevich, 'Vos'maya simfoniya D. Shostakovicha', *Sovetskaya muzïka* (1946), no. 12, 56–64 (56).

28 Plenary session of 3 April 1945, transcript in RGALI, fund 2073 (Komitet po Stalinskim premiyam), list 1, folder 11, 186–7.
29 Dm. Kabalevskiy, 'Vano Muradeli i ego vtoraya simfoniya', *Sovetskaya muzïka* (1947), no. 2, 27–39 (29).
30 'Materialï Plenuma Orgkomiteta SSK SSSR', *Sovetskaya muzïka* (1946), no. 10, 12–20 (13).
31 Yu. Kremlyov, 'Novoye i staroye', *Sovetskaya muzïka* (1946), no. 11, 3–7 (6).
32 'Vïstupleniye tov. A.A. Zhdanova na soveshchanii deyateley sovetskoy muzïki v TsK VKP(b)', *Sovetskaya muzïka* (1948), no. 1, 14–26 (20).
33 T. Khrennikov, 'Za tvorchestvo, dostoynoe sovetskogo naroda', *Sovetskaya muzïka* (1948), no. 1, 54–62 (56).
34 M.A. Glukh's speech at the meeting of Moscow composers and musicologists (February 1948), 'Vïstupleniya na sobranii kompozitorov i muzïkovedov g. Moskvï', *Sovetskaya muzïka* (1948), no. 1, 63–102 (95).
35 T. Khrennikov, 'Tridtsat' let sovetskoy muzïki i zadachi sovetskikh kompozitorov', *Sovetskaya muzïka* (1948), no. 2, 23–46 (33).
36 M. Koval, 'Tvorcheskiy put'' D. Shostakovicha', *Sovetskaya muzïka* (1948), no. 4, 8–19 (11).
37 Livanova's speech at a Union of Composers' meeting in February 1949, 'Vïstupleniya na otkrytom partiynom sobranii v Soyuze sovetskikh kompozitorov SSSR, posvyashchennom obsuzhdeniyu zadach muzïkal'noy kritiki i nauki', *Sovetskaya muzïka* (1949), no. 2, 16–36 (27).
38 Andrei Sinyavsky, 'Would I Move Back?', *Time*, 15 (10 April 1989), 75–7 (76).
39 Letter from Shostakovich to Isaak Glikman of 19 June 1960; see *Story of a Friendship: The Letters of Dmitry Shostakovich to Isaak Glikman, 1941–1975*, trans. Anthony Phillips (Ithaca, NY: Cornell University Press), 90–1.

4 | Representing Arlen

WALTER FRISCH

I

What many consider to be the Golden Age of American popular song extended across the first six decades of the twentieth century (1900–60), incorporating first the creations of Victor Herbert and George M. Cohan and then the composers who constitute the Mighty Five – Jerome Kern, Irving Berlin, George Gershwin, Richard Rodgers, and Cole Porter. A figure not normally included in that canonical group of five, but who fully deserves a place among them, is Harold Arlen (1905–86).

Arlen suffers from what might be called anonymous immortality, in that his songs are much better known than his name. This situation is reflected in an anecdote told by Arlen's principal biographer Edward Jablonski. The composer was once riding across New York in a taxi when the driver began whistling 'Stormy Weather'. 'Do you know who wrote that song?' Arlen asked. 'Sure – Irving Berlin', was the reply. 'Wrong', said Arlen. 'I'll give you two more guesses.' The cabby tried Richard Rodgers and Cole Porter. 'I wrote the song', Arlen told him. 'Who are you?' asked the cabby. 'Harold Arlen.' 'Who?'[1]

In early 2001, another Arlen composition, 'Over the Rainbow', was named the best song of the twentieth century by the Recording Industry of America and the National Endowment for the Arts, based on a national survey of 'music lovers'. It's a safe bet that most of the voters identified the singer (Judy Garland) and the movie (*The Wizard of Oz*) more readily than the composer. Indeed, Arlen's name is not even mentioned in some news reports of the ranking.[2]

Arlen's name recognition remains relatively low despite the fact that, in addition to 'Stormy Weather' and 'Over the Rainbow', many songs among the 400 or so written by Arlen during his career have become standards in the so-called Great American Songbook: 'Get Happy', 'Accentuate the Positive', 'Blues in the Night', 'Come Rain or Come Shine', 'The Man that Got Away', and 'A Sleepin' Bee'. Apart from some songs in *The Wizard of Oz*, Arlen's music is arguably the most complex among his peers in melodic, harmonic, and formal structure. In the landmark book of 1972,

American Popular Song, still the most in-depth (if idiosyncratic) analysis of the repertory, Alec Wilder claims Arlen as the most perfect and rounded of songwriters, one whose works suggest 'a greater musical thoroughness than those of other writers'. By 'thoroughness', Wilder explains, 'I mean the sense of a finished product'.[3] Arlen's melodies and harmonies are crafted such that most of his songs cannot be read, at least sensibly, off a simple lead sheet. He appears to have written out most of the accompaniments and voice leading in his songs. Ray Bolger, a close friend of Arlen who played the Scarecrow in *The Wizard of Oz*, commented to Jablonski, 'Maybe because he had been an arranger, Harold could write the song complete, with all the wonderful musical ideas written in – so that no arranger was really required.'[4]

The 'thoroughness' of Arlen has to do not just with the notes he wrote, but with his broader identity as a singer and pianist, and his clear belief in performance as a key component of the art of popular song. In these respects, I believe Arlen differs from other major composers, even Gershwin, who frequently performed as a pianist. In seeking to understand how Arlen is best 'represented' by and in the world of American popular song, all these activities must be part of the picture, including performances by the major singers such as Garland who have taken up his work. In this chapter I would like to explore some paths to understanding the 'thoroughness' of Arlen as a kind of continuum extending from the genesis of a song, its qualities as revealed by analysis, and its realization in performance. We will focus on two of his greatest creations.

II

Arlen was born Hyman Arluck as the son of a cantor in Buffalo, New York, and began his career in the 1920s not – like many of his contemporaries – as a composer and song-plugger in Tin Pan Alley, but as a singer, pianist, and arranger in jazz bands. He toured and recorded with a group called the Buffalodians.[5] This jazz world, rooted in performance, rather than the publisher-driven world of Tin Pan Alley songs by Berlin, Kern, and others, was Arlen's formation. Song composition was not on his horizon as a major activity until he was brought together with the lyricist Ted Koehler, a collaboration which resulted in his first hit, 'Get Happy', in 1930. Indeed, that song, as Arlen would later relate, originated not as a composition per se, but as a simple vamp he was improvising as rehearsal pianist for a 1929 musical by Vincent Youmans.[6]

Arlen would continue to perform and sing throughout his career in ways that went well beyond his peers. In addition to serving as pianist and/or singer on at least three dozen 78 rpm recordings made between 1926 and 1934, Arlen participated in three full-length LP albums of his music, all with Peter Matz as arranger and conductor. The first of these, a two-record set called *The Music of Harold Arlen*, was made in 1954–5 by a small independent record label, Walden Records.[7] Arlen participates as singer and pianist in performances of enormous energy, musicality, and imagination. The Walden recording was followed by another one, released in 1956, *Harold Arlen and His Songs*, for Capitol Records (T-635).[8] In 1965, Arlen recorded a third album, together with Barbra Streisand, for Columbia Records, *Harold Sings Arlen (With Friend)* (CK 52722).[9]

In 1934, the Boston critic and commentator Isaac Goldberg wrote an article on Arlen before the Boston premiere of Arlen's first big show, *Life Begins at 8:40*. He gives a compelling, articulate account of Arlen's performance style and its relationships to his music:

[Arlen does not] give an impression of Tin Pan Alley loudness. In one respect ... the man and his music are one: well-bred, soft, quietly confident, ingratiating ... About Arlen or his music there seems to be nothing raucous. You feel it in his voice, as he sings his pieces; you get it even from his touch on the piano...

He is a fine pianist and not at all a bad singer. When he lets his voice out – for he is apt to begin his songs in a soft, even introspective, legato that may be an influence of his cantor-father – he makes an excellent propagandist for his wares. These songs, often as not, have a true melodic feeling for wide yet smooth skips, and I suspect that the marked quality of what I call ingratiation comes from the frequent employment of these half-glissando leaps. As he sits at the piano, playing and singing, his face tilted upward and his eyes half-closed, you seem to detect a relationship between his manner and his matter.

He plays, by the way, as unostentatiously as he sings – as unconsciously as most people write, in privacy, a letter. His music, too, has this – shall we call it epistolary? – character.[10]

'The man and his music are one' and 'a relationship between his manner and his matter': Goldberg's well-turned phrases capture an essential part of Arlen's identity as a musician, one that has been too little acknowledged, let alone celebrated. At least one songwriter understands it very well: Stephen Sondheim, who has acknowledged more broadly the impact of Arlen on his work. In his book on Sondheim, Steve Swayne devotes more than eleven pages to a discussion of Arlen's influence on and relationship with Sondheim, much of this articulated by Sondheim himself.[11] Sondheim says of Arlen as a performer, 'I heard him sing and play, and let me tell you: If you're into songwriting, they don't come any better than that. Hearing Harold Arlen play and sing makes me cry. It was a thrill – thrilling.'[12] Swayne reports in a footnote that 'Sondheim was visibly moved at this point in his recollection of Arlen'.[13]

III

It is of course a limitation of print media such as the current volume that these qualities of performance, by Arlen and his greatest interpreters, cannot be directly demonstrated with this chapter. But it is hoped readers will seek out the recordings and videos to which I refer, as well as the notated scores. To represent the 'manner and matter' of Arlen, I will focus here on two of his greatest songs, both (as it happens) from 1954: 'The Man That Got Away', from the film *A Star is Born,* and 'A Sleepin' Bee', from the Broadway musical *House of Flowers.* We will work outwards from the text to the context of performance.

Most of Arlen's songs emerged as complete or near-complete musical structures before lyrics were added. Although there was always creative give-and-take as a song evolved, Arlen's main lyricists, who included Ted Koehler, E.Y. 'Yip' Harburg, Johnny Mercer, and Ira Gershwin, tended to work from the music.[14] This makes Arlen among the more 'absolute' of popular song composers, something that is reflected in the complexity and variety of his song structures.

Arlen's most famous song, 'Over the Rainbow', is almost a textbook example of the standard, thirty-two-bar AABA form of an American popular song.[15] But Arlen often – more frequently than his peers – transgressed that form with a type of song he himself called a 'tapeworm'. The term is perhaps unfortunate, not only for the rather gooey pathology it evokes, but also because a tapeworm implies something that grows out of control. Arlen's tapeworms achieve their length – sometimes extending to well over sixty measures – not by being through-composed in any classical sense, but by adjusting both the standard eight-measure lengths of sections and the normally equal proportions among those sections.

Jablonski asked Arlen about his frequent departures from the standard dimensions of popular song: 'Is it an attempt on your part to be different?' Arlen's answer: 'I don't think I'm trying to be different. Sometimes I get into trouble; in order to get out of trouble I break the form: I start twisting and turning, get into another key or go sixteen extra bars in order to resolve the song. And often as not I'm happier with the extension than I would have been trying to keep the song in regular form.'[16]

Nowhere are Arlen's 'twists and turns' more effective than in 'The Man That Got Away', with lyrics by Ira Gershwin. 'The Man That Got Away' was written for and made famous by Judy Garland, who sings it unforgettably in the 1954 film musical *A Star Is Born*.[17] Like most numbers in this film, it is diegetic, occurring within the plot or narrative and sung as a self-conscious 'song'. 'The Man That Got Away' appears relatively early in the film when the actor Norman Maine (played by James Mason) tracks down a singer he has admired (Esther Blodgett, played by Garland) to a small night club in Hollywood's Sunset Strip, where she is rehearsing the song, with a small group of musicians.

A true 'tapeworm' among Arlen's songs, 'The Man That Got Away' extends to fifty-six measures (plus a five-measure coda) not by abandoning the AABA structure, but by modifying its proportions:[18]

A (16 = 8 + 8) – A' (16 = 8 + 8) – B (8) – A" (21 = 16 + 5 as coda)
The A sections are each sixteen measures, double the standard length, while the B remains at eight.

It is especially characteristic of this kind of Arlen tapeworm that the melodic and harmonic impetus of the A section pushes past the moment where we would normally expect a B section to begin, at measure 8, because Arlen clearly feels the need for another eight measures to create a coherent musical unit. The tessitura of the first eight measures is low and rises to its highest point, B flat, on the last note, the '-way' of 'Away'. The next phrase, 'No more his eager call', continues the upward linear trajectory, beginning on C. This phrase is preceded by a sustained dominant under the B flat, and might seem to be initiating a B section. But that dominant is in fact V of II, not of the tonic; the melodic B flat is the thirteenth of the chord. 'No more' begins on a ii^7 chord (Example 4.1). Only at 'astray', thus after another eight measures, do we come back to the tonic F, and then its dominant, C. This is the real end of the A section.

The opening of the A' section follows A closely until the shattering high D in its seventh measure, at 'game', which replaces the original B flat and wrenches the rest of A' in a new direction. The B section of the song, remarkably brief at eight measures, contrasts strongly with the A sections. There is a wide variety of note values that give the melody an almost conversational quality unlike the steadier rhythms of A. The voice part seems to encapsulate and compress the melodic highpoints of the A section, from the B at 'on' to the D at 'fools', to the new E flat and E natural at 'gone to' (Example 4.2).

Judy Garland's iconic performance of 'The Man That Got Away' seems to create, rather than merely re-create, the emotional and musical

Example 4.1 'The Man That Got Away' (From 'A Star Is Born'), mm. 5–9. Words by Ira Gershwin. Music by Harold Arlen. Copyright © 1954 (Renewed) Ira Gershwin Music and Harwin Music Corp. All Rights for Ira Gershwin Music administered by WB Music Corp. All rights reserved. Reprinted by permission of Hal Leonard Corporation and Alfred Publishing.

Example 4.2 'The Man That Got Away', mm. 37–41. Words by Ira Gershwin. Music by Harold Arlen. Copyright © 1954 (Renewed) Ira Gershwin Music and Harwin Music Corp. All Rights for Ira Gershwin Music administered by WB Music Corp. All rights reserved. Reprinted by permission of Hal Leonard Corporation and Alfred Publishing.

architecture of the song.[19] During the short instrumental introduction she sings a wordless, seemingly casual vocalise, as if preparing for a mellow, gentle song. The first four measures of the A section continue this restrained idiom, in which, however, Garland constantly nuances the insistent, repetitive rhythmic pattern. She adjusts the lengths of the first two words, 'night is', elongating the first and abbreviating the second such that instead of the even quarter notes notated by Arlen, the proportion is more like 6:1.

As she hits the high B flat on the '-way' of 'away', Garland begins a *crescendo* and opens up into more of a 'belter' voice, which is sustained until the end of the A section. The same happens in A'. Garland interprets

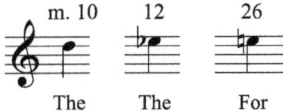

Example 4.3 Successive high notes in 'The Man That Got Away'. Words by Ira Gershwin. Music by Harold Arlen. Copyright © 1954 (Renewed) Ira Gershwin Music and Harwin Music Corp. All Rights for Ira Gershwin Music administered by WB Music Corp. All rights reserved. Reprinted by permission of Hal Leonard Corporation and Alfred Publishing.

with a special intensity what is perhaps the most unusual feature of the second half of A': the three highest notes, successively D (m. 10), E flat (m. 12), and E natural (m. 26), coincide with the article 'the' or the conjunction 'for' and fall on the weak fourth beat of the measure (Example 4.3). There is thus a disjunction – intended, of course, by Arlen and Ira Gershwin – between the climactic trajectory of pitches and the metrical and syntactical aspects of the phrases. Rather than rushing through these notes, Garland holds them out beyond the quarter-note value. The effect is completely gripping.

At the end of the brief B section, Garland scrupulously but compellingly observes the continuity Arlen creates across the transition back to A" (see Example 4.2). Almost as if not allowing the energy of B to dissipate, Arlen challenges the singer to move directly, without rest, from the high E of 'too', which ends the B section, to C on 'the' a tenth below, which begins A". Garland more than rises to the challenge, taking a breath only after 'rougher'.

In Arlen's own 1954 performance of 'The Man That Got Away', captured on film, he accompanies himself at the piano, with an orchestra (invisible) that joins in for the A" section.[20] Arlen's performance is 'thorough' in the narrower sense adumbrated by Alec Wilder: he plays the accompaniment, with all its special voicings and inner parts, largely as written in the published music – thus, incidentally, confirming that the often intricate arrangements in the sheet music for Arlen's songs must be his own.

Arlen's rendition of 'The Man That Got Away' also reveals the composer's thoroughness in the broader sense expressed by Isaac Goldberg: the man and his music are one. Arlen's eyes, his voice, his hands, and even his feet on the pedals indicate a complete absorption in the song. He begins singing with his eyes closed and opens them – appropriately and with great effect – at the line 'The dreams you've dreamed have all gone astray.' Arlen's vocal style is less sustained and continuous than Garland's; despite being a good singer, he did not have her technique. But his singing is still highly nuanced and effective. His approach to rhythm and phrasing – and even at times pitch – is freer than Garland's. In one wonderful moment, both hands temporarily leave the keyboard after playing the B flat ninth chord at the beginning of m. 17, and Arlen sings the line 'Has seen the final inning' without accompaniment, also revising the vocal melody to G–F–G–F–E natural–C (instead of D flat–D flat–E natural–E natural) and altering the first four notes from dotted rhythms to even eighth notes.

Despite these freedoms, like Garland, Arlen projects a strong sense of the song's vast architecture. The phrase 'No more that all-time thrill, / For you've been through the mill' becomes the climax of the first thirty-two measures. The B section is sung with powerful intensity; near its highpoint, at 'Fools will be fools', Arlen seems inspired to improvise a piano accompaniment that refers back to the A section.

IV

In 1954, around the same time that *A Star Is Born* was completed, Arlen began to work on the show *House of Flowers* with the American writer Truman Capote, who, although an experienced author of fiction, would be his least experienced collaborator. *House of Flowers* was an adaptation of a short story from 1951 of that name by Capote, about a young prostitute in Haiti, Ottilie, who leaves the brothel to seek true love with a young man from the island.[21] For the book of the musical, Capote expanded the plot and number of characters to encompass two competing brothels, run by Madame Fleur and Madame Tango. The producers, led by Arnold Saint Subber, assembled an extraordinarily luminous team to create a visual and musical Caribbean world. In addition to Arlen and Capote, Peter Brook was signed as director, Oliver Messel as costume and set designer, and George Balanchine as choreographer.

Pearl Bailey and Juanita Hall were cast as the duelling madams, at the head of an almost all-black cast that included a young Diahann Carroll making her Broadway debut as Ottilie. In the end, too many famous cooks ruined this broth. Peter Brook offended the cast with remarks perceived as racist. Balanchine left the show during out-of-town tryouts (and was replaced by Herbert Ross). Pearl Bailey behaved like a prima donna and often ad-libbed as in a nightclub act. Despite basically positive reviews, *House of Flowers* lasted only five months on Broadway.

Fortunately, Goddard Lieberson produced an original cast album for Columbia that has allowed several generations to appreciate this score as one of Arlen's finest.[22]

When they began work on *House of Flowers*, Arlen and Capote had never met in person. Arlen was still in Hollywood and Capote was living in Rome. In a 1960 interview Capote recalled, 'I had no true understanding of song writing (and Lord knows, still do not). But Arlen, who I suppose had never worked with an amateur before, was tolerant and infinitely encouraging and, well, just a gent about the whole thing.'[23] They sometimes spoke by phone, and developed an unusual long-distance method of collaboration. According to Capote, 'I would send him scenes and scraps of lyrics, and back came homemade phonograph records, Arlen playing melodies that the tentative lyrics had tentatively suggested, singing and talking to me.'[24] Remarkably, one of these records has survived. It is owned by the pianist and singer Michael Feinstein, who provided it to Sony for inclusion as a bonus track on the CD reissue of *House of Flowers*.

'A Sleepin' Bee' grows out of a moment in Capote's short story where Ottilie, uncertain how to distinguish a feeling of true love, goes to consult a witch doctor, a *Houngan*, who tells her that if she holds a bee in the palm of her hand and it does not sting her, she will know she's in love:

When her friends spoke of love, of men they had loved, Ottilie became sulky: How do you feel if you're in love? she asked. Ah, said Rosita with swooning eyes, you feel as though pepper has been sprinkled on your heart, as though tiny fish are swimming in your veins. Ottilie shook her head; if Rosita was telling the truth, then she had never been in love, for she had never felt that way about any of the men who came to the house.

This so troubled her that at last she went to see a *Houngan* who lived in the hills above town. Unlike her friends, Ottilie did not tack Christian pictures on the walls of her room; she did not believe in God, but many gods: of food, light, of death, ruin. The Houngan was in touch with these gods; he kept their secrets on his altar, could hear their voices in the rattle of a gourd, could dispense their powers in a potion. Speaking through the gods, the Houngan gave her this message: You must catch a wild bee, he said, and hold it in your closed hand ... if the bee does not sting, then you will know you have found love.[25]

The recording Arlen sent to Capote lasts just under six minutes and is transcribed by the author as the appendix to this chapter. The composer works with the scenario Capote created from this passage, conveying his musico-dramatic vision for the song 'A Sleepin' Bee' by speaking, singing, humming, and playing the piano. This recording is a private, working document, not a public performance like that of 'The Man That Got Away'. As such, it perhaps reveals even better the 'thoroughness' of Arlen, his complete command of the creative process.

Even though Arlen describes what he is using as a 'dummy' or provisional lyric, the first two lines of it – the image of the bee sleeping in the palm of a hand – made it into the title and final song. The central idea of the bee as sleeping seems to have come from Arlen; it is not in Capote's original story. In the final version of the lyric, however, Capote created a more poetic continuation of the first two lines than Arlen's. Capote's 'You're bewitched and deep in / Love's long look'd after land' is much more effective than Arlen's dummy 'And true love comes a creepin' / and your heart understands.' Indeed, Capote's lyrics are genuinely beautiful; we might regret that he never again worked on a musical show. But we can also see how extensively Arlen's compositional vision of the song, as captured in his recording, governed the final product. Indeed, Arlen is credited as co-lyricist for this and other numbers in *House of Flowers*.

The chorus of 'Sleepin' Bee' has a basic thirty-two-bar structure (plus a four-bar coda), arranged not in a standard AABA', but as ABA'B'. (This is a fairly common variant of the standard form in American popular song.) The first two phrases of A are a lesson in how to achieve harmonic and melodic breadth with the simplest of means (Example 4.4). The first four measures all unfold over a tonic pedal. The melody rises very quickly through a tenth, from the low C to the high E flat. It is essentially pentatonic, except for the brief neighbour note B natural. The underlying harmony, however, has sevenths, first a major seventh in measure 2, then the flatted seventh in measure 4, giving the tune the slightest blues feel. The gentle triplets are the rhythmic counterpart to the harmonic language. The second phrase begins as a sequence of the first, but the top of the rise is now a step higher on F, a surprising and wonderfully effective move. Almost as if in shocked response, the bass moves up a half step under the sustained F, thus forming a diminished seventh and the first real dissonance of the song. That F had a more or less consonant status in the pentatonic world of the first phrase, but now it is definitely a dissonant suspension to the E flat of the diminished chord.

'Sleepin' Bee' became the most popular song from *House of Flowers*. A real singer's number, it was taken up by many performers. The composer Richard Rodgers commented that for some time after the show opened, 'Sleepin' Bee' was sung at almost every audition he attended.[26] One young singer who made a speciality of 'Sleepin' Bee' was Barbra Streisand, who

Example 4.4 'A Sleepin' Bee', mm. 1–8. Lyric by Truman Capote and Harold Arlen. Music by Harold Arlen. Copyright © 1954 (Renewed) Harold Arlen and Truman Capote. All rights controlled by Harwin Music Col. All Rights Reserved. Reprinted by Permission of Hal Leonard Corporation.

declared it her favourite song and recorded it several times. It was with 'Sleepin' Bee' that Streisand, just nineteen years old, made her national television debut in April 1961, on the Jack Paar Show.[27]

One can understand why Arlen 'friended' Streisand for his later album. In the televised performance from 1961, her pitch, rhythm, and diction are precise, and she deploys the distinctive timbre of her voice with sensitivity and control. She displays hardly any of the vocal swooping and the pulling apart of lyrics that characterize (and, for this author, mar) her later singing. Streisand approaches the first high note, the '-in" of 'sleepin", as part of a legato arc. (The note is C; Streisand performs the song in F major, a minor third below the original A flat.) This note, the fifth of the scale, fits smoothly into the prevailing harmony over the tonic pedal.

The next high note, on the 'in' of 'deep in' in the parallel second phrase, is the sixth degree (here D), and thus is more distant from the tonic harmony still sounding underneath. Here Streisand emphasizes the difference, and the greater distance, by opening up her voice. She also changes the colour of the D to capture the sudden change of harmony on the third beat of the measure, where the bass moves off the tonic pedal for the first time in the song, up a half step from the tonic pedal to support a diminished seventh chord. The high D is sustained over this change and now becomes genuinely dissonant, an appoggiatura to the C natural that forms part of the diminished seventh and to which the D then resolves in the second half of the measure.

Streisand's 1961 performance of 'A Sleepin' Bee' realizes these aspects of the song, and many more. It represents perhaps the endpoint on the spectrum of 'thoroughness' of Arlen's song that extends from initial inception to a complete performance.

V

In conclusion, I would like to make briefly two points, both related to how Arlen is 'represented' in and by his songs and both of which require further thought and research. First, a great Arlen song such as 'The Man That Got Away' or 'A Sleepin' Bee' is a world unto itself. Both songs were originally part of larger music-dramatic structures (a film and musical, respectively) yet have transcended those contexts. With a clear, powerful emotional and musical trajectory, each inhabits an almost self-contained realm of expression. This is a quality – the song as creating a world, much as Mahler described a symphony – that is very hard to put in words, and I have not seen it addressed in the literature on popular song. In one of the best-known aphorisms from *Athenaeum* of 1798, Friedrich Schlegel wrote: 'A fragment, like a miniature work of art, has to be entirely isolated from the surrounding world and be complete in itself like a porcupine.'[28] The original context of that quotation is of course far removed from the context of the present chapter. But it gets at something of the 'thoroughness' of Arlen's best songs that we have been analysing in this chapter.

The anonymous immortality of Arlen, as discussed above, brings me to my second point and also back to where I began, when I noted that Judy Garland is more readily identified than Harold Arlen with 'Over the Rainbow'. The same may be the case with Garland and 'The Man That Got Away', and Barbra Streisand and 'A Sleepin' Bee'. This phenomenon, in which Arlen himself becomes almost transparent, is also ironically part of his thoroughness. Arlen would likely not have been disappointed with or surprised by this situation, because as a truly complete musician – composer, pianist, and singer – he understood that a great performance, public or private, is ultimately the best representation of a song.

Appendix

Harold Arlen, demonstration recording made for Truman Capote for the creation of the song 'A Sleepin' Bee' from *House of Flowers* (December 1953), transcribed by the author from Sony CD SK 86857.

In a discussion the other night, I thought that this might set quite a charming key for Miss Ottilie in the first scene with the Houngan, and I will give you what I *think* may be workable. I'm sure the tune has enough quality and captures the mood. I hope the dummy few lines – and I call 'em that because they *are* that – mean something to you to clarify what I'm stumbling about. Now in the first scene when the Houngan and Ottilie have their dialogue before the bee caught off a flower tree, I'm going to try to read some of it. But before I do, I want you to hear one chorus of the song. Then I will do some of the dialogue, and then go into the tune as we *might* have it, and finish the scene dialogue-wise and finish the scene with the song, with a few lines of the lyric that we *can* correct later. And if this works out, as I said before, and Audrey and Bill and Saint [Subber, producer] want to send it on to you, I'd be very pleased. [Plays chorus on piano.]

[Reads from the show's book:] [Houngan:] O many, child, many. Pluck a hair from your man's head, drop it in a glass of water. If it turns into a flower, that's one sign. Or if you find a pearl inside a coconut, that's another. But there's only one sign carries a guarantee. [Ottilie:] What do dat be, Houngan? [Houngan:] The god of hearts sets great store by *his* secrets. It'll cost you maybe a thousand francs. Ask a bee. [Ottilie:] Ask who? [Houngan:] A bee what makes the honey.

[Plays] [Speaks with the music:] 'When a bee lies sleepin' / In the palm of your hand. / And true loves comes a creepin' / And your heart understands.' [Ottilie:] I'm fear'd of bees. Suppose I do like you say, catch one in my hand. Suppose he sting me? [Houngan:] Then, child, you ain't in love; you just in misery. [Ottilie:] But if he don't sting me, or if he don't [*sic*], I know I'm in love, same as all other ladies? Now, that's a fact? [Houngan:] Absolutely. [Sings:] 'When a bee lies sleepin' / In the palm of your hand. / And true loves comes a creepin' / And your heart understands.' [Speaks:] More lyric, we hope. [Hums melody.] [Sings:] 'And true love she'll know has come for Miss Ottilie.' [Speaks:] Soft curtain.

Notes

1 Edward Jablonski, *Harold Arlen: Happy With the Blues* (New York: Da Capo, 1986; orig. ed. 1961), 19–20. This is a reprint of the first of two books Jablonski

wrote about Arlen, whom he served as a kind of amanuensis in the later years. This volume was written during Arlen's life and is full of information gleaned directly from the composer (but mostly hard to corroborate in any other source). After Arlen's death, Jablonski published *Harold Arlen: Rhythm, Rainbows, and Blues* (Boston: Northeastern University Press, 1996), which incorporates much of the information in the earlier book into a more complete life-and-works, and for which he had access to much of Arlen's personal materials.

2 www.cnn.com/2001/SHOWBIZ/Music/03/07/365.songs/index.html. This article begins, 'Judy Garland's rendition of "Over the Rainbow" tops a new list of 20th century American songs.'

3 Alec Wilder, *American Popular Song: The Great Innovators, 1920–1950* (Oxford University Press, 1990; first pub. 1972), 290.

4 Jablonski, *Happy With the Blues*, 91. The principal volumes of Arlen's songs readily available today are David Bickman (ed.), *Harold Arlen [The Harold Arlen Songbook]* (New York: MPL Communications, 1985); and *Harold Arlen Rediscovered* (New York: MPL Communications, 1996).

5 An example of Arlen's work with the Buffalodians, the song 'How Many Times', in which he sings and plays piano, can be heard (as of this writing) on the Internet Archive at www.archive.org/details/TheBuffalodiansVharold-Arlen-HowManyTimes1926, and on YouTube at www.youtube.com/watch?v=p1N66itSyMY.

6 As related by Arlen in an interview included in the excellent film documentary *Somewhere Over the Rainbow: Harold Arlen* (WinStar, 1999), at 20:51.

7 Now released on CD by Harbinger Records; also available as mp3 download from Amazon.

8 The twelve tracks from this album are included on a two-CD set, *St. Louis Woman and Harold Arlen and His Songs*, from DRG Records; also mp3 download.

9 The Sony CD reissue of this album (1993) is now out of print.

10 Cited in Jablonski, *Happy With the Blues*, 92–3.

11 Steve Swayne, *How Sondheim Found his Sound* (Ann Arbor: University of Michigan Press, 2005), 77–88.

12 *Ibid.*, 84.

13 *Ibid.*, 271.

14 Arlen, Koehler, and Mercer discuss aspects of the creative process in *Somewhere Over the Rainbow* at 4:30.

15 One of the clearest explanations of the formal conventions of popular song, including its division into verse and chorus, is given by William Zinsser, in *Easy to Remember: The Great American Songwriters and Their Songs* (Jaffrey, NH: Godine, 2000), 37–44.

16 Jablonski, *Happy With the Blues*, 234–5.

17 The original soundtrack for the film was remastered and released on CD in 2004 by Sony Legacy, CK 65965 (now out of print but available as mp3 download).

18 The song is in *The Harold Arlen Songbook*, 232–6.
19 A film clip of 'The Man That Got Away' is at this writing viewable on YouTube at www.youtube.com/watch?v=2h3SjisivsA.
20 This filmed performance can be seen in the documentary *Somewhere Over the Rainbow* at 50:11–53:04. At this writing, the A and A' sections of it can be seen on YouTube at www.youtube.com/watch?v=e0kHAwrJkjc.
21 'House of Flowers' is included in *The Complete Stories of Truman Capote* (New York: Random House, 2004), 197–212.
22 It has been remastered and released on CD by Sony, SK 86857 (2003).
23 William Zinsser, 'Harold Arlen, the Secret Music Maker', *Harper's Magazine*, 220.1320 (May 1960), 46.
24 *Ibid.*, 45.
25 *The Complete Stories of Truman Capote*, 199. Ellipsis is in the original story.
26 Jablonski, *Happy With the Blues*, 259.
27 Currently viewable on YouTube at www.youtube.com/watch?v=3DXvLD-pxms.
28 Friedrich Schlegel, *Philosophical Fragments*, trans. Peter Firchow (Minneapolis: University of Minnesota Press, 1991), 45.

5 | Video cultures: 'Bohemian Rhapsody', *Wayne's World*, and beyond

NICHOLAS COOK

Representing music

Queen's 'Bohemian Rhapsody', Freddie Mercury's operatic fantasy, is one of those songs that is deeply engrained in the early twenty-first-century Anglo-American psyche: love it or hate it, everybody knows it. Perhaps the best evidence of this is that advertisers have been capitalizing on it for years. A 2000 commercial for the American fizzy drink 'Mountain Dew' referenced the original Queen video – down to the diamond-shaped pattern of four faces which is its most enduring single image (actually borrowed from Mick Rock's photograph on the cover of the album *Queen II*). A British commercial from the following year, with the occupants of a Renault Scenic belting out Queen's music as they tear down the road, would be pointless if you didn't know the 'Bohemian Rhapsody' sequence from *Wayne's World*, the cult movie directed by Penelope Spheeris which appeared in 1992. And so it continues. As I finalized this chapter, in 2012, a commercial for the 'Cosmopolitan of Las Vegas' hotel featured a guy smooth-talking his way out of trouble when accosted by a group of thugs:[1] the spoken dialogue, entirely taken from the central section of 'Bohemian Rhapsody', would make no sense if you did not know where it came from. As Anne Desler has argued,[2] the neglect of Queen's work on the part of popular musicologists and humanities scholars more generally is a phenomenon of academia, rather than a reflection of the place the band's music occupies within the collective memory of society at large.

So how did 'Bohemian Rhapsody' acquire its canonic and iconic (hereafter canoniconic) status? Perhaps sheer musical audacity is enough to explain the song's first, record-breaking run of nine weeks at the top of the UK charts in 1975, with its extravagant generic mixture of ballad, hard rock, and opera, as well as its reckless – for a single – six-minute length. Then again, as released on Queen's 1975 album *A Night at the Opera*, 'Bohemian Rhapsody' was a landmark in complex multitrack studio production; at the same time, in a variety of simplified forms, it became a mainstay of the band's live performances, with Mercury's entry on the opening piano vamp being greeted by clapping and whistling and the audience singing along with the first verse. No song was more personally associated with Mercury than 'Bohemian Rhapsody', and its second spell in the charts (in 1991) was a nostalgic response to his death as a victim of AIDS, in the wake of which Queen increasingly emerged as an established signifier of Britishness (the name helped, of course). In the US, by contrast, chart success followed only on the release of *Wayne's World*.

But it's not just the song or even the film: it's the video.[3] As the story is usually told, when 'Bohemian Rhapsody' first topped the charts, Queen were on tour and so could not appear on the BBC television show 'Top of the Pops', exposure on which was both a condition and a consequence of UK chart success. Other versions have it that the song was too difficult to perform live on 'Top of the Pops', or that the band members were desperate to avoid having to appear on the programme: in a 2004 interview, the drummer, Roger Taylor, described it as 'the most boring day known to man and ... all about not actually playing, you know pretending to sing, pretending to play', and he added, 'we came up with the video concept to avoid playing on Top of the Pops'.[4] Either way, the video was commissioned from Bruce Gowers. It was shot in two days (or possibly four hours, depending whom you believe), on a budget usually said to be around £4,500 – though the 'Songfacts' web page for 'Bohemian Rhapsody' puts it as low as $3,500.[5] And whatever its contribution may have been to the song's canoniconic status, the video launched Gowers's career, subsequent highlights of which included direction of Bill Clinton's inaugural concert at the Lincoln Memorial and the live episodes of *American Idol*.

The 'Songfacts' page also remarks that 'at the time, it looked high-tech'. That introduces an element of historical distancing, and I shall come back to some of the dated features of the video, yet I would describe it as less a historical curiosity than an astonishingly complete realization of a genre that at the time did not exist: when I carried out my first work on what eventually turned into this chapter, in 2005, the Wikipedia entry for 'Music video' went as far as to claim that 'it featured the complete visual grammar of today's music promos'.[6] Of course, when new genres come into being apparently fully formed, this usually means they are firmly built on existing sources, and the current Wikipedia entry credits the Beatles' film *A Hard Day's Night*, from eleven years earlier, with having introduced the 'new grammar' replicated by later promotional films.[7] The solidest justifications for the frequently encountered claim that 'Bohemian Rhapsody' was the first music video are then, first, the fact that it was shot and edited on video, not film, and second, the way in which it changed expectations: as

Michael Heatley says, with this video 'Queen upped the ante in terms of costs and visual effects'.[8] But perhaps no less important to the video's historical importance and canoniconic status is the highly designed quality of the visuals. The pattern of four faces borrowed from *Queen II* is said to have been the starting point of the video, and is just one of a number of then unfamiliar special effects achieved through the use of a prismatic camera lens. Particularly striking is the visualization of the central section, which Mercury himself described as a 'tongue in cheek ... mock opera':[9] it is rather like a succession of overlaid stills, a series of singing heads. Much the same might indeed be said of the song at this point.

And that illustrates the first point I want to make in this chapter: the visuals of the 'Bohemian Rhapsody' video are an extension of the song. They are as much part of the music as is, for example, Ravel's orchestration of Mussorgsky's *Pictures at an Exhibition*. In saying this, I mean more than that the visuals throughout comprise footage of performance, or rather miming. (The soundtrack is taken from the original album.) More precisely, they are composed of footage from different performances, some more naturalistic and others more obvious products of studio artifice, as well as different views of the same performance. And it is the idea of composition – the way in which different elements are brought together to create meaning – that I want to emphasize. As one would expect of any music video, even the first, the pictures are cut to the song, but this is particularly the case of the operatic section; the outer sections, by contrast, generally fade from shot to shot. Again, while in the operatic section everyone stands still and looks straight at the camera (meaning there is no depth and so creating the effect of a succession of stills), in the outer sections the camera is usually in motion – as if it were part of the give-and-take of the group performance represented in these sections. There is also a degree of song-level organization in the relationship between stylized images based on the *Queen II* cover and more naturalistic performance footage: the former characterize the introduction, the central operatic section, and the final moments of the song before a stripped-to-the-waist Roger Taylor strikes the gong in an unmistakable reference to the Rank Organisation's 'Gong Man'.

There is also a deeper level at which sonic and visual dimensions work together. The video is constructed in the familiar cinematic manner, creating a pattern of contrasted elements, a series of juxtapositions, that conveys a sense of continuous, real-time unfolding (what one might term 'musical diegesis'), but at the same time strongly conditions its signification. The point is that, to an almost unprecedented degree, the same might be said of the audio production of the song. As the chapter 'Inside the Rhapsody' on the *Queen Greatest Hits I* DVD makes clear, 'Bohemian Rhapsody' was for its time an extreme example of multitrack production, with the tracks laid down separately and successively, and the music assembled by sound engineers.[10] (It was said that only Mercury had any clear conception of how the individual takes were to fit together.) The song is not, then, the trace of an event but a closely engineered construction of multiple fragmentary takes, and this is the source of its exceptionally tight sound quality: Queen's live performances of 'Bohemian Rhapsody' always sounded loose by comparison. To put it another way, the recording is not so much realistic as hyper-realistic. And although the visuals were added at a later stage, the continuity in terms of production process between them and the sounds is one of the reasons that they form, so to speak, a single audio-visual stack: this gives the whole a quality of integrity, in the sense that the visuals are to all intents and purposes part of the music, generously conceived.

I spoke of dated elements. Inevitably these include the 'high-tech' features referred to in the 'Songfacts' page, such as the prismatic lens effects or the visual feedback created by pointing the camera at the monitor: these now look like feeble analogue approximations of what can be done much more effectively in the digital domain. (They are, incidentally, further examples of visuals constructed on musical principles: the prismatic images in the operatic section are the exact correlate of the studio-created chorus, while feedback in the acoustic domain was a defining feature of heavy rock guitar performance until the invention of circuitry to mimic it.) But there is another aspect of the 'Bohemian Rhapsody' video which appears dated, particularly when you compare it with what is often referred to as the 'Flames' version of the video. This is a lightly re-edited version of the original, which the BBC started using for 'Tops of the Pops' a few weeks into the song's number one run, and which was long unobtainable until it was included as an easter egg on *Queen Greatest Hits I*.[11] As the name implies, its most striking feature is the flames that are overlaid during the first section, but there are many less obvious points where things seems to be done differently from the original, not so much because they might be better that way, but simply because they are different: at one point in the middle section,[12] for example, the alignment of images with the music is reversed, so that instead of images A–B–A–B you get B–A–B–A. It was, in short, a freshening-up job.

But there is one aspect that is consistently different throughout the operatic section, and here the result is to create a subtly different effect. In the original version, the beginning of almost every line in the operatic section is marked by a cut, resulting in a slightly cartoon-like quality. That is the dated element to which I referred – though it might equally be argued that it is of a piece with the farcical nature of this section, more than anything a preposterously camped-up evocation of another paragon of Britishness, Gilbert and Sullivan (the first-person/third-person alternations are an obvious give-away), with perhaps a dash of Monty Python thrown into the mix. By contrast, the editing of the 'Flames' version may be more anodyne, but it is also more typical of mainstream music video style as it became established in the years after 1975. Rather than reduplicating the rhythms of the song, as if it were just an extra element within the mix, the edit points are more often slightly offset. The essentially musical construction remains, but its execution is a concession to the codes of classic narrative film, where offsets between image and soundtrack help to make the cuts unobtrusive. The 'Flames' version is still music to see, but with eyes accustomed to the cinema. For those who regard 'Bohemian Rhapsody' as the first music video, the progression from the one version to the other might be seen as embodying the genres' instant history – a history measured not in years, or even months, but rather in weeks.

The relationship between 'Bohemian Rhapsody' as song and as video illustrates the complexities in the relationship between different instantiations of music. If we believe the story that the video was prompted by Queen's being on tour, then its purpose was to stand in or substitute for the band; it represented a performance that could not be presented in the flesh. Of course the same might be said of any audio recording, except that in popular music (unlike classical music and jazz) the original studio recording is generally regarded as the definitive version of a song. Indeed 'Bohemian Rhapsody' is a particularly clear example of a song that was conceived for recording and only translated with difficulty, and over a period of time, to live performance. The key problem was the studio-produced chorus of the middle section, which Queen could not perform live, since they had only three singers. As the Wikipedia entry for 'Bohemian Rhapsody' explains, the band initially played the other sections individually, but eventually arrived at a format whereby a recording of the operatic section was played on a darkened stage, flanked by live performance of the outer sections. (All this can be seen in the 1986 performance from Wembley available on YouTube.)[13] One might, then, think of Queen's live performances as derivative forms, representations of a studio product adapted for the stage.

But the video further confuses these categories. In the first place, its construction as a single audio-visual stack means that it is as much the presentation of a new multimedia experience as the representation of a pre-existing one (just as Ravel's version of *Pictures at an Exhibition* creates a new orchestral experience based on Mussorgsky's piano piece). And in the second place, by powerfully reinforcing the expectation that any major musical release must include a video, 'Bohemian Rhapsody' played a crucial role in the process through which the music video developed from a promo to a revenue stream, that is to say, from the representation of a product to the product itself. As so often with music, the distinction between signifier and signified is blurred.

Musical representation

Such representational issues become further complicated when a song is incorporated within a narrative film, and this brings me to the second point I want to make in this chapter. *Wayne's World*, which charts the attempts of its protagonist (Mike Myers) to develop his public access TV show, does not reference the original video: rather it offers an alternative visualization of the song. The 'Bohemian Rhapsody' sequence begins as the opening credits end, and basically coincides with a car journey. Garth picks up Wayne from the side of the road ('This is my best friend, Garth Elgar', says Wayne as he gets into the car, speaking to the camera rather than the other occupants), and as the car pulls off Wayne inserts a cassette tape into the car stereo ('I think we'll go with a little Bohemian Rhapsody, gentlemen'). The cassette proves to be neatly lined up with the beginning of the operatic section, and the music plays continuously from there to the end of the song, coinciding with the end of the journey, with the exception of two interpolations. One is when they stop to pick up Phil ('Phil, what are you doing here? You're partied out, man – again'), and the other when Wayne insists on getting out to ogle an unaffordable guitar in a shop window: 'He does this every Friday', Garth tells the camera.

This sequence employs cinematic cutting more like that of the 'Flames' version of the video than the original, but to the opposite end: rather than the visual dimension being appropriated by the musical structure, the musical dimension is subsumed within the discourse hierarchy of narrative film – but only for the first part of the sequence. It starts diegetically enough, as an element within the narrative representation, not only with Wayne's insertion of the cassette but also with the headbanging that has ever since been indelibly associated with this passage: everyone sings along, and their raucous voices are clearly audible at the top of the mix. By the time the words get to 'spare him his life from this monstrosity', however, the superimposed voices have disappeared, and so have the environmental noises: what we hear is simply Queen's song. And by 'Nothing really matters', the protagonists are miming to Queen's music in the most approved music video style. At such moments – which are broken up by the diegetic interpolations I mentioned – the music asserts its dominance over the visuals, turning the film into a visualization of the music. A generic shift has taken place: narrative cinema has turned into music video.

This transformation is facilitated by a structural similarity between the visuals of the sequence from *Wayne's World* and those of the original video (in either version). I spoke of the video being spliced together from different performance footages. Another way of expressing this is that the video track consists of a limited number of different types of shot that repeat in an irregularly permutated pattern. As I explained in my book *Analysing Musical Multimedia*, where I referred to these types as visual 'paradigm classes', this is true of most music videos, but particularly rap videos: song and video share a common mode of construction, although there is not a fixed relationship between auditory and visual paradigm classes.[14] It is also true of the 'Bohemian Rhapsody' sequence from *Wayne's World*. In one sense, this is trivial. If you are filming a car journey, there is really only a limited number of camera angles you can use (facing the front or back seat passengers, from the side, looking out of the car, showing the car from the street), so the kind of permutational patterns I have referred to are bound to occur. But the point is that in a context of musical dominance, the alternation of shot types ceases to be a more or less transparent element of the diegesis and begins instead to be experienced as a dimension of the music's rhythmical or structural articulation. One might then say there are passages in the 'Bohemian Rhapsody' sequence from *Wayne's World* when the visuals are heard rather than seen, which is basically what I said about the original video.

But as I also said, these passages are broken up by narrative interpolations when the car stops. And there are other ways in which the diegetic intrudes upon the visualization of the music. The most obvious is after Phil has first got into the car, with apparent reluctance – pinioned between the back seat passengers, he at first nods off but then comes to at the words 'will not let you go', when we hear his voice above the music: 'let me go ... let me go!' A more subtle example of this slippage between music and diegesis comes at the end of the guitar-ogling episode, when Wayne intones 'it will be mine, oh yes, it will be mine', and a few seconds later the words of the song offer sardonic commentary: 'ooh, yeah, ooh, yeah'.

(The visuals at this point show a stack of cars piled fantastically high, underlining the unlikelihood of what Wayne asserts.) But these points of slippage represent audio-visual puns, subverting the normative alignment of media. And in this way they serve to make the point: external reality intrudes as an anomaly into the world of music video, a world in which – to misquote Ernest Lindgren[15] – film is a servant art.

Or at least, film is a servant art as long as the car keeps moving. Filled with sound and subject to the laws of the music video, it is like a hermetically sealed capsule enclosed within the world of administered reality embodied in the urban landscape outside and represented by the conventions of narrative cinema. (Many of the innumerable other visualizations of 'Bohemian Rhapsody' – more on these soon – are based on the iconography of space travel, but even those that are not, such as FatSatan's 'Titanium Rhapsody', tend to adopt it at the words 'just gotta get out, just gotta get right outta here'.) As for the second interpolation, the functioning of music as a symbol or mediator of alternate worlds is even more obvious: as Wayne turns round to say 'it will be mine', the sounds of 'Bohemian Rhapsody' are replaced by *a cappella* voices singing a fragment of Palestrina-style polyphony, of all musics perhaps the one most associated with another world (and least associated with the electric guitar). In this way, music penetrates to the core of *Wayne's World*. If the film has a serious message, it is about what happens when Wayne and Garth's personal musical world is appropriated by the world of corporate business, as represented by the questionable TV executive Rob Lowe.

Whereas the dividing line between presentation and representation becomes blurred in the relationship between 'Bohemian Rhapsody' as song and as video, then, its recontextualization within the narrative of *Wayne's World* means that the process of signification takes place on quite another axis. *Wayne's World* does not in any useful sense represent 'Bohemian Rhapsody', it does not stand in for it in the way that the video stood in for Queen on 'Top of the Pops'. Instead, in the filmic context, 'Bohemian Rhapsody' serves to represent a set of values – subjectivity, authenticity, aesthetic extravagance or *jouissance* – that are seen as at odds with those of corporate America. More than that, the shifting but always oppositional relationships between musical and narrative diegesis embody the tension between these ultimately irreconcilable values: the 'Bohemian Rhapsody' sequence shows us how, through a combination of symbolic capital and illocutionary force, canoniconic cultural artefacts choreograph and articulate real-time processes of identity construction and negotiation within the multiple domains of the physical, emotional, social, and ideological. In this way, it serves as not just a metaphor but also a metonym of the underlying theme of Spheeris's film.

Beyond representation

The last point I wish to draw from 'Bohemian Rhapsody' – and the one that will take the most space to make – returns to the issue of canoniconicity, but now from the perspective of how musicology is to represent its object of study. My starting point here is something that can be established by means of a single YouTube search: the sheer multiplicity of visualizations, in part or in whole, of 'Bohemian Rhapsody' (the song also exists in a multiplicity of cover versions, of course, but that is not my topic here). There are the original and 'Flames' versions of Gowers's video, together with the 'Bohemian Rhapsody' sequence from *Wayne's World*. A new video was created to coincide with the film's release, combining clips from both *Wayne's World* (not just the 'Bohemian Rhapsody' sequence) and the original video, as well as live performance footage: new opportunities were found for meaningful juxtaposition of sounds and images.[16] (For example, the stack of cars from *Wayne's World* now appears alongside the words 'Look up to the skies and see'.) Then there are the Mountain Dew, Renault, and Cosmopolitan of Las Vegas commercials I mentioned at the beginning.

There is also the video issued in 2007 by the British vocal group G4 (the G stands for the Guildhall School of Music and Drama, where all four members had studied); they shot to fame in 2004, when they came second in the ITV talent show *The X Factor*, and their debut single, released the following year, was a cover of 'Bohemian Rhapsody'. As in the Mountain Dew commercial, the video (in which the song is hacked down to the standard four minutes) features the diamond-like arrangement of heads from the original video.[17] That is the only obvious reference, however, and the singers' trained operatic voice production curiously inverts the relationship between the rock/ballad – 'normal' for Mercury – and the operatic elements. As such, and with its full orchestral backing, G4's rendition of 'Bohemian Rhapsody' belongs to a distinct genre of audio and video covers which appropriate 'Bohemian Rhapsody' for the classical tradition: examples respectively include the London Symphony's instrumental version,[18] released in 1977 and the first track on the first LP of the orchestra's 'Classic Rock' series, and a multitracked arrangement for four violins available on YouTube (we see the performance of each part in a separate window, resulting in another echo of the original video's diamond-like arrangement of heads).[19]

But the highest-profile video remake to have appeared in recent years has to be the one released in 2009 by The Muppets Studio, a wholly owned subsidiary of The Walt Disney Company.[20] It strongly references the design of the original video, including the opening silhouettes, the diamond-like arrangement of heads, and their placing against a black background. But the song is fully assimilated into the established characters of the Muppets, with the lyrics adapted accordingly. 'Haha', writes spiderlover678 on the YouTube comments page, 'I was looking for Miss Piggy the whole way through and then I figured she would probably be doing the finale at the end :)', and indeed she does: 'Nothing really matters', she intones, lounging like some latter-day Marlene Dietrich on Rowlf the Dog's grand piano, 'nothing really matters – but *moi!*' The camera tracks back to reveal the various Muppets characters set against the black screen – and then further back to reveal that everything we have seen is one half of a video conference with Kermit the Frog. 'Scooter', says Kermit as the gong fades, 'remind me to stop setting up these videoconferences. They're not very productive.'

To get the point of the Muppets video, you have to be familiar with both the original 'Bohemian Rhapsody' video and the Muppets. The world of 'Bohemian Rhapsody' videos is intertextual through and through. Michael Strangelove writes that 'the YouTube audience ... is continually engaged with intensely intertextual media texts',[21] and each video is located a mouse click away from related videos or websites, surrounded by what Kathrin Peters and Andrea Seier refer to as 'a web of paratexts established by the functionality of YouTube'.[22] That does not of course necessarily mean that relationships between different versions are intended by their creators. It was in 2008, a year before their version of 'Bohemian Rhapsody', that The Muppets Studio embarked on a series of viral videos, released directly on YouTube and designed to raise its profile. (Others range from Beethoven's 'Ode to Joy' to Nirvana's 'Smells Like Teen Spirit'.) So there is no reason to suppose an intentional link with other puppet visualizations of 'Bohemian Rhapsody', such as one from the Scottish Falsetto Sock Puppet Theatre, the creation of comedian Kev F. Sutherland: it features a farcically recreated soundtrack, and the YouTube information box reads, 'Before the Muppets, the Socks have been playing our audiences in with this for years.'[23] The likelihood of links being intentional diminishes as the number of versions rises – and a YouTube search on 'bohemian rhapsody' AND 'puppet' yields 304 hits. While there are limitations to the YouTube search functions, a little sampling suggests that a good half of these are indeed distinct puppet visualizations of 'Bohemian Rhapsody', most of them clearly home produced.

That should give some idea of what I meant when I referred to the 'innumerable' visualizations of 'Bohemian Rhapsody' that circulate on the internet. All I can aim at is the most impressionistic overview. The Muppets video illustrates one major principle: most visualizations are based on existing, mass-mediated iconographies and draw more or less explicitly on their narratives and connotations. Examples range from animations based on 'My Little Pony' (shades of the 'Pastoral Symphony' sequence from *Fantasia*) to versions incorporating clips from *Lost*, the American television series that followed the fortunes of the survivors of a plane crash on an island somewhere in the South Pacific. There are versions based on 'Lord of the Rings', though these draw on the online role-playing game of that name (LotRO) rather than Tolkien's epic story. FatSatan's 'Titanium Rhapsody', which I have already mentioned, is based on characters from the 1980s Nintendo game Megaman: it references both the original video (in the opening diamond formation, though here we have cartoon bodies, not just heads) and the *Wayne's World* sequence, with the spasmodic head bobbing at the beginning of the heavy rock section.

Games-based visualizations do not stop there. There are versions based on characters and graphics from the Sony Playstation game 'Final Fantasy', among the most entertaining being The Spiffy Mage's 'Bohemian Fantasy' – not least because, like many other versions, it is based on 'Weird Al' Yankovic's insanely up-tempo and countrified parody of the song, 'Bohemian Polka'.[24] (Actually there is a whole genre of up-tempo countrified versions: the DVD accompanying the 'rockgrass' band Hayseed Dixie's 2010 album 'Killer Grass', for example, includes a cover of 'Bohemian Rhapsody' that features banjo and folk fiddle, and that plays not only on the singing heads from the original video but also on the miniskirted, vacuum-cleaning Freddie Mercury of the 'I Want to Break Free' video.)[25] There are even versions created using Mario Paint Composer, making Peter Kirn's point that 'For some strange reason, this creation has inspired endless musical oddities, uploaded to YouTube.'[26] And then, as I said, there is a whole genre of versions based on the iconography of space travel: one large group is based on *Star Wars*, another on *Star Trek*. Of the latter, a few simply couple the original music with film clips, in the manner of the 'Lost' versions, but most have as their soundtrack Kevin Barbare's 'Star Trek Fantasy'. Barbare is a comedian and impressionist who co-hosts the Hill-Man Morning Show on WAAF FM, a Boston-based rock station which issues occasional limited-edition CDs by its presenters: 'Star Trek Fantasy' was included on *Royal Flush: Live On-Air* (1997), and features rhythmically declaimed lyrics related to *Star Trek* ('I am the *cap*tain of the *star*ship Enter*prise*. Captain *Kirk*, this is *Spock*, please step *on* the trans*porte*r', and of course '*Let's* boldly *go* where *no*-one's gone be*fore*').

But no overview of visualizations of 'Bohemian Rhapsody' would be complete without mention of the countless anime versions, many of which may be found on YouTube, though the connoisseur of the genre will wish to explore the AMV (AnimeMusicVideos) website.[27] Since the 1980s, Japanese animated films have become a global phenomenon, with the AMV site catering for anglophone makers as well as fans. Within anime there is a large number of sub-genres associated with particular manga (cartoon) serials. For instance, Neon Genesis Evangelion anime films, such as the manga of the same name, are based on an apocalyptic scenario according to which, following an interplanetary collision that has annihilated Antarctica, the earth comes under attack from hostile aliens called Angels; the theme is similar to that of Final Fantasy or any number of other videogames.[28] All this provides a ready-made iconography and set of graphic conventions that can be used with animation software to create music visualizations of considerable complexity. An example that attracts highly positive comments from YouTube viewers is set to Queen's 1986 performance of 'Boheman Rhapsody' at Wembley, and illustrates many features of the genre.[29] As ZarathustraDK comments, the lyrics are visualized almost word for word, an approach that in other contexts might be thought naive but results in a dense succession of contrasted images that mix everyday and apocalyptic imagery, with meaning emerging unpredictably from the sometimes surreal juxtapositions between them. There are also vestiges of visual narrative, as elusive and fragmentary as Mercury's lyrics, and it is hard to know how far these might be references to the original song, to the universe of Neon Genesis Evangelion, or of a more personal nature. What might at first glance look like a private act of memorialization – a plaque that reads IKARI YUI 1977–2004 – is in fact a reference to a Neon Genesis Evangelion character.

Have I made the point yet? There are personal remixes and parodies of the *Wayne's World* episode. There is a video of a live performance by BBC newscasters from 2005, but incorporating a filmed central section, as in Queen's own performances; made for the charity Children in Need and a transparent exercise in wish fulfilment, it features perhaps the most execrable singing I heard in all this research, though it also reveals Fiona Bruce as a remarkably assured rock chick, complete with bondage collar.[30] A similarly communal version comes from the HMS *Campbelltown*, made to while away the time on patrol in the Indian Ocean.[31] There is a clutch of versions by Moymoy Palaboy, a Filipino comedy duo who built a professional career on the basis of lip-synch videos distributed through YouTube; highlights include air guitar on a broomstick, complete with only slightly overdone rock-style grimacing, and – like all YouTubers who achieve celebrity status – Moymoy Palaboy have attracted their own parodists.[32] The same applies to a number of versions posted by Gerry Philips, who refers to himself as a manualist or hand musician, though everybody else calls this hand farting.[33] Then there is a whole genre of special Christmas versions. There are time-lapse animations entirely created out of Lego (in fact there is a channel dedicated to Lego versions of Queen videos). There are animations in which the song is lip-synched by Smart cars or by the presidential sculptures at Mount Rushmore. There is one version – just one – in which the song has been lovingly recreated from the sounds made by scanners, oscilloscopes, floppy and tape drives, and other obsolete electronic detritus.[34] A detailed list of the equipment is provided.

Jean Burgess and Joshua Green observe that 'YouTube's ascendancy has occurred amid a fog of uncertainty and contradiction around what it is actually *for*',[35] and that is the first question I asked myself about the video culture that has developed around 'Bohemian Rhapsody': what are its aims, motivations, and values, or expressed in more emic language, wtf? The second question was, why 'Bohemian Rhapsody'? An obvious answer is that the very canoniconicity of 'Bohemian Rhapsody' ensures the intimate familiarity with music, lyrics, and images on which this culture depends; at the same time, the often highly personal video interpretations of 'Bohemian Rhapsody' reference one another, creating a dense tissue of intertextuality – an expanding universe of simulacra – that must in turn stimulate the production of yet more versions. (Hence CPTREX65578's Baudrillardian comment on the Muppets video page: 'I hear Queen did a cover of this'.) Then again, the suggested rather than sustained narrative of the song, coupled to the diversity of its generic references, emotional qualities, and modes of address, creates a multiplicity of routes for identification: any number of highly divergent, individual interpretations can be constructed out of it. Finally, the song offers a further advantage in the free availability of individual tracks from the studio mix through websites such as Acapellas4All:[36] the ability to include or exclude tracks allows the replacement of the vocals by new ones while retaining the original instrumental parts, as illustrated by the Muppets version and many others. It has also given rise to YouTube postings of selections from individual tracks, which create a new experience of intimate access for listeners who have internalized the original recording: 'Very nice to hear his voice without anything', comments Ferrariemil (he is referring of course to Mercury). 'We can feel the breath and the larynx also jumping (at one point), imperfections, effort, defects typical emission Freddie and all ... obviously for me it's all beautiful!'[37]

As for the first question, what may be incomprehensible in terms of standard musicological models of reception makes more sense when related to the participatory cultures that have grown up around other, better documented media genres. Fan culture – which Strangelove describes as the 'definitive example of an emerging participatory culture within our media-soaked society'[38] – is the obvious comparison. As Henry Jenkins writes, 'fans of a popular television series may sample dialogue, summarize episodes, debate subtexts, create original fan fiction, record their own soundtracks, make their own movies – and distribute all of this world-wide via the internet'.[39] Jenkins has devoted particular attention to the fan cultures that have developed around *Star Wars*, which as we have seen is a major genre within the 'Bohemian Rhapsody' videos. This goes back to the 1960s, when *Star Wars* was a principal focus for the development of fanfiction, that is to say (in the words of the Wikipedia entry on the topic) 'stories about characters or settings written by fans of the original work, rather than by the original creator'.[40] But it continues to the present day. Fans now in their teens and early twenties, says Jenkins, 'grew up dressing up as Darth Vader for Halloween, sleeping on Princess Leia sheets, battling with plastic light sabers'; in this way, '*Star Wars* has become their "legend", and now they are determined to remake it on their own terms'.[41] A more recent focus of fanfiction, to which Jenkins also devotes attention, is the *Harry Potter* stories: the largest *Harry Potter* archive, Jenkins tells us, houses over 30,000 stories and book chapters.[42] (And yes, there are versions of 'Bohemian Rhapsody' set at Hogwarts.)

Like fanfiction, then, the YouTube culture around 'Bohemian Rhapsody' represents the traces of personal appropriation of a canoniconic artefact. By creating your own video of 'Bohemian Rhapsody' you make it your own, in much the same way that you make any music your own by playing it (and in this context it does not much matter whether you do so well or badly). And more than that, you inscribe yourself into its history. There is a comparison with what Kathrin Peters and Andrea Seier describe as the 'overwhelming number of performances' of The Buggles's 'Video Killed the Radio Star' on YouTube. This was the first clip that MTV showed when it started broadcasting in 1981, and so these remakes, Peters and Seier continue, 'are attempts at reenacting what is now a historical music video'.[43] 'Video Killed the Radio Star' is in its own way as canoniconic as 'Bohemian Rhapsody'. YouTube videos are also, in many cases, the traces of prolonged labour, efforts of love or otherwise personally significant acts of self-definition or expression: several times I saw statements in the YouTube information box that a video had taken six months to make, and the levels of skill deployed can be impressive. But long hours at the keyboard do not mean that this is not at the same time a social activity, and here I would like to set the video culture of 'Bohemian Rhapsody' into a longer historical context of participatory culture.

In his book *Remix*, Lawrence Lessig puts forward a distinction between what he calls RO and RW culture. By RO or 'read only' culture, Lessig means the established concept of art as something that is normatively produced by professionals and consumed by a paying but otherwise passive public. Artistic practice is seen as condensed into marketable commodities, such as paintings and musical works, and the copyright system is designed to protect the rights of their owners against unauthorized copying. Lessig contrasts this with what he calls RW or read-write culture, although participatory would be an equally good term: art circulates through the practices of quotation or recomposition that Lessig calls 'remixing', exemplified by hip hop and the other musical cultures that developed around digital sampling. These practices have frequently been the target of successful litigation by rights holders, normally large corporations, and so Lessig argues that 'current copyright law supports the practices of the RO culture and opposes the practices of the RW culture ... RW culture is thus presumptively illegal.'[44] Lessig's book is in essence a proposal for the creation of a new legal framework that will not only recognize a major arena of cultural participation and creativity, but also stimulate a new, hybrid economy.

Because of his use of the term 'remix', it is possible to get the impression that Lessig sees RW culture as something fundamentally new, but this is not correct. On the contrary, he emphasizes the participatory nature of non-professional musical performance, and the extent to which such performance has traditionally involved elements of remixing. Lessig's point is underlined by the vast numbers of nineteenth-century arrangements for all conceivable, and some inconceivable, instrumental combinations, as evidenced for example by the *Monatsberichte* issued throughout most of the century by the Leipzig music publishers Friedrich Hofmeister: they convey an image of nineteenth-century musical culture very much at odds with standard musicological representations of it. One might, then, see the concept of RO culture as less a neutral description of real practice than a representation that skews it to the interests of a particular group. Musical aesthetics and copyright law developed hand in hand in order to constitute music as ownable property and hence bring it within the capitalist economy, resulting in the extraordinary success story that was the twentieth-century music business. It is worth pointing out that, with the exception of a few corporate contributions such as The Muppets Studio's, the entire culture around 'Bohemian Rhapsody' which I have been describing is illegal under UK legislation.

The concept of RW culture enables us to situate today's practices of digital participation in a tradition that goes back through the washboard era of post-war youth culture to the period remixing evidenced by nineteenth-century arrangements, or for that matter the 'older folk culture of quilting bees and barn dances'[45] that both Jenkins and Lessig invoke. And like its predecessors, today's YouTube culture of intertextual reference is also one of human relationships, for as Patricia Lange says, 'creating and circulating video effectively enacts social relationships between those who make and those who view videos'.[46] No less than its predecessors, this is a culture embedded in community, which is why Nick Prior refers to YouTube's 'dizzying proliferation of digital folk culture':[47] it is just that it is a digitally networked community. Burgess and Green stress that the way to misunderstand YouTube is to see it as it originally described itself, 'Your Digital Video Repository'.[48] For them, the key to YouTube's success is its social networking dimension. The commentaries and responses are obvious indicators of this: while (as Jenkins acidly remarks) 'the user comments posted on YouTube fall far short of Habermasian ideals of the public sphere',[49] flippant or plain rude postings on 'Bohemian Rhapsody' videos rub shoulders with those that offer considered criticism or constructive advice to the maker. But an even clearer illustration of the social dimension of participatory video culture is the AMV website. Not only do you have to register in order to download the videos, so gaining access to a wide range of news, discussion pages, and technical guides, but also you are invited to rate each of the videos you download. And more than this, once you have downloaded ten videos, you cannot download any more until you have completed your ratings. In this way, community participation becomes not just an opportunity but an obligation.

Referring to the constant tension and occasional litigation between corporate rights holders and the creators of fanfiction, Jenkins writes that judges 'don't know what to do with amateurs'.[50] What applies to fanfiction applies all the more to music, the prime battleground between RW culture and the copyright regime predicated on RO culture. The trouble is it is not only judges who do not know what to do with RW culture: it is musicologists too. Prior remarks that 'In the domain of music, the "amateur" has been given especially short shrift.'[51] To be sure, there have been sociological studies of non-professional culture in music, a classic example being Ruth Finnegan's study of participatory music-making in Milton Keynes,[52] while ethnomusicologists routinely work with non-professional informants, though mainly outside the context of contemporary Western practices. But mainstream musicology has generally eschewed engagement with the amateur, participatory, and relational dimensions of musical practice, and the reason is that it is a system of representation based on the ontology and the values of RO culture. It is structured around the cultural artefact rather than its reception, and as such oriented to the close examination of individual instances. It deals with the multiplicity of cultural products by valorizing the authentic, the original, the best. In short, it is a discipline built on canoniconicity. As such it has traditionally fulfilled a gatekeeper role, underpinned by the same ideologies of genius and exceptionality that underpin aesthetic theory and copyright law. These ideologies form a particular target of Lessig's critique: after commenting that 'It takes extraordinary knowledge about a culture to remix it well' (a point illustrated by some at least of the 'Bohemian Rhapsody' videos), he continues, 'The artist or student training to do it well learns far more about his past than one committed to this (in my view, hopelessly naive) view about "original creativity".'[53]

Concepts of genius and original creativity have an old-fashioned ring even in musicology. We like to think that the legacy of autonomy aesthetics was shrugged off by the 'New' musicology of the 1990s, when whole swathes of the discipline were reoriented around reception and interpretation history, with canons no longer being taken for granted but becoming the object of historical and ideological critique. But the selective, or exclusive, representation of the field of musical practice which I have termed 'gatekeeping' is not solely a function of now problematized beliefs in aesthetic universals. It is also a pragmatic reflection of working methods. Consider some statistics. As of January 2012, the various YouTube postings of the original 'Bohemian Rhapsody' video had attracted 87 million views, while the Muppets version had attracted 25 million (7 million during just the first week), and a single Moymoy Palaboy version over 7 million. Even the version based on electronic detritus has over two million. But it is not just the viewing figures. It was when I discovered the AMV website, in June 2005, that I realized traditional practices of close reading were not going to work for this project once I got past canoniconic texts such as Gowers's video and *Wayne's World*. At that time searching the AMV site for 'Bohemian Rhapsody' generated just sixty-five hits, whereas now it generates 270. But I must have forgotten the lesson, for when I got back to this chapter in

2012, I started by typing 'Bohemian Rhapsody' into YouTube and working through the results page by page. Perhaps I would not have done that if I had noticed that the search yielded 'about' 83,700 hits: while the number of hits obtained by searching on YouTube is not an easily interpretable statistic (and can vary unaccountably on different occasions), it must mean something that in June 2005 the same search had yielded just 16,200 hits. After working through twelve pages of results, looking for any video that seemed to have been designed as such rather than just being a filmed live performance, I realized this was hopeless and changed tack: having now identified various genres of 'Bohemian Rhapsody' (puppets, *Star Wars*, Lego), I conducted searches based on these terms.

But this raises the question of what you are meant to do with such vast quantities of materials once you have found them. In addition to close reading of individual videos and the comments on them, of which this initial scoping of the terrain has barely scraped the surface, YouTube provides various measures of consumption. There are statistics for individual videos that plot not only views but also ratings (likes and dislikes) against time; there is information on the sites or search engines from which views originated and on their demographics (gender and age band) and location. Unfortunately, however, uploaders can – and often do – disable these statistics. You can also see what other videos the same person has uploaded, and if you have a YouTube username and channel you can contact that person to conduct standard real-world ethnography. Videos are often reposted from other sites, however, so the uploader is often not the creator, and may in any case not wish to reveal his or her real-world identity: YouTube culture is based on user names, so anonymity is the norm. Besides, there is an argument that – as Tom Boellstorff has claimed of Second Life[54] – ethnography is better conducted in the virtual domain; in other words, through participation. Hence Kiri Miller's question, 'How could one possibly understand participatory culture without participating?'[55]

But that only brings us back to the original question. 'Scale at the level which YouTube represents', Burgess and Green observe, 'tests the limits of the explanatory power of even our best grounded or particularist accounts.'[56] Their own solution is to choose a sample of 4,230 videos gathered on three specific dates, code them according to origin, uploader, genre, and themes, and analyse the resulting data. That is reasonable given their aim to create an overview of YouTube's content regardless of specific genre or subject matter. It is, however, unlikely to provide answers to the sort of questions musicologists might want to ask. Further work on musically based video cultures, then, is likely to depend on the same mixture of close reading and participant observation through which an increasingly large proportion of musicological work is nowadays done. At the same time, we must recognize that such methods cannot represent the dimension of sheer scale that is so definitive an element of RW culture as it proliferates throughout today's digitally mediated world. But then, there have always been dimensions of musical culture that lie beyond representation.

Notes

1. 'The Cosmopolitan of Las Vegas sixty-second "Let Me Go" TV Commercial' (www.youtube.com/watch?v=9Xa7cYMD-Dc), accessed 16 February 2012; all other websites accessed 10 January 2012 except as stated. Titles retain original orthography to aid identification if urls change.
2. Anne Desler, 'History without Royalty? Queen and the Strata of the Popular Music Canon', *Popular Music* (forthcoming).
3. Queen – 'Bohemian Rhapsody' (www.youtube.com/watch?v=fJ9rUzIMcZQ).
4. *The Observer*, 12 December 2004 (www.guardian.co.uk/music/2004/dec/12/popandrock.shopping).
5. www.songfacts.com/detail.lasso?id=685.
6. http://en.wikipedia.org/wiki/Music_video, accessed 28 May 2005.
7. http://en.wikipedia.org/wiki/Music_video, citing the film critic Roger Ebert.
8. Michael Heatley, *Massive Musical Moments* (London: Collins and Brown, 2008), 143.
9. Cited in Ken McLeod, 'Bohemian Rhapsodies: Operatic Influences on Rock Music', *Popular Music*, 20 (2001), 189–203 (192).
10. DTS Parlophone 7243 4 92944 9 3 (PAL).
11. On disc 2 select 'Inside the Rhapsody', highlight 'Back to main', and type the arrow keys up, right, right, and left.
12. From 'Bismillah' to 'Never let me go' (though the cutting points are different).
13. 'Bohemian Rhapsody (Live at Wembley 1986) [Queen]' (www.youtube.com/watch?v=pe0rhTJq-OY).
14. Nicholas Cook, *Analysing Musical Multimedia* (Oxford University Press, 1998), ch. 4.
15. Ernest Lindgren, *The Art of the Film* (London: Allen and Unwin, 1948), 13.
16. www.youtube.com/watch?v=vAakY-eQOos.
17. 'G4 – Bohemian Rhapsody' (www.muzu.tv/gb/g4/bohemian-rhapsody-music-video/516511/).
18. 'London Symphony Orchestra – Bohemian Rhapsody' (www.youtube.com/watch?v=kXTtkKzLY4A).
19. 'Bohemian Rhapsody, for Four Violins' (www.youtube.com/watch?v=IG9iDNNzd-U).
20. 'The Muppets: Bohemian Rhapsody' (www.youtube.com/watch?v=tgbNymZ7vqY).

21 Michael Strangelove, *Watching YouTube: Extraordinary Videos by Ordinary People* (University of Toronto Press, 2010), 117.
22 Kathrin Peters and Andrea Seier, 'Home Dance: Mediacy and Aesthetics of the Self on YouTube' in Pelle Snickars and Patrick Vonderau (eds.), *The YouTube Reader* (Stockholm: National Library of Sweden, 2009), 197–203 (194).
23 'Bohemian Rhapsody – Scottish Falsetto Sock Puppet Theatre' (www.youtube.com/watch?v=Fj9QCoBl9Xk).
24 Download of 'Bohemian Fantasy' at www.animemusicvideos.org/members/members_videoinfo.php?v=41157, available on free registration; 'Bohemian Polka' is from Yankovic's album *Alapalooza*, released in 1993 (Scotti Bros 32020).
25 www.hayseed-dixie.com/Video%20Evidence.html.
26 'Free Mario Paint Composer for Windows and Mac; Mario Does John Cage' (http://createdigitalmusic.com/2008/04/free-mario-paint-composer-for-windows-and-mac-mario-does-john-cage/).
27 www.animemusicvideos.org/; free registration required.
28 Further details may be found at http://en.wikipedia.org/wiki/Neon_Genesis_Evangelion.
29 'Neon Genesis Evangelion AMV-"Bohemian Rhapsody"' (www.youtube.com/watch?v=qiq3pRAH8Qc).
30 'Children In Need News Presenters Bohemian Rhapsody' (www.youtube.com/watch?v=Kd_56ezMtc0).
31 'Royal Navy's Bohemian Rhapsody' (www.youtube.com/watch?v=DerD7RNMbDQ).
32 'bohemian rhapsody' (www.youtube.com/watch?v=nwTL0NRkHgg). For celebrity status and parody see Strangelove, *Watching YouTube*, 117.
33 'manualist plays bohemian rhapsody on his hands!' (www.youtube.com/watch?v=IOyEw9bT8yQ).
34 'Queen Bohemian Rhapsody Old School Computer Remix' (www.youtube.com/watch?v=Ht96HJ01SE4).
35 Jean Burgess and Joshua Green, *YouTube: Online Video and Participatory Culture* (Cambridge: Polity Press, 2009), 3.
36 See www.acapellas4all.com/?p=184.
37 'Bohemian Rhapsody stripped track by track' (www.youtube.com/watch?v=JJY9_JAQpfs).
38 Strangelove, *Watching YouTube*, 116.
39 Henry Jenkins, *Convergence Culture: Where Old and New Media Collide* (New York University Press, 2006), 16.
40 http://en.wikipedia.org/wiki/Fan_fiction.
41 Jenkins, *Convergence Culture*, 135.
42 *Ibid.*, 188.
43 Peters and Seier, 'Home dance', 190–1.
44 Lawrence Lessig, *Remix: Making Art and Commerce Thrive in the Hybrid Economy* (London: Bloomsbury, 2008), 97 and 100.

45 Jenkins, *Convergence Culture*, 136.
46 Quoted in Strangelove, *Watching YouTube*, 122.
47 Nick Prior, 'The Rise of the New Amateurs: Popular Music, Digital Technology and the Fate of Cultural Production' in John R. Hall, Laura Grindstaff, and Ming-cheng Lo (eds.), *Handbook of Cultural Sociology* (Abingdon: Routledge, 2010), 398–407 (401).
48 Burgess and Green, *YouTube*, 4.
49 Jenkins, *Convergence Culture*, 291.
50 *Ibid.*, 198.
51 Prior, 'Rise of the New Amateurs', 402.
52 Ruth Finnegan, *The Hidden Musicians: Music-Making in an English Town*, 2nd edn (Middletown, CT: Wesleyan University Press, 2007; originally published 1989).
53 Lessig, *Remix*, 93.
54 Tom Boellstorff, *Coming of Age in Second Life: An Anthropologist Explores the Virtually Human* (Princeton University Press, 2008).
55 Kiri Miller, *Playing Along: Digital Games, YouTube, and Virtual Performance* (Oxford University Press, 2012), 6.
56 Burgess and Green, *YouTube*, 7.

PART II

Sound and visual representations: music, painting, and dance

6 | 'On wings of song': representing music as agency in nineteenth-century culture

THOMAS GREY

> The function of a wing is to take what is heavy and raise it up to the region above, where the gods dwell; of all things connected with the body, it has the greatest affinity with the divine.
>
> Socrates, in Plato's Phaedrus

What does music 'look like'? On the whole, nothing, even if individual pieces will often elicit attempts at description or even visual representation. Whether lamented or celebrated, music's invisibility and intangibility are essential attributes of the medium. They suited the idealist temperament of Romantic aesthetic thought very well, of course. Even in that era, however, the impulse to represent music – in words, images, or spectacle – remained strong. This chapter considers how nineteenth-century culture tended to represent or imagine music 'on the whole', as a medium, rather than attempts to render individual compositions visible through instances of musical ekphrasis in the form of paintings, poems, or descriptive prose. At the conclusion, I do turn to a specific work, the third movement of Schumann's *Fantasy* Op. 17, to speculate on how music might be understood to represent 'itself'. That concrete example serves to illustrate, however, the question of how one imagined the representation of music – generally, as a medium – by the nineteenth century, or by what means one might imagine 'seeing' it.

Representing music: from allegory to 'agency'?

There are many ways to approach the issue of 'music and representation', and a good number of those are represented in the present volume. The most fundamental approach would be through the venerable topic of mimesis: how has music been understood to represent nature, objects in nature, feelings or emotions ('human nature'), or other works of human artifice such as lyric, epic, or dramatic poetry (ideas of music as narrative). This approach asks how music represents other things, things that are not themselves music. In asking the question the other way around, 'How does one represent *music* by other means?' (my starting point above), one might of course take a technical approach and study the practices of musical notation in different periods or cultures, as a matter of the history of musical theory. Here I am trying to ask the second question, but from the perspective of cultural history. Two clarifications about this approach will lead directly to the main argument, a claim that music might be imaginatively represented – that is, to or within our imagination – in terms of its effects or agency: we can imagine, even visualize, music in terms of what it does to its listeners.

First, in speaking of 'representation' I am mostly using it in the sense of the German word *Vorstellung* (as in Schopenhauer's title *Die Welt als Wille und Vorstellung*: 'The World as Will and Representation', the latter term sometimes also rendered as 'Idea'). This meaning is shared by English in the expression 'mental representations', that is, the way in which we picture or imagine a thing 'in the mind's eye'. This is the sense most relevant to questions about representing, or imagining, 'music on the whole', while these questions might also have implications for representing music 'in particular', visualizing, imagining, or interpreting individual works or performances. (As mentioned, I am leaving aside the technical idea of music as represented through systems of notation.)

Second, the idea of representing music 'on the whole', or music as a medium, might suggest an essentially allegorical mode of representation. In that regard music does not differ much from the other arts. If it is difficult to say what 'music on the whole' looks like, it is scarcely any easier to say what poetry or drama or even painting look like as generalized concepts rather than in specific exemplars. (With the exemplars of painting or poetry or drama we would normally be looking at an object of representational content, unlike music, unless we were to address the mechanics of writing, typography, etc., by analogy to notation as a representation of musical sounds and structures.) As generalized concepts, any of the arts might traditionally be represented through allegories, or by simple emblems – the relevant Muse outfitted with the relevant attributes. Music we could expect to see allegorized in the form of one of its legendary practitioners, Orpheus or St Cecilia. In both cases, the iconographic tradition is nearly inexhaustible (Figures 6.1 and 6.2 offer just two classic examples).

My argument about later – specifically, Romantic – cultural practices does also start from allegory. By the nineteenth century, I argue, there arises a tendency to move beyond traditional allegorical representations of music in favour of representing (i.e., *imagining* or suggesting) the invisible, intangible medium of music by means of representing its effects – representing

Figure 6.1 Benedetto Montagna, 'Orpheus', 1500–20. 26 × 19.6 cm. © Trustees of the British Museum.

not merely musical instruments or acts of performance, but also musical agency, music's effect on the listening subject.

Of course, earlier allegorical practices do very often portray agency in representing 'the power of music' as a topos. The favoured motif of earlier Orpheus pictures is the hypnotic charm exerted by his song on 'the savage beasts', no less than on gods, humans, and inanimate rocks. (In the visual

Figure 6.2 Marcantonio Raimondi (after Raphael), 'St Cecilia', *c*.1480–*c*.1534. 25.4 × 16 cm. Image © Sterling and Francine Clark Art Institute, Williamstown, Massachusetts, USA (photo by Michael Agee).

arts, Orpheus enchanting the wild beasts seems to have been routinely preferred to depictions of his power to move the hard heart of Pluto, probably because the animals were more interesting to painters and collectors.)

A trait already implicit in many examples of the earlier allegorical tradition is music's 'transfiguring' effect on the listening or performing subject. Music's effect of 'lifting up' or 'up-lifting' the subject and transporting him or her to some supra-terrestrial space, traditionally figured as heaven, tends especially to be suggested in the Christian iconographic tradition with St Cecilia. Both Orpheus and St Cecilia provide instruments for this newer representational work, and as mentioned above, it is the case of Orpheus we will return to later, from a Romantic-era perspective. By the age of Enlightenment and, even more, Romanticism, music's transfiguring, levitational properties become increasingly independent of classical or Christian iconography and independent of the allegorical mode itself. As we approach the era of 'absolute music', the representation of music likewise acquires a new kind of autonomy. In properly idealist terms, we could say that allegory is not so much rejected as 'sublated' (*aufgehoben*) to a higher plane. The figure is aptly recursive: in the Romantic imagination, music is always rising.

'On wings of song': transporting the listening subject

The poetic trope that effects this gradual shift from allegory to a more autonomous representation of musical agency is itself a venerable one. This is the trope of voice, especially musical voice (song), as an air-borne entity with the power to transport things through space – albeit mostly immaterial things such as words, thoughts, prayers, or souls.[1] The human direction of this musical transport tends to be lateral or horizontal: song as a sort of ventriloquism or telephonics, projecting the voice into the distance, sometimes immeasurably far. The overarching, divine direction is vertical: the voice is launched upwards, typically in prayer, towards heaven. It is this latter version of the figure that comes to dominate the Romantic imagination, as, for example, in the tableau of religious or spiritual redemption (discussed in the following section). Both versions of this figure of musical 'transport' develop affinities with sentimental, even kitschy cultural registers across the nineteenth century; but these affinities are enabled, even encouraged, precisely by the venerable and 'lofty' qualities of the originating figure.

A typical example from the middle cultural register of the Romantic era is Mendelssohn's still somewhat familiar setting of the Heinrich Heine poem 'Auf Flügeln des Gesanges' ('On Wings of Song').

Auf Flügeln des Gesanges	*On wings of song,*
Herzliebchen, trag ich dich fort,	*my dearest, I carry you hence,*
Fort nach den Fluren des Ganges,	*away to the shores of the Ganges,*
Dort weiss ich den schönsten Ort.	*where I know the fairest spot.*
Dort liegt ein rothblühender Garten	*There blooms a garden of red*
Im stillen Mondenschein;	*in the silent beams of the moon;*
Die Lotosblumen erwarten	*the lotus flowers await*
Ihr trautes Schwesterlein.	*their little sister so dear.*
Die Veilchen kichern und kosen,	*The violets giggle and tease,*
Und schau'n nach den Sternen empor;	*and gaze aloft at the stars;*
Heimlich erzählen die Rosen	*the roses secretly whisper*
Sich duftende Märchen in's Ohr.	*perfumed tales to each other.*
Es hüpfen herbei und lauschen	*There come leaping to listen*
Die frommen, klugen Gazell'n,	*the wise and devout gazelles,*
Und in der Ferne rauschen	*and in the distance murmur*
Des heil'gen Stromes Well'n.	*the waves of the holy river.*
Dort wollen wir niedersinken	*There we will lie down*
Unter dem Palmenbaum	*beneath the spreading palm,*
Und Lieb' und Ruhe trinken	*drinking love and contentment,*
Und träumen seligen Traum.	*and dreaming blessed dreams.*

Heine's poem is a conventional, orientalizing lyric utterance, perhaps not untinged with irony. Here the pleasing strains of song are proposed as the figurative means of escape to a lightly exotic *locus amoenus*, suggesting the world of Thomas Moore's *Lalla Rookh*. Mendelssohn's simple, fluid setting is certainly quite without irony. The 'wings of song' figure is reflected, also conventionally, in the way the lilting 6/8 vocal line 'floats' above the rippling arpeggios of the accompaniment (Example 6.1). The implied 'lateral' directionality of the figure, transporting the subject from the speaker's 'here' to a distant, imaginary elsewhere, is gently underlined by sustained high E flats at the cadences to the two musical stanzas (at 'erwarten' and 'rauschen') and the varied coda phrase (at 'Traum').

The first song of Beethoven's *An die ferne Geliebte*, 'Auf dem Hügel sitz' ich spähend', grounds the whole cycle in this trope, which is clearly suggested by the collective title of the cycle, as well. The third stanza of the Jeitteles poem expresses the insufficiency of 'sight' and even of unvocalized 'sighs' to reach across the distance:

Example 6.1 Mendelssohn, *Auf Flügeln des Gesanges*, Op. 34, no. 2, mm. 1–9.

Ach den Blick kannst du nicht sehen,	*Ah, my glance you cannot see*
Der zu dir so glühend eilt,	*as it fervently speeds your way,*
Und die Seufzer, sie verwehen	*and my sighs, they expire*
In dem Raume, der uns teilt.	*within the space that divides us.*

That spatial reach is accomplished when the voice becomes musical, the decision taken in stanzas four and five, thereby launching the remainder of the cycle:

Will denn nichts mehr zu dir dringen,	*Will nothing then reach you,*
Nichts der Liebe Bote sein?	*nothing serve as love's messenger?*
Singen will ich, Lieder singen,	***I will sing! Sing you songs***
Die dir klagen meine Pein!	*that shall lament to you my pain!*
Denn vor **Liebesklang** entweichet	*Thus before the **sounds of love***
Jeder Raum und jede Zeit,	*all space and time must yield,*
Und ein liebend Herz erreichet,	*and a loving heart thus reaches*
Was ein liebend Herz geweiht!	*what a loving heart has blessed!*

Beethoven's setting of the poem consists simply of five iterations of a single eight-measure melodic phrase, but he emphasizes the turn to song (indicated by boldface in the lines quoted) with an accelerated sixteenth-note accompaniment in stanzas three and five, suggesting the greater momentum achieved when the poetic speaker becomes a singer.

These songs, then, represent the 'lateral' or horizontal version of the topos of music's transportational agency. The 'vertical' version, which also provides the source of another large figurative repertory (music as a transfiguring agency in tableaus of heavenly ascent or 'redemption') can be seen in an anonymous parlour song called 'The Music Fays' (*c.*1820?). The musical setting, likewise anonymous, is a cheerfully sociable composition in E flat, 4/4, marked 'lively', introduced by a *cantabile* ritornello with a short, bouncy cadence which returns between the verses.

When beauty wakes the sleeping strings,
To sport with her in song or dance,
We waft the tones to earth on wings
More swift than light, or fancy's glance.

And as they fade on mortal ears
Each air-drawn sound returning flies,
Where music moves the starry spheres,
Where song harmonious never dies.

For ev'ry breath of music's birth
Is borrowed from a deathless strain,
The faintest whisper heard on earth,
Is wafted to its heav'n again.[2]

Here we have an early version of the Romantic metaphysical view later satirized by Nietzsche as music serving for a 'telephone from the beyond'.[3] In this pre-technological version, music itself has not quite become the medium of transmission; rather, it is carried back and forth from heaven, like Wagner's Holy Grail, by obliging winged messengers ('the music fays').

Wagner's inspiration in *Lohengrin* was to match the music to the messengers, omitting any text (in the Prelude, that is, where he had imagined this scenario) so that the listener's attention is focused on the etherealized sound-image.[4] For this idea he was able to draw on a more dignified pedigree than 'The Music Fays', of course. In the closing lines of 'Alte und neue Kirchenmusik', for example, E.T.A. Hoffmann expressed his hope that a revival of a 'true' style of sacred music would improve lines of communication between mankind and the otherworld: 'May music, free and strong, stir its seraph's wings and begin again its flight towards the world beyond, which is its home and from [whence] consolation and grace shine down upon man's uneaseful breast.'[5] Listening to Wagner's *Lohengrin* Prelude in 1860, Charles Baudelaire experienced something like this otherworldly transport, gratified to discover afterwards how closely his response corresponded to the hermeneutic glosses on the music by Wagner and Franz Liszt. 'I felt myself released from the *bonds of gravity*', he recalled in the essay 'Richard Wagner et Tannhäuser à Paris', 'and I rediscovered in memory that extraordinary thrill of pleasure which dwells in *high places*'. After describing the further sensations of solitude, spatial amplitude, and light, he concludes: 'Then I came to the full conception of the idea of a soul moving about in a luminous medium ... hovering high above the natural world.'[6]

Before the telephone or radio were discovered as a means to transport the disembodied human voice through space, music and song were portrayed as possessing that capacity, at least in some latent or symbolic way. Music, of a certain sort and in certain contexts, was perceived as a means of conveying the listening subject heavenwards 'on wings of song' by virtue of its disembodying, transfiguring effects. In this Romantic tradition it becomes (to anticipate another technological innovation) a 'Metaphysical Transportation Authority', not a subway, but a stairway to heaven, a celestial escalator (in the vertical version), or, to stay with the winged species, something like Lohengrin's swan-boat (in the horizontal version).

The figure of music's 'winged' agency seems to have especially crystallized in the decades after 1800. Consider the reaction of the title character in Dorothea von Schlegel's 1801 novel *Florentin* to the music of an elusive aristocratic female composer named 'Clementine'. Wandering out of doors after a performance of Clementine's music, Florentin meditates: 'My spirit was relieved from all concerns of this life. As if on angelic wings, I felt removed from the earth by the all-powerful tones and saw a new world opening up before my eyes.'[7] A play popular in Beethoven's Vienna, *Die Schuld* by Adolf Müllner (1774–1829), both begins and ends with the heroine Elvire playing her harp as a means of effecting disembodiment and transfiguration: 'So would I, one day, like to soar on high and fade away into the better life! ... Carry me softly upward to my home', she implores as the curtain rises to the fading notes of the overture.[8] Getting her wish, finally, at the end of the play, Elvire clutches her harp and whispers: 'Thus I am preserved – like the tones of a harp – drifting towards heaven, my resting place.'[9] Both of these passages from Müllner's play were copied by Beethoven in his *Tagebuch* of 1812–18.[10]

The Italian operatic *preghiera* almost always suggests this trope, more or less explicitly. Recall, for instance, one of the most famous ones, 'Va pensiero, sull'ali dorate'. The unison song of the exiled Hebrews in Verdi's *Nabucco* gives 'golden wings' to their thoughts of home, soliciting as well the aid of a psalmodist's golden harp-strings.

Va, pensiero, sull'ali dorate;	*Go, thought, on wings of gold;*
va, ti posa sui clivi, sui colli,	*go, alight on hill and in dale,*
ove olezzano tepide e molli	*where soft, warm, and sweet air*
l'aure dolci del suolo natal!	*breathes over our native land!*
....	....
Arpa d'ôr dei fatidici vati,	*Golden harp of the prophets,*
perchè muta dal salice pendi?	*why hang silent from the willow?*
Le memorie nel petto raccendi,	*Awaken memories in our breast,*
ci favella del tempo che fu!	*and tell us of times that were!*[11]

Even Nietzsche himself, at least in his younger Wagnerian phase, could invoke the figure of music's 'winged agency' in a non-satirical vein. Throughout the later sections of *The Birth of Tragedy*, he theorizes about the relation of the Apollonian image to Dionysian sound, or music, in Greek tragedy. The Dionysian musical stimulus 'discharges itself', he explains, in a heightened perception of the stage image: we 'recognize this moment when the Apolline [i.e., the Apollonian image] soars upward, as it were, borne on the wings of music, as the supreme intensification of its energies'.[12]

Music and the 'redemptive tableau'

'Winged' music is transformed from mental to fully visible representation in the tableau of redemption and celestial 'assumption' common in nineteenth-century opera, theatre, and visual culture generally. Virtually every mature work of Richard Wagner from *The Flying Dutchman* on (counting the *Ring* as a single work) involves this trope in some significant way, normally at the end. The Wagnerian canon raises two questions with respect to the representation of music as 'agency'. First, while music of course participates in the realization of these redemptive apotheoses, is it also in any way thematically *represented* by them? Second, if we *can* argue that these scenes do in some sense *represent* music, is this representation principally allegorical in nature, or could the situations be seen to represent the transfiguring *agency* of music in some more direct way? I would respond to both questions with a qualified 'yes'.

In his first attempt at a drama from Nordic mythology, *Wieland der Schmied* (Wieland the Smith), which never progressed beyond the draft of a libretto, Wagner even specifically deploys the figure of winged flight in the concluding redemptive stage picture. The titular hero is a Nordic

Icarus, a smith of mythical genius who is captured and crippled (hamstrung) by his enemy, Neiding, while trying to avenge the death of his valkyrie-like wife, Schwanhilde, part woman and part swan. Wieland forges a pair of magical-mechanical wings, traps his own captors in the smithy where they had enslaved him, sets it on fire, and then soars aloft to join the spirit of his beloved Schwanhilde in the skies. The final image is of Wieland rising above the smoking ruins of the forest dwelling where he had been imprisoned. For a moment he is invisible in the cloud of smoke (i.e., disembodied). Finally, 'All gaze in transport and amazement up to Wieland ... The dazzling steel of his wings shines like the sun in the morning splendor. Schwanhilde hovers towards him from the woods on her outspread swan wings. They meet and fly into the distance.'[13] Wieland becomes an unmistakable allegory of the Romantic artist, beleaguered but finally transcendent. The music that would have animated his flight was never composed. (Wagner also offered the material to Franz Liszt at the time the latter was contemplating operatic composition in Weimar; allegedly Adolf Hitler had designs to compose it somehow, prior to his political career.) Music as such, however, is not suggested as the agency of Wieland's flight.

Wagner's best-known tableau of disembodied transcendence is Isolde's *Liebestod* or, more properly, *Verklärung* ('transfiguration'). In the course of this famous finale, Isolde 'resurrects' Tristan in the form of disembodied traces of his former self, freed in death to join her in a noumenal beyond, like Wieland and Schwanhilde. Here, however, we might argue that the essential medium, or agency, of the transcendence is song:

Höre ich nur	*Do I alone hear*
diese Weise,	*this melody,*
die so wunder-	*that so wonderfully*
voll und leise,	*and softly*
Wonne klagend,	*cries of bliss,*
alles sagend,	*saying all,*
mild versöhnend	*gently reconciling,*
aus ihm tönend,	*sounding from him*
in mich dringet,	*and within me,*
auf sich schwinget,	*rising up*
hold erhallend	*and echoing*
um mich klinget?	*all about me?*

Although she sings of sinking or drowning, the 'billowing flood' into which Isolde imagines herself disappearing is a flood of *sound*, and breath:

'In dem wogenden Schwall, in dem tönenden Schall, in des Welt-Atems wehendem All' ('In the surging flood, in the ringing sound, in the world-breath's infinite gasp'). The preceding images reinforce this: 'Sind es Wellen sanfter Lüfte, sind es Wolken wonniger Düfte?' ('Is this the billowing of soft breezes? Are these clouds of blissful scents?') The composite gesture of Isolde's *Verklärung* has been, with good reason, associated with Wagner's well-known admiration for Titian's famous 1518 Venetian altarpiece representing the Assumption of the Virgin.[14]

The music of Isolde's *Verklärung*, the 'billowing' orchestral textures and the inexorable sequential patterns, acts like that cloud on which Titian's Virgin is riding. Isolde makes the point herself, when she asks about the music ('diese Weise') she imagines emanating from Tristan's body and surrounding her: 'Are these clouds of blissful scents?' Hearing music, she imagines it taking the visible, not to mention aromatic, form of clouds of incense. Her body may fall to the ground, but her 'disembodied' part – voice, spirit – has only one way to go: up. (The fact that Wagner himself associated Titian's painting with the conception of a different composition – the Prelude to *Die Meistersinger* when the idea for it came to him while leaving Venice by train[15] – only confirms, perhaps, that even the heaviest music aspires to float.)

The Alpha and Omega of this redemptive visual trope in the nineteenth century is the conclusion of Goethe's *Faust* and its many iterations across different mediums and cultural milieus. The end of Part I rehearses the tableau in its simpler, more conventionally Christian form with the last-minute heavenly pardon of the errant, suffering Gretchen. (Goethe's own text provides only the merest cues, such as a small voice 'from above'.) The end of Part II, Faust's own death, subjects the gesture to a sort of cosmic, pantheistic amplification. In neither case does Goethe attribute a transfiguring agency to music, specifically; but popular theatrical representations, especially in the latter half of the nineteenth century, amply supply it. Charles Gounod's *Faust* opera is the obvious case, although Michel Carré's earlier, widely circulating theatrical adaptation, *Faust et Marguerite* (the source of his libretto for Gounod), and Henry Irving's big-budget London *Faust* production of the 1880s at his Lyceum Theatre, for example, encouraged a similar marriage of spectacle and sound in Gretchen's apotheosis. (These popular dramatizations, including Gounod's, all in some sense transfer the celestial riot of the *Faust II* conclusion to Gretchen's end at the close of *Faust I*.)

At the end of Irving's production, as Mephisto sweeps Faust into the wings, 'the back wall of the dungeon opened, … rapturous music swelled in the orchestra, the voices of angels rose in the chorus, and the stage was gradually illumined by rays which seemed to descend from a cloudless sun'. To effect Gretchen's ascension, Irving constructed a virtual 'ladder of angels' illuminated by limelight against a midnight-blue backcloth so that they appeared 'floating radiantly in the empty heavens'. Each of the winged angels arrayed in this diagonal line, from the boards on one side up into the flies on the other, reached down towards Gretchen (or here, 'Margaret'), inviting her immortal part to join them. (The arrangement is reminiscent of the spiritual telecommunications system outlined in 'The Music Fays'.) 'With this tableau the play ended', Michael Booth remarks in his account of Irving's *Faust* in *Victorian Spectacular Theatre*, 'a beautiful morality painting of the frustration of evil and the salvation of good; the destruction of Wills's poor, weak, and helpless Faust' – referring to the author of the adaptation, William Gorman Wills, who was also a painter as well as the theatre manager – 'was almost an irrelevance'.[16] Reviewing the production, the writer Bram Stoker (of *Dracula* fame) was bemused by the intensely material, industrial efforts required by Irving's heavenly phantasmagoria (which provides, in fact, a good example of how the 'phantasmagoria' became a critical figure for Adorno). Another critic likened the 'inclined plane' of the angelic ladder to a touristic funicular in the Swiss Alps (the Righi-Bahn).[17] Irving probably took his cue to some extent from Marguerite's 'Anges pures, anges radieux' in the climactic trio of Gounod's by then universally popular opera. The combination of angelic arpeggios and stepwise modulation in Gounod's trio does a kind of musical heavy lifting not unlike what Stoker observed in the mechanics of Irving's tableau. (The enduring musical-iconographic tradition is aptly preserved in an educational short feature on opera from 1973, in which the final scene from *Faust* is gamely performed by Joan Sutherland and Richard Bonynge for an inquisitive audience of Muppets.)[18]

The cultural ubiquity of this religious-sentimental complex of music and image could be documented at length. Consider just one further example, the closing scene in George Aiken's adaptation of *Uncle Tom's Cabin* as a stage melodrama, which one editor describes as both 'America's first long-running hit' and 'the greatest success in the history of the American theater'.[19] At the close, Uncle Tom expires from a ruthless beating at the hands of the arch-villain, Simon Legree, who in this version is shot in a sudden mêlée, allowing for full moral closure. George Shelby, Jr, son of Tom's original upright Kentucky master, has come to rescue him from Legree, but too late. After Shelby discovers Tom's body in the penultimate scene, Act VI, scene 6, Aiken's stage directions read: *Solemn music. George covers Uncle Tom with his cloak and kneels over him. Clouds work on and conceal them, and then work off.*[20] The final scene (Act VI, scene 7) consists solely of one further stage direction, distilling the *über*-sentimental death scene of 'Little Eva' (the angelic blonde paragon of childish virtue) from an earlier portion of Harriet Beecher Stowe's novel into a wordless final tableau:

Gorgeous clouds, tinted with sunlight. Eva, robed in white, is discovered on the back of a milk-white dove, with expanded wings, as if just soaring upward. Her hands are extended in benediction over St Clare [Eva's likewise deceased father] *and Uncle Tom who are kneeling and gazing up to her. Expressive Music. Slow curtain.*

END[21]

The image may not be 'about' music in the sense that Isolde's *Verklärung* arguably is, but its performance is inconceivable *without* the music. As a stage picture, it depends entirely on the music to 'realize for the feelings' (as Wagner would put it) the redemptive dynamic of its symbols.

Orpheus, Beethoven, Schumann and the *Fata Morgana* of 'the Music Itself'

Saintly Little Eva on the wings of a dove returns us to the traditions of musical allegory mentioned at the beginning, and the question of how that mode of representing music ('on the whole') differs from what I have called representations of musical agency more characteristic of the Romantic era.

St Cecilia, not surprisingly, is often depicted in the company – or prospective company – of angels. In this iconographic context, the winged celestial beings anticipate something of the transfiguring agency later attributed more explicitly to music. Not infrequently, St Cecilia pictures thematize a contrast between the imperfections of earthly, 'broken' (or breakable) instrumental music – *musica humana* and *instrumentalis* and all these might symbolize – and the incorporeal *musica mundana* of eternity, as in for instance the much reproduced and imitated picture by Raphael (see Figure 6.2 above). John Dryden's poetic version of the allegory, the 1687 'Song for St Cecilia's Day', explicitly grants 'wings' to the notes emanating from Cecilia's pipe organ, suggesting (with a certain Enlightenment audacity) that this instrument of human invention might help to retune the neglected harmony of the spheres. In any case, music is once again seemingly implicated in a kind of celestial communications network. Moreover, Cecilia's heavenly orientation is compared advantageously to Orpheus's terrestrial focus. The 'breath' of the organ resembles that of the human voice and, implicitly, the aerial quality of the human spirit; the tones of the plucked lyre, by comparison, have a more limited range:

> But oh! what art can teach,
>   What human voice can reach
> The sacred ORGAN's praise?
> Notes inspiring holy love,
> Notes that wing their heavenly ways
> To mend the choirs above.
>
> Orpheus could lead the savage race;
> And trees uprooted left their place,
>   Sequacious of the lyre;
> But bright CECILIA raised the wonder higher:
> When to her ORGAN vocal breath was given,
> An angel heard, and straight appeared
>   Mistaking Earth for heaven.[22]

We could apply the metaphorical dichotomy suggested earlier of music's vertical vs horizontal or lateral reach to these two allegorical instrumental paradigms, respectively.

Even the pagan Orpheus, better known for his infernal descent, is often given angelic attention, at least in the modern European iconographic tradition. In G.B. Tiepolo's fresco 'Allegory of the Power of Eloquence' in the Palazzo Sandi in Venice (c.1724–5), for example, Orpheus is seen from below, lifting Euridice up to the earth's surface; the violin and bow he holds extended in his right hand point up towards the clouds and blue skies of heaven, while a winged, blindfolded Cupid or *putto* hovers above the pair, urging on their ascent in what is presumably its last moment. Eugène Delacroix's cupola painting for the Palais Bourbon from a century later (1845–7), depicting Orpheus civilizing the savage Greeks, shows the goddesses Demeter and Athena hovering in mid-air above the poet as he sings or recites from an unfurled scroll.[23] Franz Liszt's programme for his symphonic poem *Orpheus* composed a few years later also chooses the theme of Orpheus as bringer of civilization (drawing not on Delacroix but on a classical image, a Greek *krater* in the Louvre). These two nineteenth-century cases both invoke music's civilizing agency, but both also figure this in terms of raising human consciousness from the earth towards some kind of heavenly or metaphysical ideal.

Liszt's symphonic poem, moreover, concludes with a musical allusion to the singer's 'translation' into the skies as a constellation. The tradition of Orpheus's heavenly apotheosis derives from a contemporary of Virgil, Gaius Julius Hyginus, who introduced in his *Poeticon Astronomicon* the apotheosis of Orpheus's lyre as a constellation in recognition of his sufferings and his civilizing contributions.[24] Hyginus's apotheosis was perhaps conceived as a deliberate alternative to the striking poetic conceit in Virgil's *Metamorphoses* in which the head of Orpheus, having been torn from his body by the frenzied Thracian maenads, is cast into the river Hebrus where it continues to sing – or at least sigh – the name 'Eurydice' as it floats forlornly downstream. (The violent dismemberment of Orpheus by the maenads in Virgil harks back to archaic Dionysian rituals of possession or ultimately some form of fertility rites from a time before music and the arts had transformed the savage Greeks into civilized Hellenes.)

It might be possible to detect a fusion of classical or early modern allegorical traditions with the newer romantic trope of music's 'transfiguring agency' in the somewhat enigmatic final movement of Schumann's *Fantasy* in C major for piano. By way of conclusion, let us entertain briefly such a speculative reading of this piece, to see how old and new ideas of representing the art of music might be heard to inform a particular example.

Schumann, as is well known, had two different figures in mind in composing the music eventually published as the *Fantasy*, Op. 17. The opening movement (*phantastisch und leidenschaftlich*) was affiliated in his mind primarily with Clara Wieck, while the whole three-movement work was intended as a 'grand sonata' paying homage to the memory of Ludwig van Beethoven (specifically, as a gesture of support – more symbolic than practical – for the project of a Beethoven monument in Bonn). The eventual publication was formally dedicated to Franz Liszt. All these figures – Clara Wieck, Beethoven, and Liszt – were paragons of music to Schumann, in one way or another, though Beethoven was one of a different order. Only ten years dead when the work was composed, Beethoven was already a mythic figure, and it was with that figure the completed work was meant to be overtly associated, even if that association was rescinded in the end from the published text. Schumann seems to have thought of the movements as constituting three different 'fantasies', each with a different heading. Originally, these headings read: 'Ruins', 'Trophies', and 'Palms'. Collectively, the composition was to be billed as a 'Grand Sonata for the

Table 6.1 Versions of Schumann's original titles for Op. 17

Titles as of December 1836	Titles as of April–May 1838
Grand Sonata ('Obulus') for Beethoven's Monument	Dichtungen ('Poems'), Op. 12 [sic] Or: Fata morgana (?)
I. Ruinen ('Ruins')	I. Ruinen ('Ruins')
II. Trophäen ('Trophies')	II. Siegesbogen ('Triumphal Arch')
III. Palmen ('Palms')	III. Sternbild ('Constellation')

Piano for Beethoven's Monument, by Florestan and Eusebius'. Shortly before it was published Schumann was calling the collective work *Dichtungen* ('Poems'), and now the poetic headings for the separate movements read: 'Ruins', 'Triumphal Arch', and 'Constellation'. (These dates and different title versions are compared in Table 6.1.)

About the same time the second set of movement titles was proposed, Schumann also suggested calling the whole work 'Fata Morgana' – that is, a mirage, or illusion.[25] Like all the movements, the last was eventually headed simply with the composer's performance directions: *Langsam getragen. Durchweg leise zu halten*. But what, if anything, are we to make of the earlier proposed headings for the last movement? 'Palms' presumably signified Beethoven's posthumous victory as a hero of music, in the related sense of the 'myrtles' or 'laurels' of classical emblematic tradition: a musical crown to his overall 'monument'. How did the 'Palms' become a 'Constellation'? And how does the movement, in either case, constitute a 'fantasy', a 'poem', or the end of a sounding 'mirage' ('fata morgana')?

The third movement begins with simple triadic arpeggiations. In their deliberate simplicity of musical form or content we could reasonably take these opening measures to signify 'harmony', suggesting an improvisational harp- or lyre-like accompaniment to some anticipated poetic-lyrical utterance (Example 6.2a). The third relations, though uncomplicated, signal depth and interiority. Then, through the introduction of sustained chord tones in the right hand, 'harmony' generates 'melody': the lyre yields to the 'voice'. On the piano, this vocal-melodic element can emerge from *within* the harmony rather than being merely superimposed, as a real vocal line would be (see Example 6.2b, the tenor-range voice in the dotted notes of the right hand).

Soon the lyrical 'voice' predominates, but it seems as if we are tuning in only *in medias res* to some distant song, catching just some fragments. We could easily relate these melodic fragments to the lyric voice projected afar, carried 'on wings of song', according to our original poetic trope

Example 6.2a Schumann, *Fantasy* Op.17, mvt. III, mm. 1–5.

Example 6.2b Schumann, *Fantasy* Op. 17, mvt. III, mm. 5–10.

(Example 6.3). Harmony and melody, instrument and voice are afterwards presented in pure, almost symbolic juxtaposition in a way that prompted Nicholas Marston to imagine the grafting of two different compositions, a 'harmonic' and a 'melodic' one, into one simultaneous experience,[26] a musical analogue of sorts to the Romantic literary conceit of accidentally intercalated narrative texts, as in E.T.A. Hoffmann's *Kater Murr*. At first, fragments of these two different 'works' are heard juxtaposed, unintegrated (Example 6.4).

In these complementary musical figures Schumann is, I imagine, celebrating Beethoven as 'Orpheus' through sounding emblems of his lyre and his voice, respectively. Together, the lyre and the voice ('harmony' and 'melody') constitute a complete sounding emblem of music, that is, music 'on the whole', music itself.[27] However, throughout most of the movement the harp-like emblem of 'harmony' remains separate from the lyrical elements. From mm. 42 to 71, and again from mm. 99 to 122, the lyrical cantabile material coalesces into more continuous, periodic melodic

Example 6.3 Schumann, *Fantasy* Op. 17, mvt. III, mm. 15-23.

Example 6.4 Schumann, *Fantasy* Op. 17, mvt. III, mm. 30-41.

phrasing, with a straightforward harmonic bass line and chordal harmonization in simple keyboard textures. When the emblematic harp or lyre figure (pure 'harmony') returns at m. 87, however, it is again juxtaposed with the earlier melodic fragments (as in mm. 30–43). In both cases the 'lyre' figure pushes the melodic fragments in new harmonic directions, without properly joining them. These melodic fragments (see mm. 34–5 of Example 6.4) are shunted this way and that by the mysterious 'lyre' figure, which itself seems to constitute a continuous 'subterranean' current of

Example 6.5 Schumann, *Fantasy* Op. 17, mvt. III, mm. 127–41.

harmonic arpeggiation (as Marston imagines it), only now and then rising to the audible musical surface. These floating lyrical fragments, tossed here and there by the harmonic current, could even suggest the image of Orpheus's severed head, as described in Virgil, singing in fragmentary sighs as it floats down the Hebrus towards the Black Sea.

In the coda to this structurally simple yet strangely amorphous movement, these two complementary emblems of harmony and melody, the lyre and the voice, are joined at last, beginning in m. 123. The underlying gesture of the movement as a whole, completed in the coda, could be imagined – 'represented' – as an apotheosis: Orpheus, translated to the firmament as a constellation (Schumann's *Sternbild*), recalled in homage to the Orpheus of modern music, Beethoven. The gesture of apotheosis is accomplished through the agency of Schumann's musical materials. After lyre and voice have been briefly (re-)united at the beginning of the short coda, the increasingly urgent gestures of 'harmony' subsume the last, fading, sinking fragments of 'melody'. The voice falls silent as the surging harmonic arpeggios (with a new Neapolitan cadence inflection) complete the 'translation' of the Orphic subject into a perfected beyond (Example 6.5). In other words, as Orpheus's singing (mortal) head sinks beneath the waves, the emblematic (immortal) lyre is raised to the skies.

As with Wagner's Isolde, an image of sinking or drowning (the last gasp of the singing head) is merged into a larger gesture of apotheosis of the disembodied subject. In the symbolic distillation of 'melody' and 'harmony' as pure essences throughout the movement, eventually joined but only to be dissolved in a concluding 'apotheosis', Schumann's homage to Beethoven also suggests a representation of music as such. The apotheosis of an Orphic Beethoven is at the same time the ultimate, impossible act of representation – the *fata morgana* of 'music itself'.

Notes

1 On the literary and iconographic traditions of various figures relating to intangible things such as breath, spirit, soul, ghosts, and spirits from ancient to modern times, see Marina Warner, *Phantasmagoria: Spirit Visions, Metaphors, and Media into the Twenty-first Century* (Oxford University Press, 2006). Particularly relevant here are Parts II (Air), III (Clouds), and VIII (Ether), and more particularly Part II, ch. 5, 'Winged Spirits and Sweet Airs', 71–80.
2 Anon, 'The Music Fays', in a collection of vocal music *c.*1800–45, British Library music collection, H.1650f.
3 Friedrich Nietzsche, *On The Genealogy of Morals*, trans. Walter Kaufmann and R.J. Hollingdale (New York: Vintage, 1969), 103. The passage reads in full: 'With this extraordinary rise in the value of music that appeared to follow from Schopenhauerian philosophy, the value of *the musician* himself all at once went up in an unheard-of manner, too: from now on he became an oracle, a priest, indeed more than a priest, a kind of mouthpiece of the "in itself" of things, a telephone from the beyond – henceforth he uttered not only music, this ventriloquist of God – he uttered metaphysics: no wonder he one day finally uttered *ascetic ideals*.'
4 See Wagner's 1853 programme note to the Act I Prelude to *Lohengrin* in Thomas S. Grey (ed.), *Richard Wagner and his World* (Princeton University Press, 2009), 499–501.
5 E.T.A. Hoffmann, 'Old and New Church Music' (1814), trans. Martyn Clarke, in David Charlton (ed.), *E.T.A. Hoffmann's Musical Writings: Kreisleriana,*

The Poet and the Composer, Music Criticism (Cambridge University Press, 1989), 376.

6 Charles Baudelaire, 'Richard Wagner and *Tannhäuser* in Paris' in *The Painter of Modern Life and Other Essays*, ed. and trans. Jonathan Mayne (London: Phaidon, 1964), 116–17.

7 Dorothea [Veit] von Schlegel [née Mendelssohn], *Florentin, a Novel* (1801), trans. with introduction by Edwina Lawler and Ruth Richardson (Lampeter, Dyfed, Wales: The Edwin Mellen Press, 1988), 143. See also Matthew Head, 'Cultural Meanings for Women Composers: Charlotte ("Minna") Brandes and the Beautiful Dead in the German Enlightenment', *Journal of the American Musicological Society*, 57.2 (Summer 2004), 231–84.

8 Elvire: So auch möcht' ich einst verschweben / Und verklingen in das beßre Leben! Adam Müllner, *Die Schuld*, Act I, sc. 1 in *Dramatische Werke. Erster Theil* (Braunschweig: Friedrich Vieweg, 1828), 5. (Plays in this edition are separately paginated.)

9 Elvire (*halb aufgerichtet, mit sich verstärkendem Blicke*): So wahr ich – wie Töne der Harfe – die mir zum Lager dient – himmelwärts schwebe! (*Sie sinkt sterbend auf die Harfe zurück, die Hand gleitet dabei matt über die Saiten, und man hört einen leisen verhallenden Ton.*) Müllner, *Die Schuld*, 185.

10 See the annotated transcription of the Beethoven *Tagebuch* in Maynard Solomon, *Beethoven Essays* (Cambridge, MA: Harvard University Press, 1988), 233–95 (249–50). This is the first extract as copied by Beethoven, in Solomon's translation:
Elvira (alone, harp in her arm, ending the music with ever quieter and softly disappearing tones);

As the last tone dies away,
That sounds under a soft hand
From the harp's strings
Like a drop fallen
On the clear crystal pond,
....

So would I, one day, like to soar on high
and fade away into the better life! –
....

(*Her head bent over the harp, she rests awhile. A string breaks, Elvira starts up in fright, the harp falls [echoingly] to the ground.*)

11 Verdi, *Nabucco* (libretto by Temistocle Solera), Part III, sc. 4, 'Chorus and prophecy'.

12 Friedrich Nietzsche, *The Birth of Tragedy and Other Writings*, ed. Raymond Geuss and Ronald Speirs, trans. Ronald Speirs (Cambridge University Press, 1999), 112.

13 Richard Wagner, *Wieland the Smith* (a dramatic sketch), trans. William Ashton Ellis, in *Richard Wagner's Prose Works*, 8 vols. (London, 1895), vol. I, 248 (translation emended).
14 See, for example, Dieter Borchmeyer, 'Love and Objectification in the Music Drama: Tristan's Isolde and her Sisters' in Daphne Ellis (trans.), *Drama and the World of Richard Wagner* (Princeton University Press, 2003), 157–79 (161–4); and Camilla Bork, '"Tod und Verklärung": Isoldes Liebestod als Modell künstlerischer Schlußgestaltung' in Hermann Danuser and Herfried Münkler (eds.), *Zukunftsbilder: Richard Wagners Revolutionen und ihre Folgen in Kunst und Politik* (Schliengen: Argus, 2002), 161–78 (164–8).
15 Richard Wagner, *My Life*, trans. Andrew Gray (Cambridge University Press, 1983), 667–8. Wagner comments on the 'exalting impression' made on him by the painting, which re-awakened his creative impulses 'with almost their original primordial power', and immediately follows this with a simple statement about his decision to compose *Die Meistersinger* and his mental drafting of the opening paragraphs of the Prelude. A causal relation between painting and musical inspiration is not explicitly articulated. Much later, in a remark recorded by Cosima Wagner in her diary on 22 October 1882, Wagner did connect the Titian image directly with Isolde's transfiguration. Cosima and Richard had been looking at paintings that afternoon in the Accademia di Belle Arti in Venice (where at the time Titian's altarpiece was located, before being returned to the church of the Frari). 'R. looks at many things with great calmness and concentration, among them … the *Assunta*, and in respect of his appreciation of this great work, I see to my joy that he is increasingly coming around to my feeling about it … [Later] R. begins, "One cannot paint Christ, but one can portray him in music" … From this we go on to painting – that it was able to depict the Mother of God. But R. denies that the *Assunta* is the Mother of God; it is Isolde, he says, in the apotheosis of love … Thus calmed and raised above reality by the images of art, we go off to rest. However, it was not a good night.' *Cosima Wagner's Diaries*, ed. Martin Gregor-Dellin and Dietrich Mack, trans. Geoffrey Skelton, 2 vols. (New York and London: Harcourt Brace Jovanovich, 1980), vol. II, 934–5.
16 Michael R. Booth, *Victorian Spectacular Theatre: 1850–1914* (London and Boston: Routledge & Kegan Paul, 1981), 123.
17 *Ibid.*, 122–3.
18 See www.youtube.com/watch?v=Q3pAinJhdnM, accessed 10 April 2012.
19 Daniel C. Gerould, introduction to Gerould (ed.), *American Melodrama* (New York: Performing Arts Journal Publications, 1983), 14.
20 George Aiken, *Uncle Tom's Cabin* in Gerould, *American Melodrama*, 132–3.
21 *Ibid.*, 133.
22 John Dryden, 'A Song for St Cecilia's Day', lines 42–54, in Alistair Fowler (ed.), *The New Oxford Book of Seventeenth-Century Verse* (Oxford University Press, 1991), 685.

23 The full title placed in gilt lettering below Delacroix's hemicycle painting reads: 'Orphée vient policer les Grecs encore sauvages et leur enseigner les arts de la paix' ('Orpheus comes to civilize [refine, establish order among] the still savage Greeks and to teach them the arts of peace'). For the Tiepolo image, see www.artandarchitecture.org.uk/images/gallery/b03b0d57.html; and for the Delacroix, see www.assemblee-nationale.fr/histoire/bibliotheque-delacroix-paix.asp, accessed 10 April 2012.

24 See also Owen Jander, *Beethoven's 'Orpheus' Concerto: The Fourth Piano Concerto in its Cultural Context*, North American Beethoven Studies, no. 5 (Hillsdale, NY: Pendragon Press, 2009), 135–42, where Jander interprets passages from the last movement coda of the Fourth Piano Concerto (mm. 416–25, 500–7, 520–9, and 546–53) according to the 'apotheosis' of the lyre. The monograph expands on Jander's well-known reading of the *Andante con moto* in terms of the myth of Orpheus in Hades pleading for the return of Eurydice, proposing Orpheus-based interpretations of all three movements as well as offering extensive documentation of the presence of the Orpheus legend (Virgil and Ovid, as well as Gluck and subsequent operatic renditions) in Beethoven's Vienna.

25 Marina Warner discusses the 'fata morgana' as atmospheric phenomenon and its cultural history as metaphor in chapter 7 ('*Fata Morgana*; or, Castles in the Air') of *Phantasmagoria*.

26 Nicholas Marston, *Schumann: Fantasie, op. 17* (Cambridge University Press, 1992), 79–84.

27 Cf. Jander's résumé of his reading of the mythic-iconographic tradition of Orpheus's lyre in relation to Beethoven's Fourth Piano Concerto: 'In the Finale, Orpheus is destroyed by the Bacchantes, but his lyre is rescued and transfigured … [V]ictory is granted to the lyre, the symbol of music itself' (Jander, *Beethoven's 'Orpheus' Concerto*, 149).

7 | Representation and musical portraiture in the twentieth century

JOSHUA S. WALDEN

The genre of musical portraiture emerged in the eighteenth century and has remained of interest to composers to the present day, as a means of creating sonic depictions of patrons, family, friends, and historical figures. Portraiture has proven a more complex and even elusive enterprise in music than in painting or sculpture, for obvious reasons: in the absence of a means of depicting physical appearance, an element of portraiture in the visual arts that is commonly considered essential, composers have grappled with the question of how music can convey attributes of identity other than appearance in such a way that listeners will interpret the composition to represent an individual. But there is no doubt that composers expect their musical portraits to be understood as representational. With the aid of a title that indicates that a composition is to be heard as a depiction of a particular person, the musical portrait invites interpretation, as the listener constructs in his or her imagination an impression of the work's human subject. Musical portraiture therefore evinces a particularly self-conscious, interactive form of representation, in which a composition's sounds and structures, in conjunction with a name identifying it as a portrait, are constructed and heard to evoke abstract attributes of identity such as character, mood, and personality. The twentieth and twenty-first centuries have brought compelling developments to the genre of visual portraiture, as Western conceptions of identity have changed in parallel with increasing challenges to the predominance of mimesis in artistic representation. In light of these transformations, there has been renewed focus among composers on the representation of human subjects through music. This chapter examines recent efforts at musical portraiture, focusing on key examples by Philip Glass and György Ligeti, to understand how these composers depict other artists and musicians through the medium of sound.

Composers including François Couperin, Carl Philipp Emanuel Bach, Robert Schumann, Edward Elgar, Béla Bartók, Charles Ives, Virgil Thomson, Ligeti, and Glass have experimented with the genre of musical portraiture. Thomson, who between 1928 and 1985 composed over 140 musical portraits for a variety of ensembles, suggested that all composition is inherently representational, but that musical portraits aim to render a singular, identifiable image: 'Very little has ever been written down that the author did not think was about something. Some thing or some body. So every musical portrait is tied to an individual, and the composer of it tends to believe it a true likeness.'[1] In his musical portraits, Thomson employs the medium of instrumental music to depict emotion, temperament, and character with the intention of producing convincing resemblances of individual sitters.

From the earliest writings on the subject, portraiture in the visual arts has been considered a genre that relies inherently on processes of representation to fix and thus preserve the likeness of an individual subject. In his *Poetics*, Aristotle invoked portraiture as a paradigmatic representational art form, through which the artist presents again before the viewer the image of a person who is ever increasingly distant in time.[2] Reflecting Aristotle's influence, Leon Battista Alberti, in Book II of his 1435 treatise *On Painting*, writes, 'Painting contains a divine force which not only makes absent men present … but moreover makes the dead seem almost alive … Thus the face of a man who is already dead certainly lives a long life through painting.'[3] Since the sixteenth century, however, artists and critics have expressed scepticism that the depiction of mere physical likeness is sufficient to represent a sitter's identity.[4] Jerrold Seigel writes that the Western conception of the self has from the time of René Descartes and John Locke consisted of three components: the bodily, or physical existence; the relational, deriving from social interaction and cultural contexts; and the reflective, the capacity to examine and question oneself.[5] This multivalent notion of the self has had a significant impact on historical understandings of identity and its representation in portraiture. A successful visual portrait is generally understood not only to depict physical appearance, but also to provide insights into character and signs of profession or social position.[6] Of course, conceptions of what constitutes these aspects of human identity have varied considerably over time, and conventions in both visual and musical portraiture have developed alongside.

In the twentieth and twenty-first centuries, identity has increasingly been understood as something constructed and performed, rather than innate and tied to outward appearance. Identities are frequently viewed as fragmented, mutable, and defined through social interaction.[7] Madan Sarup writes, 'Identity in postmodern thought is not a thing; the self is necessarily incomplete, unfinished – it is "the subject in process".'[8] The contemporary understanding of identity as multivalent and open to varied interpretation has allowed artists to use more abstract means to represent individual subjects in a host of media. Many artists during this period have also expressed dissatisfaction with the conventions of mimesis as producing a 'mirror' of 'real' life, leading some portraitists to experiment with the elimination of literal physical likeness.[9] These artists have developed innovative methods of representing individuals without relying on verisimilitude. For example, Pablo Picasso engaged the techniques of cubism to deconstruct his sitters' bodies; Charles Demuth's portrait of William Carlos Williams *I Saw the Figure 5 in Gold* (1928) and Katherine Dreier's *Abstract Portrait of Marcel Duchamp* (1918) abandon pictorialism to offer abstract representations of their subjects; and Francis Bacon painted images of sitters with their faces and bodies contorted, often beyond recognition.[10] Thus portraiture has remained an important genre since the turn of the twentieth century, even for many artists who have eschewed mimesis in favour of alternative modes of representation.

These developments in the visual arts provide a model for describing how composers have experimented with depicting individuals through music. By analogy to cubism and other abstract representational modes of painting, composers have attempted to take advantage of music's structural qualities, creating portraits that depict the subject from various perspectives, unfolding through time and representing their sitters through the development of musical elements such as form, harmony, and style. As this chapter will show, Glass's composition for solo piano 'A Musical Portrait of Chuck Close' calls attention to the analogy between visual and musical portraiture, while Ligeti's duet for two pianos, 'Selbstportrait mit Reich und Riley (und Chopin ist auch dabei)' (Self-Portrait with Reich and Riley (with Chopin in the Background)), in which he depicts himself in the presence of composers Steve Reich and Terry Riley and their predecessor Frédéric Chopin, similarly manipulates musical structures and sounds to construct a complex representation of an artist, this time the composer himself. In these works, written for keyboard in the manner of many of the earliest musical portraits by Couperin and Bach, Glass and Ligeti employ the genre in overlapping but contrasting ways to explore in music how different artistic media can produce personal meanings and relate to contemporary notions of identity. This chapter closes with a coda, offering a glimpse at a playful variation on the intimate connection between visual and musical portraiture, Thomson's musical portrait of the artist Buffie Johnson in the process of sketching a portrait of the composer.

Philip Glass's 'A Musical Portrait of Chuck Close'

Glass's 2005 musical portrait of Close was commissioned by pianist Bruce Levingston, who was inspired to suggest the idea for the piece when he viewed Close's large-scale portrait of Glass hanging outside Caspary Hall at

Rockefeller University. The piece is constructed of two movements, though Glass originally conceived of it in another form, and its genesis is the result of serendipity.[11] Glass had prepared two alternative works before choosing one that he favoured as the final portrait, but his assistant mistakenly delivered Levingston the abandoned version. Later, when the error was discovered and Levingston received Glass's other composition, the pianist was enamoured of both, and convinced Glass to combine them into a two-movement work, also persuading him of the order in which they should be played. After hearing Levingston's performance, Glass approved, stating, 'I now think the current order is the right order. This is the fortunes of happenstance and synergy.'[12] The formal and harmonic attributes of Glass's composition in its final form suggest an emotional and creative narrative that depicts Close's career from his days as a young artist to the present, while the short modular rhythmic gestures of which the piece is built mimic the technical construction of Close's works of portraiture.

Glass and Close met in Paris in 1964 through mutual friends, the artists Richard Serra and Nancy Graves. They soon reunited in Manhattan, where for a time both worked as assistants in Serra's studio, and Glass, who raised money during periods of his early career working as a plumber, laid the pipes in Close's loft.[13] Glass was the subject of the 1969 painting *Phil*, from one of Close's first series of portraits, his oversized, highly realistic black-and-white 'Big Heads' begun that year on the basis of photographs of his friends' faces (Figure 7.1). Close has returned to many of these photographs throughout his career to paint them again, reusing none more frequently than the image of Glass, who has joked that he is the artist's haystack, in reference to the recurring subject in the paintings of Claude Monet.[14] Close has stated that his fascination with this photograph derived from the opportunities it offered him to experiment with modes of representation, taking inspiration from Glass's 'Medusa-like hair' and his 'heavy, hooded, druggy eyes and … sensuous mouth'.[15] The portraits of Glass, numbering over a hundred, appear in a variety of media including painting, spit-bite aquatint, dot drawing, finger painting, silk tapestry, watercolour, inkpad print, and paper pulp.[16] In 2001, Glass sat for Close again, to be the subject of a daguerreotype, the nineteenth-century photographic technique in which Close has produced a series of portraits.

The friendship between Glass and Close was cemented early on by their shared interest in process as a basis for the creation of new works of music and art.[17] Glass relied on process for much of his oeuvre prior to *Einstein on the Beach*, allowing formal principles such as additive rhythms and cyclical structures to govern his work on compositions including 'Two

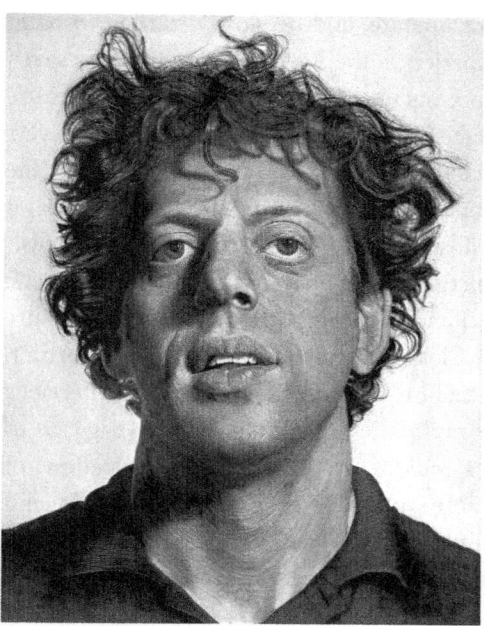

Figure 7.1 Chuck Close, b.1940, *Phil*, 1969. Synthetic polymer on canvas, 108¼ × 84 × 2¾in. (275 × 213.4 × 7 cm). Whitney Museum of American Art, New York; purchase, with funds from Mrs Robert M. Benjamin 69.102. © Chuck Close, courtesy The Pace Gallery.

Pages' (1969), 'Music in Similar Motion' (1969), and *Music in Twelve Parts* (1968–74).[18] Although Close has worked almost exclusively in the genre of portraiture, his aim, he has argued, is not to portray the sitter's character, but to find new processes for depicting facial structures in an objective way. He explains, 'I just want to present [faces] very neutrally and very thoughtfully. I don't try to orchestrate a particular experience or crank it up for high-impact emotional effect.'[19] His processes typically involve the division of the artistic surface into a grid that corresponds to his maquette, an expanded version of the original photograph overlaid with a grid.[20] He works within strict, self-imposed creative limitations to produce the final image. In an early series of large painted portraits, for example, he created images in the full spectrum of colours by building layers of diluted primary colours directly on the canvas.[21]

Close experienced a devastating health trauma in 1988, suffering a collapsed spinal artery that left him paralysed from the neck down.[22] After a long, frustrating period of rehabilitation, Close regained some movement in his arms, though he never fully recovered the use of his hands and remains in a wheelchair. His desire to return to making art inspired a determination and stamina to recuperate, and he slowly learned to paint again. Close calls this pivotal experience 'the Event', saying that art 'saved my life'.[23] Many of his works since his injury are more painterly in texture than his previous canvases though still built on grids, over which he layers circles and lozenges in intense contrasting colours. In such paintings, the face is visible from a distance, but as the viewer approaches the image, it disintegrates into repetitive, gradually changing patterns of abstract cells.

Because of his goal of depicting a generalized image, an aesthetic character at odds with the specificity typical of the genre of portraiture throughout much of its history, Close tended to avoid the word 'portrait' early in his career, preferring to call his works 'heads'. In a 1970 interview, he explained, 'I tried to purge my work of as much of the baggage of traditional portrait painting as I could.'[24] In spite of his protestations of aesthetic neutrality, however, Close's portraits of family and friends lend themselves to interpretations of his sitters' characters and emotional states. In so doing, they reveal that even when an artist focuses only on the structures of the face and makes a concerted effort to avoid manufacturing affect, many viewers will be prone to read a portrait for signs of what a person's exterior appearance can reveal about his or her interior self and identity. Close's objective distance forces the viewer to be especially creative in interpreting his portraits, complicating the task of imagining the sitter's character and identity where they are not explicitly signified. This process resembles the way listeners are invited to engage with and interpret musical portraiture, in which physical likeness is excluded.

Glass's 'A Musical Portrait of Chuck Close' offers a musical analogy to Close's portraits in the way it invites the listener to imagine the subject's character and identity, here using musical rather than visual clues.[25] Glass employs formal techniques at both low and high structural levels to convey in the temporal medium of music Close's varying affective states and life experiences over the period of their acquaintance. The shorter first movement has an air of caprice. Glass creates a sense of playful energy out of rhythmic and harmonic friction, through juxtaposition of duple and triple divisions of the measure, rapid alternation between major and minor as a result of repeated raising and lowering of the third scale degree, and brilliant fanfare-like rhythmic patterns in high tessitura. Glass appears to represent Close's tendency towards experimentation and both personal and creative unpredictability with rising and falling scalar patterns, unprepared dissonances, and recurring upward-reaching unfinished melodic phrases.

The movement concludes in F major, and is followed by the start of the second movement in the relative key of D minor, opening with a simple

Alberti-like pattern played at a significantly slower tempo. Above this ostinato, repeated arpeggios enter in groups of three pitches, in a plaintive gesture reminiscent of the *Adagio sostenuto* of Beethoven's 'Moonlight' Sonata (Op. 27, no. 2). Approximately halfway through the movement, the right hand stops playing again, and after a louder re-establishment of the Alberti pattern in the bass, the treble returns with rapid, undulating arpeggios in six-note groupings. These slower and faster passages alternate, and elements of both at times combine in a single phrase. The movement finally slows once more, to conclude in an ambivalent mood in the minor tonic.

The structure of Glass's work, with its movement from major to minor, from a fast and playful first movement to a second movement that begins with a bare texture and mournful, slow tempo before regaining speed and energy, creates a narrative arc that appears to describe Close's career. This progression maps the major periods of his life through the music's formal and harmonic structures, representing his creative and innovative work as a young artist, followed by the tragic sense of loss that followed his collapse, and the gradual return to work and the excitement of finding new ways to create his portraits. Interpreting the portrait's structure to represent Close in this way, Levingston has said, 'Every time I play the piece, I think about that phrase Chuck used about regaining his ability to paint: "loss and celebration".'[26]

If Glass's composition evokes Close's life in its overarching harmonic and formal characteristics, it mimics his art at the level of its brief structural details. In an analogous manner to Close's portraits built of dots, thumbprints, grids, and other small, repeated units, Glass's musical portrait is constructed of brief modular 'bricks' including scales, arpeggios, and rhythmic gestures that recur and gradually change in structure, pitch content, and other traits. Close has interpreted Glass's portrait of him as representing the technical qualities of his works and the ways in which his artistic methods have changed across his career: 'The first movement is more like my earliest work, much more minimal and reductive, almost black and white. And the second is the musical equivalent of a riot of color. It's celebratory in much the same way I try to build these big color images out of lots of little pieces of every color in the world.'[27] Glass has indicated that he also sees a correlation between the brief gestures out of which his piece and Close's portraits are created:

To me the second piece has an expansiveness to it, it just seems to keep going on and on. And it's like trying to find the edge of the canvas in one of Chuck's paintings. There's an edge there because there has to be an edge somewhere. But in another way you could say, well, why doesn't it keep going forever?[28]

Glass hints that the double bar at the close of the movement stands as an arbitrary ending, that the work provides an unfinished, fragmented representation of his friend, whose identity is, of course, still developing and actively being constructed beyond the completion of the portrait.

Ligeti's 'Selbstportrait'

In 1976, György Ligeti composed his musical representation of himself in the company of his contemporaries Reich and Riley and their predecessor Chopin, in the second movement of *Drei Stücke für zwei Klaviere* (Three Pieces for Two Pianos), bookended by 'Monument' and 'In zart fließender Bewegung' (In a Gentle Flowing Movement). Writing the piece at the request of the pianists Alfons and Aloys Kontarsky, Ligeti initially wished to call it 'Still Life with Reich and Riley', but partly in order to avoid the morbid resonances of the still life genre, known in French as *nature morte*, he changed the title to Portrait, and then Self-Portrait.[29] Ligeti had only first encountered the music of American minimalists in recent years, and was particularly inspired by Riley's 'In C' (1964) and Reich's 'It's gonna rain' (1965) and 'Violin Phase' (1967), which he heard on recordings at Stanford University in 1972, during his first visit to the United States.[30] Ligeti employed pastiche in 'Selbstportrait' to emphasize similarities between techniques developed independently but simultaneously in his works and those of his contemporaries in the 1960s. He also highlights striking and unexpected resonances between compositions by these musicians and the romantic pianism of Chopin.

Since at least the nineteenth century there has been a strand of music criticism and scholarship that holds a composer's works to be autobiographical and to offer revelatory insights into his character, calling to mind the Renaissance proverb, 'Every painter paints himself.'[31] Compositions explicitly identified by their creators as self-portraiture, however, occupy a rare category of the musical portrait; previous works include François Couperin's 'La Couperin' (1730) and C.P.E. Bach's 'L'Aly Rupalich' (first titled 'La Bach' and thought to be a self-portrait, 1755),[32] both for solo keyboard, as well as Benjamin Britten's 'Portrait No. 2 (E.B.B.)' for viola and ensemble (1930). The title of Ligeti's movement evokes an imaginary snapshot of him alongside his American contemporaries, with Chopin's visage in the background – a ghostly apparition, as implied by the parentheses. Ligeti uses the title to indicate that the piece situates his own compositional technique in relation to piano music's present and past.

Ligeti's group self-portrait depicts the four musicians' compositional innovations, recalling a common tendency of painters of self-portraiture to emphasize their creative endeavours by depicting themselves with their artistic implements. In self-portraits including Diego Velázquez's *Las Meninas* (1656), Rembrandt van Rijn's *Portrait of the Artist at His Easel* (1660), Jacques-Louis David's *Self-Portrait* (1794), Pablo Picasso's *Self-Portrait with a Palette* (1906), Richard Avedon's *Self-Portrait* (c.1963), and Lucian Freud's *Painter Working, Reflection* (1993), artists have shown themselves with easels, brushes, palettes, cameras, and other tools of their trade, and sometimes in the process of creating new works of art. Since the emergence of the genre of self-portraiture in the fifteenth century, many artists have sought to foreground their craft and creativity as essential elements of their identities, interwoven with character and social position.[33]

Ligeti follows in this tradition by depicting his subjects in a manner that emphasizes their profession as composers. Painted self-portraits rely on mimesis to depict artists with their tools: the self-conscious evocation of the artist's profession in these works depends on the viewer's recognition of palettes, brushes, and cameras. Without visual mimesis, Ligeti must find other means to indicate that the notes on the page do not only prescribe the structures for a performance, but also stand self-consciously for themselves as the tools these musicians employ in their art. Ligeti borrows musical techniques developed by his subjects to depict them through a stylistic pastiche that combines their compositional processes with his own.

In painted self-portraiture since the turn of the twentieth century, artists have repeatedly represented themselves not only through direct likeness, but also by emphasizing the artistic techniques they developed earlier in their careers.[34] For some artists who challenged the supremacy of mimesis in their works, style and technique took clear precedence over likeness in self-portraiture. In Picasso's 1972 *Self-Portrait*, the viewer sees the artist in the image less because it presents a recognizable likeness than because it offers an exemplar of the cubist style in which Picasso had worked throughout much of his career. Kasimir Malevich similarly turned to technique rather than likeness in self-portraiture, representing himself in *Suprematism: Self-Portrait in Two Dimensions* (1915) as an abstract pattern of quadrilaterals and a circle in primary colours and black on a white background. Even Malevich's title indicates that he and his Suprematist style are equivalent.[35]

More unusual is Ligeti's depiction of his own style in combination with the techniques of other composers. A visual analogy can be found in David Hockney's etching and aquatint *Artist and Model* (1973–4), created with

Picasso's frequent collaborator, the print maker Aldo Crommelynck. Hockney stages an imaginary meeting with the artist, in which they sit across from one another at a table, each depicted using a contrasting method of print-making. Inspired by Robert Doisneau's iconic 1952 photograph of Picasso, *Les Pains de Picasso*, and Picasso's images of artists and models, Hockney represents himself naked across a table from Picasso; he is the artist's model, and the artist his role model.[36] Like Ligeti, Hockney portrays artistic influence as deriving from a complex relationship between himself and his predecessor. Richard Hamilton, in his 1970-1 *A Portrait of the Artist by Francis Bacon*, in collotype and screen, similarly employs pastiche to represent himself in a manner that conveys the influence of another artist. Hamilton, working from a polaroid of his face taken by Bacon, manipulates the photograph, distorting his features and blurring its lines to create an image that resembles Bacon's haunting figures, including his 1969 *Self-Portrait*. Hamilton depicts his artistic self by altering his own likeness in the style of his contemporary, in a method analogous to Ligeti's merging of technical elements of the music of three other composers with his representation of his own identity.

In his programme notes for 'Selbstportrait', Ligeti wrote that he created supersaturated canons and superimposed grids as tropes to depict himself; phase shifting to evoke the music of Reich; pattern transformation to stand for Riley; and, towards the end of the movement, a parody of the melodic and rhythmic patterns of the Presto from Chopin's 1839 Sonata in B flat minor, Op. 35.[37] 'Selbstportrait' is constructed from a perpetual motion of arpeggiated patterns, following the precedent set by Chopin for continuously moving, fast-paced virtuosic fingerwork on the piano. The analysis of the first section reveals how Ligeti's composition operates as a group portrait by combining references to all four composers in a complex musical texture.

Many visual artists have viewed self-portraiture as offering a rich opportunity for experimentation, and in his foray in the genre, Ligeti likewise initiates a new compositional procedure, the blocked-key technique, whereby the left hand in each piano part silently depresses a set of keys while the right hand plays constant patterns of eighth notes in rising and falling scalar units. Because some of the same keys are blocked by the left hand, only a few of the notes make a sound. Ligeti asks the pianists to play continuously and evenly, allowing the placement of the left hand to determine the melodic and rhythmic content of each piano part, producing a sonic illusion that the pianists are playing complex arpeggiated rhythmic figurations. Ligeti attributes the concept behind this technique to the theorist Henning Siedentopf and the organist Karl-Erik Welin, with whom he worked on 'Volumina' (1961–2).[38]

The continuous undulating cells in the right-hand parts in both pianos are composed in what Jane Piper Clendinning has called Ligeti's 'pattern-meccanico' style, a technique he developed in works including his 1968 'Continuum' and String Quartet No. 2.[39] Ligeti builds melodic lines of perpetually repeating fragments that change minimally and gradually as the piece progresses, in a manner evocative of broken machinery. He associated his pattern-meccanico writing with a childhood memory of reading a story by Hungarian author Gyula Krudy about a widow who lives alone in a house full of ticking clocks. This haunting image, and a later experience of watching Charlie Chaplin's *Modern Times*, in which Chaplin's character works in a factory and is at one point swallowed into the gears of a machine, inspired a life-long fixation with the noises of functioning and broken machinery.[40] In light of its deeply personal resonances, the pattern-meccanico technique serves as a potent signifier of Ligeti's artistic identity in his self-portrait.

In the first section, Ligeti layers two lines of pattern-meccanico writing into a texture that he has referred to as micropolyphony in discussions of similarly constructed works.[41] In such compositions, the structural techniques guiding the polyphony are inaudible, as unexpected rhythmic groupings, pulsations, and harmonic structures emerge as though through lattice-works in performance.[42] In a manner he had developed since the late 1960s, Ligeti delineates the thick washes of sound with moments of greater stability and clarity in which the texture reduces to narrow intervals that he called 'signals'.[43] 'Selbstportrait' opens with the repetition of a narrow signal, a half step between E double flat (initially spelled as D natural) and D flat in the first piano, with the unison E double flat in the second piano. The texture gradually expands into a dense mist, until four discrete pitches are sounding in each voice.[44] The texture subsequently thins again (from measure 'b') with the removal of pitches in each voice, until both pianos are playing only a major second of E and D, an interval Ligeti has called a 'typical Ligeti signal'.[45] The section closes with a sustained trill on these pitches in both pianos.

Although Reich and Riley also employ continuously repeated patterns that incorporate gradual changes, Ligeti was surprised to learn of such shared compositional techniques between his works and those of his contemporaries when he first heard their music. In 'Selbstportrait', he also experiments with new compositional principles that he has learned from Reich and Riley, phase shifting and the relinquishing of authorial control by offering the performer an element of choice. Reich developed phase shifting in 'It's gonna rain', 'Violin Phase', and 'Piano Phase' (1967), in which multiple musicians or prerecorded tracks play the same musical material in unison and one gradually accelerates or decelerates while the other remains at tempo. Riley incorporated performer choice into compositions including 'In C', constructed of fifty-three brief phrases that the musicians are permitted to play any number of times before moving on to the next.

In 'Selbstportrait', a form of phase shifting occurs not because the pianists play at gradually different tempos, as in Reich's works, but because they perform continuous groupings of different quantities of eighth notes, returning at the start of each set to E double flat (until 'X', at which point the groupings begin on F flat or E, first in piano two, followed by piano one at 'Z'). As a result, they oscillate between playing unison pitches together and apart. After each new pattern of pitches, Ligeti writes a repeat symbol and indicates the number of times the pianist is to reiterate the same grouping. In the instructions at the start of the score, he explains that when the number of repetitions exceeds eight, the pianist need not be entirely precise in counting, when it is between twelve and eighteen 'a deviation of 1–2 in either direction is tolerated', and when it is above eighteen the quantity is only approximate. Ligeti's leniency offers the pianists considerable choice, and their communication in the performance is critical: they have to estimate the number of repetitions played by the other and signal to each other before continuing to subsequent pattern groupings. In this way, Ligeti creates his group self-portrait by incorporating the three composers' stylistic developments in a piece whose idiomatic pianism shows the influence of Chopin, and closing the movement with an explicit homage to Chopin's music.

Ligeti frequently stated that he conceived of strong correlations between musical and visual forms of representation. Since childhood, he had experienced synaesthetic associations between sound and colour.[46] His compositions were influenced by the works of painters he admired, including Pieter Brueghel the Elder, Hieronymus Bosch, and René Magritte, and he saw similarities between his pattern-meccanico processes and the gradually transforming tessellations of M.C. Escher.[47] Furthermore, Ligeti characterized the 'acoustical illusions' in 'Continuum' as resembling optical illusions, and considered some of his works to collapse the perception of time, unfolding as though over an area of space in a frozen instant.[48] Given this deep-seated correspondence between the aural and visual in Ligeti's perception, it is perhaps unsurprising that he would make a foray into portraiture, an artistic genre typically associated with visual media, as a mode in which to merge his compositional innovations with those of his American contemporaries.

T.J. Clark has argued that self-portraiture depicts 'the activity of self-scrutiny'; in the self-portrait, he writes, 'the self is shown representing itself'.[49] A self-portrait represents not merely the artist's likeness but also what he comes to understand about himself when he contemplates his appearance. By representing his conception of his own musical and creative self in 'Selbstportrait', Ligeti offers his audience the opportunity to listen in on what he hears when he listens to his own music and compares it with the work of contemporary and past composers. This act of self-hearing, to which the audience becomes privy, constitutes Ligeti's contemplation of his own identity as a composer. In 'Selbstportrait', the musical notes and technical guidelines in the score operate as more than simply instructions for a performer and signs of the sounds of this individual piece; they also stand for the body of works of Ligeti, Reich, Riley, and Chopin, and in doing so serve as a representation of the four composers' musical identities.

Coda: Virgil Thomson's 'Buffie Johnson', in conclusion

Thomson began composing musical portraits early in his career, and during some of his first exercises in the genre, he developed a unique method for composing these works: he created them in front of his subjects, in the manner of a portrait painter, attempting to write in a spontaneous manner, inspired by the sitter's proximity.[50] In doing so, he believed, he was best able to represent the abstract essence at the core of the sitter's identity; he explained, 'I do not try evoking visual art; in all my portraits only the sitter's presence is portrayed, not his appearance or his profession.'[51] Thomson was inspired both to work in the genre of portraiture and to create his compositions spontaneously in the sitter's presence by his friend the writer Gertrude Stein, who wrote numerous literary portraits in which she attempted to depict her subjects using language abstracted from traditional forms of narrative and grammar. Thomson saw a parallel between the modes of representation in Stein's use of language and his own music, and sought to mimic her efforts in experimenting with the representation of identities in music.[52]

In his collection *Nineteen Portraits for Piano* (1981), Thomson included a musical portrait of his friend Buffie Johnson, an artist who specialized in portraiture, among other genres, titled, 'Buffie Johnson: Drawing Virgil

Example 7.1 Virgil Thomson, 'Buffie Johnson: Drawing Virgil Thomson in Charcoal', mm. 1–6.

Example 7.2 Virgil Thomson, 'Buffie Johnson: Drawing Virgil Thomson in Charcoal', mm. 20–4.

Thomson in Charcoal'. In this portrait, Thomson depicted Johnson in the process of creating a portrait of Thomson. Whereas both Glass and Ligeti depict their subjects through the imitation of their characteristic artistic styles and techniques, Thomson once stated that his musical portraits of artists do not mimic the subjects' own works of art. It might be the case that Thomson does not imitate the style or appearance of Johnson's artworks, as he protests, but in this portrait her act of creating a representation through portraiture appears to become the subject of his musical construction of her identity.[53]

This short, neo-classical composition is written in an imitative structure in which the left hand plays the same through-composed melody as the right, always two measures behind and a minor tenth below (Example 7.1). With its canonic form, in which the melody is constantly at once presented and re-presented, 'Buffie Johnson' appears to depict a mirroring effect, as the two artists serve as both model and portraitist for one another, each depicting the other in the process of creating a representation. The conclusion of the piece comes unexpectedly in mid-phrase, as though the work is cut off while still in progress, an impression accentuated by the performance instruction 'abrupt' at the start of the work (Example 7.2). In ending the composition in this manner, Thomson emphasizes the arbitrary manner in which portraiture captures for posterity a sitter's likeness, or 'presence', in a single moment. The unending melody and perpetual imitation in this work could continue, just as does the subject's lifelong construction and performance of her identity.

'Buffie Johnson' operates as a whimsical representation of the act of producing a portrait; the portrait's subject is not only the sitter, but also the process of artistic representation. Furthermore, if, as T.J. Clark suggests, self-portraiture offers a representation of the artist's self-scrutiny, a view of what he sees when contemplating his appearance, Thomson's portrait operates not only as a portrait of another artist, but also as a peculiar form of self-portrait, in which Thomson depicts himself through the eyes of another. Thus 'Buffie Johnson' shares important attributes with both 'A Musical Portrait of Chuck Close' and 'Selbstportrait', as a depiction of another artist and also of the composer's own identity. In portraying the artists' identities through references to their works, styles, and activities of artistic creation, these three musical portraits imply that an artist's technical innovations form a crucial component of his or her identity, conceived to include not only the publicly visible aspects of the artist's self, including social position and profession, but also the private, internal attributes of self that form character and biography. These musical portraits indicate that the artist's idiomatic style offers a window onto identity. In creating musical frameworks with which to represent artists and composers, Glass, Ligeti, and Thomson construct works whose true subject, in the end, is music's capacity for representation. As their portraits demonstrate, this capacity is analogous to the kind of representation achieved in abstract visual arts, in which elements such as shapes, colours, and style can be interpreted as representative of human qualities.

Notes

1 Virgil Thomson, 'Preface' in Anthony Tommasini, *Virgil Thomson's Musical Portraits* (New York: Pendragon Press, 1986), x.
2 Joanna Woodall, 'Introduction: Facing the Subject' in Joanna Woodall (ed.), *Portraiture: Facing the Subject* (Manchester University Press, 1997), 8.
3 Leon Battista Alberti, *On Painting*, trans. John R. Spencer (New Haven: Yale University Press, 1966), 63.
4 Shearer West, *Portraiture* (Oxford University Press, 2004), 37.
5 Jerrold Seigel, *The Idea of the Self: Thought and Experience in Western Europe since the Seventeenth Century* (Cambridge University Press, 2005), 5–6.
6 Richard Brilliant, *Portraiture* (London: Reaktion Books, 1991), 15.
7 West, *Portraiture*, 210.
8 Madan Sarup, *Identity, Culture and the Postmodern World* (Edinburgh University Press, 1996), 45.
9 West, *Portraiture*, 187.
10 *Ibid.*, 194–201.

11 Charles McGrath, 'A Portraitist Whose Canvas is a Piano', *New York Times* (22 April 2005), www.nytimes.com/2005/04/22/arts/music/22glas.html?pagewanted=1&_r=1, accessed 7 May 2011.
12 McGrath, 'A Portraitist'.
13 Christopher Finch, *Chuck Close: Life* (Munich and London: Prestel Verlag, 2010), 9 and 117–19.
14 Martin Friedman, *Close Reading: Chuck Close and the Art of the Self-Portrait* (New York: Harry N. Abrams, Inc., 2005), 182.
15 N.a., 'Close Encounter', *The Metropolitan Opera*, www.metoperafamily.org/metopera/news/interviews/detail.aspx?id=3459, accessed 25 April 2012.
16 Christopher Finch, *Chuck Close: Work* (Munich and London: Prestel Verlag, 2007), 103.
17 Finch, *Chuck Close: Life*, 157.
18 See Keith Potter, *Four Musical Minimalists: La Monte Young, Terry Riley, Steve Reich, Philip Glass* (Cambridge University Press, 2000), ch. 4.
19 Friedman, *Close Reading*, 54.
20 Finch, *Chuck Close: Work*, 44.
21 *Ibid.*, 76.
22 *Ibid.*, 178.
23 *Ibid.*, 13.
24 Quoted in Robert Storr, 'Chuck Close: Angles of Refraction' in Robert Storr (ed.), *Chuck Close* (New York: The Museum of Modern Art, 1998), 44.
25 Glass's composition is not publicly available in published form, but can be heard on the CD *Portraits*, by Bruce Levingston, released in 2006 by Orange Mountain Music (0025).
26 McGrath, 'A Portraitist'. See also Bruce Levingston, 'Portraits', www.premierecommission.org/recordings/portraits.html, accessed 25 April 2012.
27 N.a., 'Close Encounter'.
28 McGrath, 'A Portraitist'.
29 Richard Steinitz, *György Ligeti: Music of the Imagination* (London: Faber and Faber, 2003), 207–8.
30 *Ibid.*, 206.
31 See Joanna Woodall, '"Every Painter Paints Himself": Self-Portraiture and Creativity' in Anthony Bond and Joanna Woodall (eds.), *Self-Portrait: Renaissance to Contemporary* (London: National Portrait Gallery, 2005), 17.
32 Joshua S. Walden, 'Composing Character in Musical Portraits: Carl Philipp Emanuel Bach and *L'Aly Rupalich*', *Musical Quarterly*, 91.2 (Fall–Winter 2008), 379–411.
33 Omar Calabrese, *Artists' Self-Portraits*, trans. Marguerite Shore (New York and London: Abbeville Press Publishers, 2006), 161 and 183.
34 Joseph Leo Koerner, 'Self-Portraiture Direct and Oblique' in Bond and Woodall (eds.), *Self-Portrait*, 68.
35 Calabrese, *Artists' Self-Portraits*, 358 and 370.

36 Wendy Wick Reaves (ed.), *Reflections/Refractions: Self-Portraiture in the Twentieth Century* (Washington, DC: Smithsonian Institution Scholarly Press, and Lanham, MD: Rowman & Littlefield Publishers, Inc., 2009), 125.
37 The programme note is reproduced in Stephen Ferguson, *György Ligetis Drei Stücke für zwei Klaviere: Eine Gesamtanalyse* (Tutzing: Hans Schneider, 1994), 265–6.
38 György Ligeti, 'Performance Instructions' in *Monument-Selbstportrait-Bewegung* (Mainz: B. Schott's Söhne, 1976).
39 Jane Piper Clendinning, 'The Pattern-Meccanico Compositions of György Ligeti', *Perspectives of New Music*, 31.1 (Winter 1993), 192–243.
40 György Ligeti, Péter Várnai, et al., *György Ligeti in Conversation with Péter Várnai, Josef Häusler, Claude Samuel, and Himself* (London: Eulenburg Books, 1983), 17.
41 *Ibid.*, 14–15.
42 *Ibid.*, 15.
43 *Ibid.*, 28–9 and 31.
44 Michael Hicks discusses this technique in 'Interval and Form in Ligeti's *Continuum* and *Coulée*', *Perspectives of New Music*, 31.1 (Winter 1993), 174.
45 Ligeti, *György Ligeti in Conversation*, 29.
46 *Ibid.*, 58.
47 Steinitz, *György Ligeti*, 206.
48 On 'acoustical illusions', see Herman Sabbe, 'György Ligeti – Illusions et Allusions', *Interface*, 8.1 (1979), 30. On Ligeti's conception of time and space, see Jonathan W. Bernard, 'Inaudible Structures, Audible Music: Ligeti's Problem, and His Solution', *Music Analysis*, 6.3 (October 1987), 210.
49 T.J. Clark, 'Gross David with the Swoln Cheek: An Essay on Self-Portraiture' in Michael S. Roth (ed.), *Rediscovering History: Culture, Politics, and the Psyche* (Stanford University Press, 1994), 280 and 296.
50 Virgil Thomson, 'Of Portraits and Operas', *Antaeus*, 21/22 (Spring/Summer 1976), 208–10.
51 Quoted in Anthony Carl Tommasini, 'The Musical Portraits by Virgil Thomson', *Musical Quarterly*, 70.2 (Spring 1984), 243.
52 *Ibid.*, 239.
53 Tommasini, *Virgil Thomson's Musical Portraits*, 17.

8 | Representational conundrums: music and early modern dance

DAVINIA CADDY

The relation between music and dance is a riddle that continues to intrigue. Particularly in recent years, under the influence of so-called post-structuralist enthusiasms (identity politics, visuality, issues of presence and embodiment), musicologists have turned their attention to the coupling of the two – that is, two complex metaphors, neither without signifying ability, yet neither secure in its signification. Questions of representation loom large. How can music represent choreographic performance, its gestures, moving bodies, and visual shape-shifting? Can particular musical parameters – melody, timbre, texture, and so forth – take on particular representational functions? Alternatively, how can dance represent music, its internal genetics, associational qualities, and expressive rhetoric? Should dance or music have priority, when, where, and why? And how can this priority be measured, let alone assured? The meaning of representation – its definition and discursive usage – can also be questioned. Describing the relation between music and dance, critics of the latter have tended to rely on loosely conceived notions of parallelism and verisimilitude, contrasting representation-as-likeness (some kind of audio-visual-physical matching) with its opposite, a condition of resistance or conflict. Yet theory and criticism across the humanities have long promoted a range of representational practices; particularly in the plastic arts (those that would appear to provide the clearest of representational paradigms), scholars have described various relational engagements and various contingencies – not least, the spectator's contribution to the image-making process (his perceptual psychology), famously dubbed 'the beholder's share'.[1] How might this more nuanced perspective – representation-as-critical-and-dialectical-process – cause us to reassess the terms of the representational contract routinely wrapped around music and dance? How, then, might we more accurately examine the coupling of the two?[2]

Questions tumble forth, far-reaching and formidable, and certainly resistant to easy answers. What interests me here is their historical relevance: the ways in which dancers of the past have envisioned and embodied their representational mandate – specifically, their relation to an accompanying music. For reasons of space and personal competence, I shall focus on dancers of the late nineteenth and early twentieth centuries, a period long regarded as the golden age of dance. During this period, Paris enjoyed an especially vibrant and diverse dance scene, one that acquired significant cultural prestige, commercial success, and general popularity. This Parisian vogue was no doubt stimulated and sustained by a number of concurrent phenomena: a burgeoning interest (in the visual arts and physical sciences) in the concept of motion; a specifically theatrical (and, perhaps, specifically French) anxiety about opera and vocal exegesis; an intellectual loss of confidence in verbal culture; the Republican promotion of sport and recreation; and the Parisian presence of impresario Sergey Diaghilev and his Ballets Russes.[3] Equally important was the emergence of a new kind of dance, outside social, folk, and theatrical traditions, known nowadays as 'early modern'. The category embraces a cluster of dance practitioners, most from North America, active in Paris around the turn of the century. The early moderns, as they are called, blurred the boundaries between the conception and performance of dance; some even acquired a Wagnerian degree of control over the various aspects of their productions. The dancers also tended to teach, to set up schools in their name, and to rhapsodize at length about their aims in newspapers, specialist journals, and autobiographical writings (which doubled as aesthetic manifestos). Their legacy, it might be argued, relies centrally on this body of literature – itself a form of representation – rather than on their actual dances, most of which were un-notated and have not survived. Indeed, the dancers may best be regarded as 'ideas' people, their dances 'a point of view':[4] in the words of one historical observer, 'in dancing, as in most other things, it is ideas that carry the day'.[5]

Names may be familiar: Loie Fuller, Isadora Duncan, Ruth St Denis, Maud Allan, Valentine de Saint-Point. Women, especially, drifted towards dance during the period, enamoured by ideals of bodily liberation and expressive licence – ideals shared and promoted by a rising tide of feminist campaigners across Europe and the US. As for their dancing, these women were regarded as 'rénovatrices en leur genre' (reformers of their genre); they groped, often barefoot, towards styles that departed from the conventions of ballet – classical technique, dramatic mime, structural formality, and essentially superfluous virtuosic display.[6] These styles did not form a homogeneous entity: Duncan believed that the source of bodily movement was the solar plexus (not the spine) and preferred simple, flowing steps and grand, expressive gestures; St Denis, in contrast, mixed movements of dubious Orientalism with popular dance and gymnastics. Nonetheless, the dancers shared a basic creative ambition. Dance, they believed, was a mode of communication, of projecting the individual impulse to movement. Moreover, it was closely bound to music. As Duncan said with characteristic hyperbole: 'I am not a dancer. I am there to make you listen to the music.'[7] Fuller spoke similarly: 'I aim only to express the spirit of the music.'[8]

This chapter digs deeper into the dancers' comments in order to better understand their representation of music: from the above quotations, this would seem the *raison d'être* of early modern dance. Building on recent scholarship that seeks to intertwine the dancers with the cultural and intellectual debates of their period, I shall explore how their musical aims and agendas were rooted in contemporary ideologies and strains of influence, ones that crossed boundaries between the arts and the sciences.[9] Close attention to the dancers' thoughts on music will not only bring valuable insights to bear on the significance of dance within turn-of-the-century creative practice; it will also encourage us to take a more nuanced attitude to issues of representation – in particular, to the representational conundrums of early modernism. Of the dancers mentioned above, I shall focus on merely a couple – Loie Fuller and Valentine de Saint-Point, women who appear to conceptualize music in contrasting ways. But I should like to begin with one man, almost entirely unknown in dance history. Jean d'Udine – dancer, teacher, and critic for the French weekly journal *Le Courrier musical* – invented a theory of art that offers a useful starting point for this study of music–dance relations.[10]

Jean d'Udine, *L'Art et le geste*

Reviewing 'L'École Jean d'Udine' for the Parisian press (July 1912), critic André Mangeot bestowed the highest of praise. Recent dance concerts of extracts from Haydn and Beethoven – played by d'Udine at the piano – flaunted students' technical skill and bodily suppleness. What is more, the dancers achieved a remarkable feat: 'la transposition intégrale de la musique dans la danse'.[11] Mangeot insisted:

> Ne croyez pas que ce fut une adaptation plus ou moins heureuse, comme la font les Russes, de la musique, par des pas et des gestes. Ce fut le mariage d'inclination de la musique et de la danse en union pure, loin de toute suggestion littéraire, et de tout l'attirail scénique.[12]

(Do not think that this was a more or less felicitous musical adaptation, like those of the Russians, in steps and gestures. This was a marriage motivated by love between music and dance, a pure union, far removed from any literary evocation and any scenic paraphernalia.)

To Mangeot, the comparison was clear. Unlike Diaghilev's dancers and their happenstance choreographic adaptations, d'Udine's students realized the most fundamental of associations between music and dance, and without recourse to pictorial or poetic impressions, or to seemingly gratuitous visual display. Their dancing, Mangeot went on, betrayed basic structural coordinates, bringing to light the metre, pulse, and rhythm of the accompanying music. Moreover, the dancers managed to tap into the composers' psyches, to make manifest onstage their musical intentions:

Non seulement tous les rythmes marquaient devant nos yeux la division du temps, mais la pensée musicale d'Haydn et de Beethoven était là tout entière.[13]

(Not only did all the rhythms indicate the division of time before our eyes, but the musical thought of Haydn and Beethoven was visualized in its entirety.)

This was not entirely unqualified. Despite his rhetoric of exceptionality, as well as his obvious enthusiasm, Mangeot reveals sharp insights into d'Udine's musical and gestural methods, disseminated in the dancer's journalistic writings and described at length in his 1910 treatise *L'Art et le geste*.[14] As the critic was aware, and as d'Udine himself acknowledged, the influence of Émile Jaques-Dalcroze figured heavily. The Swiss music pedagogue, with whom d'Udine had studied in Geneva, was known for his 'eurhythmics', a holistic system of musical education based on the gestural realization of rhythm. Designed to quicken physical responsiveness and develop musical creativity, eurhythmics emphasized the coordination of motor and mental faculties.[15] It was this coordination – the ideal of the complete, harmonious body – that inspired d'Udine.[16] Following Dalcroze, the dancer preached the possibility of dancing (rather than simply beating) all musical rhythms, bodily members at times working against themselves (legs against arms, for example) in the physical realization of complex rhythmic structures.

But d'Udine was more than a mere imitator. Pursuing the ideological implications of the Dalcroze method, the Frenchman devised a comprehensive theory of art and its representational mechanics, one that derived principally from the Romantic concept of organicism. *L'Art et le geste* also echoed one of the central tenets of literary Symbolism, the sensory 'correspondances' famously evoked by Baudelaire and Rimbaud. Indeed, at the basis of d'Udine's theory was a belief in synaesthetic equivalence – in music, gesture, word, and image as essentially and mutually imitative. But this was no mystical or alchemic ideal. D'Udine was inspired by the scientific principles of Félix le Dantec, a widely read evolutionary biologist and believer in the theory of perigenesis.[17]

Invented by the German naturalist Ernst Haeckel, perigenesis held that the physical basis of life could be reduced to one basic matter, a kind of primordial goo found inside cells and shared by all living organisms.[18] This goo, called protoplasm, could receive and store impulses from the external world; moreover, it was fluid enough to pass on these vital forces to cellular offspring. The mechanics of protoplasm thus provided a bio-physical explanation of inheritance, one that challenged Darwin's so-called pangenesis (based on the shedding of cell 'gemmules'). Perigenesis applied as much to physiological functions (breathing, muscle contraction, circulation) as to the life of the soul – Haeckel's 'Seelenleben', Le Dantec's 'sens interne'. Ideas, instincts, and feelings could also be encoded in protoplasm, and also subjected to the same mechanical methods and graphical recording devices designed to render physiological phenomena in visual script: devices such as the myograph (for recording muscular force) or sphygmograph (for blood pressure). Le Dantec dreamt of a device – 'le phrénographe' – that would record all sensory modalities, as well as all mental activities, making visible the feelings, states of minds, and primordial automatisms characteristic of protoplasmic beings.[19]

With Le Dantec firmly in mind, d'Udine erected his theory of representation on the model of perigenesis: the objective imitation of vital forces by means of protoplasm.[20] Art, he believed, had its basis in emotion ('un mouvement de l'âme', a movement of the soul), emotion that derived from physiological rhythms stored in protoplasm. The role of the artist, D'Udine concluded, was that of 'une mime specialisé': accessing the protoplasmic archive, the artist determined the rhythms that corresponded to the emotion in question, then rendered these rhythms perceptible to the beholder in the appropriate artistic medium. As for dancing to music, d'Udine hypothesized that the process – the reversal of an original scenario in which music was born from movement – highlighted the convergence of sensory modalities and thus recovered an original and undifferentiated protoplasmic unity. The body, it seems, functioned like Le Dantec's imagined 'phrénographe', inscribing both external (sonic) and internal (psychological) impulses. Dance was a visual script, the work of the bodily apparatus. Not only this, dance stimulated a condition of recognition in the spectator, activating a further link in the synaesthetic chain. Sensing the rhythms heard and visualized onstage, the spectator adduced their underlying and initiatory sentiment – that is, 'l'émotion du créateur'.

This system of 'reversibilité' (so called by d'Udine) relied on the scientifically derived theory of synaesthesia that the dancer accepted and sought to propound.[21] At base, this was a theory of innate equivalence, fixed associations, and a straightforward, immediate relationship between the artist and his audience. Contemplating another relationship, that between music and dance, d'Udine envisaged the objective encoding of the one in the other. Representation, to d'Udine, was a kind of corporeal etching or *écriture* (akin to what Le Dantec called 'direct optics'): in response to musical stimuli, the dancing body carved out the grammar of metre and rhythm, bringing (back) to life the creative impulse of conception.

Loie Fuller, *l'enchanteresse*

D'Udine was not alone in his desire to represent music through movement; as already mentioned, the early modern dancers expressed this same intention. St Denis, also influenced by Dalcroze and his eurhythmics, established the principle of music 'visualization', inventing a series of choreographic equivalents for musical structure, harmony, and melody, ones that (she argued) foreclosed interpretation of any kind.[22] Duncan, quite the opposite, exalted the interpretive endeavour. Acknowledging the emotional expressivity of music, she sought to translate this expressivity into gestural form, to surrender her body to that of her accompanying orchestra.[23]

Loie Fuller, a music-hall dancer who introduced Duncan to Parisian audiences, pushed further. Known primarily for the huge silk drapes that she tossed around her body, Fuller wanted to connect music and movement with coloured light projections; in doing so, she believed, she would create 'une nouvelle forme d'art' (a new form of art), 'un tout émouvant' (an expressive whole).[24] Audiences and critics applauded. Anatole France – the author of a preface for Fuller's 1908 autobiography – described 'une musique pour les yeux' (music for the eyes);[25] Léo Clarétie – the nephew of Jules, a prominent literary figure who urged Fuller to write that autobiography – recalled 'une harmonie universelle'.[26] Reviewing Fuller's production of Debussy's orchestral movement 'Nuages', Clarétie added:

La musique est la joie des oreilles; elle fut encore la joie des yeux. Elle rend la musique picturale. [...] Elle apporte aux yeux ce qui devrait leur échapper.[27]

(Music is the joy of the ears; it is also the joy of the eyes. She makes the music pictorial. ... She brings before our eyes that which should escape them.)

The composer seemed to agree. According to theatre producer Gabriel Astruc, Debussy praised Fuller's 'Nuages' as the ultimate expression of his music: for the first time, Debussy confided, he had heard that music come to life.[28]

Clearly, 'La Loïe' (as she was known amongst Parisians) shared d'Udine's belief in the union of music and dance; indeed, she extended the synaesthetic project, coordinating light effects with the visual scene. Nonetheless, she rejected the Frenchman's theory – and all others. 'Oh, des doctrines!', Fuller exclaimed: 'Il n'y a pas de doctrines, pas de règles, pas de formules, pas de théories, pas de discipline' (There are no doctrines, no rules, formulas, theories, discipline).[29] To students and interested observers, Fuller recommended an impromptu style of dancing based on individual intuition and experience. In her native American, she explained:

You must read your own story into a dance just as you must read it into music. No one can tell you what Beethoven thought when he wrote the 'Moonlight Sonata'; no one knows Chopin's point of view in his nocturnes, but to each music lover there is in them a story, the story of his own experience and his own explorations into the field of art. ... You can put as many stories as you wish to music, but you may be sure that no two people will see the same story. So every dance has its meaning, but your meaning is not mine, nor mine yours. Dancing is movement made beautiful. You must in it express your own true self.[30]

Dancing, Fuller might have added, is music made mobile. Subjective and spontaneous, it is the lens through which not only personal experience is envisaged. Music itself – the mobility of meaning, the indeterminacy of expression – is embodied in kaleidoscopically shifting visual forms.

Indeterminacy, polysemy, ambiguity: these were Fuller's representational principles, the motivating forces behind not only her thoughts on music, but also her movement and production design. Enveloped in vast swaths of silk, and variously illuminated from above and below, Fuller cultivated a mysterious look that appeared to deny her physical presence. Literally, her body faded from view, subsumed by billowing fabric and tricks of light; and metaphorically, the fleshy reality of her physical being dissolved into free-floating images. A flower, the sun, fire, clouds, a butterfly, a snake, leaves blowing in the wind: according to critics, Fuller metamorphosed into a range of flora, fauna, and other natural phenomena. Stéphane Mallarmé, famously scribbling at the theatre, described and delighted in Fuller's elusivity: overstepping the boundaries of conventional iconicity, the dancer was not a woman dancing, but 'une métaphore résumant un des aspects élémentaires de notre forme, glaive, coupe, fleur, etc.' (a metaphor encapsulating one of the elemental aspects of our form, sword, cup, flower, etc.).[31] For critic Jean Lorrain, doubts about the dancer's humanity became doubts about what was happening onstage:

Était-ce une danse, une projection de lumière, une évocation de quelque spirite? Mystère. Une fleur de rêve avait surgi des ténèbres, une fleur de rêve (car pouvait-on donner le nom de femme à cette fumée d'étoffes longues et légères que le moindre mouvement soulevait en lumineuses nuées?). Était-ce un être humain cet écroulement de nuances mouvantes et mourantes et de transparences de gazes et d'éther?[32]

(Was it a dance, a projection of light, an evocation of some spirit? Mystery. A flower of dreams had arisen from the darkness, a flower of dreams (as could we call this haze of long, light fabric, that which minimal movement whipped into luminous clouds, a woman?). Was it a human being this caving-in of ephemeral nuances and vaporous transparencies?)

Disembodied, dehumanized, and denying dramatic character, Fuller courted such doubts and uncertainties. Visually, she avoided the choreographed eroticism of the music hall, preferring optical illusions and metamorphosing shapes designed to divert attention from her stage presence. Musically, too, she preached the precariousness of expression – the pictorial ambiguities, characteristic of her favourite 'modern' composers (Wagner, Debussy, Chopin), that inspired imaginative reflection. She described how 'something in a bar of music suggests a movement or an attitude to the mind', 'accordingly, the body shapes itself and moves in sympathy with that idea'.[33] But this 'something' was never defined, and neither was the seemingly causal relationship between mind and body. In fact, Fuller told her students not to think too seriously about what they were doing:

Pour danser – danser – danser – danser encore – sentir – ressentir – penser, et pouvoir, mais ne pas étudier ces mouvements, et quand quelqu'un vous demande, comment vous l'avez fait, répondez: 'je ne sais pas, car je ne sais pas ce que j'ai fait, j'ai seulement fait ce que je ressentais.'[34]

(To dance – dance – dance – dance again – to sense – to feel – to think, and to control, but not to study these movements, and when someone asks you how you danced, say: 'I do not know, as I do not know what I did, I only did what I was feeling.')

Spectators were encouraged to follow suit – to follow their individual, unprompted responses. Fuller described how she wanted to arouse and extend her spectators' imagination, to open their minds to the ephemeral and indefinite forces she sought to express.[35]

Clearly, this logic – or, rather, this lack of logic – unshackled music and dance from the pre-determined bio-physical constraints imagined and imposed by d'Udine. According to Fuller, the two mediums could relate; and these relations could be intense, compelling, and coercive. Yet the representational dynamic depended not on structural coordinates, and not even on authorial intention. Fuller discarded what she regarded as a naïve theory of mimesis, based on both the objective imitation of fixed points of reference and the cultural authority of the author. Unseating this authority, she promoted the agency of the observer (the spectator inside the theatre) and that of herself, as observer of music; and she represented this music in all its imagined metaphoricity – its infinite powers of suggestion. To put this in other words, Fuller envisaged dance as profoundly deconstructive, a critique of both aesthetic perception and musical signification.

In this, Fuller partook of the destabilizing, obfuscating, and non-naturalistic strategies characteristic of artistic modernism. As is well known, the late nineteenth and early twentieth centuries witnessed more than a simple shift from representational art to abstraction. The powers of representation were put through their paces, as artists tended towards what one recent critic has dubbed 'potential images' – ambiguous, indeterminate and dependent in meaning and effect on the creative contribution of the beholder.[36] Examples embrace not only visual art (Moreau, Degas, Monet, Cézanne, Redon) but literature, including the Symbolist poetry of Mallarmé, for whom the pleasures of suggestion, the enigma of the 'Idée', and the disappearance of the author found their ultimate incarnation in Fuller herself.[37] (This is not to mention the Symbolist fascination with the poetic mystery of music, its characteristic imprecision and ineffability.) The sculptor Auguste Rodin, known for his personal association with Fuller, confessed similar ideals, acknowledging the obscurity and ambiguity of his sculptures, as well as their appeal to the observer. To Rodin, this appeal encapsulated the essence of art: suggestiveness was privileged for its ability to awaken the imagination and expand its creative capacity.[38]

Figure 8.1, dating from c.1904, provides another example. Dedicated to the French artist Eugène Carrière, this photograph of Fuller depicts her characteristic swirling motion and voluptuous veils. But the photograph conveys its own ambiguities. Indeed, despite claims (and accusations) of mechanical reproduction, the medium of photography contributed many 'potential images': techniques of photomontage, multi-exposure, and gum-bichromate printing enabled the 'blurring' of photographed objects,

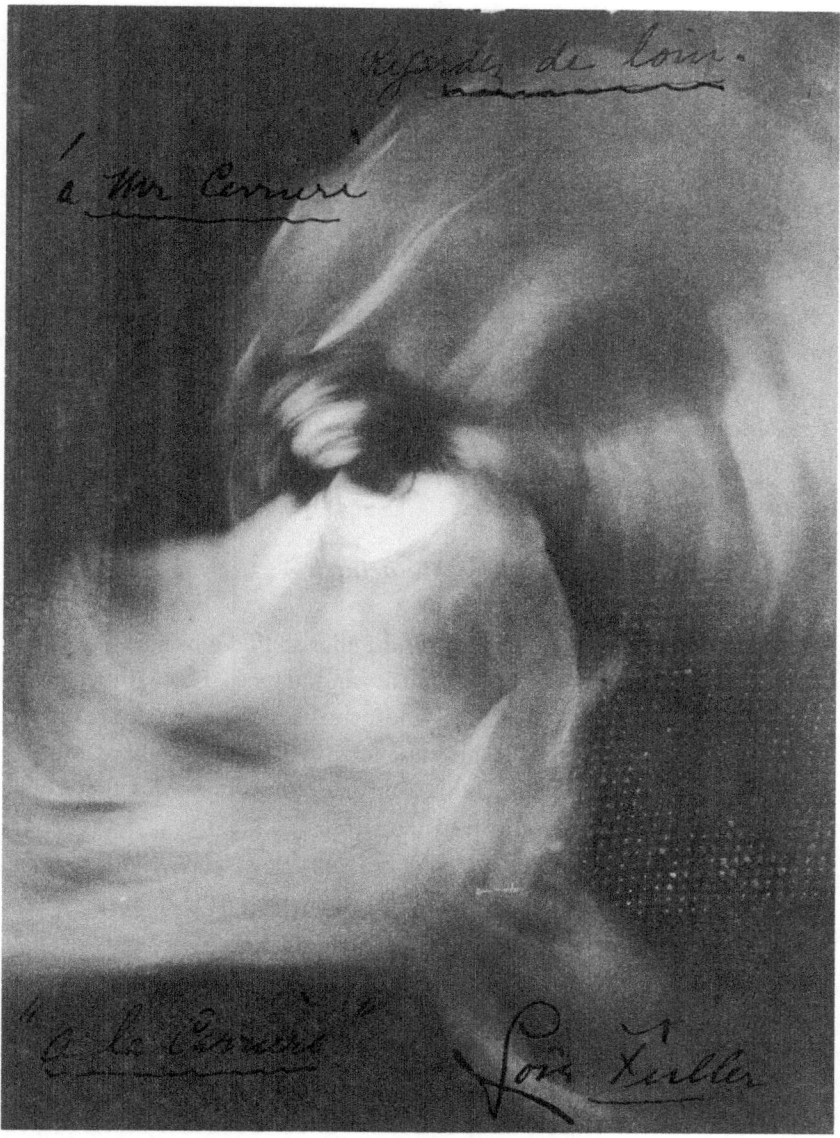

Figure 8.1 R. Moreau, *Loïe Fuller dansant* (à la Carrière), c.1904. Calotype, 15.5 × 11.4 cm. Courtesy of the Musée Rodin, Paris (Ph 1674).

foregrounding visual indeterminacy whilst engaging the observer in the creative process.[39] Here, the blurred effect – which owes in part to the calotype process (a calotype is an early photographic negative, dipped in silver nitrate and gallic acid, with a tendency to blur) – dissolves the outline of Fuller's veils, as well as her facial features. The resulting impression of movement, swift yet gentle, draws the observer into continuously reconstructing the visual scene. But look closely and, ironically, we are told to look from afar ('Regardez de loin'). Fuller's body becomes vaguer still, devoid of all detail and reference points. Eventually she/it disappears, a blotch of white on a nondescript background, a random smudge.

The effect is that which Fuller herself set out to achieve: the photograph captures her guiding principles – her aesthetics of indeterminacy – in its means and technique. At a distance of a few feet, the dancer no longer exists as a bodily totality; her veils cannot settle, cannot be pinned to a determinate spatial position. And neither, it seems, can we. There is no vantage point from which to view the image as a comprehensive and secure spatial construction, no quick-fire route to its representational meaning. The dancing object, a free-floating signifier, compels our 'reading-in'; she/it is a metaphor for both danced dissolution and imaginative response.

Valentine de Saint-Point, *La Métachorie*

Whatever their differences, d'Udine and Fuller shared a basic belief in the representational compatibility of music and dance. They mined their accompanying music for structural and/or expressive content, seeking to make manifest this content in physical form. And they idealized music's associational qualities, exploring the various correspondences that could enliven and intertwine the theatrical apparatus.

Valentine de Saint-Point, it seems, did not. Poet, playwright, painter, muse, and great-grand-niece of Alphonse Lamartine (the famous French writer and politician), Saint-Point published an article-cum-manifesto that questioned the principles upon which early modern dance – even, one might argue, the entire tradition of Western theatrical dance – was based. This article, on the theory and practice of 'Métachorie' (literally, beyond the chorus), offered what appeared to be a genuinely new written discourse, infused with a vocabulary of fracture and indifference that signalled a revolt against the age-old affiliation of music and dance. For too long, Saint-Point insisted, dance had been not only dependent on music, but also derivative. A mere accessory, obedient and slavish, dance had contributed nothing of its own – nothing unique or distinguishing – to the theatrical experience. Saint-Point described how she wanted to liberate dance from its musical shackles, to envisage a new choreographic autonomy. In its 'metachoric' realization, dance, she argued, would be impartial and independent; it would contribute its own ideational significance and thus contest the priority of music.[40]

BALDO
(*Étude d'après une figure métachorique*)

Figure 8.2 Gino Baldo, study of a metachoric figure, 1914. Lithograph of pen and ink drawing. Courtesy of the Jerome Robbins Dance Division, The New York Public Library for the Performing Arts, Astor, Lenox, and Tilden Foundations.

Yet this music was to be resisted. Saint-Point erected her 'Métachorie' on the deliberate disjunction of music and dance, a disjunction that denied the affective musical qualities that those around her sought to celebrate. Indeed, she spoke critically of dancers who succumbed to music's expressive allure, particularly those who cultivated the sensory-based, spontaneous approach: 'réduire la danse aux inspirations instinctives ou aux gestes conventionnels équivaut à la renier comme art' (to reduce dance to instinctive inspirations or conventional gestures is to renounce its status as art).[41] She imagined an artistic defence mechanism, a protective shield against the musical magnetism that rendered dance merely contingent, merely representational. Her distinctive warrior pose, sketched by the Italian artist Gino Baldo (Figure 8.2, on which more later), is evocative in this regard. Dressed as a Merovingian warrior, with metal headgear and armour, Saint-Point and her pose signify masculine power and strength – and implicitly critique the feminine bodily aesthetics of Fuller, Duncan, and followers.[42] Yet the warrior is not only emblematic of mannish muscle; he embodies Saint-Point's own aesthetics – or, rather, her *an*aesthetics. The arch-example of the autonomous, autotelic subject, the warrior cannot be controlled or influenced. He is self-sufficient, impermeable, and immune to sensory experience – to aesthetics (in the original etymological meaning of the term).[43] In her chainmail costume, bent down on one knee and with arms outstretched, Saint-Point may be similarly sense-dead. Her body appears anaesthetized by a metal construction that blocks the corporeal sensorium, rendering her cold and impassive.

Rejecting the choreographed femininity of her fellow dancers, Saint-Point thus subverted their aesthetic, inventing an anaesthetic that would rupture the representational contract – the long-standing ties between music and dance, sensation and effect. She did this, though, not without serious thought; in fact, thought was her guiding principle:

> Jusqu'à présent, on dansait pour danser, ou pour aimer, ou pour divertir, ou bien encore – lorsque l'homme s'exagérait sa propre importance – on dansait pour prier. On va danser, désormais, pour penser. Il était temps: la philosophie manquait de jambes.[44]

(Until now, we danced for dancing's sake, or for love, for entertainment, or even – when man overestimated his own importance – as a means of prayer. From now on, we will dance in order to think. It was time: philosophy has been lacking legs.)

This 'thinking' dance – philosophy in motion – was stripped of all mimetic, pictorial, dramatic, emotive, sensual, and erotic qualities. Dubbed 'la danse idéiste', it was the result of a preordained, tripartite process:[45] first, Saint-Point took an idea from one of her poems (read aloud before her danced performances); next, she visualized this idea in a geometric design (used as the floor-plan for her choreography and projected onto the backdrop of the stage); then, she embodied the idea in movement – in walking, running, skipping, jumping, lunging, crouching, and crawling steps designed to signify pure line and pure form.[46] Nothing, she wrote, was to detract from this conceptual geometry; during performance, she wore masks to conceal her facial expressions and costumes that emphasized 'les lignes essentielles du mouvement'.[47] These lines emerge clearly from Figure 8.2, Baldo's sketch – or, rather, schematic diagram – of the warrior pose. Saint-Point is rendered in two dimensions, a flat surface comprising black and white shapes. Figure 8.3, also by Baldo (and of the same pose), simplifies further, excavating the dancing body for basic trajectories of movement.

Baldo's drawings also convey something of the critical dialogue in which Saint-Point engaged. Her 'Métachorie' did not spring autochthonously to life: it was influenced by a strain of artistic modernism – associated with the avant-garde journal *Montjoie!*, in which both Baldo's drawings and Saint-Point's writings appeared – that promoted a specifically intellectual creativity. Saint-Point explained:

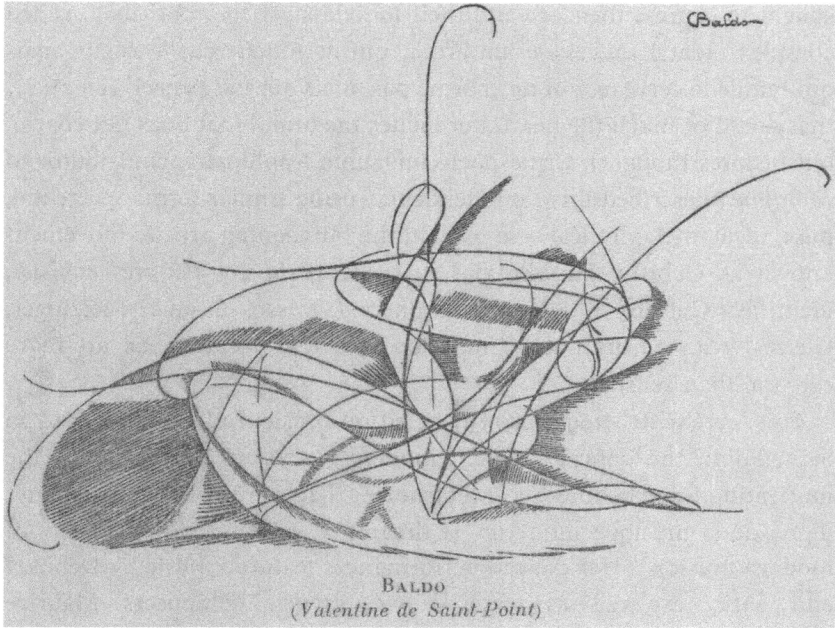

Figure 8.3 Gino Baldo, drawing of Saint-Point, 1914. Lithograph of pen and ink drawing. Courtesy of the Jerome Robbins Dance Division, The New York Public Library for the Performing Arts, Astor, Lenox, and Tilden Foundations.

Je cherchai ... à faire suivre à la danse la même évolution qui, suivie par les autres arts, met la France à la tête de l'art moderne. Cette évolution, comme tous les esthéticiens l'ont pu constater, est toute cérébrale. La musique, la peinture, etc. ... ont cessé d'être simplement instinctives, intuitives et sensuelles: la danse devait suivre la même voie.[48]

(I was trying ... to have dance follow the same evolution that, followed by the other arts, positions France at the helm of modern art. This evolution, as all the estheticians have been able to certify, is wholly cerebral. Music, painting, etc. ... have stopped being simply instinctive, intuitive, and sensual: dance should follow the same route.)

This route was mapped by *Montjoie!* editor Riccioto Canudo. In his 'Manifeste de l'art cérébriste', published in the same edition of the journal as Saint-Point's 'La Métachorie', Canudo traced a line from Baudelaire to Rimbaud, Mallarmé, d'Annunzio and Wilde, Cézanne, Gauguin, and Van Gogh.[49] These artists, Canudo declared, had turned away from the banalities of 'l'art sentimental', spurning tired and trite artistic formulae in favour of the noble, rational, and hermetic – 'le niveau fièrement intellectuel' (the proudly intellectual level). Rebelling against institutionalized dogma, they sought to express their age and their individuality in an art that excited complex mental processes: 'un art ... qui ne touche pas le coeur, mais qui remue le cerveau, qui ne charme pas, mais qui fait penser' (an art ... that does not touch the heart, but incites the brain, that does not charm, but inspires thought). Critic-poet Guillaume Apollinaire, contributor to *Montjoie!*, described this same tendency, using similar terms – cerebral, pure, ideal, metaphysical – to explain the burgeoning artistic movement known as Cubism. His seminal study of 1913, *Les Peintres cubistes*, identified Cubism and its practitioners (Picasso, Braque, Metzinger, Gleizes) with an art not of imitation but of conception, an art more cerebral than sensual.[50]

This 'cérébriste' trend also impacted on music. Indeed, to rewind to Saint-Point, the dancer credited modern music, in particular, as the motivating force behind her 'Métachorie': 'J'ai ... rêvé de créer la danse digne de la musique moderne' (I dreamt of creating dance worthy of modern music).[51] Her danced performances featured music by Debussy and Satie, as well as lesser-known French composers Maurice Droeghmans and Alexis Roland-Manuel. Yet, as Daniel Chennevière implied in a *Montjoie!* review, none of these quite convinced their audience. According to Chennevière, Saint-Point was still awaiting 'le Stravinsky français', a composer who, like the infamous Russian, could create a purely choreographic music, constructed architecturally according to geometric gestural schemes.[52]

Perhaps Saint-Point gave up waiting: her 'Métachorie' was performed but twice, once in Paris at the Théâtre Léon-Poirier (20 December 1913), then in New York at the Metropolitan Opera House (3 April 1917). Or perhaps the dancer's musical antennae were wrongly directed. One Alberto Savinio, an Italian composer active in Paris from 1910, also recognized the influence of 'une nouvelle et puissante force cérébrale' (a new and potent cerebral force);[53] moreover, his ballet music was based on the same principle of audio-visual disjunction envisaged by Saint-Point.[54] In a preview article for Savinio's first Parisian recital, Apollinaire applauded the Italian's 'musique nouvelle'. No longer bound to 'l'esthétique' and 'la beauté', this music functioned independently of its balletic scenario.[55] It functioned, one might argue, like Saint-Point's dance, bypassing conventional mimesis in order to facilitate direct, unmediated access to a poetic idea.

There was another resemblance between Saint-Point and Savinio, one that had the look of a contradiction in terms. For this poetic idea – to Saint-Point, '[une] idée nullement vague, errante et désordonnée' (an idea not at all vague, loose, and disorderly) – acted as a governing principle: it unified all artistic parameters, even those conceived independently.[56] Music and dance could thus jostle uncomfortably, creating moment-by-moment disjunctive effects. But the two were motivated by a single concept: in the words of Saint-Point, 'le même thème cérébral'.[57] The dancer spoke of synthesis, harmony, and fusion, of how she could unite music and dance with coloured lights and odours of incense (supplied by Parisian perfumier Bichara). She added: 'C'est donc l'union parfaite de tous les arts qu'apporte la métachorie' (Métachorie thus brings about a perfect union of all the arts).[58]

L'Union parfaite (conclusion)

The words are loaded with significance, themselves a union of Wagnerian, late Romantic, and Symbolist ideologies. That they crop up here, of course, is important: Saint-Point's 'Métachorie' may have rivalled Fuller's dance-and-light displays in theatrical effect, may even have matched up to the synthetic credentials of d'Udine's student concerts. The three dancers, it seems, worked towards a single goal: 'l'art total', the fusion of artistic parameters, the identification of originary unity.

If this goal had taproots in a venerable tradition, one that developed in the nineteenth century along various intellectual, pantheistic and occultic lines, it collided in the early 1900s with specifically modernist strains of influence. As Camille Mauclair acknowledged in a 1904 essay, artists' aspiration towards the fusion of the arts ('un désir de l'unité') had begun to provoke anxiety and apprehension:[59]

> Y a-t-il continuité absolue, relation constante, entre tous les ordres de pensées humaines? Notre âme le pressent. Mais pouvons-nous rendre visible cette continuité, l'extérioriser dans nos oeuvres, créer une langage d'analogies assez souple pour parler simultanément à l'esprit de tous les ordres de pensées? Est-ce à l'oeuvre d'imposer à l'âme ce travail, est-ce à l'âme de la faire? Ne courra-t-on pas, sous prétexte de synthèse, à une désolante confusion? La fusion des arts est-elle une utopie, ou la prévision d'un langage intellectuel futur? La question doit-elle être posée intérieurement ou peut-elle s'extérioriser?[60]

> (Is there an absolute continuity, a constant relationship between all the orders of human thought? Our soul urges so. But can we make visible this continuity, make it manifest in our works, create a language of analogies flexible enough to communicate simultaneously to the spirit of all orders of thought? Is it for the work to compel the soul to make this effort, should the soul do so? Are we not, under

the pretext of synthesis, heading towards a devastating confusion? Does the fusion of the arts represent a utopia, or does it provide an intellectual language of the future? Should the question be posed internally, or can it be made manifest externally?)

The ideal of an ideal union was thus interrogated, and with the intensity and self-consciousness – the 'inward turn' – emblematic of early modernism. As is often said of modernist philosophy, and extended to modern art more generally, structures of thought were brought newly to consciousness, examined critically and from various perspectives, so that, as a result, thought became its own subject.

The saying may apply to the dancers studied here. In their thoughts on music and dance, d'Udine, Fuller, and Saint-Point were self-critical, reflexive, aware and attuned to the conditions of art, to issues of agency, and to various structures of representation. Indeed, their thoughts articulate a prototypically modernist dilemma: in the words of T.J. Clark, 'what it is to "represent" at a particular historical moment – they show us the powers and limits of a practice of knowledge'.[61] D'Udine, clearly, was the most empirically minded, a man for whom representation meant reproduction, transparency, a doubling-up of the rhythmic pulsations (and, therefore, the psychological impulses) characteristic of human physiology. Fuller, quite the contrary, unleashed the representational potentiality of her materials. Certainly, she did not deny or repress representation; rather, she rendered it multiple, metamorphosing, and contingent on the creative contribution of the spectator. As for Saint-Point, her representational aesthetic incorporated its opposite, a non-representational anaesthetic. She challenged the significance of sensory experience, promoted solely cerebral activity, and suggested that the hidden unity of the arts might best be grasped in moments not of personal intuition or scientific illumination, but of disjunction between independent artistic parameters.

There is more that could be said: about specific impacting ideologies (Saint-Point, for example, was associated with the Futurists and 'Simultanéists', as well as the *Montjoie!* circle); slippage between theories (both the Symbolists and the 'Cérébristes' upheld the significance of creative ambiguity, Canudo repeating the phrase 'Suggérer, et non pas définir'); influences in later years (the Futurist leader F.T. Marinetti acknowledged the influence not of Saint-Point but Fuller); and modernist contradictions (between subjectivism and depersonalization, sensuality and schematics). These topics deserve further scrutiny; likely, they will bring the thoughts and theories aired here – the dancers', as well as my own – into sharper focus. Yet the case studies of these pages may be salutary in themselves, for they bring to critical discourse the questions with which this chapter began – questions that could help us think afresh about representation as a realm of creative possibility.

Notes

I should like to dedicate this chapter to my grandmother, Millicent Caddy, whose sudden but peaceful passing on 23 January 2012 is a reminder of the humbling fragility of life.

1 Ernst Gombrich, *Art and Illusion: A Study in the Psychology of Pictorial Representation* (London: Phaidon Press, 1960).
2 Dance scholar Stephanie Jordan is one of few to raise similar questions; see her essay 'Choreomusical Conversations: Facing a Double Challenge', *Dance Research Journal*, 43.1 (2011), 43–64. Jordan also notes the 'old hard binary of parallelism and counterpoint'; she seeks ways to address, instead, the 'dynamic interaction' and 'mutual implication' of music and dance.
3 On these phenomena, I hope it will not seem immodest to cite Davinia Caddy, *The Ballets Russes and Beyond: Music and Dance in Belle-Époque Paris* (Cambridge University Press, 2012).
4 John Martin, 1933; quoted in Selma Jeanne Cohen, *The Modern Dance: Seven Statements of Belief* (Middletown, CT: Wesleyan University Press, 1966), 4.
5 Sylvia Grey, 'Dancing', *The Theatre* (1 January 1898), 34–7 (34).
6 Please note: all primary source material is quoted in its original language, followed by an English translation (my own); translations are not provided in the notes or when the meaning of a word or phrase seems clear enough.
7 Isadora Duncan, 1927; quoted in Fredrika Blair, *Isadora: Portrait of the Artist as a Woman* (New York: McGraw-Hill, 1986), 187–8.
8 Loie Fuller, 1914; quoted in Sally Sommer, 'Loie Fuller's Art of Music and Light', *Dance Chronicle*, 4.4 (1981), 389–401 (390).
9 I think particularly of Rhonda K. Garelick, *Electric Salome: Loie Fuller's Performance of Modernism* (Princeton University Press, 2007); and Julie Townsend, *The Choreography of Modernism in France* (London: Legenda, 2010).
10 D'Udine's real name was Albert Cozanet. (The pseudonym is thought to borrow from Giovanni da Udine, a student of Raphael.)
11 André Mangeot, 'L'École Jean d'Udine', *Le Monde musical* (15 and 30 July 1912), 218.
12 *Ibid.*, 218.
13 *Ibid.*, 218. Also see Victor Debay, 'Rythmes et danses', *Le Courrier musical* (1 July 1912), 397–9.

14 Jean d'Udine, *L'Art et le geste* (Paris: Félix Alcan, 1910).
15 See Émile Jaques-Dalcroze, *Méthode Jaques-Dalcroze* (Neuchâtel: Sandoz, Jobin et Cie, 1906). Later writings are compiled in *Rhythm, Music and Education*, trans. Harold F. Rubinstein (London: Chatto and Windus, 1921); and *Eurhythmics, Art and Education*, trans. Frederick Rothwell (London: Chatto and Windus, 1930). As is well known, Dalcroze retreated from the precise structural synchronization he first advocated, envisaging freer relations between music and dance, and even the wholesale absence of music from danced performance.
16 See D'Udine, *La Coordination des mouvements et la culture de la volonté par la gymnastique rythmique de Jaques-Dalcroze* (Paris: Institut Général Psychologique, 1911).
17 In its scientific footing, d'Udine's theory may compare to that of René Ghil, a lesser-known Symbolist poet who developed a synaesthetic system linking vowels, consonants, colours, musical instruments, and emotions.
18 Haeckel was one of Darwin's leading supporters, best known for his 1875 treatise *Über die Wellenzeugung der Lebensteilchen oder die Perigenesis der Plastidule*. For a detailed explanation of Haeckel's theory and its relation to Darwin's, see Robert J. Richards, *The Tragic Sense of Life: Ernst Haeckel and the Struggle over Evolutionary Thought* (University of Chicago Press, 2008).
19 Félix Le Dantec, 'L'Intuition', *Les Arts de la vie*, 1.1 (January 1904), 30–2. The invention of the 'phrénographe', Le Dantec hypothesized, was imminent: one Monsieur Maneuvrier had already devised an instrument for determining the vintage of wine over the telephone.
20 D'Udine cited Le Dantec's *L'Unité dans l'être vivant* (1902), *Les Lois naturelles* (1904), *De l'Homme à la science* (1907), and *Science et conscience* (1908).
21 D'Udine expanded on this notion of 'reversibilité' in his later thesis *Qu'est-ce que la beauté?* (Paris: Henri Laurens, 1936), 128–45.
22 Ruth St Denis, 'Music Visualization', *Denishawn Magazine*, 1.3 (1925), 1–3.
23 According to one Franz Ruhlmann, she succeeded: 'Isadora Duncan est la Musique même, son incarnation, sa réalisation plastique. Elle est la Musique qu'on regard.' See the collection of press clippings at the Bibliothèque Nationale de France, Département des Arts du Spectacle (hereafter F-Pn), Fonds Rondel (Ro) 12073, as well as Duncan's biography, *My Life* (1927; rpt New York: Liveright, 1995).
24 Loie Fuller, interview with Coville, 'Danse, musique, lumière chez Loie Fuller', *L'Éclair* (8 May 1914), 6; also see clipping, F-Pn, Ro 12124.
25 Anatole France, cited in Louis Schneider, 'La Loie Fuller et son école de danse' (10 November 1912); clipping, F-Pn, Ro 12124.
26 Léo Clarétie, programme to accompany Fuller's appearance at the Théâtre du Châtelet, May 1914; housed at the Houghton Library, Harvard University (hereafter US-CAh).
27 *Ibid.*
28 Gabriel Astruc, *Le Pavillon des fantômes* (1929; rpt Paris: Mémoire du Livre, 2003), 369.

29 Fuller, interview with André Arnyvelde, 'Écoles de beauté', *Je sais tout* (15 November 1913), 599–614 (610).
30 Fuller, quoted in 'Lois [sic] Fuller in a Church', n.d.; clipping, US-CAh, TMC, HTC Clippings 1.
31 Stéphane Mallarmé, 'Ballets' (1886), *Crayonné au théâtre*; rpt in G. Jean-Aubry and Henri Mondor (eds.), *Oeuvres complètes* (Paris: Gallimard, 1945), 303–7 (304).
32 Jean Lorrain, 'La Loïe', *Le Journal* (29 October 1897), 1–2 (1). For more on Fuller and her aesthetics of obliquity, see Guy Ducrey, *Corps et graphies: poétique de la danse et de la danseuse à la fin du XIXe siècle* (Paris: Champion, 1996); Ann Cooper Albright, *Traces of Light: Absence and Presence in the Work of Loie Fuller* (Middletown, CT: Wesleyan University Press, 2007); and Garelick, *Electric Salome*.
33 Fuller, quoted in 'Loie Fuller on Dancing' (1 January 1910); clipping, US-CAh, TMC, HTC Clippings 1.
34 Fuller, 'Théorie la danse' (c.1911–14), rpt in *Ma Vie et la danse* (Paris: L'Oeil d'Or, 2002), 177–8.
35 *Ibid.*, 48.
36 Dario Gamboni, *Potential Images: Ambiguity and Indeterminacy in Modern Art* (London: Reaktion Books, 2002).
37 See Christoph Bode, *Ästhetik der Ambiguität: Zu Funktion und Bedeutung von Mehrdeutigkeit in der Literatur der Moderne* (Tübingen: Niemeyer, 1988). Gamboni also links the phenomenon of 'potential images' to concurrent trends in the philosophy and psychology of perception, as well as to the modernist 'subjectivization' of the observer described by Jonathan Crary in his *Techniques of the Observer: On Vision and Modernity in the Nineteenth Century* (Cambridge, MA: The MIT Press, 1990).
38 See Auguste Rodin, *L'Art: entretiens réunis par Paul Gsell* (Paris: Bernard Grasset, 1911), 213. On his sculptures, Rodin maintained: 'Ils éveillent sans aucun secours étranger l'imagination des spectateurs. Et cependant, loin de l'encercler dans les limites étroites, ils lui donnent de l'élan pour vagabonder à sa fantaisie. Or c'est là, selon moi, le rôle de l'art.' Odilon Redon, equally enthused by 'le monde ambigu de l'indéterminé', described the function of art in similar terms: 'd'obtenir chez le spectateur, par un attrait subit, toute l'évocation, tout l'attirant de l'incertain, sur les confins de la pensée'. See Redon, 'Confidances d'artiste' (1909) in *À soi-même: journal 1867–1915* (Paris: José Corti, 1961), 5–29 (26).
39 See Heinz K. Henisch and Bridget A. Henisch, *The Photographic Experience, 1839–1914: Images and Attitudes* (University Park, PA: Pennsylvania State University Press, 1994); and Michel Frizot (ed.), *A New History of Photography* (Cologne: Könemann, 1998).
40 Valentine de Saint-Point, 'La Métachorie', *Montjoie!*, 2.1–2 (1914), 5–7.
41 *Ibid.*, 6.

42 Mark Franko offers a gendered reading of Saint-Point's 'Métachorie' in his *Dancing Modernism/Performing Politics* (Bloomington: Indiana University Press, 1995), 21–4.
43 Susan Buck-Morss cites Kant (the warrior as transcendental subject) and Nietzsche (as embodiment of the Will to Power); see her seminal article 'Aesthetics and Anaesthetics: Walter Benjamin's Artwork Essay Reconsidered', *October*, 62 (1992), 3–41 (8–10). For a comprehensive account of aesthetics as 'perception by feeling', see Terry Eagleton, *The Ideology of the Aesthetic* (Oxford: Blackwell, 1990).
44 Saint-Point, quoted in Georges Pioch, 'Mme Valentine de Saint-Point et la danse idéiste', *La Revue des oeuvres nouvelles* (January 1914); clipping, F-Pn, Ro 11973(2).
45 Saint-Point, 'La Métachorie', 5.
46 *Ibid.*, 6.
47 *Ibid.*, 7.
48 Saint-Point, quoted in 'Tribune libre' (14 December 1913); clipping, F-Pn, Ro 11973(2).
49 Riccioto Canudo, 'Manifeste de l'art cérébriste', *Montjoie!*, 2.1–2 (1914), 9. (The manifesto was first published in *Le Figaro*, 9 February 1914, 1–2.)
50 Guillaume Apollinaire, *Les Peintres cubistes: méditations esthétiques* (Paris: Figuière, 1913).
51 Saint-Point, 'La Métachorie', 7.
52 Daniel Chennevière, 'La Musique chorégraphique', *Montjoie!*, 2.1–2 (1914), 13–15 (15).
53 Alberto Savinio, 'Le Drame et la musique', *Les Soirées de Paris*, 3.23 (April 1914), 240–2 (241). Savinio's real name was Andrea de Chirico; he was the younger brother of painter Giorgio de Chirico.
54 *Ibid.*, 240: 'J'ai la conception d'une oeuvre constituée à la fois d'éléments dramatiques et musicaux, mais où ces éléments – contrairement aux méthodes usées – ne se soutiendraient par aucune dépendance mutuelle.'
55 Guillaume Apollinaire, 'Musique nouvelle', *Paris-Journal* (24 May 1914); rpt in L.-C. Breunig (ed.), *Chroniques d'art (1909–1918)* (Paris: Gallimard, 1960), 382–4.
56 Saint-Point, 'La Métachorie', 5.
57 *Ibid.*
58 Saint-Point, quoted in 'Tribune libre', 14 December 1913; clipping, F-Pn, Ro 11973(2).
59 Camille Mauclair, 'L'Identité et la fusion des arts', *Idées vivantes* (Paris: Librairie de l'Art Ancienne et Moderne, 1904), 197–309.
60 *Ibid.*, 203–4.
61 T.J. Clark, *Farewell to an Idea: Episodes from a History of Modernism* (New Haven and London: Yale University Press, 1999), 165.

PART III

Musical representations in opera and cinema

9 | Allusive representations: homoerotics in Wagner's *Tristan*

LAURENCE DREYFUS

Debates on music's ability to 'represent' the world are often premised on a notion of meaning which asserts that music either does or does not convey something that can be contained within a verbal proposition, as when a musical gesture X can reasonably be said to express a proposition Y. So either the opening of Beethoven's Fifth Symphony expresses 'Fate knocking on the door' or it does not. Even in the rarefied world of Saussurean semiotics, the sense of music and its individual gestures inevitably comes up short, for even if we can point to a meaningful musical signifier, such as an interrupted or deceptive cadence, no one can give a clear account of the signified concept in the same way that words seem to depict actions or images represent objects in the external world.

If representation in the arts is an account of how one thing – a murder in a staged drama or a vase of flowers on a painted canvas – stands in for something else, music invariably fails to make the grade, since it appears almost as difficult to differentiate musical signs as it is to name what it is they stand for. What signs, for example, mark the beginning of Bach's Brandenburg Concerto No. 6 (BWV 1051)? Is it the key of B flat major, the odd canon between two solo violas *da braccio*, the anomalous use of accompanying violas *da gamba*, the static harmony, the rhythmic pulsations of the accompaniment, the absence of violins, and so on? What should we take all this to represent? Even when a musical sign depends on a clear referent – such as the sleigh bells in Mahler's Fourth Symphony – the chaining, overlapping, and proliferation of sounds heard as signs in music suggest that its representations of the world can only be, at best, part of a much larger ideational process. One can easily see why so many thinkers since the eighteenth century have been persuaded that music is a fundamentally un-representational art with few significant links to lived experience, its expression hermetic to its own materials.

These days, of course, very few people assert that the significance of art lies either in its clear articulation of propositional statements or in its unsullied reflections of life. Rather than translate from a natural language or mirror the outside visual world, art – it is generally recognized – engages with the world in a myriad of different ways. What has been crucial to the Western European canon, perhaps, is a kind of music which, instead of arguing or depicting, rhapsodizes on the world in ways that both crystallize and transform human experience. In this chapter, I will suggest that 'representation' – at least as commonly understood – is the wrong place to be searching for meaning of music. The right place to be looking is 'metaphor', not merely as an activity of figurative language but also as a fundamental and supra-linguistic mode of human understanding in which all forms of art excel. Metaphor, moreover, also helps explain how so much of what we like to think of as representation is actually allusion, with its own peculiar ways of divulging meaning.

The following observations on homoerotics in Wagner's *Tristan und Isolde* are offered so as to consider how even the most subtle musical allusions enrich musical experience via metaphor. By metaphor I mean the notion of 'understanding as, seeing as, or hearing as' rather than via the mode of classical representation which depends on the reflection of a specifiable content. What is needed, I suggest, is a move away from a model of musical representation in the sense of a string of fixed meanings towards a more shapely account of the experiential vagaries which characterize what we do when we hear, play, and reflect on music. Wagner is especially interesting in this regard, for he was caught both in his theories and in his compositional praxis between a commitment on the one hand to music which realizes the intention of verbal utterance and a belief on the other in the 'higher' status of music which surpasses words in depicting complex emotional states. So one reads in his *Opera and Drama* (1852) of 'the musician' as 'the realizer of poetic intent' (*Der Musiker, Verwirklicher der Absicht des Dichterische*),[1] while in 'the Application of Music to the Drama' (1879), he notes that 'with the help of a strangely derived harmonization' he could present two musical 'motives' knit in such a way that, 'more than Wotan's words, this musical event [*diese Ton-Erscheinung*] should impart to us a picture of the frighteningly gloomy soul of the suffering god' (*uns ein Bild der furchtbar verdüsterten Seele des leidenden Gottes gewahren lassen sollte*).[2] Wagner's ambivalence – which is the ambivalence of much of the nineteenth century – can be best understood as the inevitably hamstrung response to the inadequate terms of the representation debate, a cultural trap from which it is still hard to escape.

Homoerotics may seem an unnecessarily provocative term when applied to Wagner, but I mean it to encompass themes of passionate desire and closeness between members of the same sex, even if it is only one character who exhibits these feelings towards another.[3] Sentimental and eroticized same-sex friendships were a staple of late eighteenth- and early nineteenth-century German literature and culture, but by the 1850s were beginning to be regarded by some as suspect once erotic friendships between men and women came to dominate bourgeois sensibilities. Writing about the 'great passionate and ideal friendships' of the past, the Swiss writer Gottfried Keller, for example, thought that it was 'becoming more and more awkward [*unpassend*] for two [men] to want something so very special and exquisite between them; ... As for a relation to women it is rather different'.[4] Wagner stands out as a man of the past by embedding several sentimental friendships within *Tristan und Isolde*. The erotic pathos of this opera in fact gains a heretofore unheard-of intensity, not only because of the impossible Love–Death between Tristan and Isolde, but because even the minor characters are in love with one of the protagonists. This point was first put forward in a book from 1903 by Hanns Fuchs entitled *Richard Wagner und die Homosexualität*.[5] Brangäne, Fuchs notes, is far from a merely devoted and bungling servant. Her life 'has only a single goal – the happiness of her mistress', which is why she has no choice but to supply the Love potion instead of the Death philtre.[6] Her distressed diction betrays a desperate attachment to Isolde, as when she 'showers her mistress with pet names' in an attempt to placate Isolde after having cursed Tristan:

O Süsse! Traute!	My sweetheart! Beloved!
Teure! Holde!	Precious! Charmer!
Gold'ne Herrin!	Golden mistress!
Lieb' Isolde!	Dear Isolde!

Four short lines – six exclamation points.

The stage directions evoke a similar delirium. First Brangäne 'flings herself upon Isolde with unrestrained affection [*mit ungestümer Zärtlichkeit*]' and then 'gradually draws her to the couch'. Hanns Fuchs treats only the text, but Wagner's music too traffics in 'unrestrained affection', blurring in the process Isolde's erotic torment with Brangäne's own. Thereafter, as Brangäne hatches her plan to bind Tristan to her mistress with the love potion, we soon perceive her own erotic impulse in 'conjuring up the power of love', above all in the music often called Brangäne's Consolation. In fact, this leitmotif might better be dubbed *Freundesliebe* or Romantic Friendship. As can be seen from Example 9.1, the motive emerges directly out of the original pitch collection of the *Tristan* chord.

As John Deathridge clarified in 1979, Wagner composed what he called this 'motive' in 1857 without connecting it to any concrete words or ideas

Example 9.1 *Freundesliebe* of Brangäne (for Isolde) and King Marke (for Tristan) – (Act III, sc. 3).

and only subsequently found a match to some verses in *Siegfried*. As he wrote to Mathilde Wesendonck several days later:

> The Muse is beginning to visit me: does it betoken the certainty of your visit? The first I found was a melody which I didn't at all know what to do with, till all of a sudden the words from the last scene of *Siegfried* came into my head.[7]

The words from Act III of *Siegfried* that came into Wagner's head occur just as Brünnhilde, shocked by Siegfried's sexual overtures, says: 'My senses are confused, my knowledge is silent: must my wisdom vanish?' To which Siegfried replies: '*Sang'st du mir nicht, dein Wissen sei das Leuchten der Liebe zu mir?*' (Did you not sing of your knowledge that would radiate your love for me?) (In fact, the music for the verses in the ultimate version in the opera *Siegfried* – the so-called World Inheritance motive – was not composed until 1864.) *Tristan* was actually much on Wagner's mind in 1857, and the composer found himself writing music for both operas at once. In fact, he found a far better use for his sketches in Brangäne's loving entreaty to her Mistress.[8] What is clear is that Wagner associated the music – in an instinctive personal reaction – with a gentle erotic charge as he awaited a visit from Mathilde. It was, however, a charge with a nuance, as Wagner marks the sketch *Anmuthig* – 'agreeable' or 'charming' – thereby revealing one shade of the music's character.[9]

Even in the earliest sketch, one can see that the motive embodies the sweet lyrical expression of two lovers in a particularly poignant way. As shown in Example 9.1, not only does the double counterpoint invert the two contrasting themes at the octave as the melodic first voice and subsidiary voice trade places, but also there is a telling (and very sensuous) overlap before the end of the weak notional fourth 'beat' of the (hypermetrical) phrase, where the bass line interrupts and impatiently re-inaugurates the lyrical outburst in the form of a voice-exchange. The lilting reference to the waltz which underlies this version of the motive evokes a feminine grace as do the two swooning falls of a minor seventh, though Wagner – still thinking of the music for *Siegfried* – also tried his hand at a version of the motive in a more 'masculine' duple metre with a syncopated theme, a significant move because of the use he made of it for King Marke in *Tristan*, Act III.

King Marke is certainly the greatest of Wagner's homoerotic companions. Here is a man who loved Tristan so much that when his Queen died, he saw no need to remarry. Instead, he wished to turn over all his wealth to Tristan and 'loved you then so much that never again did Marke wish to wed' (*So liebt' er dich / Dass nie aufs Neu / Sich Marke wollt' vermählen*). What torments the king is the pain which Tristan – not Isolde – inflicted on him, for he forgoes any mention of his wife's guilt. In Act III, when

Tristan lies dead before him, he rejoices that Tristan – not Isolde – was innocent of intentional guile. As he puts it:

Da hell mir ward enthüllt,	Since it was clearly disclosed to me
Was zuvor ich nicht fassen konnt'	What before I couldn't grasp,
Wie selig, dass ich den Freund	How blessed, that I found the Friend
frei von Schuld da fand!	Free from blame!

The Friend, indeed. What Fuchs, in addition to a few opera guides, did not notice, however, is that Marke sings the duple version of the same orchestral leitmotive (which accompanied Brangäne), as can be seen in the lower stave of Example 9.1.

Kurwenal is yet another of Tristan's super-loving Friends and the composer casts this character's final hyperbolic outburst in a somewhat different, tragic mode modelled on the homoerotic bond between Spartan lovers. So great is Kurwenal's loyalty to Tristan that it causes his death. When the ship arrives with Marke and Melot, he throws himself on the arrivals whom he takes for enemies, and sinks mortally to the ground from the blows he has received from the defenders. Eight years earlier, in 1849, Wagner had already foreshadowed Kurwenal's selfless act in the Artwork of the Future when he wrote about a *Männerliebe* which 'knit the fellowships of love into battalions of war and military order which prescribed death-defying tactics to rescue the threatened lover or to exact vengeance if he fell in battle'.[10] Kurwenal's mortal affection for Tristan offers therefore a 'classical' example of homophilia in sacrificing himself for his beloved in the precise terms which Wagner had specified:

Tristan! Trauter!	Woe! Tristan! Beloved!
Schilt mich nicht,	Scold me not,
Dass der Treue auch mit kommt!	So the faithful one may follow you!

Kurwenal enunciates these words as he dies trying to take hold of Tristan's hand. 'There he lies', Kurwenal sings to the king, 'where I lie' (Act III, sc. 3).

Kurwenal's bond to Tristan presupposes the exclusion of women, in keeping with time-honoured values of *Freundesliebe* between men. Most important to Kurwenal is that Tristan not denigrate himself before a woman:

Ein Herr der Welt	A master of the world
Tristan der Held!	The hero Tristan
Ich ruf's: du sag's	I cry: Say it this way, even if
und grollten mir tausend Frau Isolden.	a thousand Dame Isoldes resent me.

As a paradigmatic Spartan companion-lover, Kurwenal serves as the ideal Friend to nurse Tristan in Act III, and, against the vassal's own wishes, 'sends for the one female physician who can help his master'.

Der einst ich trotzt',	To whom I once defied,
Aus Treu' zu dir.	Out of troth to you
Mit dir nach ihr	With you towards her
Nun muss ich mich sehnen.	Must I now crave.

(Act III, sc. 1)

The music Wagner crafts for Kurwenal's demise is rich in erotic allusions, though at the beginning, as Kurwenal 'staggers, mortally wounded, before King Marke', the music of Isolde's Curse which resolves to the *Tristan* chord might embrace Marke as much as Tristan's manservant (Example 9.2). But the stage is entirely – if briefly – Kurwenal's as he clutches at Tristan's hand, gasping between his words as the orchestra plays a version in tragic Adagio of a musical motive linked biographically to Wagner's passion for silk (illustrated in Example 9.3).[11] In the first statement of Silken Longing in Act III, scene 1, Tristan 'draws Kurwenal towards him and embraces him', and in the act of thanking the Friend, shares with him his ecstatic world. That Kurwenal's own music at his Death alludes to Desire ensures that his erotic world – like that of Brangäne – is heard in conjunction with luckless Desire and the Love–Death of Tristan and Isolde. In scene 1, in fact, Tristan calls Kurwenal 'my shield, my shelter in war and strife, in joy and sorrow, always ready at my side' (*mein Schild, mein Schirm / in Kampf und Streit, zu Lust und Leid mir stets bereit*). And even though Tristan believes that compassionate Kurwenal cannot understand the full extent of Tristan's erotic misery – 'this frightful yearning that sears me' (*Dies furchtbare Sehnen, das mich sehrt*) – at the moment of Kurwenal's death, Wagner recalls Tristan's declaration of *Freundesliebe* in his hopeless longing, now dragged down by the heavy-laden tones heard in the bass register at half the tempo. What originated in a longing for silk now alludes to Wagner's commentary on Kurwenal's tragic love for Tristan.

It is no great surprise that in the opera all these homoerotic desires have to end badly: death for Kurwenal, misery and unhappiness for King Marke and Brangäne. Yet none of these characters is deemed sick or perverse. To the contrary, their aspirations for love are noble and ennobling, for they reflect the mores of Romantic Friendship, values which Wagner esteemed in his own life, though it is fair to say that, apart from exceptional moments (such as his infatuation in 1864 with King Ludwig II), he preferred to be the *object* of homoerotic devotion rather than its

Example 9.2 Death of Kurwenal, *Tristan und Isolde* (Act III, sc. 3).

Example 9.2 (cont.)

Example 9.3 Silken longing, sketch and voice-leading of a nameless leitmotive for *Tristan und Isolde* (Act III, sc. 1).

practitioner, preferred, that is, to play Tristan over Kurwenal or King Marke. In the end, the musico-dramatic acuity and sympathy Wagner brings to these characters create a sexual universe made all the more compelling by its overlapping sets of magnetic erotic attractions.

The rich context for Wagner's views on homoerotic love show him ironically – in light of his endemic anti-Semitism – to be something of a liberal in sexual matters: not only did Wagner name Spartan *Männerliebe* as the emblematic model for the most ideal form of heterosexual love, but he was also still giving thought to this idea in notes he jotted down shortly before his death.[12] Across the course of his life he encouraged a succession of younger men to express undying and passionate devotion to him. His relationship to the first singer of the role of Tristan, Schnorr von Karolsfeld, was particularly intense, and at the time of Schnorr's mortal illness and early death, Wagner's diary entries are rife with histrionics and loving epithets. Wagner's letters from 1864 to King Ludwig II as well as to close female friends at the time bear witness to his patent infatuation with the young king. Wagner in fact wrote approvingly of two men living together in an openly acknowledged pairing, as with two musicians who entertained him while he was in London in 1855 named Sainton and Lüders. As for the music, the display of the motivic transformation from the triple to duple metre shown in the musical example makes it clear that Wagner linked the idealized and passionate, if sexless, attraction of Brangäne shown in Act I of *Tristan* to the similar kind of attraction expressed by King Marke in Act III. Most strikingly, Wagner's set designer for *Parsifal*, Paul von Joukowsky, lived for three years in the Wagner household with his young Neapolitan lover Pepino, whom Wagner treated as a member of the family, involving both members of the couple in frequent family soirees, even Christmas entertainments. Wagner, as someone whose own sexual interests centred on obsessions with pink satin and rose perfumes, seemed even to associate his own fetishes with Joukowsky's sexuality, to judge from an anecdote recounted in Cosima's diaries.[13]

The musical associations articulating the devotion of Brangäne to Isolde and King Marke and Kurwenal to Tristan therefore echo a sensibility for which there are ample biographical references, and, in a small way, then transforms the way one hears the music. But does the music for *Freundesliebe* in *Tristan* represent homoeroticism? To even put the question this way is, I think, to misconstrue what is going on when we speak of musical meaning and typifies what is wrong with most debates on musical representation.

Far better, it seems to me, is to allow Wagner's allusion to enter into a metaphorical process which results in a rising spiral of cognition, not a set of definitions, or an appeal to musical abstraction. Let me explain what this might mean. The plain fact is that it is impossible to establish – in the metaphorical content the music arouses – which is the tenor and which is the vehicle, to use terms made famous by I.A. Richards. A simple example might be the leitmotive from Wagner's *Ring* universally recognized as Alberich's curse. We can equally say 'hear this music as the curse' as we can say 'hear the curse as this music'. Although we might like to transfer the qualities of a curse to a passage of music, we also transfer perceived qualities of the passage of music to curses – here the raw ugliness of a half-diminished chord collection on F sharp followed by a rude juxtaposition of a C major triad blaring a demonic fanfare. The metaphorical content only arises when both terms of the metaphor are considered invertibly. It is fair to say therefore that we experience a reciprocal isomorphism between the two realms (music and expressive content) rather than infer a clear dependency of one upon the other. With this reciprocity, moreover, the musical curse-motive and the notion of curse inflect one another in a process of ever deepening associations. While we can and do reflect singly on the concept of curse (without the music) and on the musical content of the motive (without thinking of curses), the affective experience of Alberich cursing Love in *Das Rheingold* is transformed until – three operas later – Hagen plunges his spear into Siegfried in *Götterdämmerung* accompanied by the same chilling invocation in a wholly different setting.

The reciprocity between Alberich's curse in the drama and Wagner's music for the Curse motive does not even stop there, since the binary metaphorical pairing gives rise to a cognitive spiral, with each new insight coaxing a renewed return to the metaphorical inversion permitting an ever more enriched aesthetic moment to be recognized and further distilled. This resulting novel experience – the bringing together of the auditory and the conceptual realms in their reciprocity – helps explain how art shapes lived experience as much as (or even more than) it reflects it, and why we face such a conundrum in trying to explain in language what the devil is going on. Implicit here might also even be a rudimentary theory of artistic value, which posits that in less inspired works of art the reciprocal spiral set off by the two metaphorical operations is halted at an early stage: in mediocre arts, one exhausts the possible number and quality of outcomes instantiated by each metaphor at a relatively early stage. To assert a work's greatness is to point to unexpectedly and continually ingenious outcomes between the reciprocal stages of experiential 'hearing as'.

Returning to Wagner's homoerotics in *Tristan*, we can see how a host of metaphorical pairings give rise to a spiral of enriched meanings all the while sidestepping the question of direct representations. The following list of invertible metaphors illustrates certain cognitive operations through which the musical experiences might be funnelled.

Brangäne (*Tristan und Isolde*, Act I) – FREUNDESLIEBE (1)

a) FREUNDESLIEBE (1) as 'unrestrained affection' [*mit ungestümer Zärtlichkeit*]
b) falling sevenths as Brangäne's swoons
c) the text ('Wo lebte der Mann, der dich nicht liebte?') as Brangäne's own erotic feelings
d) waltzing reference in FREUNDESLIEBE (1) as 'charm' (marking of *anmuthig*)

e) *Tristan* chords in FREUNDESLIEBE as 'sweetened' Love-Death (*dolce* marking)

King Marke (*Tristan und Isolde*, Act III) – FREUNDESLIEBE (2)

a) FREUNDESLIEBE (2) as FREUNDESLIEBE (1)
b) duple-metre, lower pitched, syncopated FREUNDESLIEBE (2) as Marke's noble and tragic masculinity
c) Marke–Tristan as Spartan lovers (1849)
d) Marke–Tristan as Sainton–Lüders (1855), Ludwig II–Wagner (1864), or Joukowsky–Pepino (1880)

Kurwenal (*Tristan und Isolde*, Act III) – SILKEN LONGING

a) SILKEN LONGING (3) as FREUNDESLIEBE (2)
b) Kurwenal–Tristan as Spartan lovers (1849)
c) Tristan–Kurwenal as Schnorr von Karolsfeld–Wagner (1865)
d) Kurwenal–Tristan as Sainton–Lüders (1855), Ludwig II–Wagner (1864), or Joukowsky–Pepino (1880)

First there is the grasp of the motive's sense in its connection to Brangäne's 'impulsive or unrestrained affection' noted in Wagner's stage direction. The motive here does not especially amplify the text which speaks of any man falling for Isolde, but rather is heard far more as a musical metaphor for Brangäne's own feminine fantasy of what it would be like to be smitten by a glance at Isolde. Not only does the gentle waltz-like 'charm' of the gesture romanticize Isolde as an object of love, but the feminine swoons heard in the two falling minor sevenths likewise embody Brangäne's own same-sexual affections. The emergence of the Freundesliebe motive out of the prime collection of the *Tristan* chord and the saturation of the music with *Tristan* chords at the end of the passage (marked in the musical example) likewise invite us to hear the sweet lilting marked *dolce* in light of the more tormented pangs of the protagonists' own love–death.[14] As much as the bodily gesture of Brangäne's 'unrestrained affection' imprints itself on the music of Freundesliebe, so the specific qualities of the music's lilting sweetness are transferred to the understanding of the specific nature of her unrestrained affection. When the two metaphorical operations have completed their work, there is a new experiential quotient which did not exist before.

The transformation of the motive into music for King Marke in Act III takes the rejected music for the character of the young Siegfried and raises it to a higher, nobler station fit for a king, transposing it downward and adding the tragic heaving syncopes as Marke rhapsodizes over his guiltless

Friend to whom he had bequeathed all. The fact that we have previously heard something similar in a different context causes an associative link: so we hear Marke's emotive outburst in light of Brangäne's in Act I. They are not equivalent, of course, but Marke's affection gains in allusive significance because of the musical experience of Brangäne's impulsive tenderness. Brangäne's affection, in turn, gains retrospectively as seen through the lens of Marke's noble valediction which names Tristan, as the blessed Friend. The tragic music for Kurwenal's death gains as it is overlaid in references to silk, and to the positive references to Spartan lovers and other same-sex pairings, much as Wagner highlights what he took to be a noble, tragic dimension inhering in these pairs of male relationships. One musical experience imposes its pattern and values on another, thereby giving rise to what the philosopher Christopher Peacocke calls new metaphorical content.[15] Both these sets of feelings and their related music, in the next turn of the cognitive wheel, profit from varied biographical contexts – such as the touching story of the pair of London musicians Sainton and Lüders which Wagner recounts in *Mein Leben*, or the ecstatic apostrophes to the perfect love between Friends found in the composer's correspondence with King Ludwig. The reflexivity of these metaphorical operations – whether between music and concept, music and words, music and gesture, or even music and music – thrives in a spiral of figures in which one transfers qualities reciprocally from one or the other term of the metaphor, allowing each continuously to shape the cognitive content of the other.

Whereas it is vitally important in poetic metaphors to distinguish between Richards's tenor and the vehicle – where the order of the terms is fixed – the cognitive reciprocity I have been postulating shows how we are able to bounce back and forth fruitfully between the realms of the two metaphorical terms, especially in the most allusive kinds of art that encourage a continual to-and-fro. In the supra-linguistic and cognitive process I am trying to describe, we experience musical gestures and allusions and embed them in historical and biographical contexts not to fix the meaning of music or open it up to unbounded interpretation, but rather to restore and capture musical sense without ever exhausting its expression. There is no doubting the vivid concreteness of the music itself: the problem arises only when we try to pin down metaphorical associations to clear representations. Instead, these rich allusions to human experience may well be what draws us to music whose patterns challenge us to divine their meaning and savour their significance.

Notes

1 *Oper und Drama* in Richard Wagner, *Sämtliche Schriften und Dichtungen* [*SSD*], 6th edn, 16 vols. (Leipzig: Breitkopf & Härtel, 1911–14), vol. IV, 201.
2 'Über die Anwendung der Musik auf das Drama', *SSD*, vol. X, 188.
3 I treat this topic in the last chapter of *Wagner and the Erotic Impulse* (Cambridge, MA: Harvard University Press, 2010), 175–217, from which some of the material in the current chapter is drawn.
4 Letter to Johanna Kapp in Jacob Baechtold, *Gottfried Kellers Leben* (1894; Berlin, 1903), vol. II, 215, as cited in Lilli Jung, *Dichterfreundschaft und ihr romantisches Eigengepräge* (Saalfeld, 1934), 11.
5 Hanns Fuchs, *Richard Wagner und die Homosexualität: mit besonderer Berücksichtigung der sexuellen Anomalien seiner Gestalten* (Berlin, 1903).
6 *Ibid.*, 153.
7 See John Deathridge, 'Wagner's Sketches for the "Ring": Some Recent Studies', *Musical Times*, 118 (1977), 386; and also Robert Bailey, 'The Method of Composition' in Peter Burbridge and Richard Sutton (eds.), *The Wagner Companion* (New York, 1979), 317–27, where there is a transcription of these musical sketches for *Siegfried* and *Tristan*, along with the translation of Wagner's letter and a detailed commentary.
8 In an entry from 1878 in Cosima Wagner's diaries – *Die Tagebücher*, ed. Martin Gregor-Dellin and Dietrich Mack, rev. edn, 4 vols. (Munich: Piper, 1982), vol. III, 142 – Wagner's wife reveals that the World Inheritance motive set to the passage in *Siegfried* was originally intended for the Buddha in *Die Sieger* (*The Victors*), presumably when he gains a new insight about the stilling of sensual desires. Wagner describes this moment in a letter to Mathilde Wesendonck from 1858, speaking of how this insight marks the Buddha's final progress towards a state of supreme enlightenment. A woman, now understood compassionately, could be accepted into the 'community of the saintly' as long as she also renounced sensuality as a component of her love for a man.
9 I discuss the connection to *Die Sieger* in 'Siegfried's Masculinity', *The Wagner Journal*, 4 (2010), 16–18, translated as 'Siegfrieds Männlichkeit' in Tobias Jans (ed.), *Wagner in der Diskussion* (Würzburg: Königshausen und Neumann, 2011), 90–3.
10 Richard Wagner, *Dichtungen und Schriften: Jubiläumsausgabe*, ed. Dieter Borchmeyer, 10 vols. (Bayreuth, 1983), vol. VI, 111.
11 I treat Wagner's silk fetish in *Erotic Impulse*, 135–55.
12 Richard Wagner, *Nachgelassene Schriften und Dichtungen* (1895; Leipzig, 1902), 141.
13 Dreyfus, *Erotic Impulse*, 31–2, 175–81, 196–204, 213–17.
14 This torment-tinged sweetness – one can show analytically – forms the basis for a significant reappearance of the same modal mixtures in *Die*

Meistersinger, especially the Quintet in Act III. See Dreyfus, *Erotic Impulse*, 112-13.

15 See Christopher Peacocke's 'The Perception of Music: Sources of Significance', *British Journal of Aesthetics*, 49 (2009), 257-75; and my reply, 'Christopher Peacocke's "The Perception of Music"', *British Journal of Aesthetics*, 49 (2009), 293-7.

10 | *Der Dichter spricht*: self-representation in *Parsifal*

KAROL BERGER

For Hermann Danuser

In Hans Jürgen Syberberg's 1982 *Parsifal* film, there is one moment only when we catch a glimpse of any of the orchestral musicians: at the beginning of the Act III section usually called the Good Friday Spell, a spectral figure of the conductor, Armin Jordan, in a polo shirt, appears for a moment 'like a floating bird' in the skies above the scenic landscape – an apparition from another world, different from the fictional world of the drama, the world of shirtsleeves rather than costumes, our world (Figure 10.1).[1] After twenty-five seconds, the ghostly flying conductor disappears behind the prominent nose of the Wagner death mask of which the landscape is constituted. While I do not intend to come back to Syberberg's image explicitly, this chapter is an implicit gloss on this intrusion from the real world.

1

If there is one thing that everyone knows about later Wagner, it is that in his music dramas he assigned a demanding role to the orchestra, giving its part a melodic and motivic content of unprecedented density. As a result, the orchestra abandoned its subordinate, accompanimental role and became, some of the time at least, an equal partner of the voices.

But who is it, actually, that speaks through the orchestra in Wagner's music dramas, whose voice does the orchestra represent? To ask this question is to give the subject of representation in Wagner a somewhat unusual slant: normally, no sooner is the subject mentioned than someone will talk of leitmotifs, and no sooner are leitmotifs mentioned than someone will ask, 'What do they represent?' My question here is not so much, 'What is represented by leitmotifs?' as, 'Who does the representing, who expresses himself through the leitmotifs?'

Like so many interesting questions about Wagner, this one was also asked on a number of occasions by Carl Dahlhaus.[2] Leitmotifs, Dahlhaus argued, sometimes embody the memories, conscious or not, of the singing character. At other times, however, they represent the narrative voice, for Dahlhaus identical with the voice of the author, who speaks about the

Figure 10.1 Richard Wagner, *Parsifal*, director Hans Jürgen Syberberg, Act III, at 39:45.

characters and their dramatic situations directly to the audience, above the characters' heads.

This answer might seem right at first – right and attractive, since the presence of the narrator resonates with epic qualities of Wagner's dramas. One soon realizes, however, that the situations when a leitmotif has to be attributed to the narrator are exceedingly rare, if they can be found at all. Let us put aside for the time being passages of purely orchestral music. True, such passages may perhaps be attributed to the narrator: who else might be the speaker in such cases? But if we are looking for situations when the narrator speaks to us above the heads of the characters, we clearly need to concentrate on those moments when there are characters onstage. In such moments, we quickly discover that, for the most part, the orchestra, although remarkably eloquent and motivically rich, functions in late Wagner similarly to how it had long functioned in earlier opera: normally, rather than revealing a new, separate subjectivity, it provides the audience with access to the inner workings of the mind of the character onstage; occasionally, it also paints the external environment of the characters, the scenery in which they find themselves, the atmosphere they breathe – at least to the extent that this external environment impinges upon the characters' subjectivity. The leitmotifs, then, transmit the inner world, tell us what is on the character's mind, whether or not the character is fully conscious of what it is, just as an agitated accompaniment to a traditional operatic aria tells us that the personage is, well, agitated. To attribute such information to a separate speaker is unnecessary – a needless multiplication of entities against which Ockham would be justified in wielding his razor. For the most part, then, in later Wagner it is not that the narrator raises himself up from the pit to provide us with the information; it is, rather, that a window opens up in the character through which we may peek inside and access the intentional mind behind the gestural and verbal behaviour. Wagner's orchestra, like the operatic orchestra in general, acts usually as an extension of the singer's body, amplifying and supplementing his comportment, gestures, tone of voice, so that we might know better what is on the character's mind. It is, of course, true that, where in the traditional opera the orchestra usually tells us only of the character's mental state, his mood or emotion, Wagnerian leitmotifs extend this narrow range of reference considerably to include also the thought of such items as specific persons, objects, and even fairly abstract notions that cross the character's mind. But, for the most part, the Wagnerian orchestra does not speak in the name of a separate subjectivity. Rather, it simply amplifies our insight into the subjectivity of the presently acting and speaking character – just as the traditional operatic orchestra does.

Does a true narrative voice ever emerge in the orchestra? Perhaps this happens when the orchestra stops speaking in isolated motifs and begins to provide a longer continuous discourse, a discourse that makes musical sense independently of the vocal lines even when these are present? Perhaps it is at such moments that we become aware of the emergence of a voice that seems to emanate from a subjectivity independent of the characters onstage? The length and in particular the continuity of the independent orchestral discourse, I am suggesting, would make the crucial difference in such cases. This would be probably at least in part because continuity is the essential attribute of human consciousness. It is characteristic of us that we are aware not only of what is happening in the present moment, but also of how this experienced present is connected with the remembered past and anticipated future. Melody, which can be comprehended only when its continuity is grasped in terms of the constantly shifting interplay of the experienced present with the remembered past and anticipated future, has frequently served philosophers – from Augustine, through Schopenhauer, to Husserl – as the key example of how consciousness works.[3] Once an independent orchestral melody acquires a

Table 10.1 Good Friday Spell

Parsifal's prologue ('Wie dünkt mich doch die Aue heut' so schön!'; in B; III.626–63)
Transition ('Das ist – Karfreitags Zauber, Herr'; III.663–74)
Gurnemanz's monologue ('Du siehst, das ist nich so'; in D; III.675–770)
Parsifal's epilogue elegy ('Ich sah' sie welken, die einst mir lachten'; in D; III.770–99)

---

certain length and a degree of continuity, it would become less and less plausible that what we hear is the voice of the character's subconsciousness or unverbalized consciousness, and more and more tempting to attribute the orchestra's discourse to a new subjectivity, that of the narrator, speaking independently of the characters.

2

But is this temptation ever irresistible? I would like to consider one particularly tempting case, the so-called Good Friday Spell from Act III of *Parsifal* – tempting simply as a singularly elaborate and sustained piece of orchestrally articulated continuous discourse (Table 10.1). The melodic substance here is carried almost entirely by the orchestra, with the voices superimposing their counterpoints above it: not much rewriting is needed to present the whole as an orchestral piece, and, of course, it has often been so presented. Its main portion, in D major, is given to Gurnemanz; this is framed by Parsifal's prologue in B major and Parsifal's epilogue (which, Wagner's authorized biographer Glasenapp tells us, the composer himself called 'Elegy')[4] in D major.

What is striking about the Good Friday music, in its context, is how deliberately, serenely stable and regular it is (Example 10.1) – a complete reversal of the character of the music that opened Act III and pervaded it until now. After three introductory measures (III.626–8), Parsifal's prologue begins with two almost identical phrases of eight measures each (III.629–36 and 637–44; marked A in the example), the first one ending on the dominant and the second on the tonic chord, but otherwise harmonized with utmost simplicity: four measures of the tonic followed by four measures of the dominant for the antecedent; four measures of the tonic, three measures of the dominant, and a final tonic measure for the consequent. This is followed by a new eight-measure phrase (III.645–52; marked B in the example), this one also sounding like an antecedent and ending on the dominant, though harmonically more animated than the

Example 10.1 Parsifal's prologue, Good Friday Spell, *Parsifal*, Act III, mm. 626–63.

Example 10.1 (cont.)

first. The consequent, however, is less regular this time: consisting of only six measures (III.653–8) and ending on the dominant, it sounds inconclusive, and so does its even shorter repeat (III.659–63) that brings the main body of Parsifal's prologue to an end. But by this point the harmonic stability and the regularity of phrasing have been so firmly established that the inconclusive ending does nothing to erase them.

All this expressive serenity serves a dramatic purpose, of course. In order to understand this purpose fully, however, we need to look back at what has happened before this music begins – a series of highly symbolic actions, presented to a considerable extent in wordless, orchestrally accompanied pantomime (the sort of pantomime that has been prominent in Act III from the start), and all involving the pouring of liquids. As Parsifal reacts to Gurnemanz's story of the moral and physical decay of the Monsalvat community with despair and is about to faint, Kundry fetches some water with which to revive him. Parsifal's fainting and Kundry's gesture add to the many prominent parallels between Acts I and III, as they echo similar events in Act I. In Act III, however, the water Kundry brings triggers a whole cascade of flowing liquids. First, Gurnemanz orders that Parsifal be washed of the dust of his pilgrimage in the water of the nearby 'holy spring' ('heil'ge Quelle'; III.463), where indeed Kundry bathes the pilgrim's feet, while Gurnemanz sprinkles his head. Next, Kundry produces a phial of ointment and, in a gesture that clinches our suspicion that her figure is partly modelled on the traditional image of that other repentant sinner, Mary Magdalene (and, by the same token, provides Parsifal with yet another Christ-like feature), anoints the pilgrim's feet and dries them with her own hair. At Parsifal's own request, the phial now passes from Kundry to Gurnemanz, who uses its content to anoint the pilgrim's head and thus to proclaim him the new king. And finally, the new king performs his first office, using the water of the spring to baptize Kundry, who 'sinks her head deep to the ground; she appears to weep fervently' ('senkt das Haupt tief zur Erde; sie scheint heftig zu weinen').

This is where the Good Friday music begins. According to the stage direction, 'Parsifal turns around and looks in mild rapture at the forest and meadow which now glow in the morning light' ('Parsifal wendet sich um, und blickt mit sanfter Entzückung auf Wald und Wiese, welche jetzt im Vormittagslichte leuchten'). The ointment, the water of the spring, Kundry's tears, and the morning dew blend together, bringing Parsifal, Kundry, and the meadow a new life. Kundry, recall, has been associated with 'wild' nature already in Gurnemanz's Monologue of Act I. And at the beginning of Act III, nature's renewal with the coming of spring after harsh winter and Kundry's revival after a deep coma are explicitly correlated: 'Up! Kundry! Up! Winter has fled and Spring is here!' ('Auf! Kundry! Auf! / Der Winter floh, und Lenz ist da!'; III.71–4), Gurnemanz addresses her as he tries to wake her up from her hibernation. But now, thanks to the baptism, 'nature' is no longer 'wild' – it has been brought under the dominion of the spirit. On this spring morning, nature is renewing itself and Parsifal looks at it with new eyes: 'How beautiful does the meadow seem to me today!' ('Wie dünkt mich doch die Aue heut' so schön!'; III.639–41). And he contrasts the present serenity of the transfigured meadow with the remembered wild erotic temptations of Klingsor's enchanted garden. The black magic of untamed desire has been defeated by the white magic of spiritual transformation. Gurnemanz explains: 'This is ... the Good Friday spell, my Lord' ('Das ist – Karfreitags Zauber, Herr'; III.663–7).

Gurnemanz's words usher in a transition between the prologue and the main portion of the Good Friday music (III.663–74), a brief modulatory intrusion of passionate suffering as Parsifal recalls that Good Friday is the day of the crucifixion and thus should be one when all the creation mourns and weeps. His tutor's answer (III.675–770) is both musically and verbally the core of the scene – a lecture in theology, or rather a sermon, that lies at the centre of the opera.

Musically, Gurnemanz's sermon is constructed on the scaffolding made of the two diatonic phrases of Parsifal's prologue, whose periodic reappearances, all in the tonic key of D major, are separated by two new heavily chromatic and modulatory interpolations (see Table 10.2, where the material based on Parsifal's first phrase, III.629–36, is marked A, that based on his second phrase, III.645–52, is marked B, and the interpolations are marked x and y). It begins with an introduction made of Parsifal's first phrase, shortened and inconclusive, presented in two overlapping statements (III.675–84). There follows as the first part of the sermon the first interpolation (III.685–98) and this culminates in a single repetition of Parsifal's first phrase (III.699–704), again incomplete and inconclusive. The second interpolation (III.705–15) begins the second part of the sermon and again issues seamlessly in a presentation of, this time, Parsifal's second phrase (III.716–37), much developed and consequently much longer than in its original form, as well as, equally seamlessly, the first phrase (III.738–52) repeated three times and given this time a triumphant conclusion. The whole is rounded off with a peroration based on the second phrase (III.752–70).

Once the sermon is finished, Parsifal completes the Good Friday music with an elegiac epilogue-peroration of his own, consisting, first, of a brief chromatic interpolation (III.770–80) and then of the first phrase of

Table 10.2 Gurnemanz's Good Friday sermon

Introduction:
A (III.675–84)
Part 1:
x (III.685–98)
A (III.699–704)
Part 2:
y (III.705–15)
B (III.716–37)
A (III.738–52)
Peroration:
B (III.752–70)

his prologue, presented this time in a complete and conclusive form (III.781–8) and rounded off with an echo of Gurnemanz's peroration (III.788–99) that dissolves into a transition ushering in the immediately following Transformation music.

The periodic refrain-like returns of the diatonic phrases in the tonic key calm down and neutralize the tortured quality of the chromatic interpolations, just as the divine love redeems and consoles the suffering and mortal creation – the sermon's theme. Parsifal has been mistaken, Gurnemanz teaches, when he thought that this day is the occasion for all the creation to mourn and weep only. This, after all, is the day when God's loving self-sacrifice redeemed man 'who feels liberated from the burden of sin and dread' ('der fühlt sich frei von Sündenlast und Grauen'; III.713–16). Thus today's tears have a regenerative power and the day itself calls for rejoicing.

So far, so traditionally Christian. But Gurnemanz goes further and it is here that the Christian message acquires an unmistakably Wagnerian accent. The sacrifice of the cross has a significance that extends beyond man to all nature. Through man's mediation the divine act of redemption spreads to the rest of the creation. To be sure, 'it [the creation] cannot itself glimpse Him [the Saviour] Himself on the Cross' ('Ihn selbst am Kreuze kann sie nicht erschauen'; III.705–9), but 'therefore it looks up to the redeemed man' ('da blickt sie zum erlös'ten Menschen auf'; III.710–12). And 'the sinner's tears of repentance ... besprinkle field and meadow with holy dew and thus make it flourish' ('Des Sünders Reuetränen ... / ... mit heil'gem Tau/beträufet Flur und Au: / der ließ sie so gedeihen'; III.684–94) so that 'all the creation rejoices' ('freu't sich alle Kreatur'; III.695–6). More: the repentant sinner becomes nature's guardian rather than exploiter. Here is the key passage of the sermon: 'Now grass and flower in the meadows notice that today the foot of man does not step on them, but rather that – as God with heavenly patience pitied him and suffered for him – so also man today in pious grace spares them with soft steps' ('Das merkt nun Halm und Blume auf den Auen, / daß heut' des Menschen Fuß sie nicht zertritt, / doch wohl – wie Gott mit himmlischer Geduld / sich sein' erbarmt' und für ihn litt – / der Mensch auch heut' in frommer Huld / sie schont mit sanftem Schritt'; III.722–40). Just as God has shown man His compassion, so now man is compassionate towards 'all that blooms and soon dies here' ('was all' da blüht und bald erstirbt'; III.745–7). Thus also nature is 'made free of sin' ('entsündigte'; III.748–9) and regains its 'day of innocence' ('Unschuldstag'; III.752–4).

In short, the divine compassionate love poured its redeeming grace over the sinful man, whose tears of repentance, in turn, poured in love and compassion over dumb and mortal nature, included it in the salvation plan, and made it flourish and rejoice. In Wagner's recension, thanks to man's channelling of divine love further down, the good tidings embrace all of nature. Wagner's Christianity takes on a distinctly ecological colouring. Thus the question suggested by Gurnemanz's Monologue in Act I – how to redeem wild nature by bringing it under the spirit's dominion – finds its answer in his Good Friday sermon.

Parsifal's epilogue elegy is designed to make sure we understand that nothing escapes this embrace – neither the blooming meadow in front of his eyes, nor the remembered flowers of evil, the seductive Flowermaidens in Klingsor's enchanted garden, nor, finally, the most evil flower of them all, the 'rose of hell' ('Höllenrose'; II.112) herself, Kundry, now repentant and newly baptized. He wonders if Klingsor's flowers he once saw wither 'today long for redemption' ('heut' sie nach Erlösung schmachten'; III.775–7). He assures Kundry that her tears of repentance are a 'dew of blessing' ('Segenstaue'; III.781–2): 'you weep, … behold, the meadow smiles!' ('du weinest, – sieh', es lacht die Aue!'; III.783–8). And he seals this assurance with a chaste kiss on her forehead – a kiss of charity that reciprocates the erotic kiss she had given him in Klingsor's garden.

We can now come back to the initial question. In the Good Friday music, the melodic substance belongs almost entirely to the orchestra; the voices play a subordinate role and can be removed without significant damage to musical sense or continuity. But who speaks through the orchestra, whose subjectivity gets expressed here?

In this case as well, one is initially inclined to reach for Ockham's razor. At the outset of the Good Friday Spell, Parsifal is seized by a philosophical-religious vision of 'wild' suffering nature transfigured by spirit, consoled by divine compassion, of Eros brought under the dominion of Agape, a vision he cannot coherently and rationally articulate in words, but which is nevertheless his own, and is articulated for him by the orchestra speaking the language that can access deeper layers of the self than his words could at this stage. Subsequently, the more experienced Gurnemanz brings this orchestral vision into fully rational linguistic awareness in his sermon. Throughout, the orchestra articulates a way of experiencing the world that Parsifal and Gurnemanz share, even if only the latter is able to express this way in words, to make it fully conscious and rational. Thus, there seems to be no need to postulate that the orchestra speaks for a separate subjectivity, that it assumes the narrator's voice.

3

But things begin to look differently when we consider the Good Friday Spell in a larger context, the context of the whole opera. The Good Friday music plays a peculiar role in the music–dramatic organization of this opera: it is at once central and eccentric. In one sense, it does not belong to the drama at all; in another, it is its core. Let me explain.

Parsifal is put together of three principal kinds of structural music–dramatic events, each performing a distinct role (see Table 10.3, where I have used bold typeface to indicate formally closed sections and bold italics for the formally open sections). First, there are the opera's main structural pillars of closed-form stability – the two Communion sequences that close Acts I and III, the first sequence shaped as an asymmetrical arch with the Communion itself serving as its capstone, the second shaped as a teleological linear progression with the Communion as its goal. Retrospectively, the Prelude is assimilated as a component of the first sequence, once we realize that its first forty-three measures anticipate the first Communion service. (The two Communion services themselves emerge in this reading as the most important sections of the whole.) According to Cosima Wagner's testimony (diary entry of 11 August 1877), it was while composing the first Communion sequence in the summer of 1877 that Wagner came to see that 'this scene of the Holy Communion will be the main scene, the core of the whole work'.[5] Second, these two pillars of closed-form stability are separated by the opera's largest open-form sequence – the Parsifal–Kundry confrontation of Act II, with the pivotal Kiss, the drama's turning point, at its centre. Third, standing outside of this symmetrical ABA' structure, there is the unique combination of a closed-form orchestral discourse with

Table 10.3 *Parsifal*: Main structural events

Act I:
Prelude (I.1–113; in A flat)
Gurnemanz's Monologue (I.373–741)
Communion Sequence I (I.1073–1666) with the **Communion** (I.1422–1574; in A flat) at its centre
Act II:
Choral Dance of the Flowermaidens (II.567–702; in A flat)
Parsifal–Kundry Confrontation (II.739–1539)
Act III:
[*Prelude*] (III.1–44)
The first monologue complex:
Parsifal's Monologue (III.285–332)
Gurnemanz's Monologue (III.332–419)
The second monologue complex:
Good Friday Spell (III.626–799; in (B)/D)
Communion Sequence II (III.800–1141) culminating in the **Communion**
 (III.1088–1141; in A flat)

superimposed monologues – the Good Friday Spell directly preceding the second Communion sequence, the only structural element of Act III without a parallel in Act I.

The dramatic function of the first of these structural elements (the two Communion sequences) is to enact the ritual which is the main content and point of the opera – which, in a sense, *is* the opera. The ritual has to be performed twice, since it is not fully successful the first time: it accomplishes everything it is meant to accomplish only on the second try. The ritual action has two aspects: it is, or is expected to be, at once a communion and a redemption. The first of these two roles it successfully accomplishes even on the first run-through, but not the second, since the designated redeemer is not yet ready. The second run-through of the ritual action, the emphasis now shifting from the communion to the redemption, is a full success.

The dramatic function of the second structural element (the Parsifal–Kundry confrontation pivoting on the Kiss) is to show how the merely potential redeemer was transformed into the actual one, how the conversion of the saving hero was accomplished. If the ritual enacted by the first structural component is the essential content of the opera, the conversion enacted by the second component is the prerequisite for the ritual's success.

The dramatic function of the third structural element (the Good Friday Spell) is different in kind: it is not to present an action, but rather to offer a commentary on it. Strictly speaking, the Good Friday music is not part of the drama at all: even without it, the drama would be complete. Rather, like any sermon, the Good Friday Spell offers an interpretation of the ritual action it accompanies. It is in this sense that the section is at once the centre of the opera and a component external to it. Wagner, a practical man of theatre from the beginning, was increasingly aware in his later years that his task does not end with the creation and publication of the dramatic poem and score, increasingly interested in shaping and controlling the initial productions and performances of his dramas and thus establishing performance traditions for each one of these. The Festival Theatre at Bayreuth was only the most visible and permanent institutional embodiment of this awareness and interest. But in *Parsifal*, Wagner went one step further. In addition to assuming control over the way his dramas would be performed as well as the conditions under which they would be seen and heard, with *Parsifal* the composer also attempted to control the way in which the drama would be understood. This, in a nutshell, is the function of the Good Friday Spell. To be sure, the sermon is delivered by Gurnemanz, not by Wagner himself, but the temptation to identify the two in this case is strong simply because the views expressed by Gurnemanz are consistent with the views Wagner was putting forward in his later years.

While hardly incontrovertible, these then are my two interrelated arguments in favour of yielding to the temptation and considering the orchestral voice of the Good Friday music as speaking for the narrator: first, that the section stands outside the drama, that it does not serve to present the story, but rather to interpret it; and second, that there are good, and yet to be presented, reasons to think that the interpretation is Wagner's own. The shifting of the melodic substance from the voices to the orchestra is at most merely a hint that the author's voice may be taking over.

It is significant, by the way, that, when he recalled in his autobiography – that is, many years after the fact – how he wrote the first (now lost) prose sketch of his poem on the Good Friday of 1857, the composer stressed that the thoughts of Good Friday were the inspiration: 'From the idea of Good Friday I quickly sketched out an entire drama.'[6] There are good reasons to think that Wagner's recollection was inexact and that the sketch could not have been written on that particular day, 10 April 1857.[7] But this does not seem terribly important. What is important is that in Wagner's memory the work was conceived 'from the idea of Good Friday'. The communion services are the central components of the represented story, but the Good Friday Spell that interprets these services is indeed the spiritual and musical core of the work. In his autobiographical writings, Wagner was less interested in factual accuracy than in the symbolic significance of the recollected events. A note in Cosima's diary for 22 April 1879 confirms:

'R. today recalled the impression which inspired his "Good Friday Music"; he laughs, saying he had thought to himself, "In fact it is all as far-fetched as my love affairs, for it was not a Good Friday at all – just a pleasant mood in Nature which made me think, 'This is how a Good Friday ought to be.'"[8]

4

But are we really justified in attributing the views expressed by Gurnemanz in his sermon to its poet? Attempts to elucidate Wagner's own understanding of *Parsifal*'s significance usually invoke his so-called Regeneration essays of 1880–1 – 'Religion und Kunst' (1880) supplemented by 'Was nützt diese Erkentniss' (1880), 'Erkenne dich selbst' (1881), and 'Heldenthum und Christenthum' (1881). Since the poem was completed before these texts were written, on 19 April 1877, to be exact, the essays are treated as retrospective attempts at self-interpretation. I do not doubt the relevance of the Regeneration essays to our question, but would like to pursue a different strategy here and concentrate on much earlier documents, documents having to do with the opera's origin. In the remaining part of this chapter, I would like to use these documents as my evidence for the claim that, in his sermon, Gurnemanz does speak for the composer and, consequently, can be taken to articulate by means of concepts what the composer's voice embodied in the orchestra is telling us directly.

The world as it is in itself, *Parsifal* tells us, the world of 'wild' nature, is the domain of senseless and endless longing and torment. To live is to desire, and to desire is to suffer and inflict suffering. This is not only because any attempt to satisfy a desire involves some sort of effort and struggle. It is also because of the endless character of desire: individual longings may find temporary fulfilments, but, as long as life goes on, the movement of desire itself never stops and can never find ultimate appeasement.

Sexual desire lies at the heart of this vision of the world. But the exact role played by sex in this worldview should be neither underestimated nor overestimated. Above all, the role of sex in the outlook projected in the opera should not be simply attributed to the long tradition of Christian condemnation of Eros. Rather, the erotic in *Parsifal* is the powerful emblem of the most fundamental structural feature of the natural condition, the condition in which humans participate, but which is not exclusive to them.

Up to this point, Wagner's vision remains consistent with that of Schopenhauer, and, for that matter, of Darwin. Moreover, it does not go beyond the vision of things embodied already in *Tristan und Isolde*. But

Parsifal also contains an attempt to look beyond *Tristan*, to glimpse a horizon beyond that opera's 'desolate and empty' sea.

The two operatic projects were closely intertwined. In his autobiography, Wagner recalled that in the autumn of 1854, that is, at the time when he was beginning to sketch his *Tristan* poem, he planned to have Parsifal, on his long erratic way back to Amfortas's Grail domain, visit wounded Tristan in Brittany. The reason for the visit was the close similarity Wagner discerned between the figures of Tristan and Amfortas: 'I identified Tristan, wasting away but unable to die of his wound, with the Amfortas of the Grail romance.'[9] The similarity is indeed unmistakable and goes beyond the wounds with which the two heroes are afflicted to what these wounds stand for – the unappeasable erotic longing. The composer continued to entertain the idea of the visit until at least late August 1857.[10] It was probably also by April 1857, and certainly by 1 October 1858, that is, at the time when he was working on *Tristan*, that Wagner began to think of a Parsifal opera.[11] Wagner's early thoughts on a *Parsifal* opera are mostly documented in his letters to Mathilde Wesendonck dating from the time of his work on *Tristan* and immediately afterwards, 1858–60.[12] Even after the idea of a Parsifal visit to Kareol was dropped, the affinity of the two operatic projects, and specifically the affinity between Tristan and Amfortas, continued to haunt the composer. On 30 May 1859, as he worked on the music of the first part of Act III, he wrote from Lucerne to Mathilde Wesendonck in Zürich:

This last act is now a real intermittent fever: – the deepest and most unprecedented suffering and yearning, and, immediately afterwards, the most unprecedented triumph and jubilation ... It is this thought that has most recently turned me against Parzival again. You see, it has again dawned upon me of late that this would again be a fundamentally evil task. Looked at closely, it is *Anfortas* who is the centre of attention and principal subject ... It suddenly became dreadfully clear to me: it is my third-act Tristan inconceivably intensified.[13]

Further down in the same letter we read: 'And you expect me to carry through something like this? And set it to music, into the bargain? – No thank you very much! I leave it to anyone who has a mind for such things; *I* shall do all I can to keep my distance from it!'[14] Composing the music of Tristan's Delirium was an emotionally draining experience. That the composer might have been reluctant to revisit these sorts of emotional states yet again on account of Amfortas is not difficult to understand.

But if Amfortas is an intensified Tristan, Parsifal has no counterpart in the earlier opera. 'Over coffee, when our conversation turns to Eros and Anteros, scorned love, R. says that Anteros is Parsifal', noted Cosima Wagner in her diary entry for 20 September 1881.[15] Richard got the meaning of Anteros, who was the god of love requited, wrong, but no matter – it is easy to follow his line of thought: Parsifal is the anti-Eros, the answer to what afflicts Tristan and Isolde, Amfortas and Kundry, to what afflicts all nature in its wild state. His role is to heal the erotically afflicted, to redeem raw nature.

In a 31 January 1865 letter to King Ludwig II of Bavaria, Wagner explained the programme of a concert to take place next evening:

We want to begin with the tone picture of the most untroubled repose of the most sublime blessedness of love that we imagine as the original source of all pure, transfigured love, the love of the world redeemer: 1. This will be proclaimed by the *orchestral Prelude* to *Lohengrin* – the mystery of the holy Grail. 2. We should then be made to feel the opposed unsatisfied longing of love by the Prelude to *Tristan*: the Liebestod, however, should be followed by the Transfiguration (the final section) leading us through the highest ecstasy finally back to this state of highest purity of love which allows us again to glimpse the Holy Grail.[16]

At this point *Parsifal* is an as yet unrealized project and it is the Prelude to *Lohengrin* that has to represent the significance of the Grail symbol. But the letter illustrates Wagner's understanding of how the love monumentalized in *Tristan* is related to the love celebrated in the Grail temple. The former is a yearning that brings torment and can never be fully appeased; the latter is the transfiguration of the former, the bliss of appeasement itself, the ultimate fulfilment of all desire, that comes from the 'original source of all pure, transfigured love, the love of the world redeemer'. Wagner's Anteros, the answer to Eros, is Agape, the Christian love of neighbour, charity, pity.

This is the one possible answer to the Schopenhauerian–Darwinian world of *Tristan*, the meaningless world of raw natural unending desiring and suffering, the world driven by the self-serving Eros. As an alternative *Parsifal* proposes a vision of nature transfigured and redeemed by charity, the world guided by the other-serving anti-Eros, the world in which natural desires and torments find their ultimate appeasement and meaning in a vision of supernatural bliss that such symbols as the Grail allow one to perceive in the only way that finite beings can perceive the infinite, mediated by signs, as if in a dark mirror. 'Knowing through compassion', that is, feeling pity for another suffering being and understanding this feeling, is one act capable of stopping the meaningless wheel of torments and imbuing dumb nature with sense.

If *Tristan* asks a Schopenhauerian question, the answer provided by *Parsifal*, its Christian components notwithstanding, is no less consistent with the philosopher's ideas. There can be little doubt that the Christianity of *Parsifal* takes on a distinctly Schopenhauerian colouration. More explicitly than Jesus, Schopenhauer was ready to extend the love of neighbour to animals, since he saw no essential break between the human and animal worlds; animals suffer, and hence deserve pity, no less than humans, he thought.[17] Wagner was clearly impressed, as his preoccupation with such issues as vegetarianism (which he was for, at least some of the time) and vivisection (which he was against) in his late years shows.[18] A 27 January 1882 entry in Cosima Wagner's diary suggests just how central a role the notion of compassion played in the composer's understanding of religion and how closely the issue of vivisection was intertwined with this notion in his mind: 'In the evening, after telling us that the antivivisection petition has again been rejected (Reichstag), he says that he recognizes no religion except compassion.'[19] It is this religion of compassion that is preached in the Good Friday Spell, compassion extended not only to unmistakable humans (such as Amfortas), but also to creatures whose fully human status may be somewhat in doubt, creatures that bridge the gap between the human and the animal (wild, erotically supercharged Jewish females, such as Kundry), or even the human and the vegetal (such as the Flowermaidens), and finally to all living beings, even the flowers of the meadow. In the eco-theological vision of *Parsifal*, the divine compassion is channelled through its elected male vessels (such as Parsifal himself) to the rest of living nature, and man becomes not the exploiter, but the loving guardian of the creation.

In fact, long before his late years, at the time of Wagner's initial involvement with the *Parsifal* project which, we have seen, was contemporary with the composition of *Tristan*, the compassion for dumb nature seems to have been even more important to him than the compassion for fellow humans. Self-consciousness gives humans the ability to rise above their sufferings and embrace resignation, he thought; suffering animals lack this ability and hence deserve compassion even more. A fascinating entry of 1 October 1858 in a diary he kept for Mathilde Wesendonck deserves to be quoted at length:

But I am also clear in my own mind why I can even feel greater fellow-suffering for lower natures than for higher ones. A higher nature is what it is precisely because it has been raised by its own suffering to the heights of resignation, or else has within it – and cultivates – the capacity for such a development. Such a nature is extremely close to mine, is indeed similar to it, and with it I attain to fellow-joy. That is why, basically, I feel less fellow-suffering for people than for animals. For I can see that the latter are totally denied the capacity to rise above suffering, and to achieve a state of resignation and deep, divine calm. And so, in the event of their suffering, as happens when they are tormented, all I see – with a sense of my own tormented despair – is their absolute, redemption-less suffering without any higher purpose, their only release being death, which confirms my belief that it would have been better for them never to have entered upon life. And so, if this suffering can have a purpose, it is simply to awaken a sense of fellow-suffering in man, who thereby absorbs the animal's defective existence, and becomes the redeemer of the world by recognizing the error of all existence. (This meaning will one day become clearer to you from the Good Friday morning scene in the third act of Parzival.)[20]

Animal suffering plays a similar role in Wagner's thinking to that played by the suffering of infants and small children in the thinking of Augustine and Dostoevsky: it is the stumbling block in any effort to make sense of existence. The suffering animal, able to die and thus terminate its torment, but not to rise above it, shows existence to be meaningless. The only glimpse of sense appears with human compassion for the suffering animal: it is this act of compassion that allows self-conscious humans to recognize the senselessness of existence and thus to redeem it by world-transcending resignation.

It thus seems that the core ideas of Wagner's last opera were in place even before the completion of *Tristan*. It is clear, again, that these ideas go beyond the horizon of *Tristan*. A slightly later letter to Mathilde Wesendonck, sent from Venice on 2 March 1859, may perhaps suggest that much – that Wagner sees *Parsifal* as an answer, enrichment, and completion of the Schopenhauerian drama he was then composing: 'Then I occupied myself a lot with philosophy and succeeded in that to reach great results, which supplement and emend my friend Schopenhauer ... Parzival occupied me a great deal.'[21] Even before he settled on the Parsifal project, the composer was thinking of *Tristan* as the first part of a diptych of sorts, a statement of the problem to which another opera would provide the answer, planning to complement, or answer, *Tristan's* portrayal of the erotic torment with a redemptive solution, embodied at this point in a drama on a Buddhist subject: 'in addition to the Nibelung dramas, I have in my head a Tristan and Isolde (love as fearful torment) and my latest subject "the Victors" (supreme redemption, Buddhist legend)', he wrote to August Röckel from Zurich on 23 August 1856.[22] Soon thereafter the position of the answer to *Tristan* was taken over by *Parsifal*. And the two dramas remained coupled in Wagner's mind to the end. On 6 October 1882, his wife noted in her diary: 'He observes that *Tannhäuser, Tristan,* and *Parsifal* belong together.'[23] They do belong together, obviously, because all three centre on a hero suffering erotic torments. But the contrast of Eros (the sinful love of Venus) and Anteros (the redeeming love of Elisabeth) that in the 1840s could have been handled in a single drama, was by the next decade developed and distributed between two separate instalments.

It is undoubtedly true that the Christianity of *Parsifal* departs in its ecological emphasis from strict orthodoxy. But it is also the case that Wagner, for all his devotion to Schopenhauer, was well aware of the Christian sources of the ideas he was exploring in this last opera, just as he was aware of where the difference between *Tristan* and *Parsifal* lies. We have already seen that from the start the two works were closely associated with one another in his mind and he frequently liked to confront them. Spurred by his wife, he did so again on 18 December 1881 in Palermo. (This was the time when *Parsifal* was constantly in his thoughts, as he was completing the orchestration of Act III.) On that day his wife made this note in her diary: 'When we are alone, I say to him, "Tristan and Parsifal, one dies because of his will to live, the other lives because of his dying will." R: "You must always have a *mot*," then, after a pause, "Parsifal sees Tristan" (in Amfortas), and, after another pause, "Something has come between them – the blood of Christ."'[24] If *Parsifal* is to be seen as an answer to, or an amplification of, *Tristan*, it is precisely the ideal of compassion, and moreover compassion for all suffering nature, that it adds to the earlier work's ideal of renunciation. Where exactly this ideal comes from, whether from Jesus, or Schopenhauer, or, most likely, Jesus rendered philosophically respectable by Schopenhauer, matters less. What matters is that the ideal, articulated by Gurnemanz in his sermon, can be consistently attributed to Wagner himself. And this, ultimately, is the main justification for imagining that we hear the composer's orchestral voice speaking above the heads of his characters.

Notes

1 *Parsifal*, DVD, directed by Hans Jürgen Syberberg, Act III, at 39:42–40:07. For Syberberg's commentary on this image, see his *Parsifal. Ein Filmessay* (Munich: Wilhelm Heyne Verlag, 1982), 206f., from whence the expression 'wie einen schwebenden Vogel' is taken.

2 See, in particular, Carl Dahlhaus, 'Entfremdung und Erinnerung. Zu Wagners *Götterdämmerung*' in Christoph-Hellmut Mahling and Sigrid Wiesmann (eds.), *Kongreßbericht Bayreuth 1981* (Kassel: Bärenreiter, 1984), 416–20; rpt in Carl Dahlhaus, *Gesammelte Schriften*, ed. Hermann Danuser (Laaber-Verlag, 2004), vol. VII, 486–92.

3 See St Augustine, *Confessions*, Book XI, ch. 28; Arthur Schopenhauer, *Die Welt als Wille und Vorstellung*, paragraph 52; and Edmund Husserl, *Vorlesungen zur Phänomenologie des inneren Zeitbewußtseins*, ed. Martin Heidegger, in *Jahrbuch für Philosophie und phänomenologische Forschung*, 9 (1928), ch. 2.

4 'Jene Stelle, welche er [Wagner] selbst die "Elegie" nannte', Carl Friedrich Glasenapp, *Das Leben Richard Wagners* (Leipzig: Breitkopf & Härtel, 1911), vol. VI, 183.

5 Cosima Wagner, *Diaries*, ed. Martin Gregor-Dellin and Dietrich Mack, trans. Geoffrey Skelton, 2 vols. (New York and London: Harcourt Brace Jovanovich, 1978), vol. I, 977.

6 Richard Wagner, *My Life*, ed. Mary Whittall, trans. Andrew Grey (Cambridge University Press, 1983), 547. 'Von dem Karfreitag-Gedanken aus konzipierte ich schnell ein ganzes Drama.' *Mein Leben*, ed. Martin Gregor-Dellin (Munich: List, 1963), 636.

7 Martin Geck and Egon Voss (eds.), *Dokumente zur Entstehung und ersten Aufführung des Bühnenweihfestspiels Parsifal*, in Richard Wagner, *Sämtliche Werke* (Mainz: B. Schott's Söhne, 1970), vol. XXX, 13.

8 Cosima Wagner, *Diaries*, vol. II, 295.

9 Richard Wagner, *My Life*, 511. 'Dieser an der emfangenen Wunde siechende und nicht sterben könnende *Tristan* identifizierte sich in mir nämlich mit dem *Amfortas* im Gral-Roman' (*Mein Leben*, 523f.).

10 Gabriele E. Meyer and Egon Voss (eds.), *Dokumente und Texte zu 'Tristan und Isolde'*, in Wagner, *Sämtliche Werke*, vol. XXVII, 28.

11 Geck and Voss (eds.), *Dokumente zur Entstehung und ersten Aufführung des Bühnenweihfestspiels Parsifal*, nos. 6, 7, and 9, pp. 12–14.

12 *Ibid.*, nos. 9–13, pp. 13–17.

13 Richard Wagner, *Selected Letters*, trans. Stewart Spencer and Barry Millington (New York: W.W. Norton, 1987), 456f. 'Dieser letzte Act ist nun ein wahres Wechselfieber: – tieftest, unerhörtestes Leiden und Schmachten, und dann unmittelbar unerhörtester Jubel und Jauchzen … Das hat mich auch allerneuestens wieder gegen den Parzival gestimmt. Es ging mir kürzlich nämlich wieder auf, dass diess wieder eine grundböse Arbeit werden müsse. Genau betrachtet ist *Anfortas* der Mittelpunkt und Hauptgegenstand … Mir wurde das plötzlich schrecklich klar: es ist mein Tristan des dritten Aktes mir einer undenklichen Steigerung.' Meyer and Voss (eds.), *Dokumente und Texte zu 'Tristan und Isolde'*, 73.

14 Wagner, *Selected Letters*, 458. 'Und so etwas soll ich noch ausführen? und gar noch Musik dazu machen? – Bedanke mich schönstens! Das kann machen wer Lust hat; ich werde mir's bestens vom Halse halten!' Geck and Voss (eds.), *Dokumente zur Entstehung und ersten Aufführung des Bühnenweihfestspiels Parsifal*, 15.

15 Cosima Wagner, *Diaries*, vol. II, 720.

16 Translation mine. 'Wir wollen beginnen mit dem Tonbilde der ungetrübtesten Ruhe erhabenster Liebes-Seligkeit, wie sie uns vorschwebt als Urquell aller

reinen, verklärten Liebe – der Liebe des Welterlösers: 1. diess soll uns das *Orchestervorpiel* zu *Lohengrin* verkünden – das Mysterium des *heiligen Grals*. Der Gegensatz der unbefriedigten Liebessehnsucht soll uns dann 2. durch das Vorspiel zu *Tristan* zu Gefühl kommen: dem Liebestod soll aber die *Verklärung* (der Schlussatz) folgen, und diese uns durch höchste Entzückung zuletzt in jenen Zustand höchster Liebes-Reinheit zurückführen, welcher uns wieder den heiligen Gral erblicken lässt. –' Meyer and Voss (eds.), *Dokumente und Texte zu 'Tristan und Isolde'*, 154.

17 See, for example, Arthur Schopenhauer, *The World as Will and Representation*, trans. E.F.J. Payne (New York: Dover, 1969), vol. I, paragraph 66, 372f.

18 See, in particular, Richard Wagner, 'Offenes Schreiben an Herrn Ernst von Weber, Verfasser der Schrift: *Die Folterkammern der Wissenschaft*' [1879], *Sämtliche Schriften und Dichtungen*, 5th edn (Leipzig: Breitkopf & Härtel, 1911–14), vol. X, 194–210.

19 Cosima Wagner, *Diaries*, vol. II, 797.

20 Wagner, *Selected Letters*, 423f. 'Ich bin mir aber auch darüber klar geworden, warum ich mit niedreren Naturen sogar mehr Mitleiden haben kann, als mit höheren. Die höhere Natur ist, was sie ist, eben dadurch, daß sie durch das eigene Leiden zur Höhe der Resignation erhoben wird, oder zu dieser Erhebung die Anlagen in sich hat, und sie pflegt. Sie steht mir unmittelbar nah, ist mir gleich, und mit ihr gelange ich zur Mitfreude. Deshalb habe ich, im Grunde genommen, mit Menschen weniger Mitleiden, als mit Tieren. Diesen sehe ich die Anlage zur Erhebung über das Leiden, zur Resignation und ihrer tiefen, göttlichen Beruhigung, gänzlich versagt. Kommen sie daher, wie dies durch Gequältwerden geschieht, in den Fall des Leidens, so sehe ich mit eigener, qualvoller Verzweiflung eben nur das absolute, Erlösungs-lose Leiden, ohne jeden höheren Zweck, mit der einzigen Befreiung durch den Tod, somit durch die Bekräftigung dessen, es sei besser gewesen, wenn es gar nicht erst zum Dasein gelangt wäre. Wenn daher dieses Leiden einen Zweck haben kann, so ist dies einzig durch Erweckung des Mitleidens im Menschen, der dadurch das verfehlte Dasein des Tieres in sich aufnimmt, und zum Erlöser der Welt wird, indem er überhaupt den Irrtum alles Daseins erkennt. (Diese Bedeutung wird dir einmal aus dem dritten Akte des Parzival, am Karfreitagsmorgen, klar werden.)' *Richard Wagner an Mathilde Wesendonck. Tagebuchblätter und Briefe 1853–1871*, 42nd edn (Leipzig: Breitkopf & Härtel, 1913), 52–3.

21 'Dann trieb ich viel Philosophie, und bin darin auf große, meinen Freund Schopenhauer ergänzende und berichtigende Resultate gelangt ... Der Parzival hat mich viel beschäftigt.' *Wesendonck-Briefe*, 110.

22 Wagner, *Selected Letters*, 359.

23 Cosima Wagner, *Diaries*, vol. II, 923.

24 *Ibid.*, 773.

11 | Memory and the leitmotif in cinema

GIORGIO BIANCOROSSO

Wagner's disciple and advocate Hans von Wolzogen is still being singled out not only for inventing the term 'leitmotif' (which he did not) but also for spreading a view of leitmotifs as mere 'tags', fixed in both meaning and shape, a view that was to become prevalent in commentaries on film music as well.[1] Yet one could argue that just as damaging as the influence of Wolzogen's ready-made labels was the tendency, possibly also initiated by his thematic guides, to hear leitmotifs as carrying their associations on their sleeve, as it were, from their very first presentation. To dispel this retrospective illusion, and bring out the full extent of the work of memory in the apprehension of leitmotifs in the cinema, in this chapter I wish to examine a key moment in the celebrated 'neo-noir' *Chinatown* (1974).

Jerry Goldsmith's music for the film has been hailed as one of the high points of Hollywood film scoring.[2] But exquisite as the title theme undoubtedly is, the success of the score is due to the timing of its cues, and the intuitive understanding of the functioning of memory it entails. This is best demonstrated at the conclusion of Gittes's (Jack Nicholson) visit to the Mar Vista Rest Home, some eighty-three minutes into the film (Figures 11.1 and 11.2). As the surreal comedy of the retirement home gives way to a brutal altercation with one of Gittes's former colleagues by the entrance, the jarring intrusion of a percussive piano cue signals yet another change in register, intimating that the worst is indeed about to happen. Sure enough, two armed thugs are seen approaching the inn's entrance from outside. Just then, however, Evelyn (Faye Dunaway) enters stage with a spectacular, and superbly timed, car manoeuvre, in the process saving Gittes's life. Riding on, and contemplating his good luck, Gittes turns towards her – at which point we know he is besotted with his as yet unsuspecting rescuer. It is the music, a clever reprise of the opening phrase of the lyrical title theme, that tells us so (Example 11.1).[3] How does it do that and why is memory at all involved in it? Part of the answer is that at this juncture Goldsmith's languid melody, last heard in the credits, gains the status of a so-called leitmotif: not the 'visiting card' decried by Debussy – and later, Adorno and Eisler with respect to film – but a short, memorable, self-standing motto or expressive gesture with a clear, and

204   GIORGIO BIANCOROSSO

Figure 11.1 Evelyn Mulwray rescues J.J. 'Jake' Gittes, *Chinatown* (dir. by Roman Polanski, 1974)

Figure 11.2 Evelyn Mulwray rescues J.J. 'Jake' Gittes, *Chinatown* (dir. by Roman Polanski, 1974)

Example 11.1   The first reprise of the trumpet theme.

deeply affecting, informative function, and liable to subsequent transformations. But this raises the question: how do leitmotifs function in cinema?

In a short but important article published just over a decade ago, Justin London shed new light on the use of leitmotifs in two studio films of the classical era – *Mildred Pierce* (1945) and *All About Eve* (1950) – by reference to proper names.[4] More specifically, London pointed to the theory of proper names attributed to American philosopher Saul Kripke, and sometimes known as the causal theory of reference.[5] According to this theory, (proper) names are 'rigid designators': rigid, in that they apply to one and one person only irrespective of the contingencies of the name bearer's life (or, in the language of modal semantics, 'in every possible world'); and designators, in that their primary goal is not so much to describe, let alone connote, as simply to 'pick out' a person, thereby identifying him or her to a third party or an assembly of listeners or readers. A person's 'baptism', as the process by which a person acquires a name is sometimes described, is typically an instance of ostension. A parent or publicly appointed officiator points towards a newborn, in the presence of others; then, he or she proclaims this person to be named 'such-and-such'. Such an act inaugurates the reference. For the reference to be cemented, however, a chain of speakers must also refer to the same person by the same name, 'causing', as it were, the reference to be fixed.[6] The reference of a name, then, is for Kripke a socially bounded phenomenon. This is not to say that Kripke is interested in the social life of names; if he were, he would acknowledge that people behave as if names were descriptors as well as designators, just as he would concede the culturally determined constraints on names – that is, male versus female – all of which point to a descriptive import, or at least residual (not to say a connotation). Rather, what Kripke is interested in is the socially channelled manner in which the reference is fixed, and the causal process – via the chain of speakers – that underpins the consensus about the name's reference and seals its 'rigidity'.[7]

My aim in this chapter is not to follow through Kripke's argument in detail, let alone trace its reverberations in such fields as metaphysics and epistemology. My focus is the role of memory in sealing the association between a leitmotif and a character or, as in the case of *Chinatown*, an event. I will first discuss the process in the terms suggested by London's analogy between leitmotifs and proper names. I will then broaden the field of possible applications of the analogy, and the model of musical meaning it implies. As might perhaps be anticipated, the analogy will eventually break down. Yet this is not to say that it is without value. Indeed, if

I use the analogy as a foil to my own discussion, this is not to expose the limitations of London's proposal but rather to stress just how complex the issues he has tackled actually are, and how little explored they remain.

Introducing a film's 'topics'

London bases his analogy on the following grounds. Like a proper name, a leitmotif is attached to a person or, more accurately, fictional character, which it comes to refer to.[8] Like names, moreover, leitmotifs exhibit morphological constraints and distinctiveness, both of which attributes are necessary for the sake of easy recall and subsequent manipulation. Film composers, in devising them, avoid conventional or stock musical gestures in something like the way writers avoid identifying their characters by common nouns ('a boy') or proper names whose sheer commonality renders them forgettable and whose evocative purchase has been wholly exhausted.[9] Following Kripke, London also stresses the semantic emptiness, as against their capacity to refer, of names and leitmotifs alike. "'Richard Nixon" still refers to the same person even if we imagine a possible world in which he was not elected President. Thus, ... proper names ... are not yoked to any specific property or set of properties their referents may have; in this sense [they] are said to be semantically empty or meaningless.'[10] This may seem more controversial. People, as hinted above, do use names as if they possessed a semantic dimension. One thinks of the propitiatory use of names in many cultures (which is predicated precisely on their semantic meaning). But, and this is one of the key points of Kripke's theory, the *raison d'être* of proper names hinges on their ability to pick out their bearers and, what is just as important, the semantic meaning such names might accrue subsequent to the bearer's baptism is not needed for them to refer. A name successfully refers to someone not because it describes the person in question but rather because of the social consensus that has emerged, through the causal chain of users, around its 'target' (i.e., its intended referent).

'The fact that proper names are semantically empty', continues London, 'has important implications for reference in musical contexts. If there are linguistic structures that are semantically empty but nonetheless able to refer, then semantic content is not a general requirement of reference. Thus, even though music lacks a semantic component, this lack does not rule out the possibility of musical reference.'[11] Talk of semantic emptiness, however, may unduly suggest that it is a *property* of names (and hence, to follow through London's argument, leitmotifs).[12] Yet Kripke, at least indirectly, rejected this when he questioned whether names referring to the same person, such as 'Cicero' and 'Tully', are universally substitutable and thus equivalent for all semantic purposes.[13] In fact, 'Cicero' and 'Tully' not only imply different communicational contexts but also carry different connotations which nuance our picture of the referent; they are equivalent, and may be said to behave as if semantically empty, then, only as far as their ability to point to the same person is concerned.

Pure indexicals are virtually impossible, 'this' and 'that' being the proverbial exceptions that confirm the rule. London acknowledges this when he goes on to extol – and describe – music's expressive force. But what about semantics? When he adduces that if 'rigid designation is good enough for names then it's good enough for music', the assumption seems to be that if a verbal sign can function non-semantically, then music, in something like its 'default state', does too (indeed, given its non-verbal status and lack of propositional content, only more so).[14] But this turns on a matter of definition. For the idea that music lacks a semantic dimension depends on another bias, which reinforces it, namely that when we make theoretical claims about music we ought to treat it as a self-sufficient art form – rather like poetry, say, or sculpture – best exemplified by instrumental genres, and in isolation from other media; otherwise, insistence on semantic emptiness would be difficult to maintain. Which brings me to the second horn of the contention, namely whether music, even when construed so narrowly, lacks a semantic dimension in the first place. This is naturally a formidable subject, one that I cannot hope to treat comprehensively in the context of this chapter. What I wish to do instead is to draw attention to an aspect of musical semantics via a brief detour into the theory of musical topics. The theory, as is well known, grows out of the intuition that, in the eighteenth century, composers made deliberate use of melodic and rhythmic material drawn from music such as one might have come across in everyday life: hunting calls, various types of dance music, music employed in rituals, and so forth. When recognized, these *topoi* would call up a constellation of images and concepts associated with the milieu referred to by them and create a common ground, a shared 'existential space', between composer, performers, and the audience (all of whom are assumed to enjoy at least some degree of familiarity with them).

Strictly speaking, and short of elaborate variants or parodies thereof, topics are signs referred to by way of a two-tiered process of indexical signification. According to Raymond Monelle:

> Many topics are in the first place not iconic, but indexical; the dance measures listed by Ratner and Allanbrook, the 'fanfare' motive, the topics of 'French overture' and 'Turkish Music' do not signify by virtue of resemblance, but because they reproduce styles and repertories from elsewhere. Insofar as the slow movement of the 'Jupiter' Symphony is in sarabande meter, it presents the dance measure itself rather than an imitation of it, and thus signifies indexically ... But this is not the level of indexicality which marks a topic ... Mozart's signification in the 'Jupiter' is *seriousness* and *decorum*, not merely 'sarabande'.[15]

This is persuasive as far as it goes, but it stops short of highlighting what is most distinctive about listening to the kind of repertory Monelle has singled out for scrutiny. If *topoi* were employed singly to perform tasks such as announcing a call to arms, inviting people to dance in a court setting, or inciting people to prayer, then they would be returned to their original context and primary function. As juxtaposed elements of a symphony movement, they shed this primary mode of existence. Contemplated as aesthetic objects, at one remove from the necessities of communication in daily life, topics follow one another in a free play of 'target-less' references that do not link up in a meaningful chain of musical utterances except as a reinforcement to a reading of music as syntactically ordered structure, rhetorical discourse or, as tantalizingly suggested by Harold S. Powers, a string of poetic images.[16]

Be that as it may, underpinning the referential power of a musical topic is the ability to, in Michael Long's words, 'trigger a recognition response that tends to proceed from the listener's experience (memory) on one hand, or from an intuition that beyond what has been heard, its phenomenal portion, lies a greater whole'.[17] The beginning credits of a film exploit this aspect of music to create suspense. Like an opera overture, the title theme often lays out the most important motives of a score. Their combination, it is said, 'sets the mood' for a film. A congeries of innuendos, as yet unanchored to specific dramatic situations, a title theme often comes across as a collection of 'musical gestures in search of a character'. It is for this reason that beginning credits function as a tease, riddle, or even enigma.[18] In *Chinatown*, Goldsmith's music goes so far as to thematize its own status as a riddle by way of a learned musical reference: the particular way in which the solo horn floats above the other instruments, both in the credits and throughout the first half of the film – particularly the 'Orange Groves' sequence – calls to mind Ives's *Unanswered Question* (famously scored for solo trumpet, flutes, and string orchestra).

But title themes are also a balancing act; their distinctive features are not entirely opaque in that they exhibit recognizable 'hooks' that are key to our growing acquaintance with the film. For instance, the opening gambit of Goldsmith's score – a diatonic cluster followed by a distant 'howl' – suggests the exotic and inscrutable, and thus the mystery film. The brooding solo trumpet that quickly segues from the first two written credits, for its part, functions as an elaborate reference to doomed romance as well as the film noir.[19] In concert with the deliberately retro design of the written credits and the carefully highlighted appearance of the credit to 'John Huston', who plays a major role in the film, the music also hints at the fact that *Chinatown* will pose as a film from an earlier era of studio filmmaking.[20]

Though far from unambiguous propositions spelling out in detail specific states of affairs, these are nevertheless densely informative musical statements. The topics 'femme fatale', 'romance', 'film noir', and 'mystery film', as the musical references heard in Goldsmith's title theme may be re-christened, are subsumed under a general appraisal of the features of the film one is about to sit through (these may include, but are not limited to, a film's style, narrative scope, place in a tradition or series of similarly themed films, degree of dependence on previous works, and so forth). They help us grasp defining aspects of the ensuing narrative by reproducing musical tropes, and adopting the tone and register found in representative instances of the relevant genres, according to the two-tier indexical process of signification outlined by Monelle with respect to topics (and whose phenomenology Long has so succinctly captured). To be sure, the remarkable effectiveness with which Goldsmith's theme achieves this is not due to some immanent properties; such a capacity is, to use Nicholas Cook's term, *emergent*, the result of the productive encounter of different media as interpreted by the viewer-auditor cued up to the role traditionally performed by title sequences.[21] But this does not answer the question whether music carries semantic meanings in the negative; rather, it makes that very question moot, exposing the limits of an approach that takes 'music alone' as the paradigm.

The beginning as a 'set-up'

Music performs not one but many tasks simultaneously when employed as a title theme.[22] Among these is 'setting up' the spectator so that he or she will recognize key thematic material at important junctures later in the film (should it return). Leitmotifs often do make their appearance in the credits, fulfilling many of the functions I have just referred to albeit without revealing – not yet, that is – their full identity. Noting the over-determined character of main title cues, London quotes Gorbman on *All About Eve*: 'Does this melody, first heard over the credits, and subsequently at most emotional moments when Eve (Anne Baxter) appears, signify Eve herself, or Eve's emotional impact on her "audiences" (the characters and film viewers she manipulates), or is it simply a signature for the film *All About Eve*?'[23] London's interest in proper names stems precisely from the desire to, as he himself puts it, 'sort out Gorbman's questions'. In this he succeeds admirably. The analogy to proper names allows him to parse out continuity cues and thematic material, whose main role is the expression of connotations, from identifying – that is, referential – leitmotifs 'proper'. What London omits to note, however, is the significance of position. During the credits, leitmotifs, though morphologically distinct, play a role similar to continuity material for the simple reason that we merely hear them for the first time and, as such, only in their 'topicality' (or register). Leitmotifs, like names, must be learned.

In keeping with the broad consensus that in classical Hollywood cinema motifs are of the identifying kind, the reference is taken by London to consist mostly of a character. But, as we will see, the range of references a musical motif is capable of is actually broader, encompassing abstract concepts, personality traits, and even processes: the province, in other words, of nominal phrases as much as names.[24] Kripke, for his part, directed his analysis at the conditions of reference: put bluntly, the analysis of naming, as distinct from names. Now if Kripke is right, it is the reference-fixing naming ceremony, and not some kind of descriptive import a name possesses prior to it, that ensures that it dispatches the desired reference. If London is correct in suggesting an analogy between names and leitmotifs, in turn, the same applies to the latter (notwithstanding other functions they may be asked to perform through their broadly recognizable stylistic traits). And yet it is precisely the nature of a leitmotif's 'baptism' that remains most in need of analysis. When does a theme or motive actually begin to refer, and if so, how?

Reviewing the literature on leitmotifs in Wagner, for instance, one is struck by how much attention is lavished on their meaning, transformations, fluctuations, and role as structural devices. Carl Dahlhaus does go as far as admitting that 'one must start with a basic idea and gradually differentiate it; the infinite wealth of instinctive understanding at which Wagner aimed does not come into existence at the first impact of immediacy, but – if at all – at the second stage, when immediacy has combined with reflection'.[25] Yet hardly a word is spent on the all-too-overlooked yet crucially important instant in which a motif is, for the first time in the course of a work, heard as pointing to that 'basic idea'. Presumably, the question has been thought either too banal or, worse, not worth raising. That the simultaneous presentation of a motif and its stage, or verbal, counterpart results in the welding of an association between them must have seemed intuitive enough not to merit further discussion. But that is far from being the case. So, for instance, discussing the prelude to Act III of *Tannhäuser*, Dahlhaus interprets the anticipations of motifs from the narration as having 'more to do with overture traditions than with leitmotivic technique', thereby failing to take note of the significance of our remembering the motifs once they are sounded out – *again*, for us – in the narrative scene itself.[26] When, at the end of *Rheingold*, we hear the 'Sword' motif for the first time, on stage Wotan is greeting Valhalla and expressing the idea of begetting a progeny of 'demigods'. Commenting on the fact that Wagner 'thought of having Wotan pick up a sword left behind from the hoard', Dahlhaus adds wryly that 'inept though the idea may have been, it illustrates his obsessional desire to have everything fully justified and explained to the point of obviousness'.[27] But a simpler reason for Wagner's (aborted) idea is that he must have understood that, under such circumstances, the motive cannot be heard as pointing to a sword at all. As far as *Rheingold* is concerned, the 'Sword' motive has nothing of the sword about it after all: it is a 'presentiment'.[28]

Film music and the 'aesthetics of the hindsight'

My brief summary of a prominent musicologist's approach to the interpretation of leitmotivic technique in Wagner suggests that, to echo a distinction made in the philosophy of language, scholars have shown more interest in a meaning theory, a theory of what leitmotifs refer to, than in a 'foundational' theory of musical meaning, that is, a study of the conditions through which their meaning is acquired. To begin to sketch the latter, as is my interest here, we must look at a leitmotif's 'baptism'. Let us then return to the moment when many a leitmotif is first heard: the beginning credits. Does a title theme, or distinctive motif cast therein, possess a work-specific association? It is doubtful that it does so. A reference may well be planted there by the composer, but the spectator cannot as yet appreciate its import. In the title sequence of *All About Eve*, for instance, 'Eve's' lyrical theme enjoys an emphatic orchestral presentation. But this is true of all three major themes of the tripartite overture. It is only when mixed to the voice-over introduction, over an image of an award statuette bearing her name, that the theme may be said to refer to Eve. This is made possible, in keeping with London's morphological criterion, by the fact that the theme's status as a discrete entity is here clarified; but it is also due to the simultaneous visual presentation onscreen of her name, the numerous references made to her by DeWitt's (George Sanders) voice-over introduction, and, just as crucially, our own memory. It is upon hearing it, again, that the theme is liable to become Eve's.

Together, the shot of the statuette and the music form something like an initial, stereotypical sketch of the award-winning, eager-yet-modest aspiring young actress. As captured by the stylized sculptural form – the award statuette, like an Oscar, looks the same no matter who wins it – the nascent image of Eve is injected with a veneer of sophistication and restraint via the expressive power of the music.[29] The music does more than identifying; transfigured into an element of a physiognomy, it is subsumed under the putative portrait-in-progress of the protagonist. I say 'putative' because the film forces us time and again to revise the associations we forge between motifs, be they visual, verbal, or musical, and their referent (Eve – or so it seems). *All About Eve* sets us up not only in the sense of training us to appreciate the significance of a motif by planting it at strategically chosen points in the narrative, but it also *deceives* us as to what Eve's personality is like and, in a stunning final twist, as to what the subject of the film really is. Like *Citizen Kane*, though tempered by a good measure of irony, the film disavows the final destination of its narrative till the very last sequence. There, Eve is (again) offscreen, displaced by her double, that is, another young, aspiring actress by the name of Phoebe (though, come to think of it, she may as well be dubbed 'Eve' which, by the end of the film, becomes a proverbial moniker: the opposite of a uniquely identifying tag). Phoebe is trying on Eve's robe, the very symbol of the transferability of the possessions and features that, till a sequence before, had characterized the person we thought was the subject of the film (Eve or, more accurately, 'Eve'). By a splendid irony, in other words, *All About Eve* turns out to be not about Eve at all as much as what Eve is the vehicle for: the irrepressible desire for fame, the pursuit of which consumes a person till she becomes the mere expression of her own empty ambition. Triumphant, the tripartite musical overture is played again in its entirety. Ringing at long last in all its glorious falsity, as Phoebe sees herself reflected in a dazzling display of images of what she aspires to be, the true character of the music is finally unveiled. A medley of musical topics, it is not the unmediated expression of the defining traits of a genuine personality; rather, it presents in musical form three different faces of a contrived persona fashioned after the clichés of the world of show business. Eve's alleged theme, however detachable it may seem on purely morphological grounds, is an integral component of this three-pronged musical portrait. How appropriate, therefore, that just as the film comes to an end it retreats into its ranks, so to speak, thereby losing its all-too-easily gained status as a discrete, self-standing, *and* identifying 'leitmotif'.

Learning to fear the shark

One of the tasks of criticism is to avert the dangers of a facile 'aesthetics of the hindsight': to try to restore a sense of just how little we know as a film unfolds, 'unlearn' one's foreknowledge, as it were, and fight the complacency that often results from the critical consensus surrounding a canonical work. With respect to leitmotifs, whether in cinema or opera, one way of doing this is to remind ourselves that if an analogy were made, this ought to be not to names but more specifically to naming, that is, the actual situation in which speakers fix a name's reference or learn about it for the first time. We need to move, in other words, from morphology to pragmatics. Now, as London acknowledges, naming typically occurs through an act of ostension.[30] Ostension, however, displays characteristics that make the analogy to leitmotifs increasingly difficult to entertain. Elsewhere I have shown how the notorious shark motif in *Jaws*, for example, acquires its remarkably specific reference – that the shark is mounting an attack – only after as many as three different presentations over the course of six minutes of screen time.[31] The beginning of the film both displays and effaces the meaning of the motif. The minor second is emphasized just so the spectator may recall it at a critical juncture (the first attack); yet its significance is simultaneously also effaced, largely through the use of additional thematic material and complex textures. The strategic blend of repetition and concealment means that the recognition of what the motif entails is experienced as hard-earned knowledge by the spectator. This, moreover, is accompanied by the admixture of anxiety and titillation typical of suspense.[32] Add to this already potent mix our instinctive skill for threat appraisal and you come close to a picture of how the reference is sealed. But the process is very different from a classical case of ostension. The motif is not paired with a corresponding image in a demonstrative, and unambiguous, fashion; rather, it takes the guise of a sonic presence which the spectator, upon recognizing its increasingly ominous recurrences, eventually concedes he must contend with.

In the context of a naming ceremony, ostension is underpinned by the sanctioned wish or need to inform a community of listeners what a certain name refers to. The communicative intent behind the performance of such an act is explicit. For an analogy in the musical realm, think of Prokofiev's *Peter and the Wolf* or Haydn's *The Creation*: there, a specific referent is explicitly assigned to a motif, theme, or episode (and further specified by the use of particular instruments or combinations thereof). These are – justly famous – exceptions, however. Even in symphonic poems the link between musical motifs and poetic or pictorial images is seldom sealed with such exactness. In *Jaws*, the 'naming' ceremony of Williams's motif is disavowed altogether: the opposite of the didactic intent that underpins ostension. Disavowing the link between the musical motif and its referent encourages us, as per the aesthetic dicta of Hollywood cinema, to harbour the illusion that what we see onscreen is a transparent record of a self-generating world. The music is merely *synchronized* to what we only gradually learn to be a corresponding event: the shark charging against a prey, the animal being, significantly, offscreen, its presence intimated via a camera movement (as well as the music itself). The exact nature of the relationship between what we see and what we simultaneously hear discloses itself gradually, as it requires one or more repetitions: to wit, a *pattern*. To be sure, through analysis the didactic intent of the deployment of Williams's notorious motif becomes clear. But to a viewer sitting through the film for the first time, grasping the role of the motif is more akin to learning a new name while attending a play one does not know and in which no naming ceremony is consummated, or eavesdropping on a conversation in which the meaning of a technical word is taken for granted (i.e., in which no definition of it is ever offered). In the absence of a definition or naming ceremony, the unique – and uniquely identifying – meaning of a term we do not know becomes clear, if at all, only as one 'goes along'.[33] Similarly with leitmotifs in cinema: it follows that while at the level of morphology names do provide a useful counterpart, the pragmatics of naming and that of the deployment of leitmotifs seem too far apart for the analogy to hold.

From reference to embodiment

It is now time to return to the extraordinary case of 'delayed' association with which I began this chapter. Like *Jaws*, *Chinatown* is a successful reinvention of a past genre (while *Jaws* revives the monster film,

Chinatown revisits the noir). It too, moreover, features music that is at once an homage and an imaginative reinvention of classical scoring practices. Its score is neatly divided into two. An interlinked series of cues written for piano, trumpet, harps, strings, and percussion, of clear modernist derivation, mark different stations in the 'water mystery' plot that dominates the first half of the film. Using the same ensemble, Goldsmith also conjures an alternate score through the sole – yet crucial – addition of a melodic solo theme for the trumpet, which plays heavily on the audience's memories of the jazz-inflected scores written in the 1950s for a number of seminal film noirs. The two scores are really two sides of the same coin, however. Not only are they made of the same musical cloth but the parallel narrative threads they underpin – the 'water' plot and the 'doomed romance' plot – are in the last instance bound up with one another in a most disturbing knot. This is hinted at musically at the very beginning. Over the image of the logo and the first two written credits, a glissando on the modal scale a–a^1, obtained by directly striking the strings of the piano and resulting in a diatonic cluster, sets the tone for the only seemingly – and in retrospect, misleadingly – 'Chinese' reference in the entire score: an embryonic, nearly unrecognizable version, as if anamorphically distorted, of the opening minor third of the main theme played by what sound like the violins and a piccolo at a high register (g^3–b flat^3). This segues into a complete, 'straight' statement, led by the trumpet, of the main theme, transposed a fifth below. Here the ensemble 'flips' into a jazz duo, complete with a string envelope and the addition of dreamy harps. In a nutshell, this opening gambit would seem to give away the two faces of the score and, by an ingeniously economic musical synecdoche, the film as a whole. But, catching the spectator unaware, such a deliberate juxtaposition is likely to be overlooked. Naturally, this is for the better, for parading the intimate relationship between the two aspects of the score would unduly give away the much later – and devastating – revelation that the two parallel plots, though underpinned by two such seemingly distant musical styles, are in fact intertwined. That moment is the pivot of the film's tragic dénouement and must be concealed for as long as possible for the narrative to retain momentum.

While the credits plant a link that goes overlooked, *Chinatown*, unlike *Jaws*, does nothing to efface the main theme itself; to the contrary, it glorifies it. Even so, the moment it appears again, as Evelyn rescues Gittes, it strikes the spectator with the force of an epiphany. Held back for an astonishing eighty-three minutes, it is reduced here to its skeleton: all we hear is a subdued version of the theme's antecedent on the trumpet, in d, stripped of the sinuous figurations with which the piano was circling all around it during the credits. The theme itself is played without grace notes or ritardandos and is served up, in keeping with the dynamically charged image of two lovers on the run, on a bed of string tremolos. The ingenious arrangement notwithstanding, what renders this moment one of the high points of film scoring in all of Hollywood is its timing. Coming a full hour and twenty-three minutes after its first – and till then, sole – presentation, the reappearance of Goldsmith's famous theme is a gamble of sorts; though we have by this point forgotten to have heard it, our capacity to recall it is still – barely – intact.[34] As a result, our realization that Gittes is hooked by his mysterious and fragile client is shot through with surprise and exhilaration. The near-identical second phrase follows suit after a cut to the swimming pool of Evelyn's villa. Taken up by Orphic harps, it conveniently sets the ground for a conversation between the two soon-to-be lovers. This has the effect of 'severing' the theme into two, stressing the status of the opening phrase as a short, self-standing musical entity, liable to manipulation (that is, a leitmotif).[35]

Few will deny that repetition and a new context are somehow implicated in investing the opening phrase of the trumpet theme with a new, and much more specific, function. The question is, how? Imagine, for argument's sake, that instead of using a variant of the title theme Polanski had insisted on a different cue; let this cue be in roughly the same style, over a similarly scored tremolo. Given the context, and the actor's body language, the gist of the scene would come across just as clearly: Gittes is falling for Evelyn. If so, what is gained by deploying a variant of the theme previously heard over the credits instead? One way to answer this question is to posit the intention of a maker, or at least an 'intelligent design', as a fundamental property of a film. This is not to reaffirm a director-as-*deus-ex-machina* view of cinema but rather to acknowledge that our grasp of the action is contingent on the belief that the sounds and images presented to us have been consciously laid out by a controlling intelligence whose strategic use of recurring musical motifs begs for interpretation. Given this, to recall a motif is not merely to recognize specific features of the music as being the same, or a variant thereof; it is also to grasp the *sense* of a recurrence by establishing a correspondence between various instances of the same music and, ultimately, reckoning the presence of a communicative intention. In such a context, memory is much more than a retrieval mechanism, for it is bound up with the very coming into being of the association between the theme and the event it points to. A leitmotif is not a floating capsule whose associative content simply awaits downloading, like a shipped good upon arriving at a dock; recognizing it as being a recurring element, deliberately dispatched to us, is a constitutive stage in the activation of that very content (without such recognition the ship will moor at another port). It is a musicological truism that the basis of leitmotifs lies in the ability of music to make us recall the circumstances in which it was first heard.[36] I would put it quite differently: upon hearing a motif or theme a second time, and recognizing it, it is the concurrent circumstances, specific to the drama's 'here and now', that attach themselves to the music for future retrieval.[37]

To be sure, the proper understanding of a generic, non-recurring piece of 'mood' music is also contingent on our memory of certain features; it, too, is the result of a strategy that a spectator can intuitively attribute to an agency responsible for the presentation of a film. Yet such music, no matter how distinctive, will not elicit the process of recall and review of a past perception that I see as key to the discharge of meaning of a leitmotif. Upon walking into a movie theatre, we are already cued in on the associations of an excerpt of conventional 'mood' or genre-identifying music. Goldsmith's trumpet theme, were it not repeated after the credits, would be a good example of this. The specific associations it acquires later, however, must be learned anew in the course of the film. When that happens, the motif, as a conventional sign, 'topic', or vehicle of familiar registers, morphs into a much more individualized utterance, one that demands full apprehension of its unique features. That is why the first appearance of a leitmotif is what I have called a 'set-up'; its purpose is to make sure that the music will at some point be more than just heard in terms of inherited schema but rather recalled in its specific – not generic – features, its evolving and uniquely 'fitted' meanings showing only through repeated presentations.[38]

Of course, the idea that at the beginning of *Chinatown* we are not privy to the 'true' or 'complete' meaning of the title theme is itself a retrospective distortion. For, at that stage in the film, there is no need for the music to function in the specific manner exhibited later; as far as the beginning credits are concerned, its broad connotations of romance and sophistication, as well as its captivating beauty, serve it very well indeed. After all, as Roger Scruton suggested, 'the true leitmotif *earns* its meaning, from the dramatic contexts in which it appears'.[39] And yet that is not how we feel once a new and more specific association is forged, and with good reason, at that: for the interest of leitmotifs also lies in their ability to convince us that they were pregnant with a specific meaning from their very first presentation, thereby creating the sense of the unfolding of the film as a journey during which we initially missed the significance of some of the signposts on our way. Memory, then, is the condition not only for the recall of the identifying features of the theme but also for the revisiting of its first appearance in the light of the newly acquired association. By encouraging a reflexive play on memory, leitmotifs heighten the spectators' appreciation of their own experience – not just those of the characters – as one being projected simultaneously towards the future and the past.[40]

The impression that we are uncovering an aspect of the music that was, as it were, 'there to begin with', is of a piece with the illusion of immanence. It is as if the motif's association had an existence well before our encounter with it: upon recognizing the motif, we are merely acquiring knowledge about its place in the world presented onscreen, a place it had been occupying long before we make our acquaintance with it. That is also why a leitmotif is not replaceable or, put another way, it cannot sound any different than it does. Herein, then, lies another important difference between a leitmotif and a generic, non-recurring cue: while the latter does a fine job at dispatching narratively salient information – say, that one of the two leads is experiencing anger – the former identifies or, better, *embodies* the emergence of that particular kind of anger at that particular point, and as a result of the encounter between just those two characters. Individualization greatly reduces a leitmotif's applicability; indeed, so strong is the association of Goldsmith's theme to the (largely unspoken) romance in *Chinatown* that, quotation aside, it will resist integration into a different work (rather like an organ refusing to function in its new host body following a transplant). In this respect, a leitmotif truly is like a proper name, be it applied to a person ('Jack') or a recurring event ('Christmas Day') in that the reference is to a unique item, not a class (as is the case with common nouns).

Yet describing proper names as 'picking out' their referents, as Kripke does, implies an unbridgeable gap between them: a given name, for one, shares none of the properties of its referent (a person). This is a state of affairs that the dynamic, embodied nature of musical representation resists. While too heterogeneous with respect to their *representata* to be unequivocally called 'mimetic', leitmotifs unfold, and evolve dynamically, over time, as if embodying – as much as referring to – an event, person, or quality, fleshing out, in the form of sound, their presence.[41]

Notes

I would like to thank colleagues of the Graduate Institute of Musicology, Taiwan National University (Taipei), where I was Visiting Professor in spring 2010, for their help and hospitality in the early stages of my research on this topic. Also at an early stage of preparation, John Winzeburg kindly invited me to lecture on this topic at Baptist University (Hong Kong). Su Yin Mak, Stephen Matthews, and Paisley Livingston, finally, offered precious leads and helped me refine my argument. Research for this chapter was partly funded by a grant administered by the University Grants Committee, Hong Kong S.A.R. (Ref. no. HKU 740610H).

1 For a nuanced early history of the term, as well as a partial rehabilitation of Wolzogen himself, see Thomas S. Grey, '... wie ein rother Faden: On the Origins of "Leitmotif" as Critical Construct and Musical Practice' in Ian Bent (ed.), *Music Theory in the Age of Romanticism* (Cambridge University Press, 1996), 187–210. For a (re-)definition of the term 'leitmotif' in the context of cinema, see James Buhler, David Neumeyer, and Rob Deemer, *Hearing the Movies: Music and Sound in Film History* (Oxford University Press, 2009), 17 and 200–2.

2 Goldsmith's score was ranked ninth among the top twenty-five scores in the American Film Institute's *100 Years of Film Scores* presentation in Los Angeles on 23 September 2005. It is worth remembering that Goldsmith was called in at the eleventh hour to rewrite the music of the film after a disastrous 'test' screening featuring a score by Phillip Lambro. For Lambro's own account of the events, see his 'Chinatown Syndrome' in *Close Encounters of the Worst Kind* (Lulu.com, 2007), 272–339.

3 In the 1995 Varese Sarabande CD of the soundtrack (VSD 5677), the cue is titled, pointedly, 'Jake and Evelyn' (the CD is a re-release of the original 1974 vinyl recording, long out of print). Though he does not mention the music, Michael Eaton observes how, following the rescue, 'the terms and conditions for a closer liaison have been set'. Michael Eaton, *Chinatown* (London: BFI Publishing, 1997), 53.

4 Justin London, 'Leitmotifs and Musical Reference in the Classical Film Score' in James Buhler, Caryl Flinn, and David Neumeyer (eds.), *Music and Cinema* (Hanover, CT: Wesleyan University Press, 2000), 85–98.

5 Saul Kripke, *Naming and Necessity* (Cambridge, MA: Harvard University Press, 1980).

6 Kripke's notion of causality, as used in *Naming and Necessity*, is sometimes understood to apply to the grounding of a name, whether by ostension, a naming ceremony, or baptism; see also Joseph Laporte, 'Rigid Designators' in *Stanford Encyclopedia of Philosophy* (2006), esp. 2.3, plato.stanford.edu/entries/rigid-designators/#DirRef, accessed 9 March 2012. I think this is mistaken. Kripke, it seems to me, brings up causality to explain the cementing of the name's reference, the socially stipulated consensus that causes, through a chain of speakers, the reference to 'stick'.

7 Thus there are echoes in Kripke's appeal to the chain of speakers of the view of language as an essentially public phenomenon (such as one finds in, for instance, late Wittgenstein).

8   On fictional names, see also Thomas Pavel, *Fictional Worlds* (Cambridge, MA: Harvard University Press, 1986), 31–42.
9   Naturally, context is key in reviving the distinctiveness of a name. A novel about the 'common man' requires a fittingly stereotypical name; an absurdist play will take this a step further and defamiliarize its audience with it; a film such as *Bicycle Thieves* (1948) declines to emphasize its protagonist's name (Antonio) altogether – he is merely 'the father', just as his son Bruno is 'the son'.
10 London, 'Leitmotifs', 86.
11 *Ibid.*, 87.
12 This much is claimed by 'direct reference' theorists, for whom the meaning of a name, and even a proposition, amounts only to its referent in the real world. Direct reference is often imputed to names on the basis of Kripke's theory but this derivation is incorrect (see also Laporte, 'Rigid Designators', esp. 2.1).
13 Kripke, *Naming and Necessity*, 20.
14 London, 'Leitmotifs', 87.
15 Raymond Monelle, 'The Search for Topics' in *The Sense of Music: Semiotic Essays* (Princeton University Press, 2000), 17–18 (emphasis in the original).
16 Harold S. Powers, 'Reading Mozart's Music: Text and Topic, Syntax and Sense', *Current Musicology*, 57 (1995), 36–40. It is partially in response to the vexing question of whether topics may be said to be meaningfully ordered that both Kofi Agawu and Robert S. Hatten have built highly sophisticated, if strikingly different, analytical models centred on the music of the Classical era. See V. Kofi Agawu, *Playing with Signs: A Semiotic Interpretation of Classic Music* (Princeton University Press, 1991); and Robert S. Hatten, *Musical Meaning in Beethoven: Markedness, Correlation, and Interpretation* (Bloomington: Indiana University Press, 1994). For an interpretation of the sequence of topics in terms of rhetorical ordering, see Elaine Sisman, *Mozart: The Jupiter Symphony* (Cambridge University Press, 1993), 46–50.
17 Michael Long, *Beautiful Monsters: Imagining the Classic in Musical Media* (Berkeley and Los Angeles: University of California Press, 2008), 26. Long is discussing register here but his point applies to a whole range of mnemonically instigated references tapping into what he suggestively calls the 'vernacular imagination' (8).
18 Roger Odin, 'L'entrée du spectateur dans la fiction' in Jacques Aumont and Jean Louis Leutrat (eds.), *Théorie du film* (Paris: Editions Albatros, 1980). Unfortunately, Odin's discussion hardly touches on the role of music. James Buhler, by contrast, lavishes a great deal of attention on the opening music of *Star Wars*, describing the first measure of the score thus: 'The opening measure of Williams's score ... resembles the title it accompanies: radiant but indefinite; world-defining and timeless. More and less than the B-flat chord it seems to be, this sound is a *cipher in need of decoding*.' (Buhler, '*Star Wars*, Music, and Myth' in *Music and Cinema*, 35; emphasis mine.) In the context of Wagner's

Ring, Carl Dahlhaus, too, refers to motives that are not realized on the stage as an 'unsolved cipher', in *Richard Wagner's Music Dramas*, trans. Mary Whittall (Cambridge University Press, 1979), 86.

19 David Butler has revisited the commonplace according to which jazz *is* the sound of noir. First, he shows how precious little jazz was actually used in the noirs of the 1940s and 1950s, as studios preferred to employ jazz-inflected scores by their own (white) in-house composers instead; second, he aptly invokes Chion's notion of 'retrospective illusion' to explain the taken-for-granted assumption that jazz was a staple of classical film noir. See David Butler, *Jazz Noir: Listening to Music from* Phantom Lady *to* The Last Seduction (Westport, CT: Greenwood Publishing, 2004). One reason behind the phenomenon, one might add, is the wide distribution of films such as *Chinatown* (1974), *Taxi Driver* (1976), and *Body Heat* (1981), all of which did not merely reflect the illusion but played an active role in creating it.

20 The promise is not quite fulfilled. Indeed, as Michael Eaton notes, *Chinatown* 'avoids all the pitfalls of a retrospective soundtrack' (Eaton, *Chinatown*, 50). Goldsmith recalls how he had to convince producer Robert Evans that it would be a mistake for the whole score to have the flavour of Bunny Berigan's 'I Can't Get Started', as Evans had initially hoped. See Mervyn Cooke (ed.), *The Hollywood Film Music Reader* (Oxford University Press, 2010), 225. The song is heard, as a subtle irony, during Gittes's first assignment. Also resonant is the appearance of Jerome Kern–Dorothy Fields' 'The Way You Look Tonight', first in a piano version at the restaurant where Gittes and Mrs Mulwray meet after her husband's death, then as hummed, whistled, and finally sung by Gittes himself while waiting to meet Mulwray's successor at Water & Power, Russ Yelburton; see Robert Miklitsch, 'Audio-Noir: Audiovisuality in Neo-Modernist Noir' in Marck Bould, Kathrina Glitre, and Greg Tuck (eds.), *Neo Noir* (London and New York: Wallflower Press, 2009), 34–5.

21 Nicholas Cook, *Analysing Musical Multimedia* (Oxford: Clarendon Press, 1999).

22 Giorgio Biancorosso, 'Beginning Credits and Beyond: Music and the Cinematic Imagination', *ECHO: A Music-Centered Journal*, 3.1 (Spring 2001), www.echo.ucla.edu.

23 London, 'Leitmotifs', 85.

24 On the difficulty of separating out the reference to an object or person and that to a process, see Émile Benveniste, 'The Nominal Sentence' in Mary Elizabeth Meek (trans.), *Problems in General Linguistics* (Coral Gables, FL: University of Miami Press, 1971 (1966)), 131–44.

25 Dahlhaus, *Richard Wagner's Music Dramas*, 61.

26 *Ibid.*, 33.

27 *Ibid.*, 115.

28 Richard Wagner, *Opera and Drama*, trans. William Ashton Ellis (Lincoln: University of Nebraska Press, 1995), 330–1.

29 London, 'Leitmotifs', 89–90.
30 *Ibid.*, 87.
31 Giorgio Biancorosso, 'The Shark in the Music', *Music Analysis*, 29.1–3 (March–October 2010), 306–33.
32 It is instructive to compare the first attack to the unannounced – and terrifying – appearance of the shark itself as Brody is luring it towards the boat during the hunting episode that ends the film. The shock experienced by the spectator at this juncture, documented by an endless stream of anecdotes, is contingent on our utter lack of knowledge about the shark's whereabouts and thus inability to anticipate its moves. I thank Richard Taruskin for bringing the scene to my attention during the discussion following my presentation at the conference 'Music and Representation'.
33 The conventions regulating our understanding of a pattern may be termed, after philosopher David Lewis, a form of 'nonexplicit contract', and their effectiveness the result of 'coordination behavior and games' (Pavel, *Fictional Worlds*, 119).
34 As Gittes spies on Mulwray, there is a faintly distinguishable version, also in D minor, of the opening of the theme, played on the harp. But here the melody functions as background texture and plays, in my opinion, no role in strengthening our memory of it.
35 Thanks to Yeneling Liu for drawing my attention to the Orphic theme in the film. In their insightful summary of the score, William Darby and Jack Du Bois observe that the return to prominence of the main theme marks the moment at which 'the film can proceed to its second mystery – Evelyn's background and personality'. See their *American Film Music: Major Composers, Techniques, Trends, 1915–1990* (Jefferson, NC, and London: McFarland & Company, 1990), 505.
36 An early, stimulating articulation of this truism is Leonid Sabaneev, 'Remarks on the Leit-Motif', *Music and Letters*, 13.2 (April 1932), 200–6.
37 There is something like the adumbration of a similar point in Dahlhaus's claim, with regard to the motifs of Amfortas and the 'fool' in *Parsifal*, that 'the exposition of a motive [sic] is not necessarily the first time it is heard, but only when it is represented on the stage in some way' (Dahlhaus, *Richard Wagner's Music Dramas*, 149).
38 The most memorable sound effect in the whole film is, too, the resolution of a strategically placed 'set-up': the sound of the car horn, harbinger of the terrible news that Evelyn has been fatally shot. It is first heard in the scene outside Evelyn's home when, under pressure from Jack's questioning, she accidentally knocks the steering wheel of the car with her head.
39 Roger Scruton, *The Aesthetics of Music* (Oxford: Clarendon Press, 1997), 137.
40 A prolepsis creates a different kind of distancing effect, namely the impression that a voice outside the world of the characters 'looks back upon' the action at the very moment that same action is presented as happening in the present time. See Carolyn Abbate's discussion in *Unsung Voices* (Princeton University Press, 1991), 169.

41 I am reminded here of Karol Berger's claim that '[a] depicted figure does not "refer" to anything, it simply appears. Like a musical voice, it says something without our being able to tell what it says, or, more precisely, without our being able to distinguish its appearance from what it says.' Karol Berger, '*Diegesis* and *Mimesis*: The Poetic Modes and the Matter of Artistic Presentation', *Journal of Musicology*, 2.4 (Autumn 1994), 417.

12 | Self-representation in music: the case of Hindemith's meta-opera *Cardillac*

HERMANN DANUSER
TRANSLATED BY J. BRADFORD ROBINSON

TMI – 'the music itself' – does not exist, no matter how earnestly its champions, from Arthur Schopenhauer to George Steiner, wished it for this most immediate of all the arts. Schopenhauer, in his early magnum opus *Die Welt als Wille und Vorstellung*, raised a claim for music's special status vis-à-vis verbal and pictorial language, arguing that only music is capable of expressing *Wille* ('will' or 'volition'), whereas the other languages inhabit a realm of *Vorstellungen*, a German term that has been variously translated as 'ideas', 'representations', or, more recently, 'presentations'.[1] Steiner even went so far as to expressly and radically detach the 'language' of music, for whose referential potential Nelson Goodman claimed the term 'exemplification', from the system of 'references'.[2] Now, I do not wish to deny that the semblance of immediacy can be very important for aesthetic experiences in general and for musical experiences in particular. Yet prophets of aesthetic immediacy, such as Steiner and Hans Ulrich Gumbrecht, with their 'real *presences*' and '*presence* culture',[3] make terminological use of precisely the same lexical root that is contained in the word 'representation' (Lat. *repraesentatio*, *repraesentare*) in its sense of 'to bring something distant or absent before the mind' or 'to make something present to the imagination', which, as philosophers since late Antiquity have pointed out, necessarily involves mediation. Those who notice this will find it hard to suppress an ironic smile. Moreover, philosophers of language have stressed the same point in their critique of an object-theoretical approach.[4]

Theoretically, we can distinguish between four media in which music can exist as a text (see below) and between various modes of a musicological concept of context.[5] For example, music may manifest itself in an extra-textual context by referring to non-aesthetic systems, by expressing praise of God in church hymns, say, or the power of a ruler in secular music (indeed, these were central functions of earlier art). When it does, it partakes of the representation of something outside itself. Our above examples, important as they may be, are only two of a great many more possibilities. However, the contextual modes of music can also be elevated to a musical text, as when a rehearsal, which normally lies outside the work rehearsed and must be done prior to its execution, is made part of the work itself and its performance. When this is done, and when music's existential media are mutually reflected, music no longer represents something outside itself; rather, it evidently represents itself in a different guise. This raises some important questions: How can we separate representation through music from music's own self-representation? Under what textual and contextual conditions can self-representation in music occur at all? And in what forms does self-representation, viewed from the standpoint of musical self-referentiality, exist in the generic realms of metamusical theatre? I will attempt to provide comprehensive answers to these and similar questions in my book *Metamusik*, currently in preparation. In the limited confines of this chapter, I will simply draw up a few theses in the first section (without breaking down the contextual dimensions) and, in the second, point out some aspects of musical self-representation in Paul Hindemith's meta-opera *Cardillac*.

I

Each of the four media in which music can exist as a text – a) sound, b) notation, c) words, and d) images – represents music in its own way and can stand for one or more of music's other forms of existence. Because each form – sonic, notational, verbal, and pictorial – can represent any of the others and signify music as a whole, we are dealing in these processes with music's self-representation. My definition basically posits that these four forms are equal in value, a presupposition at odds with the conventional notion of what music is.

The conventional notion proceeds from a hierarchical order among these four forms, beginning with the sonic text as the genuine and central form and ending with the pictorial text as the most remote and least 'genuine'. For a conventional aesthetic, then, music exists mainly as sound in its primary form of existence (a), whereas the other forms of existence (b to d), though not really music, are capable of representing music as sound by standing for something which is not there. At the same time, however, music is an evanescent art, one considered to be what Adam of Fulda called a *meditatio mortis*. Viewed in this light, the sources representing sound have come down to scholars in the exact opposite chronological order. The earliest items of evidence are iconographical depictions of music-making that illustrate, in pictorial form, musical practices (whether for private entertainment, sacred worship, or the public display of secular power). Then comes literary and religious evidence of these practices, as has been expressed verbally for millennia in the poetry of the world's populations. Later we find the sound of music captured in notation in various contexts, some liturgical, some theoretical. Only much later, since 1880, has technology made it possible to store and reproduce music, thereby creating documents that convey music in its existential medium of sound. Let us now briefly go through the four media in which music can exist as a text, proceeding from d) to a).

d) Being suspended in time, *images* – the visually intelligible representation of music-making – are particularly apt for capturing the evanescent manifestation of sound. They represent music by showing men and women in the act of singing and playing. Musical iconography, or music history in pictures, teaches us about the practices of past and present cultures, providing information not only by depicting instruments and their use, but also by mapping theoretical models. Here musicology verges on a science of images. It therefore comes as no surprise, for example, that the Eikones Research Institute at Basel University has recently opened a musicological branch. Nor is there any question that video, performance art, and film, by combining existential media of image and sound (d and a), have created new art forms that override the former distinction between these textual modes. This, of course, applies perforce to music theatre as a whole.

c) Though often underestimated, the existence of music in the form of *words* is, as Carl Dahlhaus pointed out, central not only to the perception, interpretation, discussion, and criticism of music, but also to the various types of description with which a verbal text can represent music. In a work of music, or music in general, poietic description accounts for its genesis, analytical description for its construction and multi-layered complexities, theoretical description for its structure and form, musicological description for its text and contexts, and poetical description for its literary exegesis. The latter also encompasses literary fiction with conceivable but non-notated works of music, such as the imaginary compositions in Thomas Mann's novel *Doktor Faustus*, which has spawned no small number of attempts to translate them into written-out works.[6]

b) The *notational text* of a score – the form in which a work written by a composer exists – represents, with its virtual sonic text, something that is either no longer or not yet extant. The score thus represents the 'work' as the summation of sonic relations within a compositional nexus, which, however, is identical neither to the sounds imagined by the composer nor to any audible performance, whether by the composer or by anyone else. The work is thus something remote, absent, and ineffable – something which, as all TMI adherents know, is represented better by a score than by any other medium.[7]

a) If a *sonic text* stands only for itself, as it does in early non-Western musical cultures and in new technology-based types of music-making (tape and computer music, turntablism, and so forth), it can represent the religious, ritualistic, and cultural context that sustains it, the image of God or community for whose sake the music resounds, or even, provided that the music is identical with the 'work', it can represent itself. Otherwise, if it is a sonic text based on an underlying score, it is mediated by the notational text. An individual sound-text, though it represents the 'work', is not the work itself; it is one, and only one, of infinitely many other sonic texts that likewise represent the work.

In this way, self-representations and non-self-representations interlock among all the media in which music can exist as a text; there is no form of musical existence without representation. And all the existential forms of musical text coincide in that all four, when mutually reflected, partake of processes of music's self-representation. But these processes achieve aesthetic relevance only when they boldly stand out, as they do, for example, in meta-opera, the subject of our case study in section II.

A conventional aesthetic, given that it denies music per se the capability of reference, much less self-reference, can only doubt the possibility of self-representation in music. In contrast, the postulate advanced above – that the four media of music's textual existence are equal in value (this being one of the premises of *Metamusik*) – opens up many previously unimagined vistas onto this area. Works of music theatre encompass all four of these existential forms – sound, notation, words, and images – albeit in different ways. They particularly do so when the musical self-representation gives rise to a meta-opera whose multiple references resemble a 'play within a play' or a 'picture within a picture'. The 'directional character' (Ernst Cassirer)[8] points in two directions: from the outside in, and from the inside out, that is, the outer opera represents the inner one and vice versa. In Paul Hindemith's *Cardillac* (premiered in Dresden in 1926), we have the extraordinary case that it was only with the second version (premiered in Zurich in 1952) that the opera became a meta-opera, and that the meta-operatic insertion was taken from a historical work, *Phaëton*, a *tragédie en musique* by Jean-Baptiste Lully (premiered in Versailles in 1683).[9]

II

The turn to meta-opera. Hindemith's 1948 revision of his lyrical song-cycle after Rilke, *Das Marienleben*, Op. 27 (1923), affected the musical idiom and its level of dissonance but not the verbal text. Exactly the opposite was the case with his opera *Cardillac* after Ferdinand Lion: the revision primarily affected not so much the music as the libretto and the dramatic structure.[10] Previous studies of this second version[11] have emphasized its dramatic structure, characterization, linguistic style and philosophical content;[12] but these factors attain their full significance only through the generic concept that has lent its name to Hindemith's revision: 'meta-opera'. The idea of transforming *Cardillac* into a meta-opera was by no means apparent when Hindemith set to work on his revision. When he first re-encountered the work after the war, at a Venice performance in September 1948, he was satisfied with the music but almost repulsed by Lion's expressionist libretto. 'I've decided', he wrote to his publisher Ludwig Strecker on 15 November 1948, 'to rework the old Cardillac into a usable opera ... The plot will be largely altered, the words *completely* changed.'[13] Accordingly, Hindemith wrote the libretto afresh, drawing on the opera's original pre-text, E.T.A. Hoffmann's novella *Das Fräulein von Scuderi* (1819).[14] He recast the minor part of the 'Dame' in the first version to create the central role of the 'Erste Sängerin' (the *prima donna*), who, in the second version, represents a performing artist on a par with the goldsmith Cardillac. It was apparently only relatively late in the process of revision, presumably in the course of 1951, that he lit on the possibility of inserting elements from Lully's *Phaëton* into the work in compressed form.[15]

Why did he happen to choose this particular work by Lully? Part of the answer lies in the time and place of the subject matter. Hoffmann's novella bears the subtitle 'A tale from the age of Louis XIV', and the 1926 version of the opera reads, 'The plot takes place in 17th-century Paris.' It was thus natural to look to Lully for a fitting contemporary piece of music. The new version reads, more narrowly, 'Time: Paris in the final decade of the 17th century.' Of Lully's oeuvre, *Phaëton* stands out because of its affinities with *Cardillac* in their title figures. Though it was premièred in Versailles in 1683, and though Lully died four years later, Hindemith's work assigns its première, with Lully's participation, to some time after 1690. This transports the meta-opera's historical dimension into the realm of fiction and relieves it of the need to be historically accurate.

The meta-opera is constructed in the form of a *mise en abyme*, that is, a self-referential process reflecting a work on a smaller scale, whether musically or intermedially, and thereby revealing its underlying meaning in such a way as to produce a thrill of recognition or a sense of special vividness and clarity. The Lully arrangement in *Cardillac* fulfils the conditions that set a *mise en abyme* apart from a *mise en série*, a *mise en cadre*, or any 'play within a play' – namely, 'a relation of homology or similarity and a hierarchy of levels'.[16] Further iterations enrich the work to brilliant effect.

Multi-layered complexities. A meta-opera results when at least two plot levels (rather than a single plot) intersect so as to make the genre and practice of opera the object of artistic creation, thereby reflexively undergirding the resultant work and releasing an enhanced artificiality within it. *Cardillac* follows just such a generic model. It is not only the insertion of a 'play within a play' that satisfies this model; rather, the meta-opera only becomes defined through the manner in which the plot lines interweave rather than neutralizing each other. But how can a closer balance be struck in the relative weight assigned to the main plot and the implantation, that is, between Acts I, II, and IV, and Act III, with its interpolated 'Lully opera'?

Hindemith had to come up with something different from previous solutions in the meta-opera tradition, which above all, from *Der Schauspieldirektor* to *Capriccio*, had tended to make the plot turn on opera production itself (with impresario, librettist, composer, singers, audience, etc.). In the case of *Cardillac*, the role of the artist was already taken from the gallery of master artisans by the figure of the goldsmith; neither the composer and *maître de chapelle* (Lully), nor the librettist of *Phaëton* (Philippe Quinault), nor even an impresario could be stitched into the meta-opera's fabric. Instead, Hindemith transformed the 'Dame' of the first version into the central figure of the meta-opera: the 'Erste Sängerin', using the German term for 'prima donna' familiar from the contest between Madame Herz and Mademoiselle Silberklang in *Der Schauspieldirektor*. In Act III she plays the Lydian princess Theo in the 'Lully opera'. Splitting the identity of a role within a work is a sure indication of a meta-opera. The double role of Erste Sängerin/Theo is constitutive rather than optional (as when Masetto and the Commendatore were taken by the same singer at the première of *Don Giovanni*), and it tightly interlocks the two plot lines of the 1952 *Cardillac*.

The climax of the Act III *mise en abyme*, the ensemble no. 14, brings about a clarification and a compression. Cardillac, at first concealed, enters stage right at the beginning of the section '*Chor und Soli*' (rehearsal letter G) and rejoins the action at the moment when Phaeton sets out in the sun chariot, setting the tragedy on its irrevocable course. In this sense, he replaces the parallel figure in the 'Lully opera'; the frame of the drama impinges on the internal action. At this moment something previously unthinkable gives Cardillac the signal to alter the course of events. 'But the Erste Sängerin', we are told by a stage instruction, 'notices him [Cardillac] from the stage. While the chorus sings, their eyes meet; we see that at this moment the Erste Sängerin understands all the connections.'[17] Here it is the Erste Sängerin/Theo who assumes the double role described above: she is a virtuoso soprano in the main plot (the lack of a proper name emphasizes her function), but a princess in the 'Lully opera', which at this point is still being performed. The plot lines thus directly intermesh. In the exchange of glances between two potential lovers, seeing, which has been associated since time immemorial with the acquisition of knowledge, becomes a key situation for the possibility that things might work out differently. The Erste Sängerin, and only she, returns one of the goldsmith's pieces of jewellery – indeed, the diadem, the most precious of them all. The work now resides with its creator rather than its purchaser, who reified it into a commodity and divested it of its quality as art. But Cardillac, rather than altering his criminal nature (which is identical to his artistry), reverts to the business of serial murder at the end of Act III, following a duet with the Erste Sängerin.

Postmodernism 'avant la lettre'? Different layers of time are at work in the 1926 and 1952 versions of *Cardillac*. First of all, as in any opera on a historical subject, there is a gap between the time and place of the action (late seventeenth-century Paris) and the date when the opera was written (the 1920s in the first case, and basically in the second as well). This gap forms a musico-linguistic foil in which a work is shaped, quite apart from the question of which historical or mythical age is illustrated in sound by the work's subject.[18]

In the first version, neo-baroque music accompanies a plot borrowed from the baroque era: the French classical period. (Incidentally, 'neo-baroque' does not imply a regression to the style of an earlier age, but is quite definitely an idiom of contemporary music.)[19] The baroque number opera that Giselher Schubert has unveiled in the early version of the work[20] became virtually a mainspring of modern music, an engine of acceleration and a lever for parallel developments. The separate layers of the stage work, being independent, interact in a great many ways.

The second version abandons the idea of a uniform musico-linguistic space that undergirds the neo-baroque work. As in a postmodern aesthetic, musical quotations are important; what is abandoned is the notion that the composer wished to create a world unto itself. In *Cardillac*,

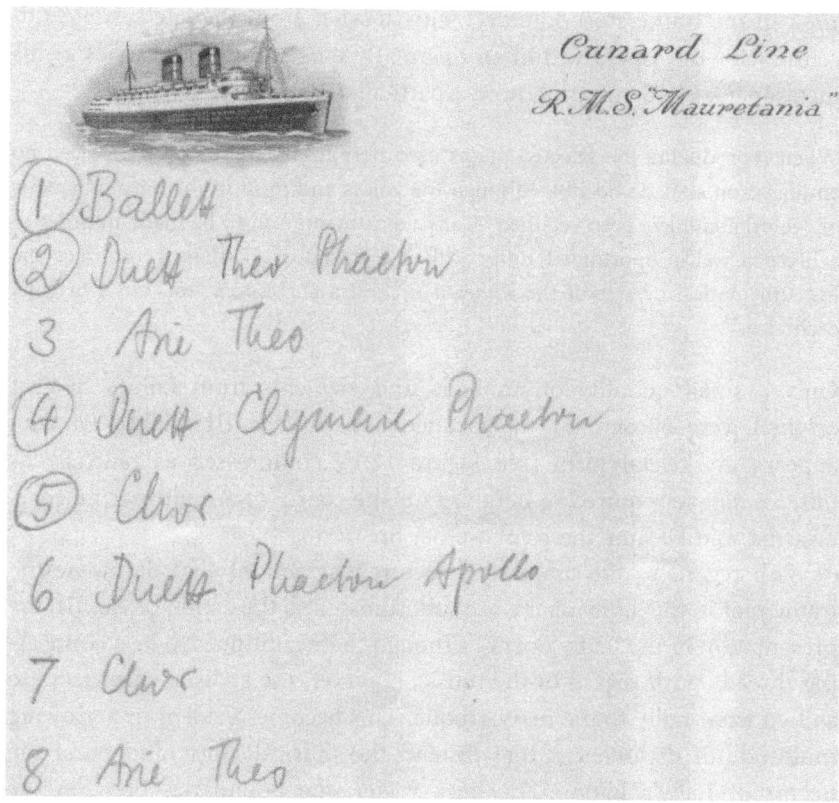

Figure 12.1 Paul Hindemith, note on the sequence of numbers in the plan for Lully's opera *Phaëton* in Act III of *Cardillac* (1952). Source: Hindemith Institute, Frankfurt am Main.

however, Hindemith not only offers contrasting temporal layers and musical languages, but also embeds a work from music history – Lully's *tragédie en musique*, *Phaëton* – in condensed form in Act III (Figure 12.1),[21] just as Strauss and Hofmannsthal had done with Molière's *Bourgeois gentilhomme* in the first version of their *Ariadne auf Naxos* (1912). A baroque and neo-baroque musical language, a modernist and pre-modernist style, stand juxtaposed in a pluralist stylistic whole that may with full justification be called post-modern.

Yet the spheres are separated less neatly in the meta-opera than in the diagram. By no means are Acts I, II, and IV governed by an original neo-baroque musical language and Act III by a borrowed baroque musical language à la Lully. Even if this had been Hindemith's intention, one problem would remain: to what extent do these languages reflect the lines in the history of musical performance?[22] Thus, a musical style of 1926 and

1952 in the frame story interacts with another from the late seventeenth century for the 'opera within an opera'. By embedding these styles in his meta-opera, Hindemith followed a particular stratagem:

When reproducing the selected pieces used here from Lully's opera, I placed no emphasis on stylistic fidelity, although the voices and most of the harmonic basis of the original have been retained. Many adjustments had to be made in order to achieve a well-proportioned unity with the music of *Cardillac*. Nor does the instrumentation or size of the *Phaëton* orchestra correspond to Lully's original orchestra.[23]

Only a small quantity of numbers and elements from Lully's five-act original were chosen for the arrangement. In Act III, Lully's *Phaëton* appears in skeletal form (see Figure 12.1), compressed as radically as *mise en abyme* required in heraldry for the centre of a multi-partite coat-of-arms, and became the rule in other art forms.[24]

With regard to the dramatic structure, the actions that dominate the frame plot in the 'Lully opera' are subordinated to the action of Act III, the presentation of the 'Lully opera', although there continues to be a connecting thread. With regard to the music, however, the stylistic emphases are shifted from Lully to the neo-baroque. This becomes evident in a growing multitude of dissonances that distend the musical fabric and burst the norms of Lully's idiom. The lines waver; the boundaries between the spheres blur. At the end of the 'Lully opera' a monophonic line bursts through in a blaze of dissonance (Example 12.1).

The chorus in the 'Lully opera' ends its number in a 'baroque style', its reflections on Phaeton merging with the hope for light from Apollo's spirit. A monophonic line proceeds from the C minor chord on which the chorus's cadence comes to a close. This line handles tonality in a completely free manner fully in keeping with contemporary music, as is clearly audible in its melodic ascent of four fourths (m. 5 after G5). The neo-baroque style thus sustains the modern work; the interpolations of the 'Lully opera' are addenda with which performance history impinges on meta-opera. This dramatic structure reinforces the ties between the protagonists in the two sections: Phaeton and Cardillac. The hubris of the one mirrors the hubris of the other. Phaeton, the son of Apollo, travels to certain doom in the sun chariot, which is not intended for human beings; and instead of a royal pardon[25] Cardillac, the imperious *homme supérieur*, suffers a violent death at the hands of the People. For the status of the meta-opera, the differences between Cardillac and Phaeton in their hubris and their destinies are as important as the identities that bind the myth to history and reflexively shore up the work.

Example 12.1 Hindemith, *Cardillac* (1952), Act III, excerpt from scene 14, ending of '*Chor und Soli*', 6 mm. before G5 to 6 mm. after G5.

A dual monologue. Yet the *mise en abyme* in *Cardillac* resides not only in general analogies, with the frame story and interior plot reflecting the downfall of megalomaniac protagonists; it resides equally in structural details. In the second version, and only there, a brief aria ('*Symbole überstarker Kräfte*') occurs twice at contrasting locations, once in Act III and again in Act IV.[26] In other words, we are not dealing with two stanzas of a single poetic construct; rather, the musico-theatrical reflection proceeds from the meta-opera, of which it is a constituent part. Similarly, the relations to the pre-text bear witness to Hindemith's technique of collage and montage: the source, an 'Air' for Théone's antagonist Lybie taken from Act I of the *tragédie en musique* (scene 1; see Example 12.2), bears no dramaturgical relation whatsoever to the target text in *Cardillac*. In no other part of the work is reflection more patently manifest than here, where the *mise en abyme* tradition announces its formative presence, magnifying realities. Hindemith deliberately duplicated the 'Air' in order to bring about a 'staggered iteration'[27] by switching between two levels with the same musico-theatrical material. The identities and differences reside in several factors.

To begin with, the identities reside in the characters who sing the 'Air': initially Theo, the Lydian princess, then the Erste Sängerin, who plays this role. Second, they reside in a romantic attachment (in both cases concealed but obvious) between this character and the male protagonist in the respective subplot: Apollo's son Phaeton, and the goldsmith Cardillac. Third, they reside in the location in the dramatic structure where the 'Air' is heard: initially in the interior plot at the end of the 'Lully opera', with the contemplation of Phaeton's corpse, then in the moralistic 'Finale' at the end of the frame story, with the contemplation of Cardillac's corpse. Fourth, they reside in the structure of the sung melody, which differs insignificantly between the two sections. Fifth and lastly, they reside in commonalities in the text, which stand out so clearly that the one becomes a variant of the other, creating an intertextuality that disengages the positions of the first and second texts from their locations in the work (Theo's 'Air' in Act III, and the Erste Sängerin's in Act IV).

These differences result first and foremost from the fact that the interior plot and the frame story have different functions to fulfil in the overall design. The exceptional circumstance that the interior plot and the frame story both derive from pre-texts has no bearing on '*Symbole überstarker Kräfte*'. Second, they result from the almost antithetical manner in which the melody is inserted into a contrapuntal orchestral texture: in Theo's Act III 'Air'[28] (divided into a recitative and a lyrical section in 'calm minims'),

Example 12.2 Lully, *Phaëton*, Act I, excerpt from scene 1, Lybie's 'Air'. Vocal score, mm. 1–10.

the voice is continuously supported by strings, and gentle departures in the harmony reveal the meta-opera's 'Lully style' to be an adaptation of early music in a twentieth-century vein. For example, the diminished octave *a flat*^{1}/*a* in the accompaniment at '*uns-re Ver-nunft*', with its ascending leap to *a flat*^{1} and its descending leap to *a*, is a particularly conspicuous departure from Lully's harmonic idiom (Example 12.3). Yet a wealth of dissonance of a completely different kind dominates the part of the Erste Sängerin in Act IV, where, at the beginning, quartal chords are combined with parallel fifths added to the vocal melody in the bass (Example 12.4).

Third, the sonic character of the orchestra in the Erste Sängerin's 'Air' in Act IV contrasts with the 'Lully opera' in instrumentation and dynamics. Previously the sustained string writing had formed a continuous basis, but now the orchestral writing is broken down into phases at a lower dynamic level, as if direct speech were being inwardly committed to memory. The strings accompany with gentle homophony while instruments omitted in the 'Lully orchestra', such as clarinet and bass clarinet, are added.

Fourth and lastly, the librettos in these two passages, for all their similarity, have some important differences (Table 12.1).[29]

Phaeton is no more identical to Cardillac than Theo is to the Erste Sängerin; their parallels all the more clearly highlight their differences. Phaeton, the object of Theo's 'Air' in Act III, is a power-hungry young man obsessed with honour, not an artist. The six substantives in the second line of verse ('*Überkommenes ...*') identify the motives for his actions; he pays for his megalomania ('heap up things we want') with his life. The princess, born into the uppermost reaches of society, is content with her status; but when she preaches 'subordination' to those who seek to reach the pinnacle of the hierarchy, her admonitions sound hollow.

The lines of the Erste Sängerin towards the end of the work generalize the goldsmith's fate into a précis reflected in the subsequent Finale by the soloists and chorus: the People. The lower forces holding humankind in thrall ('dark and bestial things') point in Cardillac to a set of complex drives, the source of ineffable beauty as well as unspeakable suffering. 'Defiance and resolve', denigrated by Theo because they result from blind ambition ('the poorest of shelters'), become positive once they are illuminated by Cardillac's personality ('the richest of shelters'). What sort of 'triumph' the bystanders are meant to learn from Cardillac's death remains unclear. Perhaps the Erste Sängerin is referring to triumph over egoism – a triumph she herself demonstrates when she returns the diadem to its creator. The vague linguistic relations and musical affinities strengthen the ties between the two 'Airs' within the tension of the *mise en abyme*.

Self-representation: Hindemith's meta-opera Cardillac 237

Example 12.3 Hindemith, *Cardillac* (1952), Act III, excerpt from Ensemble no. 14, Theo's 'Air' in the 'Lully opera'. Vocal score, 4 mm. before H1 to 9 mm. after H1.

Example 12.4 Hindemith, *Cardillac* (1952), Act IV, excerpt from the Erste Sängerin's 'Lied' no. 21 (Air). Vocal score, 3 mm. before B to 12 mm. after B.

Table 12.1

[Act 3] Theo (beside the corpse):	[Act 4] [Erste] Sängerin:
Symbole überstarker Kräfte: mehr als unsre Vernunft.	Symbole überstarker Kräfte, mehr ist unsre Vernunft.
Überkommnes, Verbrieftes, Besitz und Macht und Kron und Schwert:	Tierischdunkles, Gemeinstes, Gelüste, Laster, Hass und Schwert:
Sie lächeln wissend, wenn wir stürmen, Ein Selbstgewolltes aufzutürmen.	Wir lächeln wissend, wenn sie stürmen, Bedrohung um uns aufzutürmen.
Was gewinnt, wer mit Trotz und Entschluss aufbegehrt?	Was gewinnt, wer mit Trotz und Entschluss aufbegehrt?
Leib, Lust und Leben ärmste Unterkunft.	Leib, Lust und Leben reichste Unterkunft.
Dein Tod lehrt uns: Unterwerfung erweist unsern Wert.	Dein Tod lehrt uns: Überwindung erweist unsren Wert.
Symbols of puissant forces: greater than our reason.	*Symbols of puissant forces: greater is our reason.*
Things obsolete and certified, possessions and power and crown and sword:	*Dark and bestial things, the meanest of all, cravings, vices, hatred and sword:*
They smile knowingly when we rage to heap up things we want.	*We smile knowingly when they rage, heaping up peril around us.*
What does he gain who rebels with defiance and resolve?	*What does he gain who rebels with defiance and resolve?*
Body, desire, and life, the poorest of shelters.	*Body, desire, and life, the richest of shelters.*
Your death teaches us: subordination proves our worth.	*Your death teaches us: triumph proves our worth.*

Reflections on artistic murder. The years 1926 and 1952, when the first and second versions of *Cardillac* were respectively premiered, are each seven years removed from that disastrous period in German history when a 'Führer' who had failed as an artist erected and destroyed a 'Third Reich' with criminal decrees, terror, war, and genocide. In both versions the figure of the goldsmith, the incarnation of a man monomaniacally obsessed with his art, could only have seemed untimely. At the height of the New Sobriety aesthetic that brought forth the *Zeitoper*, the trends of the 1920s were embodied in that 'New Orpheus' with whom Kurt Weill, in his like-named cantata, elevated the normal human being into an anti-genius, and not into the romantic artist who proclaims his works to have supreme value, as exemplified by Cardillac's crimes. But there is no denying that the first version of 1926 gained much allure and depth from the tension between a neo-baroque, inexpressive style of music and the demonization of the artist. How did Hindemith respond to this in the second version, after twelve years of a regime that had driven him into exile?

A comparison between no. 18 in the first version ('Schlussgesang') and nos. 21–2 in the second version ('Lied' and 'Finale') sheds some light on this question. The words of the Officer, the lover of Cardillac's daughter in version 1, unambiguously express veneration for, and even mythification of, the artist. 'He was the victim of a sacred madness', we hear just before Cardillac's death, and thereafter the Officer calls him a 'hero' and a 'victor' whom he envies.[30] Heroics along these lines, though bolstered in the 1920s by such mythical modernist figures as Charles Lindbergh, had been rendered obsolete by the disaster of political romanticism, which left behind a mountain of debris in 1945. At that time Hindemith, who sought to give aesthetics a moral foundation by reconciling them with ethics, could no longer accept such heroics. This was yet another reason for his decision to rework *Cardillac*. The second version of the opera ends with a 'Finale' following the Erste Sängerin's 'Air'. Compared to the expressionistic iconoclasm at the end of the first version, it feels like a sermon, a valuation of justice and injustice, guilt and mercy. The combined forces of four soloists and chorus bring the work to what is at least a plausible conclusion. Cardillac is portrayed as a man of the people who merely drove to extremes things lurking in each and every one of us:[31]

The four soloists:

'Is there not something of Cardillac in us all? We too are filled with the inclination towards Beauty, and Darkness drives us to misdeeds with the same force. But we lack the courage to take both to extremes as he did ... May [fate] mercifully preserve us from the most grievous of sins: ceaseless excess. We must forgive him with pity, not reproach, for his tragically wayward spirit is neither remote from nor alien to us.'

The chorus:

'May he be forgiven, he trusted in his rightness. May we be forgiven, we trusted in our rightness ... Who is guilty, who is pure? Who is true, who untrue? Who is a brute, who a healer? Who is a criminal, who a judge? Each of us seems both at once. Rightness is what shields our coexistence and gives it meaning.'

Here individual murder is confronted with collective murder; no one pursues a 'legal process'. In this way a fatal pattern characteristic of the years around 1930 is laid bare: an antagonism between the individual and the crowd. To be sure, Hindemith's 'sermon' in the second version, with its appeal to salvation from the 'most grievous of sins: ceaseless excess', feels weak, falling well short of what the meta-opera displays onstage.

In the opera's background we find, namely, not only the romantic glorification of the artist, which figured in E.T.A. Hoffmann's original tale of 1819, but also an early modern tradition familiar since the Renaissance: the immunity of the genius from criminal prosecution. Horst Bredekamp has recently produced a revealing study of this subject[32] that adds several new facets to the opera's historical horizon. Cardillac's understanding of himself merely radicalizes the view that the artist of genius, because he and only he is capable of creating supreme works of art, stands above the law, and should be pardoned by princes, popes, and emperors should he ever commit a crime. Benvenuto Cellini writes in his autobiography that he murdered a competitor for the office of master of the papal mint in September 1534, and that the newly elected Pope Paul III told the victim's family, 'Take note that men like Benvenuto, who are unique in their profession, need not be subject to the law.'[33] All the same, when sovereigns exonerated artists from the consequences of their crimes, they did so less for the sake of their past achievements than with an eye to works they had yet to create. Thus, despite the capital crimes they had committed – crimes punishable by death – Michelangelo Buonarroti was pardoned by Popes Julius II and Clement VII, the goldsmith and sculptor Leone Leoni by Emperors Charles V and Philip II and the sculptor and architect Gian Lorenzo Bernini by Pope Urban VIII, all for the sake of their art. They were placed on a superior footing outside the legal system that bound their fellow men.

It is in this tradition that Hoffmann's figure René Cardillac, the outstanding master goldsmith in the age of Louis XIV, evidently and not unjustifiably sees himself. Even Mademoiselle de Scuderi is situated in this nexus of relations: for one thing, one recipient of Cardillac's jewellery, as we learn from the apprentice Olivier Brusson, is an 'operatic ballerina' whose lover, a 'gentleman at court', pays for the gift with his life.[34] For another, the title figure of the novella is a woman of letters, an aged noble lady whose maxim 'Un amant qui craint les voleurs / n'est point digne d'amour'[35] hovers magically above the entire story, and whose obstinate intelligence finally discloses the crimes. It is ultimately she who causes the king to pardon the apprentice suspected of murdering Cardillac.[36] 'Ceaseless excess' is precisely the personality trait that would be applied to artists of the Renaissance and the French classical period. Hindemith, in other words, misconstrues the historical roots of his subject matter when he feels that he can derive a regulatory mechanism for the human community from a reduction of this personality trait. To be sure, the deed of a consummate artist – individual murder – falls into a completely different category from collective murder perpetrated by a raging crowd, the more so when the artistry of the criminal well-nigh coincides with the criminality of the artist. In light of the atrocities of the 'Third

Reich', the chorus's speech ('May we be forgiven, we trusted in our rightness') seems almost chilling.

No matter what value we attach to them, the lines of argument in the 'Finale' remain important to the conception of this *Künstleroper*. Already in the first version Hindemith had proceeded from the primacy of musical invention by occasionally attaching the words to previously composed music (in this respect he was no different from Mozart or Richard Strauss).[37] On this basis, a textual parody, that is, retexting the first version to create the second, could be brought off without insurmountable difficulty, allowing Hindemith to replace Lion's words with his own to produce a meta-opera. The primacy of music in the neo-baroque number opera remained untouched.

The author in mirror reflection – an epilogue. Every piece of music theatre contains the four auditory and visual media in which music can exist as a text: a) the *sound* of sung words with instrumental accompaniment; b) the *notated score*, with textual and paratextual elements, which forms the basis of that sound; c) the *words*, the libretto's contribution to the work's text and a tool for its understanding through commentary and critique; and d) the *visual level* of stage sets, costumes, choreographed movement, gestures, performative declamation, and much else besides. My discussion in part II of this chapter has, I hope, made clear which strategies and forms allowed the second version of *Cardillac* to substantially shift the dimensions of representation vis-à-vis the first version in the direction of self-representation. In meta-opera, however, music not only reflects itself by allowing the work's levels – interior and exterior – to reflect each other. Since time immemorial there has always been another vehicle of potential self-representation, one even more remote and mediated, yet culturally ever-present: the work's author.

The time has apparently arrived to stop reading the 1952 *Cardillac* as a neo-conservative text in the light of the elderly Hindemith's moralistic intentions. Instead, we should view it in its highly complex and not always smoothly executed mirror reflections as a work of art whose subject is art itself, and restore it to the repertoire in imaginative new productions. The stage director's art is creative in many ways and should be capable of compensating for the weaknesses of the text and the meta-operatic construction; for example, the stereotyped depictions of the audience reaction, the maecenatic role of the wealthy Marquis and the superficial success-mongering of the singers at the beginning of Act IV. That said, any attempt at an autobiographical reading – for example, by seeing the 'creative artist' in Cardillac and the 'performing artist' in the Erste Sängerin – must bear in mind that Hindemith himself was not only a composer but also a virtuoso of the violin, viola, and conductor's baton, and is thus represented by Cardillac and the Erste Sängerin alike. In this way, the Erste Sängerin's emotional urgency at the climax of the work – 'Our lots must be joined into a single destiny'[38] – is a tribute to Paul Hindemith's own artistry.

Notes

1 Arthur Schopenhauer, *Die Welt als Wille und Vorstellung* (Leipzig: Brockhaus, 1938), vol. I, 301–16; English translations by R.B. Haldane and J. Kemp as *The World as Will and Idea* (London: Trübner, 1883–6); E.F.J. Payne as *The World as Will and Representation* (Indian Hills, CO: Falcon's Wing, 1958); and Richard E. Aquila and David Carus as *The World as Will and Presentation* (New York: Pearson Longman, 2008).
2 George Steiner, *Real Presences: Is There Anything in What We Say?* (London: Faber and Faber, 1991), 7ff.
3 Hans Ulrich Gumbrecht, *Production of Presence: What Meaning Cannot Convey* (Stanford University Press, 2004).
4 See Eckart Scheerer's entry on 'Repräsentation' in *Historisches Wörterbuch der Philosophie* (Basel: Schwabe Verlag), vol. VIII, cols. 790–7; Ernst Tugendhat, *Vorlesungen zur Einführung in die sprachanalytische Philosophie* (Frankfurt am Main: Suhrkamp, 1976), 86f., 190, 476ff., and 482ff.; and especially Charles O. Nussbaum, *The Musical Representation: Meaning, Ontology, and Emotion* (Cambridge, MA: MIT Press, 2007), 1–22.
5 See Hermann Danuser, 'Der Text und die Texte: Über Singularisierung und Pluralisierung einer Kategorie' in Hermann Danuser and Tobias Plebuch (eds.), *Musik als Text: Bericht über den Internationalen Musikwissenschaftlichen Kongreß Freiburg 1993* (Kassel: Bärenreiter, 1998), vol. I, 38–44; and Danuser, 'Die Kunst der Kontextualisierung: Über Spezifik in der Musikwissenschaft' in Tobias Bleek and Camilla Bork (eds.), *Musikalische Analyse und kulturgeschichtliche Kontextualisierung: Für Reinhold Brinkmann* (Stuttgart: Franz Steiner, 2010), 41–63.
6 See Hermann Danuser, 'Erzählte Musik: Fiktive Poetik in Thomas Manns "Doktor Faustus"' in Werner Röcke (ed.), *Thomas Mann: Doktor Faustus 1947–1997*, Publikationen zur Zeitschrift für Germanistik, new ser. 3 (Bern and New York: Lang, 2001), 293–320.
7 Another kind of notational text is provided not by a composer but by a musicologist: the transcription of a sonic process, whether captured in the act of listening or taken from a sound recording. Here the score does not represent a work to be performed but a sonic text in musical notation.
8 '*Richtungscharakter*'. See Ernst Cassirer, *Philosophie der symbolischen Formen, Dritter Teil: Phänomenologie der Erkenntnis*, ed. Julia Clemens, Gesammelte

Werke XIII (Hamburg: Meiner, 2002), 232; English translation by Ralph Manheim as *The Philosophy of Symbolic Forms* (New Haven: Yale University Press; Oxford University Press, 1953–7). Dietfried Gerhardus offers the following summary: 'To represent thus means, in general, to place something in relation to something else, where this placing in relation has a "directional character" (Ernst Cassirer) from the object to the symbol ("bringing a thing to mind as representational") or from the symbolic object to the object ("bringing a thing to mind as thing").' See his entry on 'Repräsentation' in Jürgen Mittelstrass (ed.), *Enzyklopädie Philosophie und Wissenschaftstheorie* (Stuttgart and Weimar: Metzler, 1995), vol. III, 590f. (590).

9 The following discussion of Hindemith's opera is an abridged version of the present author's article 'Hindemiths Metaoper *Cardillac*', published in the *Festschrift* for Giselher Schubert's sixty-fifth birthday: Susanne Schaal-Gotthardt, Luitgard Schader, and Heinz Jürgen Winkler (eds.), *"… dass alles auch hätte anders kommen können": Beiträge zur Musik des 20. Jahrhunderts*, Frankfurter Studien: Veröffentlichungen des Hindemith-Instituts Frankfurt am Main, 12 (Mainz: Schott, 2009), 194–217. I wish to thank the firm of Schott for kindly granting permission to publish.

10 The first version of *Cardillac*, Op. 39 (1926), was edited by Christoph Wolff in series 1, vol. IV of *Paul Hindemith: Sämtliche Werke* (1979–80). See also Giselher Schubert's 'Zur Konzeption der Musik in Hindemiths Oper "Cardillac"', *Hindemith-Jahrbuch*, 17 (1988), 114–28; and 'Hindemiths Bearbeitungen eigener und fremder Werke: Ein Überblick' in Schweizerische Musikforschende Gesellschaft (ed.), *Bearbeitung in der Musik: Colloquium Kurt von Fischer zum 70. Geburtstag*, Schweizer Jahrbuch für Musikwissenschaft, new ser. 3, 1983 (Bern and Stuttgart: Paul Haupt, 1986), 105–14.

11 *Cardillac: Oper in vier Akten nach einer Bühnenhandlung von Ferdinand Lion, Text und Musik von Paul Hindemith* (Mainz: Schott, 1952) (vocal score, full score, and libretto).

12 See Elisabeth Schwind, 'Die Künstlerproblematik in Hindemiths "Cardillac": Zur zweiten Fassung von 1952', *Hindemith-Jahrbuch*, 22 (1993), 97–132; Thomas Seedorf, 'Des Goldschmieds neue Kleider: Zur Zweitfassung des "Cardillac"', *Hindemith-Jahrbuch*, 22 (1993), 133–57; and Susanne Schaal, 'Wahn und Wille: Hindemiths Bearbeitung des Duetts Nr. 16 aus "Cardillac" (1952)', *Hindemith-Jahrbuch*, 23 (1994), 103–23.

13 The source references from the Hindemith Institute (Frankfurt am Main) are listed in Schaal, 'Wahn und Wille', 104ff. (105). In actual fact, the reworking of the opera continued beyond the Zurich première of the new version (spring 1952) and lasted until autumn of that same year. A final revision, the duet between the Erste Sängerin and Cardillac (no. 16), even dates from 1961; see *ibid.*, 103–11.

14 See the richly informative study by Caroline Gommel, *Prosa wird Musik: Von Hoffmanns 'Fräulein von Scuderi' zu Hindemiths 'Cardillac'*, Rombach Wissenschaften, Reihe Cultura 24 (Freiburg im Breisgau: Rombach, 2002).

15 Seedorf, 'Des Goldschmieds neue Kleider', 135f. After joining the Music Department of Yale University, Hindemith resumed, with great commitment, the early music activities he had formerly conducted in Berlin. It was for these purposes that he obtained, in the United States, photographic reproductions of a vocal score of Lully's *Phaëton*, published in the series *Chefs-d'œuvre de l'opéra français* (1900).
16 See Werner Wolf's entry on 'Mise en abyme' in Ansgar Nünning (ed.), *Metzler Lexikon Literatur- und Kulturtheorie: Ansätze – Personen – Grundbegriffe*, 2nd edn (Stuttgart and Weimar: Metzler, 2001), 442f.
17 Vocal score, 168.
18 The second version deleted several especially garish stylistic elements of the Roaring Twenties, such as the four jazz drums, and made the orchestration leaner as a whole. Seedorf, 'Des Goldschmieds neue Kleider', 153.
19 A functionalistic view of this concept can be found in Hermann Danuser's entry on 'Neue Musik' in Ludwig Finscher (ed.), *Die Musik in Geschichte und Gegenwart*, Sachteil, 2nd edn, 10 vols. (Kassel: Bärenreiter; Stuttgart and Weimar: Metzler, 1997), vol. VII, cols. 75–122.
20 Schubert, 'Zur Konzeption'.
21 Hindemith, as we are told by Seedorf in 'Des Goldschmieds neue Kleider' (136), travelled from New York to Le Havre in summer 1951, sailing with the Cunard Line on the RMS *Mauretania*.
22 The 1994 CD recording of Lully's *Phaëton* with solo vocalists, the Vocal Sagittarius Ensemble and Les Musiciens du Louvre, conducted by Marc Minkowski (a co-production of Erato and Radio France, MF 4509-91737-2), departs markedly in sound and performance aesthetic from the ideals that Hindemith might have espoused for a mid-century performance of this work.
23 Vocal score, 140.
24 See Lucien Dällenbach, *Le récit spéculaire: Essai sur la mise en abyme*, Collection Poétique (Paris: Seuil, 1977); Eng. trans. by Jeremy Whiteley and Emma Hughes as *The Mirror in the Text* (Cambridge: Polity; Oxford: Blackwell, 1989).
25 See Horst Bredekamp, *Der Künstler als Verbrecher: Ein Element der frühmodernen Rechts- und Staatstheorie*, Reihe Themen 90 (Munich: Carl Friedrich von Siemens Stiftung, 2008).
26 Libretto, 31f. and 44; vocal score, 171ff. and 250ff; full score, 227f. and 363ff.
27 See Harald Fricke's entry on 'Potenzierung' in Klaus Weimar (ed.), *Reallexikon der deutschen Literaturwissenschaft* (Berlin and New York: Walter de Gruyter, 2003), vol. III, 144–7 (144).
28 Full score, 226–8.
29 Libretto, 31 and 44.
30 See the libretto of the first version, *Cardillac: Oper in drei Akten (vier Bildern) von Ferdinand Lion, Musik von Paul Hindemith*, Op. 39 (Mainz: Schott, 1926), 36.
31 Libretto of 1952, 44.
32 Bredekamp, *Künstler als Verbrecher*.

33 Quoted in *ibid.*, 11.
34 E.T.A. Hoffmann, *Das Fräulein von Scuderi: Erzählung aus dem Zeitalter Ludwig des Vierzehnten* (Stuttgart: Reclam, 2002), 57.
35 *Ibid.*, 18.
36 *Ibid.*, 32.
37 Seedorf, 'Des Goldschmieds neue Kleider', 139ff.; see also Thomas Seedorf, '"Prima la musica": Über einige Sonderfälle musikalischer Lyrik' in Camilla Bork et al. (eds.), *Ereignis und Exegese: Musikalische Interpretation – Interpretation der Musik: Festschrift für Hermann Danuser zum 65. Geburtstag* (Schliengen: Argus, 2011), 459–67.
38 'Unsere Lose müssen sich zu einem einzigen verbinden'; vocal score, 187, from the 'Duett' no. 16 towards the end of Act III.

PART IV

Music, representation, and the concepts of East and West

13 Doing more than representing western music

RACHEL BECKLES WILLSON

While it is still pragmatically convenient to talk about 'western' music, there is little doubt that those of us who do so are on shaky ground. Robert C. Young's reflections on the broader context capture the provisionality and precariousness very neatly: 'Western culture', he writes, is 'a culture which consistently fantasizes itself as constituting some kind of integral totality, at the same time as endlessly deploring its own impending dissolution.'[1] And Edward Said's *Orientalism*, Young argues, was not only trapped in the dichotomy of 'west' and 'non-west' that it sought to problematize. Rather, while constructing 'the Orient' as an invention of western thought, it neglected to address the 'dislocation' that the invention revealed. 'Western culture' must be seen as fundamentally fractured, an imagined entity whose 'others' are products of internal heterogeneity rather than external boundaries.

One of the ways in which relationships between musical 'westernness' and 'non-westernness' have been posited is through the conceptualization of music as a system of representation. In such work, western music is treated analogously to Said's 'colonial discourse', understood as an instrument that categorizes, controls, and erases its 'others', as desirable in the prevailing political or aesthetic frames of reference.[2] But this way of working with music is open to the same critiques that have risen to meet the analysis of colonial discourses more broadly. To what extent, after all, can one reconcile the gulf between the aesthetic or bureaucratic languages under analysis, and the actions of colonial powers on the ground? What is the relationship between the representation and material conditions? Bhabha's intervention may help, as he notes that the ambivalence of discourse allows us to gain a more dynamic grasp of the interaction between colonizer and subject; but his own framework (drawing on psychoanalytic and poststructuralist theory) is often extremely remote from the site of colonization.[3] And much work on music is locked, similarly, in a sphere of symbolic representation.

In recent years, humanities and social science research has benefited from a new concern with materiality. Alongside anthropology's affective turn, of particular note is the rise of 'non-representational theory', which seeks explicitly to move beyond surfaces, forms, and meanings to grasp practice, process, embodiment, and performativity.[4] Whereas attention to representation often tends to create a flattened reading, over-determined by pre-existing categories, non-representational theory strives to trace the indiscipline of the world, its vitalities and virtualities. Such endeavours cannot escape the use of sources that are representations, however, especially when scholars attempt to write about the past; and Lorimer has suggested that a better term may be 'more-than-representational', which embraces a range of approaches to representations. It does not entirely neglect, but nevertheless looks beyond, their formal and symbolic dimensions.[5]

In this chapter I explore the west's 'dislocation' as identified by Young, and attempt also to use historical representations as a means to thinking *beyond* representation. On one level, I am interested in what happens if we consider how the (fractured) entity of 'western music' might be read away from home, namely in the colonizing contexts from which its various systems of representation sought to separate it. On another level, I am concerned to move beyond the sharp dichotomy between the western entity on the one hand, and the colonial contexts on the other – a dichotomy that has tended to be established by scholars themselves.

One of Said's claims in *Orientalism*, after all, was that visitors to the Middle East who wrote about their experiences tended to 'excise' themselves from their texts. This was, he argued, related to the disguises that they often wore and their deception of the people they met (wearing Muslim dress and feigning devotion), which allowed them the position of unseen observers. Their apparent invisibility, he suggested, facilitated apparently 'objective' accounts of what they had seen.[6] Timothy Mitchell took the argument further in his exploration of Egypt's colonization, connecting the hidden spectator to modern practices of surveillance and control.[7] Notwithstanding their enticing acuity, these interpretations establish problematically sharp differences between observers and observed, rendering the infiltration of colonial figures smoothly clinical. And they do not consider how disguises and deception often fail, that there is indeed a great deal of indeterminacy involved in encounter. Thus my concern is to examine texts that allow us some insights into these neglected dimensions, and to set in motion some new ways of reading both representations and (the imagined boundaries of) western music.

Whereas in the first section below my examples are taken from visitors' reports on late Ottoman Palestine, in the second section I consider a school song book published in Jerusalem in 1921, a year in which the British were ruling Palestine under a League of Nations Mandate. Recent scholarship addressing 'westernness' has argued persuasively that it is something under constant production and appropriation in a range of places and for a range of agendas and uses.[8] This book is a case in point: 'westernness' is a productive practice in Arab circles, as much as an idea that can be represented. So I place this songbook in the context of broader political currents in order to reflect how it can be read as a great deal 'more-than' a representation.

Representation and excessive feeling

One of the most-discussed examples of a European response to music in 'the Orient' is by Guillaume André Villoteau (1759–1839), who contributed writings to the collected reports of the Napoleonic Expedition. As A.J. Racy has eloquently demonstrated, Villoteau's texts strive to represent the highly charged emotionality of music-making among Arabs in Egypt, yet also reveal his shock, a product of 'this European's musical upbringing and his intellectual background, which was rooted in the climate of the enlightenment that engulfed late eighteenth century Europe'.[9]

Villoteau's shock, and the comparable consternation (and fascination) of European writers hearing Arab music in subsequent decades, must indeed be grasped through the changing conceptualization of music in Europe. During the late eighteenth and the nineteenth centuries, claims about music's inherently beneficent qualities were disseminated increasingly broadly, and a set of basic ideas became normative through the entry of music into schools. Newly constructed as a medium of harmony and moral elevation, institutionalized forms of music were represented and practised as if they were tools of betterment, superior to 'other' types of music. David Gramit has observed the secularizing impulse of the change. A rationally systematized 'nature' effectively replaced the received chorale as the ground of musical knowledge, he argues, just as new methods of teaching literacy replaced traditional dependence on the Bible or the catechism.[10] He reads the resultant pedagogical ideas of Hans Georg Nägeli and contemporaries as an example of Foucault's disciplinary practices in the modern age.[11]

On one level, an awareness of this newly disciplined and secular background has already been used to explain writers' representations of 'the Orient'. Charles Hirschkind has observed that European travellers tended to find the Middle East excessively noisy and gestural (in distinction from the quiet orderliness in their lives at home), and a range of music scholars have discussed western disparagement of 'Oriental' music in the context of enlightenment thought.[12] On another level, however, there is an unexplored space to consider. Namely, such texts need not be read so much as representations of an 'Orient', but can equally be considered as expressions of emotion and even physical discomfort that the writers themselves experienced, but sought to project away from themselves.

For example, in the following text we can trace the orderly representation that British surveyor Lieutenant Mantell was required to deliver. But we also note that when he refers directly to sonorities, he breaks out of the mould and intimates discomforting experiences – experiences that were his own, and were at least in part visceral.[13]

The Zikr now began in earnest, with the beating of drums and clashing of cymbals; of the latter there were three pairs, which were used in turn by different derwishes in the ring. Two of the drums, being large, were beaten by men standing up behind the ring; the remaining drum was much smaller, and could be managed by a performer who was sitting down. This music was exactly the same as that which is heard at the time of the pilgrimage to the shrine of Moses, and on Mohammed's birthday, and other similar occasions. At intervals one or two of the number would break out into a loud and tuneless Arab song…

The performance on the drums and cymbals described above lasted some seven or eight minutes, becoming towards the end rather painfully loud. At a pre-arranged signal it suddenly ceased, and one of the derwishes was left singing a rude chant…

This was followed by a third prayer, and this prayer by a short but very violent Zikr. The sound certainly greatly resembled the barking of dogs, to which it has been frequently compared.[14]

The sharpness of the representations lies in their implicit dichotomies: tuneless/tune, painfully loud and rude/pleasurable and polite, animal/human, and so on. If a particular kind of 'western' music is evidence of goodness, so apparently dissimilar practices can be read as a sign of something being amiss. But the sensual discomfort of the writer has contributed to the creation of the representations, which retain traces of embodiment and emotionality. Seeking this out more broadly, I suggest in the next two examples, allows us some new perspectives.

First, a text by Swiss physician Titus Tobler (1806–77), who was probably the most prolific and incisive German-language writer on Palestine in the nineteenth century.[15] Even while his intellectual and financial independence allowed him a certain detachment from the primary institutions of academic and religious intervention, he was taken as a model for the endeavours of the Deutsche Palästina Verein when it was formed in the year of his death.[16] He is still respected for his cartographic and bibliographic work, although research remains to be done on his immense output as an author of books and popular articles.

The text I discuss here, including an account of a visiting choir from France, is one of a number of popular articles. It describes parts of a pilgrimage to the region that involved (among other things) singing at a Christmas mass in Bethlehem, and the rebaptism of some young people in the River Jordan. The trip to the Jordan was hazardous, so the choir's director Mr Roland had to employ a large number of guides from a range of localities, hiring no fewer than thirty men from the sheikh in the village of Abu Dis alone. Tobler joined the group.[17]

His narrative about the initial arrival at the Jordan indicates that the ceremony started well. A gentle celebratory humour may be sensed from his suggestion that the music was so pleasurable that the land itself stood to benefit:

Holding up the singers' flag depicting harps and inscriptions, Mr Roland led sixteen singers to the bank of the Jordan, and had them kneel down in a semi-circle looking towards the river; he consecrated the flag, and rebaptized the youths by sprinkling them with water from the Jordan and exhorting them to be good Roman Catholics. Then they intoned a powerful song facing the river and the land once assigned to the tribe of Ruben, and it sounded glorious under the roaring applause of the Jordan. Scarcely can this river have heard such a harmonious song.[18]

Moving on in his account, however, Tobler suggests increasing restlessness about the whole matter, which extended over three hours:

I have to admit that the ponderous ways of the Director, the little stewards, the superstitious dunking of various objects into the Jordan, the gathering of reeds and willow branches, were embarrassingly tedious.

Finally, Tobler reports that Roland was so involved with these pious activities that he repetitively disregarded the local guides on whom he depended, and who attempted to communicate with him. Fed up, they took off, taking with them the donkeys carrying provisions. The party was left waiting for Roland, and then facing the long and hazardous trip onwards, unguided, unprotected, and without food or drink.

One of the interesting qualities in the text is that it presents a western visitor, as opposed to local people, as gripped by religious fervency to the extent that he loses his grasp of material realities. First, the bare fact of the religiosity is worth noting, for the post-Saidian narrative of Orientalism has been, as Marchand has put it, a 'secularization story'.[19] In other words, the idea has prevailed that Enlightenment replaced religion in the 'west' to the extent that research became a 'secular' practice; and that this secular vision or growing 'western rationality' became a means to degrade 'irrational' and 'religious' practices elsewhere. In fact religious practices and beliefs were a constituent part of Orientalist research even when it was practised in academic environments. In Germany in particular, research into the Bible was one of the animators of research into the Middle East, and debates over religious doctrine played out as powerfully in academic departments as in the church and state institutions.[20]

Second, the religious use of music is telling: as I indicated above, nineteenth-century European music education has been understood as a secular trend in which rational principles replaced religious ones. But in fact there was not a full displacement: music did of course continue to be closely entwined with religious practices.

Roland's loss of control over the precarious situation into which he had brought a large party of people, then, undermines the dichotomy between the spiritual East being captured for representation by the rational West. Tobler's account introduces the emotional turmoil that visitors lived through while visiting, and the sheer materiality of the region itself. The guides apparently left Roland at the Jordan because he did not listen to them. And they were doing a contracted job, whereas the visitors were immersing themselves in a religious experience. The *shared result* was chaotic.

My second example takes us further into the question of shared materialities. This is an article by one Reverend Raimund Graf, printed in a journal published by the Institute for Archaeology of the Holy Land in 1917. This institute was mooted at the time of the German Emperor's much-celebrated visit in 1898, and was formally founded in 1902 by the German Evangelical Church.[21] Theologian, linguist, and Bible scholar Gustaf Dalman was director from its opening until 1917, during which time he hosted a group of visiting researchers every year.[22] Dalman generally invited one senior scholar to be with him for nine months, and six less experienced researchers for periods of three to five months (they were often pastors – and Graf is one such case). Dalman created a curriculum and led the visitors on trips through the region, editing an annual collection of research papers, some of which included references to local music.[23]

Dalman had asked Graf to collect songs, and he guided his efforts to do this.[24] It was unusual for the time to cherish rather than denigrate the local music, and music found indeed a rather special place within Dalman's research framework. The land was for him always 'the Holy Land', even in its very climate, geology, and ecology;[25] and music seemed to Dalman to be a *part of that land*. As he later reflected, when he had undertaken his first research in Palestine in 1899, he found that song accompanied him everywhere, wove itself into his image of the country to such an extent that he could not think of it without those tones.[26] So his subsequent research process, understood as an encounter with *the land*, necessarily involved not only the land's visible elements such as mountains, lakes, and forests; rather, it would also involve aural ones, namely the 'wistful tones' of the shepherds' pipes and the songs of the ploughmen.[27]

If Dalman's attitude to the land was romantic, it was also prescriptive. The destiny of the people there, he claimed, was to be agrarian, because he perceived *the land* lending itself to that use.[28] In his vision, then, the people were simply functions of the land. One can trace a form of this stance in an article by one of his visitors, who noted that both folk songs and folk tales were inseparable components of agrarian practices. The visitor had wanted to hear a song sung at the mill, and the woman he asked told him he would have to come back when she was at the mill.[29] If song was inseparable from (agricultural) practice, then it was in fact a part of that practice (which was a destined product of the land). But the point of encountering the land and the music was not primarily intended to lead to a deep understanding of agricultural practice in the region. Rather, musical and other experiences of the land, according to Dalman, would have the function of bringing the Bible to life, and making the book a lifelong friend.[30]

Read as a whole, the work of Dalman's institute might be viewed as a classic case of Said's 'textual' reading of Orientalism, which Kirchhoff developed for the case of Palestine in his book *Text to Land*, and Nassar has explored with reference to photographic images.[31] Visitors came to the region with a textual representation in mind (in this case the Bible), and they sought to verify this, and, in some cases, to bring the land closer to the text. But to observe these trends is to echo what the visitors did. And it is not the only way to consider the resultant encounters, as I will now demonstrate.

One of Raimund Graf's articles provides six song texts and eight melodies gathered in the field, along with some quite detailed discussions about how he gained access to them.[32] One such discussion describes a session in the house of Graf's host, the teacher of Arabic at one of the German schools in Jerusalem, who arranged for a Muslim singer to come to his house in the village of Birzeit. Graf reveals that the musician performed his task for a fee, and was photographed in the courtyard; his account also includes a description of his exotic physical appearance: the player had an aquiline nose, for instance, and a 'fiery gaze'; he was wearing traditional dress and an overcoat, and seemed very self-assured. Graf also noted that the musician did not join 'the Christians beside us at the table', but sat on a mat from the wall. This was most likely a function of playing *rebaba* (spiked fiddle), yet the fact that Graf mentions all these material objects and sets up that distance at the outset is important. For in the ensuing description the relationship between these objects, the player, and Graf changes, and this intimates a change in dynamic that is disconcerting for Graf.

On describing the musical performance, it is initially another material object that comes into focus, namely the *rebaba*. Graf provides a detailed material description of the object (shape, measurements), and then elaborates how the musician's soul melted into the instrument. It seemed to him not only that the musician coaxed the instrument to produce a range of dynamics and colours, but also that the instrument coaxed the musician to give voice to his soul. Graf had animated the instrument, then, and set up an intimate union, one that was separate from himself.

Yet going on in his text, Graf admits to being astonished that the singer's passion could give way to 'cool calculation'. He observes his host laughing during the performance, but he himself does not understand what is happening; when the host explains, it emerges that the musician has made an appeal to him for a new overcoat.[33] During a subsequent piece, when Graf attempted to write down a melody being played, the musician noticed, and asked for an increased fee. This request, reported Graf, was repeated after the ensuing song too, and the singer *came over to the table where Graf was sitting*, and requested energetically. The separation, then, is broken: the musician has transgressed the territorial boundaries that had initially seemed fixed.

At the end of the account, Graf reports that the musician, on his way out, snatched a bag of onions from his host's father entering the house, whose response was to remark 'so sind sie' (that's what they're like). The comment sets up a new distance between the player and the others in the text, one that has been constantly apparent, but also in flux throughout the session. It reveals that the positioning of the mat, the table, the fee, the *rebaba* – all of which are signs that Graf is sensitive to the musician's apparently ambivalent relationship with physical objects – all these must also be imagined within a house in which the musician himself may well feel wholly a stranger.

There were plainly some local differences that may have created strangeness – the Muslim musician in a Christian establishment for instance – but we are in no position to interrogate those here. More pressing is a more fundamental strangeness, or a fundamentally estranging dynamic, namely that the musician was a representation in Graf's scheme even before the encounter had taken place. Across the threshold, his function was to slot into a role, to enable Graf to capture him on film, place him within a texted scenario, and create a textual form of his music to come in line with other representations of music in the west. In other words, the musician was to be harnessed in a process of objectification and acquisition. He was a specimen. (And had in fact already been 'collected' by Graf's landlord, whose reference to 'they' suggests that he understood him as an example of a type – as opposed to a singular human being.)

But as a collectable object the musician turned out to be 'excessive': he overflowed the boundaries of the representation that Graf sought to make of him. On the one hand, we might impute to him Bhabha's 'sly civility': he seemed to play the role expected of him for some time.[34] Yet, on the other hand, we can also sense his apparently tacit acceptance breaking down when he drew attention to the fact that he was – in Graf's world at the table – essentially a living commodity, not just a representation.

Representation and embodiment

In this section I discuss a songbook dating from 1921, the very early years of the Mandate government. It was published in Jerusalem by Khalil Totah (1886–1955), the then director of the Arab Teacher Training Institute that prepared teachers for schools throughout Palestine.[35] Figure 13.1 shows its front cover, an illustration signed by the lithographer Avraham Leib-Monsohn, a Jewish resident of the walled Old City who had established a printing press there in 1892. His montage brings together representations of violin, *oud*, *ney*, and musical scores, and the art nouveau-influenced style of decoration is complemented by olive branches, representative of local vegetation. Additionally, we see a woman perched upon a column and playing a lyre.

This reference to classical antiquity may well be the most telling element. Europe's self-construction in the nineteenth century had involved a rise of philhellenism among artists and writers (an enthusiasm for Greek remains in Italy and the work of Homer, for instance), and the institutionalization of 'Classical Antiquity' and 'Classical Archaeology' as fields of academic research. The latter were instrumental in creating a notion of European cultural 'roots' that by definition excluded 'the Orient' and Hebraic peoples completely.[36] By digging its foundations in Greece, 'Europe' managed to annex ancient Greece from its hinterland, erasing the manifold Hellenic

Figure 13.1 Front cover of *The School Song Collection*, ed. Khalil Totah (Jerusalem, 1921).

impact on other peoples in subsequent centuries: while ancient Greece was inextricably linked to Europe, 'other' cultures such as Hebraic and Islamic ones were apparently wildly different. Philhellenism, in other words, was one of the ways in which 'Europe' separated itself from 'Arab' and 'Jew'. The cover of this songbook, however, was provided by a Jew as a symbol of Arab education. It combines icons of classical antiquity and Europe with symbols of the Middle East more broadly. 'The Orient', then, has been integrated into the project of Enlightenment through a representation.

Totah himself presented his songbook in the Foreword as a contribution to Arab progress on the model of what he called 'advanced countries'. His autobiography offers a broader sense of what he meant. There he wrote, 'having known America and the West, I was consumed with the passion of doing my bit towards the creation of a new Arab World ... A new mutuality was needed, a fresh outlook and a modern approach.' He hoped the book would accomplish three things; namely, make students wish 'to seek knowledge', 'implant in them the love of the homeland', and provide them with 'a refreshing recreational activity to recharge their minds'.[37]

Postcolonial scholarship has demonstrated that the imitation of modern practices by colonized people is always simultaneously an exercise in producing difference. As a school songbook, Totah's collection was on the surface a production of sameness, for the genre of 'school song' was widespread in missionary establishments. But whereas the Anglican St George's School (to mention one example) used such songs to promote loyalty to various symbols of Englishness, royalty, and 'the Holy Land', the compilers of this songbook sought something close to their own aspirations. Even while not articulating an explicit claim to 'Palestine' by name, they express pride and loyalty to the place in various ways, in texts that were written afresh. The melodies, meanwhile, stemmed mainly from Europe, and one example is shown in Figure 13.2. Here the German song 'O Tannenbaum', well established as a Christmas Carol, has been adapted to fit the following text celebrating the work of the Teacher Training Institute. The western stave notation is adapted to be combinable with the Arabic text, which must be read from right to left.

The Song of the Institute for Teacher Training[38]
O Institute for Teacher Training, you remain the home of glory
For the ailment of ignorance is cured by those you graduate

Chorus: We cherish our homeland and those who live in it
          as long as for knowledge we have the teachers' school.

Figure 13.2 'The Song of the Institute for Teacher Training', from *The School Song Collection*, ed. Khalil Totah (Jerusalem, 1921).

The Institute for Teacher Training in the land of Palestine provides
Knowledge to cure our inner ailment

An institute where, if the thirsty stopped by, he would have his thirst quenched
And then leave the source of knowledge, his strength recharged

We are the soldiers of wisdom, who raise the flag of knowledge
With books and a pen we walk on to kill the humiliating ignorance

We would not relinquish knowledge, but rather we attain it
By sacrificing for it all that is precious to us

Go on, friends, walk on and strive so that you find success in knowledge
For you will never do well except with the education of children.

While 'difference' is often produced by a colonized people, the same process can be observed on the side of the colonizer as well. This is Bhabha's 'almost the same but not quite' (or 'white'), referencing the way that ruling authorities tend to retain hierarchies despite performing apparent inclusion.[39] It is germane here with respect to the differential relationships that the British government developed with its subjects. Palestine's majority population under the Ottomans was Arab Muslim, and even in 1914, following the mass immigration that had commenced in the early 1880s, the proportion of Jews was only 7.5 per cent.[40] Nevertheless, when the British took over Palestine, Foreign Secretary Arthur James Balfour's statement of 1917 became the basis for the region's organization in the following way:

> His Majesty's Government view with favour the establishment in Palestine of a national home for the Jewish people, and will use their best endeavours to facilitate the achievement of this object.

The majority population, however, emerged in his declaration as 'non-Jewish', and was to be somehow allowed to retain its rights despite a new state (predominantly of immigrants) in its midst:

> It being clearly understood that nothing shall be done which may prejudice the civil and religious rights of existing non-Jewish communities in Palestine.[41]

The effect was not only an ideational dichotomy between Jew and non-Jew, for when British rule in Palestine was formalized by the League of Nations in 1922 it became legally official. We do well to note that a parallel development inside Europe would lead the Nazi regime to make a distinction between Jew and non-Jew as well. There the polarization was 'Jew' against 'Aryan', whereas in Palestine the British set 'Jew' against 'Arab'.

One consequence was that Jews were given autonomy over their educational system and were thus at liberty to develop a proto-national structure, system, and curriculum. They were, then, allowed to make their own way towards existence as a modern nation. Arab education, however, was kept under colonial direction, and – according to colonial reports published at the end of the Mandate – neglected.[42] There was no comparable chance, then, for Arabs to establish themselves in the same way. Khalil Totah would go on to become director of the renowned Quaker Friends' Schools, and complained at the end of his time that attempts to take control of the Arab curriculum and integrate subjects such as music into it had been constantly obstructed by the British government.[43] It is this that makes the songbook particularly intriguing, because it runs so strongly against the grain of the ruling polity for Arabs. By commissioning such a potent illustration by a Jew for the front cover, moreover, Totah subverted the separation of 'Jew' from 'Non-Jew' that was the British government's strategy. So the songbook was an Arab-led collaboration with a Jew.

We can also use the book to think about a 'more-than' character. It is not only a representation of an interest in western practices, nor even just a critical 'production of the west'. It is also a material remnant of both more intimate and also broader interactions on a physical level. First, it required a face-to-face collaboration between the Kurdish Iraqi poet Marouf Al-Rusafi and Khalil Totah. According to one witness's recollections, Totah and his wife played the tunes on the piano in order that Al-Rusafi could write appropriate texts.[44] Second, Al-Rusafi's then residence in Jerusalem reminds us that Palestine was part of a network of regional connections with a broad hinterland. One of the chosen melodies amplifies this further for us, namely a popular song that had spread throughout the region during the Ottoman Empire, the Turkish title of which was 'On the way to Üsküdar' in reference to a district on the Asian side of Istanbul. Adopting this melody for words appropriate to local situations was standard practice in the region. Recalling the collaboration between Totah and the Jew Mohnson, and considering the use of a poem by an Iraqi Kurd and a regionally popular tune, we have a reminder that Palestine existed in a complex network of peoples in the region which Western forces separated out and reorganized, but did not wholly displace.

The absence of complete displacement is what enables us to reflect on the songbook today: its sheer materiality allows it to emerge. I discovered it in 2007 at the Friends School in Ramallah, where it was stored in a small archive that had been organized by an American teacher who worked there.⁴⁵ I have no sources regarding the number of copies that were printed in 1921, and no idea how many other copies have survived. It is the only copy that I have traced. The contextual information available about it comes from an article by Totah's daughter, Joy Totah Hilden, who interviewed one of her father's students from the teacher training college, Nicola Ziadeh. From her account, the songbook develops four further more-than representational dimensions.

First, we understand that Ziadeh developed a personal attachment to the songbook (for which he had paid one shilling). It was important to him as a physical object: 'he kept [the] book and took it with him everywhere he went'.⁴⁶ It was also something that he came to carry internally. Even in 2003, the date of the interview with Totah's daughter and over half a century after losing the book, he could recite several of Rusafi's poems, and tell her with which melodies they had been conjoined.

Second, when he graduated and worked as a teacher and historian, he used the songs at the school where he worked in Acre. Indeed, he taught 'the students to stand in formation in the yard and sing before going to class'.⁴⁷ The songbook was part of a practice of physical disciplining, then, which Ziadeh had learned as a student and transferred on to his students.

Third, it was a mediator of ideas about patriotism that was ambiguous, indeed overflowed itself, thanks to its music. According to Ziadeh, the British police came to investigate a report that children were singing the Marseillaise in the yard of the school where he taught. On receiving an explanation, the officer 'laughed and the matter was dropped'. Ziadeh does not elucidate the nature of his explanation, but if it involved an account of the song text published with the melody in the songbook, the officer could have been reassured that the intent was not revolutionary. Rather, the text evinces a somewhat embattled heroism, and a plural, implicitly *generic* concept of 'homelands', as if making a general point about the virtue of patriotism.

Finally, the materiality of the songbook, along with the emotional attachment to it and the ideas it embodies, prefaced loss, and subsequent emotion. For Ziadeh, it was among his many possessions that were destroyed in the war of 1948 that displaced Palestinian Arabs. Hilden's article states that 'everything' was lost, but mentions family photographs, academic books, and this songbook specifically as concrete examples. Thus the songbook was a material trace of a lost land and a lost network. It had embodied resistance in 1921 – in the form of collaboration with a Jew, and with Arab self-development – but these ideas and the book itself had become mourned reliquaries. As an object, the songbook could be remembered and named: it was a tangible trace of lost worlds.

Notes

I address this material more broadly in *Orientalism and Musical Mission: Palestine and the West* (Cambridge University Press, 2013).

1 Robert J.C. Young, *White Mythologies: Writing History and the West* (New York and London: Routledge, 2004), 180.
2 Georgina Born and David Hesmondhalgh (eds.), *Western Music and Its Others: Difference, Representation, and Appropriation in Music* (Berkeley and Los Angeles: University of California Press, 2000).
3 Homi Bhabha, *The Location of Culture*, 2nd edn (New York and London: Routledge, 2004).
4 Nigel Thrift pioneered early work. See Nigel Thrift, *Spatial Formations* (London: Sage, 1996); and 'Afterwords', *Environment and Planning D: Society and Space*, 18.2 (2000), 213–55.
5 Hayden Lorimer, 'Cultural Geography: The Busyness of Being "More-than-Representational"', *Progress in Human Geography*, 29.1 (2005), 83–94.
6 Edward W. Said, *Orientalism* (London: Vintage Books, 1978), 160–4.
7 Timothy Mitchell, *Colonising Egypt*, 2nd edn (Berkeley and Los Angeles: University of California Press, 1991), 27–8.
8 Alastair Bonnett, *The Idea of the West: Culture, Politics and History* (Hampshire and New York: Palgrave Macmillan, 2004); Xiaomei Chen, *Occidentalism: A Theory of Counter-Discourse in Post-Mao China*, 2nd edn (Oxford University Press, 2002).
9 A.J. Racy, *Making Music in the Arab World: The Culture and Artistry of Tarab* (Cambridge University Press, 2003), 2.
10 David Gramit, *Cultivating Music: The Aspirations, Interests, and Limits of German Musical Culture, 1770–1848* (Berkeley and Los Angeles: University of California Press, 2002), 103.
11 *Ibid.*, 106–9.
12 Charles Hirschkind, *The Ethical Soundscape: Cassette Sermons and Islamic Counterpublics* (New York: Columbia University Press, 2006), 14–15. For a discussion of French disparagement in the context of nineteenth-century racial theory, see Jann Pasler, 'Theorizing Race in Nineteenth-Century France: Music as Emblem of Identity', *Musical Quarterly*, 89.4 (Winter 2006), 459–504. See also Bennett Zon, '"Violent Passions" and "Inhuman Excess": Simplicity and the Representation of Non-Western Music in Nineteenth-Century British Travel Literature', in Martin Clayton and Bennett Zon (eds.), *Music and Orientalism in the British Empire, 1780s-1940s* (Aldershot and Burlington, VT: Ashgate, 2007), 209–36. For reflections on musicology's grappling with non-western sounds, see also Alexander Rehding, 'Wax Cylinder Revolutions', *Musical Quarterly*, 88.1 (Spring 2005), 123–60.

13 A.M. Mantell, 'A Zikr Ceremony', *Palestine Exploration Fund Quarterly Statement*, (1882), 160–3 (160).
14 *Ibid.*, 161, 162, and 163.
15 Tobler was not trained as a Palestine researcher. Early in his career he spent his spare time encouraging further education among doctors, researching regional dialects, then studying local demography and editing a newspaper. The big change came in 1835, when he took a holiday to Egypt, also visiting Bethlehem, Jaffa, and Jerusalem. For recent accounts of Tobler's biography, see Alex Carmel, '"Jerusalem muss unser werden." Titus Tobler und der "Christenstaat"' in Heiko Haumann (ed.), *Der Traum von Israel: Die Ursprünge des modernen Zionismus* (Weinheim: Beltz Athenäum Verlag, 1998), 65–88; and Haim Goren, *'Zieht hin und erforscht das Land'. Die deutsche Palästinaforschung im 19. Jahrhundert* (Göttingen: Wallstein Verlag, 2003).
16 Markus Kirchhoff, *Text zu Land: Palästina im wissenschaftlichen Diskurs 1865–1920*, Schriften des Simon-Dubnow-Instituts Herausgegeben von Dan Diner, vol. V (Göttingen: Vandenhoeck & Ruprecht, 2005), 167.
17 The trip provided Tobler with material to publish an extended, serialized article three years later (see next note) and relieve his difficult financial situation thereby. For discussion of Tobler's financial difficulties in that period, see Heinrich Jacob Heim, *Dr. Titus Tobler der Palästinafahrer. Ein appenzellisches Lebensbild* (Zürich and Trogen, 1879), 63.
18 Titus Tobler, 'Spaziergang von Jerusalem nach dem Jordan und toten Meere', *Das Ausland*, 57.8 (1947), 225–7, 230–1, 234–5, and 238–9. For this quotation see page 238.
19 Suzanne L. Marchand, *German Orientalism in the Age of Empire: Religion, Race, and Scholarship* (Cambridge University Press, 2009).
20 Kirchhoff, *Text zu Land*; Goren, *'Zieht hin'*; Marchand, *German Orientalism*.
21 Goren, *'Zieht hin'*, 347.
22 Dalman is under-represented in English-language research. For a detailed introduction to his life and thought, see Julia Männchen, *Gustaf Dalmans Leben und Wirkung in der Brüdergemeinde, für die Judenmission und an der Universität Leipzig 1855–1902* (Wiesbaden: Harrassowitz, 1987); and *Gustaf Dalman als Palästinawissenschaftler in Jerusalem und Greifswald 1902–1941* (Wiesbaden: Harrassowitz, 1993).
23 Goren, *'Zieht hin'*, 350–1.
24 Raimund Graf, 'Durch das Heilige Land westlich und östlich des Jordans im Jahre 1911', *Palästinajahrbuch*, 13 (1917), 103–38; and 'Ostertage auf dem Gebirge Ephraim', *Palästinajahrbuch*, 14 (1918), 111–34.
25 Männchen, *Gustaf Dalman als Palästinawissenschaftler*, 207–8.
26 Gustaf Dalman, *Palästinischer Diwan. Als Beitrag zur Volkskunde Palästinas* (Leipzig: J.C. Hinrichs'sche Buchhandlung, 1901), VII.
27 Gustaf Dalman, 'Das religiöse Ziel unsere Arbeit', *Palästinajahrbuch*, 9 (1913), 3–5 (4–5).

28 Männchen, *Gustaf Dalman als Palästinawissenschaftler*, 210.
29 Hans Schmidt, 'Die Kunst der Volkserzählung bei palästinischen Bauern', *Palästinajahrbuch*, 9 (1913), 133–54 (134).
30 Dalman, 'Das religiöse Ziel', 4–5.
31 Kirchhoff, *Text zu Land*; Issam Nassar, *European Portrayals of Jerusalem: Religious Fascinations and Colonialist Imaginations* (Lewiston, Queenston, and Lampeter: The Edwin Mellen Press: 2006).
32 Graf, 'Durch das Heilige Land'.
33 Graf states not only that this plea occurred 'at the end' of the performance, but also that it occurred before the musician finished playing. The implication is that the plea was sung, and indeed sung in many variations. *Ibid.*, 128.
34 Bhabha, *The Location of Culture*, 93–101.
35 Housed in the Archive of the Friends School in Ramallah.
36 In the broader political sphere the movement led in 1830 to the support of a Greek uprising and 'liberation' from the Ottomans. Kirchhoff, *Text zu Land*, 39–66. See also Marchand, *German Orientalism*, 106–13.
37 Khalil Totah, *Biographical Statement* (n.d.), www.passia.org/images/personalities/totah-khalil/khalil-text.htm, accessed 17 February 2012.
38 The translation is by Nada Elzeer. The Arabic original has rhyming lines, but the purpose of this translation is simply to render its primary content, rather than its literary style.
39 Bhabha, *The Location of Culture*, 85–9.
40 An estimated 10,000 Jews lived there prior to the first wave of Russian arrivals (1882–1903), and after the second wave of immigration (1905–14) the community had increased to an estimated 60,000, within a population of 798,389 people (657,377 Muslim, Druze, Shia, including estimated nomadic figures, plus 81,012 Christian). These figures include estimates for many who were not registered as citizens. Justin McCarthy, *The Population of Palestine: Population History and Statistics of the Late Ottoman Period and the Mandate* (New York: Columbia University Press, 1990), 13 and 22.
41 For a more detailed discussion of the matter see Avi Shlaim, *Israel and Palestine* (London: Verso, 2009), 3–24.
42 The classic work on the subject is A.L. Tibawi, *Arab Education in Mandatory Palestine* (London: Luzac & Co, 1956).
43 Thomas M. Ricks, 'Khalil Totah: The Unknown Years', *Jerusalem Quarterly*, 34 (2009), 51–77 (65).
44 Joy Totah Hilden, 'Totah and Ziadeh: Mentor and Student', *Jerusalem Quarterly*, 32 (Autumn, 2007), 94–102 (99–100).
45 Donn Hutchison. My thanks to Donn for relocating the songbook after the archive was moved, and to the staff at the Friends School for scanning images on my behalf.
46 Hilden, 'Totah and Ziadeh', 100.
47 *Ibid.*, 99–100.

14 | The persistence of Orientalism in the postmodern operas of Adams and Sellars

W. ANTHONY SHEPPARD

Representation of exotic peoples, places, and performances has long been prevalent in multiple genres of Western music, but it has particularly inspired the operatic imagination.[1] Opera is, of course, more generally concerned with musical representation as composers are called upon to depict setting, period, character type, and dramatic situation. Over the course of its four-century existence, opera has developed multiple representational systems that have proven resilient in the face of stylistic change. For example, specific techniques for characterizing the unification of lovers, madness, or the supernatural can be traced across periods and national traditions. Techniques for representing the exotic also appear quite durable.

Exoticism is simultaneously just another form of dramatic representation in opera and is treated and experienced differently from other modes of representation. In representing characters and performances that the intended audience will consider distinctly foreign, operatic composers may be viewed as displacing exotic others and their performances. When a composer, librettist, director, and performers represent two lovers on the operatic stage, we do not normally protest that this representation has displaced actual lovers who might have mounted the stage themselves. Rather, our critical discussion focuses on whether the depiction of love was convincing and moving. Of instrumental genres, we query whether the representation of such emotions and dramatic situations is possible without some reference to prior systems of representation in dramatic and texted genres. The situation is somewhat reversed when it comes to the operatic representation of exotic peoples, places, and performances. In conjunction with the libretto and staging, musical representation of the exotic in opera is not normally considered problematic in terms of efficacy, but instead has prompted questions concerning its political and social ramifications. It is generally taken for granted that audiences recognize the musical signals of the exotic, whether consciously or not, or that at least this form of representation succeeds in marking some characters, locales, and performances as separate from the world of the intended audience, thereby marking other characters, locales, and performances as 'normal'. Critical discussion is more animated by the question of whether this system of representation materially shapes an audience's views of those represented.

The terms 'exoticism' and 'Orientalism' have increasingly been used interchangeably. Indeed, 'Orientalist opera' serves as something of a genre label and (misleadingly) as a period designation, referring particularly to the late nineteenth and early twentieth centuries. It was especially during this period that specific representational devices were so frequently employed as to become codified. Throughout its history, Orientalist representation has involved a 'presenting again' of devices and stereotypical signs that have worked effectively in the past and that are repeatedly recycled. These representational devices stem from a variety of sources. Composers of musical Orientalism (and thus scholars) tend to work at the intersection of representation and influence, with specific gestures towards 'exotic authenticity' helping to shore up the work's claims to represent the other in the opera house.

Composers of Orientalist opera face two crucial representational tasks: clearly marking certain characters as exotic and realizing exotic performances within the narrative. Most nineteenth-century Orientalist operas feature at least one scene devoted to the spectacle of exotic performance, often in the form of a ballet or a performed song. Indeed, representations of exotic performance were so prevalent that they even appear in operas not otherwise devoted to exotic representation, as in the 'gypsy' performance in Act II, scene 2 of Verdi's *La Traviata*. In such operas devoid of exotic characters, European characters may be inspired to Orientalist cross-dressing in order to allow for exotic spectacles nevertheless. It is in these sections of the score – the representation of exotic performances within the opera – that the composer attempts most clearly to match in sound the exotic decor of the production.

Getting over Orientalism?

Is exotic representation a feature only of the operatic past? Modernism is frequently represented historically as having been inhospitable to musical representation *in toto*. Similarly, the new political awareness accorded to postmodernism is thought to have made certain forms of representation inadmissible in recent decades. Multiple studies assume that the techniques and motivations of Orientalist representation belong to the genre's past, that opera, at some ill-defined moment, moved 'beyond exoticism'.

For instance, Ralph Locke – the scholarly dean of musical exoticism – has referred to the 'discouraging impact of musical modernism on overt explorations of the musically exotic' and, with reference to contemporary operas, Herbert Lindenberger has stated, 'it is clear that the operatic Orient visible in recent works is scarcely orientalist in any earlier sense'.[2] When faced with undeniable elements of exotic representation in recent operas, scholars and critics have repeatedly argued that parody is in play or, at least, that the signifiers of exoticism are no longer potent. Numerous composers, librettists, and directors likewise have declared their distance from the Orientalist past in reference to their own representations of exotic subject matter. However, these alleged ruptures with past forms of musical representation have been exaggerated. Neither modernist abstraction nor postmodern political sensitivity has inoculated operas composed in the past century from Orientalist representation. In short, operatic Orientalism is not dead yet.

My focus in this chapter is less on the political and social implications of Orientalism in postmodern operas than it is on revealing the persistence of this form of representation and suggesting that our scholarly categories and period designations have obscured this feature of contemporary opera. Rather than aiming critical barbs at specific composers for failing to avoid Orientalism in their exotic representations, my true target here is the undying concept of historical progress in the arts, specifically the notion that Romantic and modernist means and meanings in musical representation of the exotic have been overcome in the postmodern era. I will focus neither on artistic intent nor on audience reception, but instead offer my observations on the continuity that we may hear and see between operatic examples of exotic representation from the recent and more remote pasts.

A necessary next step will be to determine whether these recent operas are Orientalist in the same ways as are exemplars from the nineteenth century or whether exotic representation functions differently in postmodern works. Noting the presence of traditional Orientalist representational techniques in recent works is not necessarily the same critical assertion that these works are themselves to be labelled 'Orientalist'. Are the parallels with earlier Orientalist opera another sign of the general postmodern recycling of the artistic past? Whether or not parody is in play, are these works inadvertently perpetuating stereotypes? Is it possible that, regardless of authorial intent, such operas continue to teach contemporary audiences how to think about the exotic culture being represented and that this representation supports larger political agendas?

To test these claims I have investigated operas and music theatre works from the past three decades by a variety of composers, including (from A to Z) John Adams, John Corigliano, Philip Glass, Meredith Monk, Wolfgang Rihm, Bright Sheng, Tan Dun, Judith Weir, and Evan Ziporyn.[3] I have likewise considered recent trends in the production of canonical Orientalist operas, such as *Madama Butterfly*, *Turandot*, *Samson et Dalila*, and *The Mikado*.[4] The issues raised by productions of old Orientalist works and by new operas engaging in exotic representation are similar. To a surprising degree, the musical methods and specific signs of nineteenth-century Orientalism persist in contemporary works and exotic 'influence' and exotic 'representation' remain tightly intertwined. This is evident even in cases when composers and directors have struggled to create forms of exotic representation devoid of all Orientalist overtones and, conversely, in works that deliberately incorporate and reframe the Orientalist musical past in the attempt to undermine it. The continued popularity of certain older Orientalist operas results in intertextual influence on the creation of new works and inevitably shapes audience expectations and experiences of contemporary opera. Representational intent may well be radically different from the past, but execution and, I suspect, impact exhibit strong strands of continuity. Despite what may seem a contradiction in terms, this chapter offers examples of postmodern operatic Orientalist representation.

John Adams and Peter Sellars as postmodern multiculturalists

A particularly promising opportunity for investigating exotic representation in contemporary opera is offered by the collaborative works of Adams and Sellars, two of the most prominent American figures in the history of opera. Both are routinely celebrated for their postmodern and multicultural sensibilities; thus, their operatic collaborations should serve for the most rigorous of test cases seeking to determine whether Orientalist representation has been transcended in recent opera and music theatre. Exotic influence and exotic representation are prominently featured in all of their major collaborations and their techniques of representation and specific musical and theatrical details in these works repeatedly echo the operatic past. Indeed, certain examples of their exoticist collaborative work point back to specific modernist models.

Adams's interest in both cross-cultural influence and exotic representation has been evident throughout much of his career. He has pointed to the music of George Harrison as sparking an interest in traditions beyond the Euro-American sphere and has said that non-Western music 'opened up my ears in a radical way', introducing him to new scales, approaches to improvisation, and inflection in intonation.[5] When asked about future directions for opera, Adams once remarked: 'It is also possible that things could go in another direction, something far more ritual, like what Meredith Monk does, or something far more influenced by music theater from other cultures, like Gagaku or Noh, or ritual music theater from Sufi culture or Indonesia.'[6] Several of his instrumental works exemplify Adams's delight in revelling in exotic associations and the musical multicultural. For example, the electronic synthesized piece *Hoodoo Zephyr* (1993) includes a track entitled 'Tourist Song' which features a tabla-like line. The liner notes include the following programmatic offering from Adams:

Tourists everywhere. / (Where are we now?) / Madras on my mind. / Potted plants in the lobby, / Wicker furniture, men in white Panamas. / Pipe dream: a Benares Song in just intonation. / Naked sirens glissening, beckoning. / Tablas ticking. / Nocturnal transmissions.

Perhaps this hep, fragmented, exotic reverie was offered as an ironic and distancing comment by the composer on this track. The music, with its ticking tabla, does not tell.

For several of their collaborative projects, Sellars clearly served as a multicultural guide for Adams. Throughout his career, Sellars has been engaged in cross-cultural explorations.[7] His is likely one of the first names in American theatre that the phrase 'Pacific Rim outlook' calls to mind and he consistently presents himself as an enthusiastic citizen of the multicultural world. He has long taught in the University of California, Los Angeles Department of World Arts and Cultures and served as the director of the Pacific Rim Festival in 1990. As a teenager, he apprenticed with a marionette company in Pittsburgh where he encountered *bunraku* techniques. At Harvard, he studied with a retired *kabuki* performer and his interest in Japanese theatrical forms has been furthered by numerous trips to Japan. Sellars has declared that Noh is 'the most profound theater I know of' and he has repeatedly staged Noh plays.[8] His directorial work has included a 1983 production of *The Mikado* set in present-day Japan for the Chicago Lyric Opera, a collaboration with Tan Dun on an adaptation of the classic Chinese *kunju* opera *The Peony Pavilion* in 1998, and a staging of Bach cantatas in 2001 that incorporated Tibetan Buddhist ritual elements. The impact of non-Western theatrical traditions on Sellars is also more subtly evident in the stylized movements of the vocalists in his (in)famous stagings of Mozart and Handel.

Adams once declared 'I am not a modernist', thereby claiming a post-modern status for his music and deflecting any accusations of being a fellow traveller of that suspect twentieth-century aesthetic.[9] For Sellars, the label 'postmodern' is an artistic birthright habitually assumed in discussions of the director's work. In what ways do their postmodern sensibilities intersect with Orientalist representation in their operas? An ironic engagement with the Orientalist past seems evident in such other exemplary postmodern works as John Corigliano's 1987/1991 *The Ghosts of Versailles*. However, only in *Nixon in China* do I detect traces of a satirical tone in exotic representation by Adams and Sellars. In their other operas, exoticism seems to be played straight. I will now focus on the representations of the Chinese in *Nixon in China* (1987), an Indian folktale in *A Flowering Tree* (2006), the Palestinian and Jewish choruses in *The Death of Klinghoffer* (1991), and the Native Americans in *Doctor Atomic* (2005), before considering Adams and Sellars's own views on cross-cultural influence and exotic representation.

Are the Chinese exotic in *Nixon in China*?

One might assume that *Nixon in China* (1987) would offer the most promising example to investigate whether Adams and Sellars engage in Orientalist representation or somehow transcend it. Should we not ask of this opera: How do the white American composer, white American director, white American choreographer (Mark Morris), and white American librettist (Alice Goodman) represent the Chinese people in an opera in which white Americans travel to an exotic land?[10] And yet, most discussion of this opera has focused instead on the representations of the three principal American characters: Richard and Pat Nixon, and Henry Kissinger. In fact, in raising the topic of exotic representation in *Nixon in China* in public lectures I have been asked whether the Chinese are primarily presented as Communists in the opera rather than as exotic others. Does this 'CNN opera' bypass exotic representations entirely by focusing so intently on recreating iconic political images of Nixon's trip? In the Cultural Revolution ballet scene and in his music for Mao's secretaries (the Maoettes), for example, we assume that Adams intended to mock Socialist Realist music and propagandistic prose rather than Chinese music and people. Clearly, this opera's elements of parody and particular political subject matter complicate an attempt to consider it in light of the Orientalist operatic past, and yet the fact remains that an exotic people, place, and performance are on display. Again, most commentators have assumed, even before the opera's premiere, that the crucial question is: How does this opera shape our historical views of Nixon? Few have asked: How does *Nixon in China* shape our views of the Chinese?

'History' serves as one device in the opera for distinguishing Nixon from the main Chinese characters. Nixon clearly is infatuated with the word while the Chinese figures detest or at least lament the concept. (Of the principal characters, only Pat and Kissinger do not utter the word.) Nixon repeats the phrase 'as we made history' three times and delivers the word 'history' itself a total of eight times in his first aria after landing in Beijing. He rocks back and forth with a minor third, as though caressing the word in his line 'the eyes and ears of hiss-tory' and, in a more emphatic ejaculation, 'hiss-to-ry' is hit with a high E. In Adams's setting, Nixon seems to swoon as he sings 'The Eastern hemisphere / Beckoned to us, and we have flown / East of the sun, west of the moon', framing his trip to the exotic East as a historical expedition of discovery, parallel in grandeur to the contemporaneous moon landing. In the second scene, 'History' becomes gendered and stable with fifths as Nixon sings, 'History holds her breath.' Further in this scene Nixon appears to slip into the style of a hymn, with shades of the 'Negro spiritual' dialect, as he tenderly intones on C 'History is our mother, we / Best do her honor this way', rocking gently up a minor third to E flat on 'mother' and then achieving the high E on 'way'. At the very end of Nixon's restatement of this line the Maoettes and Mao interrupt with their own take on 'history'.

Mao maintains the gender of history, but views her as a repulsive mother: 'History is a dirty sow. If we by chance escape her maw she overlies us.' His intrusive high *fortissimo* 'tutta forza' A flat on 'history' clashes with the F major chord of his accompanying Maoettes and entirely negates Nixon's positive testimonial to mother history. The violent contrast in style between Nixon and Mao here is shocking. Madame Mao also offers a blunt statement of her relationship to mother history at the end of Act II: 'At the breast of history I sucked and pissed.' Her rocking of 'history' pivots on a dissonant tritone sonority. Chou En-lai, consistent with his more philosophic character, offers a wistful view of history in the opera's final scene: 'A bankrupt people repossessed the ciphers of its history.' Here 'history' receives a resigned falling seventh. The contrast between the dissonant leaps underscoring Chou En-lai's regretful views of history, and the Maos' nasty disdain for the concept, with Nixon's hymns of praise to mother history, represents a clear clash of political positions. It also serves musically to suggest that we should identify with one character (Nixon) rather than with the others (the Chinese).

The audience is alienated from the Chinese people from the very opening of the opera. The overture, with evocations of the opening of *Das Rheingold*, offers an ominous musical depiction of the Chinese setting through repeated A minor scales, low pedal points, and staccato brass jabs. We do not appear to be visiting an enticing exotic land. In the chorus that follows, the Chinese are presented musically and visually as a rather robotic, soulless people. Sellars's static staging of this grey chorus reinforces this impression. The musical setting here was not dictated by the text, for Mao's 'Eight Points of Attention' quoted in the libretto is a rather praiseworthy code of military conduct that offered a positive impression of the Red Army during the Chinese civil war. Nothing in the musical setting would indicate this. The melodic line, like the text itself, is choppy, the setting is rigidly syllabic, the range is quite narrow, and the mode is minor. The choral style recalls the ominous chanting of native priests in nineteenth-century Orientalist operas. The phrase 'the people are the heroes now' is not set in a celebratory, patriotic fashion, but instead resembles musical clockwork, with a tense, hushed expectancy. The repetitions of this line, with this musical setting, prod us to consider the foreboding implications of the statement. Adams has stated that in *Nixon in China* he employed the chorus 'largely to evoke the enormity of the landscape and the mystery of China's past'.[11] This is clearly not a positive or neutral introduction to the Chinese people and we are not signalled by the music or libretto or staging to identify with this chorus. The style may not be marked as 'Chinese', but that does not preclude this chorus functioning in terms of exoticism. In short, from the very start it is clear that 'they' are presented most definitely as not 'us'. Adams's representations of Mao and Madame Mao draw more directly on Orientalist tradition to similar effect.

Mao's entrance is marked by a gong-like gesture in the orchestra (low octave Gs) and, in Sellars's production, he approaches monumentally, but as a puppet manipulated by his three secretaries who both repeat and anticipate his words throughout Act I, scene 2.[12] Mao is cast as a very high tenor, the only tenor in the opera, and thus contrasts comically with the mezzo-soprano voices of his secretaries. Towards the end of the scene, Mao and the Maoettes repeatedly declare: 'Founders come first, then profiteers.' The musical setting of this statement is one of the catchier rhythmic licks in the score, but its repetition is ambiguous in intent. Is this offered as an important slogan, a shrewd statement of political philosophy, a bitter complaint, or a directive for seating arrangements at a banquet? Sellars's choreographed gestures for the Maoettes at this point suggest either ritualistic performance or Cholly Atkins-style choreography for a group of Motown backup singers. The suggestion that exotic others speak nonsensical and repetitive text was common in nineteenth-century Orientalist opera.

Clearly, this opera is lampooning the rote repetition of Mao's sayings, but Mao and his Maoettes are also marked as exotic. In fact, this scene concludes with a direct echo of that landmark of modernist exoticism, *The Rite of Spring*, specifically 'The Augurs of Spring: Dances of the Young Girls' section. Here Adams extracted, and raised by a half step, half of the famous bitonal Stravinsky chord as he closely approximated Stravinsky's ostinato with unexpected accents, although in a more constrained form. (Adams moves even closer to a quotation of Stravinsky when he adds a G natural on the accented beats.) What motivation is there for this allusion, beyond the fact that Adams draws on Stravinsky in most of his scores? Perhaps this musical correspondence suggests the sacrifice and political rites of the Cultural Revolution that will be represented onstage later in the opera. Perhaps the Maoettes are equivalent to the 'Young Girls' performing the violent, ancient rites imagined by Stravinsky. In *Nixon in China*, this near quotation appears to depict the mindless, aggressive sloganeering of the Cultural Revolution Chinese; that is, the mindless, aggressive exotic other.

Finally, I turn to the operatic Madame Mao, depicted here as a sinister sister of Stravinsky's outraged and outrageous Baba the Turk, a coloratura monster rivalling the Queen of the Night, a Turandot stripped of her enticing *chinoiserie* garb. Madame Mao is first heard at the end of Act II. She obsessively declares 'I speak according to the book', with music supporting the perception that she is doctrinaire and utterly hysterical. (Offering another side of the exotic femme fatale, this dragon lady is accorded chromatic 'Ah' melismas in Act III.) The Cultural Revolution Ballet scene in Act II presents a bald parody of the historical Madame Mao's 1964 model ballet *The Red Detachment of Women*. In his choreography for this scene, Mark Morris wittily quoted from the original ballet, while adding his own stylistic twists. Adams has explained that he wanted his music for this ballet to sound as though composed by a Cultural Revolution committee: 'I'd noticed when watching films of these Chinese Communist ballets that the music, rather than being indigenous Chinese music, faithful to the sources of the stories, had sounded instead like very bad imitations of Russian and French ballet music.'[13] In creating an imitation of an imitation, here Adams has vaulted into the realm of the simulacra. Adams succeeds in producing a particularly banal repetition in this music featuring simple triads in parallel motion and with deliberately awkward text setting. Whatever associations the art of the Cultural Revolution might prompt in an audience, this scene teaches us to laugh out loud at its expense. Attempts by the exotic other to imitate the West are apparently always good for a laugh.

Whether or not these examples suffice to classify *Nixon in China* as an Orientalist opera, the exoticism of the opera has been traded on in some productions. At the 2011 Metropolitan Opera production, I noted that in the gift shop one could purchase Mao-style jackets, *Nixon in China* chopsticks, and Mao's *Little Red Book* in a 1972 English translation. 'Founders come first, then profiteers' indeed. Only two copies of the *Little Red Book* remained on the lobby table by the end of intermission on 5 February 2011.[14]

The magical multicultural mélange of *A Flowering Tree*

Standing as an apotheosis of their multicultural approach is the more recent 2006 opera *A Flowering Tree*. In Adams and Sellars's treatment of this Indian folktale, we encounter Javanese dancers, costumes inspired by traditional Indian fashion, a passage referencing Balinese *ketjak* (the 'monkey dance' drama), and clear allusions to the operas of Mozart, as well as Adams's trademark stylistic gestures towards such modernist composers as Stravinsky, Bartók, and Orff along with blatant references to Strauss and Wagner. Several passages in the score (particularly in Act II, scene 3) not only recall Indonesian gamelan music more generically – interlocking patterns, colotomic structure, and stratified textures featuring the celesta, chimes, gong, glockenspiel, Japanese bowl gongs, and harp – but specifically resemble the translations of gamelan music by Messiaen, McPhee, and Britten. The Balinese *ketjak* musical reference in Act II, scene 4 – consisting of interlocking male voices (briefly joined by altos) producing short, shouted nonsense syllables and enhanced by a Chinese cymbal and a section featuring glockenspiel, castanets, bongo, and celesta – is framed within the narrative as a representation of an exotic musical performance by Indian beggar minstrels. A women's chorus singing in a 'mocking, piercing' style that Adams has referred to as 'Gypsy-like' is eventually layered on top of this music.[15] Given that the 'grab bag' approach to musical exoticism – the easy substitution of one exotic cultural reference for another – has been intensely criticized, this musical mash-up is a striking move by Adams.

In Adams and Sellars's literary source, the magical transformations of the heroine into a tree are related in a rather matter-of-fact manner.[16] Adams transforms these moments musically into magical events. For example, in Act I, scene 1 we hear a wordless exotic female chorus during the first magical transformation of the heroine. These women sing 'Do' and 'Mi' with an 'absolutely pure vocal sound, without vibrato'. Adams has explained that to 'add to the pan-cultural flavor of the piece, I set all of the chorus texts in Spanish'.[17] Adams turns to nonsense text and the juxtaposition of languages to enhance operatic exoticism.

The opera's narrative frame suggests that this exotic story will serve as a morality tale. What does the exotic teach us in this tale and what can we learn about contemporary exotic representation from this opera? In her essay accompanying the 2008 Nonesuch recording, Sarah Cahill states that Adams avoided creating a 'multicultural pastiche' and instead 'chose a more subtle route, delving beyond cultural differences into the essence of the story'. Cahill points to the influence of *ketjak* in Act II but claims that the music 'reminds us more of his own *Harmonielehre* than it does Balinese traditional music'. Whereas Cahill appears to de-emphasize the elements of exotic representation and multicultural embrace in *A Flowering Tree*, Adams's own accounts of the work's genesis make clear that this composer consciously embarked on a trip of exotic exploration. Adams has recounted his journey to Venezuela to meet the musicians who would perform in the opera's premiere in Vienna. He has described his first impressions of this exotic land where 'music is everywhere',[18] and how when he arrived at his destination he discovered the youth orchestra playing Saint-Saëns's 'Bacchanal'.[19] Adams also alludes to the anxiety he felt as a 'straight, white, middle-aged, male'[20] engaged in such exuberant multicultural creation – a self-awareness that I will return to later in this chapter.

Glamorous and unglamorous exoticism in *The Death of Klinghoffer*

Clearly the most controversial exotic representations by Adams and Sellars are found in the 1991 opera *The Death of Klinghoffer*, as both artists are acutely aware. In his autobiography, Adams has cited Richard Taruskin's reference to the musical representations of the 'glamorously exotic

Palestinians' in that opera.[21] Taruskin's comment was partly provoked by an aria delivered by one of the young terrorists that is itself a celebration of Arabic music. We might also turn to the two opening choruses in the opera. The Chorus of the Exiled Palestinians embodies both Orientalism's enticing *and* repulsive manifestations of the exotic as we first hear decorative, hugely melismatic music (with one melisma lasting more than fifteen measures) and then threatening, aggressive music marked by a primitivist drum beat and a ferocious vocal texture. In contrast, the music of the Chorus of Exiled Jews remains within a recognizably western European choral style and is thoroughly syllabic and distinctly unglamorous. To my ear, the parallels with, for example, Saint-Saëns's *Samson et Dalila* – in which the Hebrew chorus is differentiated from the music of the Philistines in much the same way – seem clear, as does the implication for the target audience's identification with one group of characters over the other.

Lindenberger also notes the striking musical differences between the two choruses, and yet claims that in *The Death of Klinghoffer* Adams treats both the Western Jewish characters and the Eastern Arabs in 'as evenhanded a way as is conceivable'.[22] However, Lindenberger cites Adams himself as saying that he wanted to depict 'otherness' in his musical representation of the Arabs and that he turned to the music of a Syrian composer for inspiration. Lindenberger attempts to save *Klinghoffer* from the 'Orientalist' label by arguing that the 'Near Eastern coloring of this music ... never suggests the sexuality or the glamour of nineteenth-century orientalist opera, nor does Adams [employ it] ... to suggest threats of violence', and he concludes that 'Adams's is an orientalism stripped of its traditional meaning, if indeed we can call it an orientalism at all'.[23] Again, as in much scholarship on contemporary opera, although Orientalist representational techniques and musical stereotypes are undeniably present, we are asked to consider them as having lost all of their referential meaning. This suggests a modernist and postmodernist 'emancipation of Orientalist signs'. However, as with early atonality, in which dissonance continued to have its traditional associations even in the hands of composers proclaiming its emancipation, an 'emancipation of Orientalist signs' remains rather utopian.

Native song and dance in *Doctor Atomic*

My final example is perhaps the most telling. In addition to drawing upon the *Bhagavad Gita* – thereby inviting comparisons with Glass's *Satyagraha* – Adams and Sellars's 2005 *Doctor Atomic* prominently includes representations of Native Americans through words, music, and dance. (Japan is only briefly, but powerfully, evoked at the end of the opera – just after the test explosion has occurred – as we hear the recorded voice of a woman requesting water. This untranslated Japanese voice concludes the opera and thereby impels the audience to consider the impact of the bomb on the people of Hiroshima.) The exotic representation of Native Americans has inspired very little commentary in the extensive critical response to *Doctor Atomic*. In this opera, the representation of the Native American servants partakes of techniques from the tradition of operatic Orientalism. The most striking melismatic lines in *Doctor Atomic* are given to Kitty Oppenheimer in her drunken state and to her exotic maid Pasqualita, a low mezzo soprano role, as she delivers 'authentic' ritualistic texts. Adams has explained that both 'Kitty and her Tewa Indian maid, Pasqualita, embody differing aspects of Goethe's *ewig Weibliche*. Both possess Cassandra-like powers, but their utterances are delphic, cryptic, ambiguous',[24] and he has stated that '[a] lot of what Pasqualita sings verges on the incomprehensible'.[25]

All of Pasqualita's lines were derived by Sellars from a 1933 translation of a Tewa lullaby and from a 1944 poem by Muriel Rukeyser, which in turn drew upon Native American material.[26] Rukeyser's poem is in the voice of Native Americans lamenting their devastation at the hands of the white invaders. In the original production by Sellars, the Native American servants employed a great deal of symbolic hand gestures, marking them as embodying a ritualistic essence wholly distinct from the white characters. Pasqualita's particularly exotic and mysterious nature is projected most clearly by her repetitive utterances, melismatic flights, and wordless vocalizations. Her lullaby – a recurring exotic performance – features a chromatic melismatic 'Ah', the augmented second sonority, octave leaps, and a roll on the tam tam. Her visions are accompanied by an orchestral tattoo, her reference to 'the drumbeat hope' elicits a steady timpani beat, and her proclamation that the 'dead are on the march' is accompanied by offstage female 'Ahs', eerie bowed cymbals, tuned gongs, tam tam roll, and a cluster chord. Some of her vocal passages resemble the exotica of Yma Sumac. Like so many other exotic women in earlier Orientalist operas, in her limited vocal utterances Pasqualita always seems to be performing: singing a lullaby or channelling a ritualistic vision. Of course, we might well ask: When is a melismatic 'Ah' just an 'Ah'? Whereas Corigliano's Samira in *The Ghosts of Versailles* seems to sing a send-up of the Orientalist musical past in her excessive melismas, the Palestinian choral laments and Pasqualita's mystic utterances in Adams's operas suggest a straight representation of the mysterious other. I note that the contralto who played Pasqualita in the original production, Ellen Rabiner, has also portrayed Verdi's gypsy mama Azucena in *Il Trovatore* – in both works the exotic woman is presented as a mysterious oracular figure. The degrees of separation between nineteenth- and twenty-first-century Orientalist opera are few.

In addition to representations of Pasqualita's exotic lullabies and prayers, *Doctor Atomic* places a Native American ritual performance on display, but with a crucial twist. In Act II, scene 3 Pasqualita sings of visions of her people 'dancing to bring the dead back' and Sellars enlisted the choreographer Lucinda Childs to create a Corn Dance as 'an evocation of the traditional Tewa ceremony'.[27] In the original production, a simple circle dance, with the dancers holding pine branches and making gestures and dancing steps similar to the Native American model, was accompanied by Adams's evocations of *The Rite of Spring* in the orchestra and some choral 'Ahs'. The dance is rather similar to the exotic-inspired choreography of Ruth St Denis or Ted Shawn from a hundred years prior. This is an extremely tense dramatic section of the opera and as the dancers encircled the entire setting they appeared to represent an ominous machine of interlocking gears – the primitive and the futuristic were conflated once again as the opera moved inexorably closer to the explosion of the bomb. But unlike the primitivist stagings of St Denis and Stravinsky/Nijinsky in which white dancers assumed exotic identities, in this scene US military characters perform this 'Tewa' dance themselves. This is why the dance proves so frightening and intense – the 'normal' characters, coded within the opera as 'white' despite Sellars' multiethnic casting, have succumbed to the terrible tensions of violent expectation and are themselves possessed by the exotic.[28]

Adams and Sellars critiquing the Orientalist critique

Sellars and Adams have repeatedly informed us that Orientalism is not in play in their operas. In fact, they have specifically referred to the ways in which *Nixon in China* differs from the Orientalism of *Aida* and how it even parodies Verdi's opera.[29] Again, this raises the question whether one can parody operatic Orientalism without repeating it. Adams has clearly stated: 'At no point in this opera did I want to write fake Chinese music; the music is inexorably American, no matter who is singing.'[30] Of course, even when this is the case, musical borrowing and influence are not the most crucial factors in the dynamics of Orientalist musical representation. When Matthew Daines asked Sellars whether he was concerned that *Nixon in China* repeats the Orientalist trope of Westerners going abroad to achieve self-realization, Sellars replied that he hoped 'we are commenting on that in an interesting way rather than just extending that'.[31] Daines, like most other critics of the opera, took Sellars and Adams at their word and declared that 'for once, the Chinese are not just "the natives"' and that by giving the Chinese an 'identity of their own', the authors separated this work from the tradition of Orientalist operas.[32]

Adams and Sellars are certainly well aware of some aspects of the Orientalist critique in operatic scholarship from the past few decades. In many of their published remarks they seem simultaneously sympathetic towards and dismissive of such critical concerns, at least as these concerns might pertain to their own works. However, both Adams and Sellars focus almost exclusively on cross-cultural influence and charges of cultural appropriation – issues of representation do not appear to cross their radar screens. Yet, as I have shown, exotic representations of characters, settings, and performances are central to their works. Here is Sellars praising Adams for avoiding what he refers to as 'musical Orientalism':

Nixon in China, for example, has no overt Chinese reference in it musically, but sets up a world which you regard as Chinese – in some amazing way that goes beyond *The Mikado*. [laughs] Instead of using a kind of musical orientalism, it's quite the opposite: what is the *shared* world here? One of the most important things about John's music is that it's not a colonialist viewpoint tapping into someone else's music. It presents the texture of a world we are actually sharing, in which this interpenetration of influence and aspiration from all sides is creating something that is itself a new culture.[33]

Sellars does not appear to consider how the exotic was represented in these works. Indeed, I imagine the director proclaiming: 'Ask not how the exotic is represented, but in what spirit and to what ends exotic borrowing has been transacted.'[34]

When asked about the possible 'rules' that might govern Western engagement in cross-cultural appropriation, Sellars has replied that as long as the Western artist has a 'kind of integrity' this transaction is legitimate. The crucial issue for Sellars has to do with 'an artist's depth of feeling and range of response'. As a white American male he feels that 'the degree of permissibility there has to do with the degree of my honesty and specificity about my own reactions'. Sellars argues that at a certain point cultural products become 'common property' that a director must be free to rework and that artists need 'to cut loose' in such intercultural transactions in order to create new works of transformative art.[35]

The most revealing reflections on these issues appear near the very end of Adams's autobiography. In discussing the negative critical response to the 'multiculturalist aspirations' of *A Flowering Tree*, Adams first defends his opera by proclaiming that the 'actual native-born artists who performed the piece … ate up the transcultural mix of music, dance, and texts'. He goes on to make snide reference to Western scholars who fret over 'the dangers of multicultural miscegenation' and, while acknowledging the academic critique of 'cultural appropriation', denies suffering from any 'anxiety of influence'. However, his stance begins to oscillate rapidly between an outright dismissal of these critical concerns and a sympathetic understanding of the dangers of cross-cultural activity. Adams fears that when 'indigenous art forms' are 'taken out of their societal setting' they may well 'lose their power as signifiers, lose their strangeness and their magic', and he envies the (supposed) tendency of 'traditional societies' to remain culturally 'consistent'. But he also argues that the largest original leaps forward in art have occurred through cultural appropriation. He, like Sellars, seems to conclude that this is simply the price we must pay for new art and that, in any event, such appropriation is a 'two-way street' since 'they' are engaged in this activity also. However, he actually ends this discussion by stating that the 'argument persists' that such cross-cultural appropriation is detrimental. His wording here is quite ambiguous – it remains unclear whether on some level he agrees with the argument's rationale or whether he just wishes the argument would end.[36]

After first presenting my views on Orientalism in the operas of Adams, I was asked what advice I would offer the contemporary composer seeking to represent such characters as Pasqualita or the Indian beggar minstrels or the Chinese chorus on the tarmac. My answer at the time was that I am not in the business of advising composers on what to represent or how to do so. Knowing that the interlocutor had once provocatively suggested in the most public of forums that *Madama Butterfly* should no longer be performed, I suspected that the conversation might lead to questions of censoring Orientalist representation. I remain unable/unwilling to offer a precise answer, but might modestly propose that composers attempt to represent exotic characters more fully and with more variety, rather than presenting, yet again, the dark and cryptic (yet nurturing) native woman; the soulless, robotic mass of chanting anonymous others; and the frightening and enticingly primitive 'traditional dances'. If Adams and Sellars set out to represent the other – and, of course, all the characters in these operas are 'other' and separate from them, and from 'us', but to differing degrees – perhaps they could take care not to perpetuate stereotypes for those characters who will be deemed most exotic by the majority of their audience members.

As new operas and operatic productions are heralded for their attempts to move beyond the traditions of exoticism, their creators (and defenders) appear to presuppose an audience sophisticated enough to see through signs of Orientalist representation. Scholars and critics alike have not tended to focus on exotic representation in contemporary operas. A certain manufactured obsolescence seems to be in play as we declare the Orientalist critique outdated and postmodern opera devoid of Orientalist representation. Our apparent perpetual need for new critical terminology can obscure connections to the past as we investigate recent works. Despite authorial and scholarly claims to the contrary, this survey of the operas of Adams and Sellars indicates that Orientalist representation persists. It should come as no surprise that composers and directors of contemporary opera would turn to exoticism given the intense competition they face from the operatic canon, which so frequently engages in Orientalist representation. To a large extent opera is a genre of exotic representation and this particular past remains close behind.

Notes

I delivered preliminary versions of this chapter at: Merton College, University of Oxford; Williams College; the American Musicological Society; Harvard University; the Metropolitan Opera Guild; the University of Michigan; and Princeton University. I would like to thank participants and audience members at each of these venues for their comments and thought-provoking questions and maestro Alan Gilbert and Eric Owens for discussing *Doctor Atomic* with me at the New York City Japan Society in October 2008.

1 For a broad consideration of what exoticism in opera entails, a survey of developments in scholarship devoted to this topic, and a brief discussion of the persistence of exoticism in twentieth-century opera, see my 'Exoticism in Opera' in Helen Greenwald (ed.), *The Oxford Handbook of Opera* (Oxford University Press, forthcoming). For a general summary of scholarship on exoticism, see my 'Exoticism' entry in *The Oxford Bibliography of Music Online*.
2 Ralph P. Locke, 'Cutthroats and Casbah Dancers, Muezzins and Timeless Sands: Musical Images of the Middle East' in Jonathan Bellman (ed.), *The Exotic in Western Music* (Boston: Northeastern University Press, 1998), 105. Herbert Lindenberger, *Opera in History: From Monteverdi to Cage* (Stanford University Press, 1998), 175.

3 I consider works by Corigliano and Rihm in 'Exoticism in Opera'. For a discussion of Tan Dun and Orientalist representation, with brief reference to works by Sheng and Weir, see my 'Blurring the Boundaries: Tan Dun's *tinte* and *The First Emperor*', *Journal of Musicology*, 26.3 (Summer 2009), 285–326.

4 On Anthony Minghella's production of *Madama Butterfly* at the Metropolitan Opera, see my review in *Opera Quarterly*, 24.1 (Winter 2008), 139–47.

5 John Adams, *Hallelujah Junction: Composing an American Life* (New York: Farrar, Straus and Giroux, 2008), 201.

6 Matthew Daines, 'An Interview with John Adams', *Opera Quarterly*, 13.1 (Fall 1996), 54.

7 See Valentina Valentini, 'Interculturalismo e modernismo nel teatro di Peter Sellars' in Maria Delgado and Valentina Valentini (eds.), *Peter Sellars* (Catanzaro: Rubbettino, 1999), 57–77. A brief overview of his career is offered by Delgado in 'Making Theatre, Making a Society', *New Theatre Quarterly*, 15 (1999), 204–17.

8 Sellars quoted in John J. Flynn, 'Transiting from the "Wethno-centric": An Interview with Peter Sellars' in Bonnie Maranca and Gautam Dasgupta (eds.), *Interculturalism and Performance: Writings from PAJ* (New York: PAJ Publications, 1991), 186, 189–91.

9 K. Robert Schwarz, *Minimalists* (London: Phaidon, 1996), 179. Of course, modernism was not/is not a single aesthetic and one might argue that the sensibility and styles typically labelled 'postmodern' might also fit within a broadly conceived 'modernist' category. Commentators tend to agree with Adams in designating his works as postmodernist. For example, see Matthew Daines, *Telling the Truth about* Nixon: *Parody, Cultural Representation, and Gender Politics in John Adams's Opera* Nixon in China (PhD diss., University of California, Davis, 1995), 136; and Annette Kreutziger-Herr, 'Politik und Postmoderne: Die Oper *Nixon in China* von John Adams', *Hamburger Jahrbuch für Musikwissenschaft*, 17 (2000-1), 323–50. Robert Fink refers to Adams's score as an example of 'virtuoso postmodern pastiche'. See Fink, '(Post-)minimalisms 1970–2000: The Search for a New Mainstream' in Nicholas Cook and Anthony Pople (eds.), *The Cambridge History of Twentieth-Century Music* (Cambridge University Press, 2008), 554.

10 My discussion of the staging of *Nixon in China* is based on the original Houston Grand Opera production by Sellars and the 2011 revival at the Metropolitan Opera.

11 Quoted in 'The Myth of History', Metropolitan Opera *Playbill* (February 2011), 10.

12 Sellars has explained that the staging here is deliberately stylized and that the specific blocking for Nixon's meeting with Mao was 'taken from classical Chinese opera: that is the way two kings enter'. Matthew Daines, '*Nixon in China*: An Interview with Peter Sellars', *Tempo*, 197 (July 1996), 12.

13 Adams, *Hallelujah Junction*, 141.

14 This 'historic' production at the Met was well received by an audience trained on such Orientalist spectacles as *Aida* and *Turandot*. The Met offered Sellars's production as a museum piece that had made operatic history and that was making history again. During Madame Mao's Act II, scene 2 aria I suddenly imagined we might all, caught up in the spirit of the occasion, join her by waving our copies of the *Little Red Book* in the air, participating in the spectacle as though at a screening of *The Rocky Horror Picture Show*. I would like to thank Anne Shreffler for informing me after the fact that this form of participation was incorporated into the 2000 production of the opera directed by Lynn Binstock at the Theater Freiburg.

15 Adams, *Hallelujah Junction*, 302. I should note that this performance by beggar-minstrels is not found in Adams's literary source but was added to allow for an exotic musical spectacle. Adams refers to the female chorus as singing 'obscure, cryptic lines from a bhakti devotional text'.

16 Adams and Sellars based their libretto on the version of the tale presented in A. K. Ramanujan, *A Flowering Tree and Other Oral Tales from India*, ed. Stuart Blackburn and Alan Dundes (Berkeley: University of California Press, 1997), 53–62.

17 Adams, *Hallelujah Junction*, 302.

18 *Ibid.*, 295.

19 *Ibid.*, 304.

20 *Ibid.*, 297.

21 *Ibid.*, 170. For a useful selection of reviews, including a reprint of Taruskin's essay and a chronicle of the general controversy inspired by this work, see Thomas May (ed.), *The John Adams Reader: Essential Writings on an American Composer* (Pompton Plains, NJ: Amadeus Press, 2006), 297–342. For a discussion of the Jewish characters that counters Taruskin's charges of anti-Semitic representation, see Robert Fink, '*Klinghoffer* in Brooklyn Heights', *Cambridge Opera Journal*, 17.2 (2005), 173–213. On how the representation of the Palestinians has evolved through multiple productions, see Ruth Sara Longobardi, 'Re-producing *Klinghoffer*: Opera and Arab Identity before and after 9/11', *Journal of the Society for American Music*, 3.3 (2009), 273–310. Longobardi quotes Adams as stating that he had 'read a great deal of Edward Said's writing' as he worked on the opera (275) and she posits that Alice Goodman's libretto appears to 'heroicize the Palestinians' and not the Jewish characters (281–2).

22 Lindenberger, *Opera in History*, 177. My brief discussion of *The Death of Klinghoffer* and of Lindenberger's critique also appears in my forthcoming 'Exoticism in Opera'.

23 Lindenberger, *Opera in History*, 178.

24 Adams, *Hallelujah Junction*, 286.

25 Interview by Thomas May, 'John Adams on *Doctor Atomic*' in *The John Adams Reader*, 229.

26 Herbert Joseph Spinden, *Songs of the Tewa* (New York: Exposition of Indian Tribal Arts, Inc., 1933); Muriel Rukeyser, 'The Dream-Singing Elegy', *The Kenyon Review*, 6.1 (Winter, 1944), 59–63.
27 Adams, *Hallelujah Junction*, 291–2.
28 Later in Act II, scene 3 the Chorus is similarly possessed by an unspeakable fear ('At the Sight of This') and is accompanied by a 'Low Chinese Gong', described in the score as a 'Deep, "Fu Man Chu" gong with a bright "flare"'.
29 See, for example, Daines, '*Nixon in China*: An Interview with Peter Sellars', 18–19.
30 Daines, 'An Interview with John Adams', 46.
31 Daines, '*Nixon*'s Women: Gender Politics and Cultural Representation in Act 2 of *Nixon in China*', *Musical Quarterly*, 79.1 (Spring 1995), 29.
32 Daines, 'Telling the Truth About *Nixon*', 176. Daines also claims here that the 'complexity and detail with which events from the Cultural Revolution in *Nixon* are recreated demonstrate a more sophisticated understanding of Chinese culture'. Daines's appreciation of this detailed historical recreation derives from Sellars's own somewhat tenuous explanations. It is unlikely that audience members notice any of these details.
33 Thomas May, 'Creating Context: Peter Sellars on Working with Adams' in *The John Adams Reader*, 244–5.
34 It must be said that Sellars is a persuasive champion of progressivism and I have long found his political liberalism inspiring. However, even the most socially and culturally observant among us have our blind spots.
35 Flynn, 'Transiting from the "Wethno-centric"', 188–9.
36 Adams, *Hallelujah Junction*, 308–10.

~ | Afterword: What else?

RICHARD TARUSKIN

It is not as though representation were a neglected field, even within musicology. What else do we talk about these days? Semiotics, hermeneutics, intertextuality, topical and discourse analysis have been musicology's growth industries for decades now, and all of them take representation for granted. Even musicologists, scholarship's diehard romantics, have accepted by now that language and art are artful, and that art is meaningful. It is rather a long time since I have seen the formerly obligatory scarequotes around the word 'meaning' in musicological titles. A decisive moment for me was the appearance in 1994 of the essay collection *Theory, Analysis and Meaning* [no scare quotes] *in Music*, edited by Anthony Pople. To see such inroads even within the world of music theory and analysis, formalism's last redoubt, meant the fight was over. Why belabour it now?

I

But what was the fight about? It was never really about the actuality or the possibility of musical representation. No one ever denied it, not even the usual suspects. When Stravinsky, through his ghostwriter, laid down the famous gauntlet we all know by heart:

[M]usic is, by its very nature, essentially powerless to *express* anything at all[1]

he (or his ghostwriter) took pains to italicize the word *express*, and by doing so implied that the word had been carefully – artfully – chosen. He knew perfectly well that if he had written 'represent' instead of 'express', the assertion would have been absurd on its face, and it would not have become a point of endless debate, no matter how commanding Stravinsky's authority. The argument is not between expression and its absence, but among the many available alternatives: 'express', 'evoke', 'arouse', and so on, in addition to 'represent'. Among these alternatives, 'represent' certainly makes the most modest claim.

But, perhaps more importantly, it has been a debate about the place of representation in the scheme of things musical. That is what Hanslick, for one, debated. He never denied the existence or the possibility of representation in music; he merely claimed that it was beside the point, and that to insist on seeking out musical representations, or to claim that therein lay the value of music, was in a fundamental way to misunderstand the musical experience. Specifically, he claimed – beginning with the implicit claim of his title – that the representational side of music was not the source of *das musikalisch-Schöne*. If aesthetics was the study or elucidation of beauty, Hanslick maintained, then representation was aesthetically irrelevant. The claim could easily be expanded into other realms or media, and was. What else could Walter Pater have meant when he wrote, all in italics, that '*All art constantly aspires to the condition of music*'? He wrote this almost immediately after conceding that 'some of the most delightful music seems to be always approaching to figure, to pictorial definition', which shows that he admitted representation even in the case of music, and also that it was pleasurable and to that extent valuable. But when it came to what really mattered, music had an edge: 'While in all other kinds of art it is possible to distinguish the matter from the form, and the understanding can always make this distinction, yet it is the constant effort of art to obliterate it.' He went on, in the nearly impenetrable syntax that was a sign of ecstasy:

> That the mere matter of a poem, for instance, its subject, namely, its given incidents or situation – that the mere matter of a picture, the actual circumstances of an event, the actual topography of a landscape – should be nothing without the form, the spirit, of the handling, that this form, this mode of handling, should become an end in itself, should penetrate every part of the matter: this is what all art constantly strives after, and achieves in different degrees.[2]

Music was the medium, Pater assumed, that owed the least to all those 'mere' things – matter, subject, incidents, situation, circumstances, topography – and most to the form and spirit of the handling. Music was pre-eminently the medium – quoting now from Susan Sontag, one of Pater's innumerable progeny – 'that dissolves considerations of content into those of form'.[3] That is from *Against Interpretation*, Sontag's aestheticist manifesto of 1964, and Sontag was not speaking of music. She was speaking of the arts in general, which is why I take her remark as a paraphrase of Pater's. For if critics, over the near century between Pater's 1870s and Sontag's 1960s, could look forward to the day when content would disappear into form, this only shows how baldly the form/content dichotomy was drawn in all arts media, and how unequally the members were weighted.

But we musicians were always out in front of the aestheticist wave. We are the ones, after all, who coined the word 'extramusical' to denote objects of representation. I have never seen the face in a portrait described as extrapainterly, or the plot of a novel described as extraliterary, but I have actually seen musical allusions of an intertextual kind – quotations such as 'Columbia, Gem of the Ocean' in Ives, or the *Dies Irae* in the *Symphonie fantastique*, or references to 'characteristic' idioms as in Mendelssohn's 'Scottish' or 'Italian' symphonies, or even Liszt's 'Gypsy' scale – described as extramusical.[4] How can actual music be extramusical? My God, but we are squeamish.

The word *extramusical*, surprisingly enough, is not to be found in the *OED*; the Merriam-Webster Online Dictionary gives 1923 as the date of earliest use.[5] The date, right in the middle of the Pater-to-Sontag century, seems plausible; but Merriam-Webster's definition – 'lying outside the province of music' – is clearly inadequate, unless Liszt's Gypsy scale can be so described.

So what *does* it mean, then, and why?

I was first drawn into debate over musical representation when Peter Kivy began issuing his books on musical aesthetics. Until then I was a proper little formalist and had been one ever since my senior year in college, when I first read Hanslick. It was an assignment, and it came with a Svengali-like suggestion from the professor who assigned it. 'You'll be amazed to find how much of it you agree with', he said. And, of course, agree we did. Hanslick seemed so much more sophisticated than his antagonists; his appreciation of art was so refined. I proselytized for him when I began teaching music appreciation, making all the usual arguments; that is, that describing form was objective, while meaning was 'merely' subjective, or that when you described form you were describing the music, whereas when you described its meaning you were merely describing yourself, and how interesting do you think *you* are?

Kivy's first book, *The Corded Shell*, was an attempt to show that, *pace* Hanslick, expression in music was not merely relevant to its beauty, but virtually tantamount to it. Kivy called his theory of expression the 'contour and convention' theory, from which it was already evident that he saw expression in terms of representation. He claimed that the expressive content of music could be objectively determined, understanding objectivity as intersubjective consensus, amounting in practice (imaginary practice, that is, consisting of hypothetical polls of imaginary listeners) to an appeal to majority vote. Reviewing Kivy's book, I tried to nail him with a counter-example.[6] Twice Kivy cites the opening measures of Mozart's Symphony in G minor as a self-evident paradigm of sad music, for all that it is marked *Molto allegro* which of course literally means 'very happy'. 'No one', Kivy remarked, 'has ever been tempted to characterize [those opening measures] as "spritely" and "good humored".'[7] I was able to cite two dissenters.

One was Schumann, refuting the characterization of G minor in Schubart's *Ideen zu einer Aesthetik der Tonkunst* (1806). 'In G minor he finds discontent, discomfort, worried anxiety over an unsuccessful plan, ill-tempered chewing of the lips', wrote Schumann. 'Now compare this idea with Mozart's Symphony in G minor, full of Hellenic grace!'[8] But the other counterexample was the one I really thought conclusive. It came from Sigmund Spaeth's *Great Symphonies: How to Recognize and Remember Them*, in which symphonic themes were fitted out with mnemonic texts. The opening of the G minor, Spaeth assures us, is 'a very happy tune, … full of laughter and fun'.[9] And here are the words:

With a laugh and a smile like a sunbeam,
And a face that is glad, with a fun-beam,
We can start on our way very gaily,
Singing tunes from a symphony daily.

Proof positive, this (I thought), that musical affect was not immanent but attributed. I was therefore quite astonished to find, in Kivy's subsequent book, *Sound Sentiment* (actually a reissue of *The Corded Shell* with some extra chapters to answer his critics), Spaeth dismissed as a 'merely subjective' outlier and the principle of majority vote upheld without a qualm.[10] Now there is a complacent fellow, I thought. Would that I possessed his mental insulation.

II

But I have changed my mind. I now think that I was wrong to hold up Spaeth or Schumann against Kivy's characterization of Mozart's theme – not because (as Kivy suggests in his complacency) outliers are 'seriously deficient in a basic human accomplishment',[11] but because (like me at first) they did not properly appreciate the mechanisms through which musical representation works. Representation is constrained – gladly and fruitfully constrained – by convention, just as language is constrained; and therefore the sadness in Mozart's theme, being the product of a long-standing signifying practice or device, relied on insider knowledge for its correct interpretation. No party to the representational tradition that governed Mozart's choice would have mistaken the 'pathetic' message that this device was designed to send, and Spaeth or Schumann's dissent merely showed that even by Schumann's time the device in question had atrophied through desuetude.

The device, of course, was the *pianto*, or *Seufzer*, originally an imitation of a sigh or moan, and rife in seventeenth-century Italian operas and cantatas whenever characters or singing personas had reason to weep. Its history has been traced through the nineteenth century (as Schumann might have known; as Wagner surely did), despite the weakening hold of convention, and into the twentieth.[12] The main eighteenth-century event in its history was the wholesale transfer of the device from vocal music into instrumental genres. This can be as easily illustrated in Bach as in Mozart – for example, by comparing, say, the famous aria 'Seufzer, Thränen, Kummer, Noth' from Bach's cantata BWV 21 (*Ich hatte viel Bekümmernis*) with the F minor prelude from Book II of the *Well-Tempered Clavier*. True, the *Seufzer* is usually identified with dissonant appoggiaturas and their resolutions, whereas Mozart uses the descending slurred half-step as a pickup. But its pervasiveness as a motive, in conjunction with the tonality and the extra-dark scoring at the outset (like one of Mozart's late quintets with extra viola), makes its expressive – that is, representational – intent clear enough. It is the pervasiveness that makes what for me is the essential point – that is, that there is no sense trying to separate the representational role of the gesture from the constructive role of the motive, and therefore no earthly reason even to call the affect of the music an extroversive reference, let alone an extramusical one.

Pinning the proper label on the music may seem like an accomplishment, but what has actually been accomplished? The signified attribute, the 'affect' if you will, is static. It pervades the music, and the ingenuity with which Mozart manipulates the signifier – turning the *Seufzer* over or around, embedding it in strettos, sneaking it into inconspicuous corners of the texture – all of that is fascinating to ferret out and describe, but we are no longer describing a representation when we describe that. The interesting stuff still seems to be formal, or at least syntactic, as Kofi Agawu suggests when he complains that topics, to which he has devoted so much scholarly energy, 'can provide clues to what is being "discussed" in a piece of music [but] do not seem to be able to sustain an independent and self-regulating account of a piece; they point to the expressive domain, but they have no syntax'. Thus when topic succeeds topic, as they do so prodigally in Mozart, accounts quickly devolve into lists – again static, inert. No one, Agawu admits, has found a way to tell us 'why', in the introduction to the 'Prague' Symphony, 'the singing style should come after the outbursts of sensibility, or why fanfare is used towards the conclusion of the period'.[13] Wye Allanbrook, the most accomplished topical analyst by far, echoed Agawu's verdict even more pessimistically. 'We have not yet been able to contribute a topical syntax, in which principles for the combination of topics are laid out', she agrees, then adds, 'I have some doubt that such a thing is possible.'[14]

Peter Kivy himself, in his second book, *Sound and Semblance: Reflections on Musical Representation* – after mounting a vigorous, not to say vehement case for the existence of 'examples of music ... that can properly be called pictorial or representational' – admits, in the book's very last paragraph, that he has not argued, let alone shown, 'that music is a representational art, if by that one means an art essentially, primarily, or even *importantly* representational'.[15]

Could the implied or threatened judgement of triviality be among the reasons why interpretive studies of instrumental music, once the topical analysts gave the green light, so quickly spun out of control into gross exaggeration and fantasy? Why messages read were so confidently taken for messages sent? Why topics were inevitably teased and tarted up into all-embracing narratives and allegories? Never was a burgeoning or resurgent field more quickly plagued with abuse, it seems, than the one Carolyn Abbate so memorably dubbed, and debunked, as 'low hermeneutics'.[16] The article in which she did this, 'Music – Drastic or Gnostic?', was a reverberation of Sontag's 'Against Interpretation', and replayed Sontag's tactic of equating a practice with its abuse. Sontag's essay would have been more accurately titled 'Against Overinterpretation', and Abbate's should have been called 'Music – Drastic and Gnostic', but in that case we would not be quoting them today. Withal, the abuses they detailed were plain as day and needed to be called out. Low hermeneutics has given us the Shostakovich Wars and Bach the Jacobin. It has reduced composer after composer to essentialist stereotypes – sexual, national, racial, gendered – and the narratives it has proposed have been elementary, repetitious, and predictable: yes, boring.

I will instance Susan McClary's reading of the opening movement of Mozart's 'Prague' Symphony because it seems a direct answer to Kofi Agawu's query as quoted above. McClary organizes what for Agawu is just a random sequence of topics into a political narrative:

Although the introduction's military rhythms and instruments suggest absolutist power ... it begins quite benevolently. But the constant intrusion of sentimental gestures eventually seems to provoke this power into revealing itself in its most oppressive form: it turns suddenly from radiant D major to malignant D minor, and while a pleading violin line seeks to rise, the brass and timpani repeatedly come in to thwart all movement. The introduction closes locked on a dominant pedal from which there appears to be no escape.[17]

But does not (practically) every slow introduction end with a dominant pedal? And do contrasts always imply dialectics? McClary's assumption that sensibility is Us and fanfare is Them presupposes a subject persona implicitly identified with the composer (and thus with the listener). That subject persona, 'the protagonist of the movement', as McClary calls it, is given its main portrayal in the opening theme of the Allegro. Observe the lengths to which McClary is prepared to go – or perhaps I should say the leniency she is prepared to show – in order to uphold the coherence of the narrative:

> Mozart does not show us how the protagonist of the movement's main part manages to pull out of that apparently hopeless situation. After a fermata, the new subject simply takes over – shaky at first, but without a trace of the events that might be posited somewhere in the gap between the fermata and the Allegro. Just as a film might fade on a prison scene, then move directly to a scene we understand to be situated some years later, so Mozart suggests 'that was then, this is now'. Yet what causes us to accept without much hesitation this fairly abrupt juxtaposition ... is the fact that however much the materials associated with that dominant pedal imply the impossibility of progress, the harmonic function itself stands in a cause/effect relationship with the tonic. Thus when the main part of the movement begins in D major ... the new materials serve as the proper, even inevitable resolution of the old. No struggle, no Bastille, certainly no Reign of Terror. We just find ourselves relocated in the new order (102, 104).

So an imagined French Revolution, or at least a bloodless coup, has occurred between the fermata and the Allegro – and all because dominant has resolved to tonic. The shape of the exposition, from quiet first theme to ebullient codetta, is also read as a political allegory, this time of the perpetually ascendant bourgeoisie.

Once past the introduction, the opening movement pursues two agendas – both crucial agendas in most areas of culture at the time: first, the self-generation of the self from relatively unformed beginnings to full maturation, and second, the demonstration that the persona thus fashioning itself also harbors deep inner feelings. Again, the critical distinction in German thought between aristocratic *Civilisation* and bourgeois *Kultur* demands this articulation of inside versus outside ... Mozart satisfies the external narrative of becoming by starting with an unusually insecure theme that ... even seems uncertain about which of its elements – melody or bass – constitutes its identity. Eventually, however, it develops into a triumphant closing theme that is every bit as powerful ... as the materials in the militant introduction (104–5).

But again a quite ordinary sequence of events is given a very particular reading, cast moreover not as the listener's interpretation but as the composer's strategy. A chance hearing on the radio of the overture to *Il Re Pastore*, K. 208, a two-act serenata by the nineteen-year-old Mozart to a libretto by Metastasio, composed eleven years before the 'Prague' Symphony for performance at the palace of the Archbishop of Salzburg, made me wonder whether McClary would read its opening, too, as the formation and maturation of the bourgeois subject. There really is nothing to stop her, or any of us, from imposing the narrative of our choice on any favourite piece of music if doing so inspires us or enhances our pleasure, but attributing the move to the composer is a particularly flagrant example of what I call the poietic fallacy, and what Abbate, long before me, called ventriloquism. It is a bid for the composer's authority.

Let us call it an esthesic abuse. But abuses connected with representation occur on the poietic side as well as the esthesic. Berlioz once made bold to censure Beethoven for mimetic excess. In his essay, 'De l'Imitation musicale', he complained that, when Rocco the jailer and Leonore move a big rock out of the way while digging a grave for Florestan in Act II of Beethoven's *Fidelio*, Beethoven has the double basses and contrabassoon accompany the rolling rock with a clumsy phrase in sixteenth-notes that makes the audience titter. 'This imitation', Berlioz fumed,

being in no way necessary either to the drama or to the effectiveness of the music, is really an end in itself for the composer: he imitates in order to imitate – and at once he falls into error, for there is in such imitation no poetry, no drama, no truth.[18]

I read these words with astonishment the first time, not because Berlioz was writing disparagingly about a composer he would have us revere, but because his words confirmed misgivings I had had (and have) about a composer we have been taught to revere even more, namely J.S. Bach. In the 1970s and 1980s I was active as a viola da gamba soloist. Like any working gambist, I looked forward every year at Easter time to participating in performances of Bach's Passions, in each of which there is an aria with a juicy gamba obbligato. The one in the St Matthew, 'Komm, süßes Kreuz', is one of the pinnacles of the literature. I was always honoured to be asked to play it, and always leapt at the chance, even though Passion gigs had their drawbacks. The chief one was having to sit for an hour or so onstage with nothing to do except play along occasionally with the chorales to make sure you were still in tune, and gawk at the audience. After the solo, there was nothing at all to do but gawk. So I noticed something curious that always happened at the recitative, 'Und siehe da, der Vorhang im Tempel zerriß', in which the evangelist tells of the violent earthquake that follows the death of Jesus. The virtuoso continuo part, which I always envied the cellist, is pure imitation or illustration of the most literal kind. And what I noticed was that the audiences I was gawking at invariably smiled, even chuckled at it, despite the terrible events it depicted, and despite the solemnity of the moment in the context of the Good Friday Gospel narrative. In rehearsals, the musicians would always laugh aloud and shout teasing encouragement to the cellist. ('Stick a fork in him' is one I have never forgotten.)

This is obviously no place for a joke; but that, it struck me, is what Bach's imitation of the earthquake inevitably was. No matter how lofty the context or exalted the theme, such imitations rely on the mechanisms of humour: puns (plays on similarities of sound), wit (apt conjunctions of incongruous things), caricature (deliberate exaggerations that underscore a resemblance). When they are good, it is because the intractability of the medium has been adroitly circumvented. When they are not, it is because they call excessive attention to their own contrivance, as is so often the case with puns. Jean-Jacques Rousseau already knew this, complaining in his *Dictionnaire de Musique* of 1768 that representationally inclined composers 'have to follow the example of the inept painter who must label his figures: *this is a tree, this is a man, this is a horse*'.[19] 'Of course music *can* represent', I thought (and wrote when I came to review Kivy's *Sound and Semblance*), 'just as a man can breathe underwater. In both cases, however, special equipment is required, special constraints are imposed, and special allowances must be made. In neither case is the thing done especially well or naturally, nor can invidious comparisons be avoided: music with painting, man with fish.'[20]

Did Bach actually think of musical mimesis in terms of jokes? At times, I think, he surely did, not to say that his intention necessarily redeems them. Consider the very popular cantata BWV 67 (*Halt im Gedächtnis Jesum Christ*) for the Sunday after Easter. One of its aria texts proclaims, 'Mein Jesus ist erstanden', so of course an ascending melodic line was *de rigueur*. The tenor soloist enters with the same incipit as the ritornello. The second time he does so, Bach playfully accompanies the incipit with six reiterations of the ascending motive. So far so virtuosic and appropriately merry – even inevitable. (After all, the *ascendit/descendit* antithesis was depicted by Palestrina pretty much the same way in the Credo of every one of his 104 Masses.) But in the second part of the aria Bach evidently got a little tired of the device and started to mock it by turning it around so as to make it do the opposite of what Christ is doing. I do not know whether making the viola the one going the wrong way was part of the joke, nor do I think Bach's congregation was supposed to notice and laugh. I would guess it was just a little wink between Bach and the viola player. But it certainly seems intentional: a comment on the artificiality of the device, and perhaps, even, a comment on its banality.

But with Handel, I feel certain that he not only knew that musical imitations were humorous, but that he often intended his audience to find them funny and laugh, even when the ostensible subject was anything but merry. Take *Israel in Egypt*. Berlioz, who did not know it (citing it by hearsay and inaccurately), singled it out for rebuke right after rebuking Beethoven for his lapse in *Fidelio*. 'The same could be said of Handel', he wrote:

> if it be true – as is commonly said – that in his oratorio *Israel in Egypt* he tried to reproduce the flight of locusts, and this to the point of shaping accordingly the rhythmic figure of the vocal parts. Surely that is a regrettable imitation of a subject even more regrettable – unworthy of music in general and of the noble and elevated style of the oratorio.[21]

But the imitation of the locusts takes place not in the voices but in the orchestra, when the cellos, basses, and bassoons come in with a running bass line in sixteenth notes to join the violins, who had already been imitating flies in thirty-seconds. Nobody who hears this passage ever receives it with a straight face. Before this the audience had made merry over Handel's imitation of frogs in the first and second violins, who play overlapping leaps – that is, who play leapfrog. And yet, what Handel is imitating here is no benign menagerie but rather the Ten Plagues God visited on the Egyptians. Handel turns this harrowing biblical episode into one of the funniest twenty minutes in all of dramatic music, and it has long been a classroom standby.

When I play it for my music history students, I stop to examine Handel's portrayal of the darkness, which relies on chromatic harmony and murky timbres (bassoons doubling violins now instead of the basses), which gives us a chance to explore a more sophisticated – because a more indirect – sort of mimesis. But then comes 'He SMOTE all the FIRST-born of EEE-GYPT', and we are all laughing again. Here is where I wheel around and ask the students, 'Hey, what are you laughing at?' And we all realize that we have been had, that Handel has manipulated us into withholding empathy from the suffering Egyptians. That withholding is an essential part of the biblical account of the Exodus, and the scorn of the biblical Israelites and their religious descendants in Handel's audience for the ancient oppressor is what enables the success of Handel's strategy of turning an awful tale into a merry entertainment. This musically engineered separation of self and other plays also into the ideology of nationalism, on which Handel was very successfully trading. A great deal of English national pride (or anybody's) depends on a perception of separateness from other nations, and superiority to them.

But such chauvinism and self-interest is at considerable variance with the liberal ideas we propagate nowadays in institutions of higher learning, and when the political message of Handel's oratorio is broached, and juxtaposed with contemporary events unfolding in the Middle East, the students are apt to feel embarrassed at the way Handel's music has persuaded them to dissociate their reactions as listeners from their ethical sentiments. It is what we now call 'cognitive dissonance', and 'a teachable moment', and what I am particularly intent on teaching by means of this example is the power of music – exactly through its representational aspects – to influence thought and behaviour.

III

So minimize or deride them though we may, musical representations are potent – and (again *pace* Kivy) important. Nor have we even begun to take their measure, for mimesis hardly exhausts the possibilities of musical representation. Nor is musical representation exclusively or even primarily the business of the composer, even though all the examples discussed so far have been examples of composers invoking or resorting to some form of mimesis. This is how musical representation is still usually conceived, in accordance with the poietic fallacy. If we wish to break the fallacy's hold, and open up the process of representation to a wider social agency, where shall we look to see it happening?

One area in which I see the esthesic side in effective balance with the poietic is the discourse of musical nationalism. Certainly composers have represented themselves as nationalists, but just as often communities of listeners have made the decision as to what music represents them. One standard example of this is Weber's *Der Freischütz*, a work that is stylistically quite French, but which since its première as the initial offering in an officially designated National Theatre has become an unshakable emblem of Germanness in music (just ask Wagner). Even more suggestive of the role of esthesis are the contests over the right to represent the nation in music that have taken place over the years, involving many national groups: Hungarians, Jews, Roma, and particularly (in terms of social contentiousness, length of debate, and breadth of attendant issues) Americans. Issues such as these – that is, issues of social mediation and contention – are no longer new to musicology, but they still offer tremendous scope for innovative research, particularly as regards representation. Whom does what represent, for what purpose, and who gets to decide? Such questions are not confined to nationalism, but they are always political, because they involve the claim and exercise of power. Whole repertories can be contested in this way, but also individual musical artefacts that work as social or political catalysts. Handel's manipulation of the audience's response to the plagues in *Israel in Egypt* already shows the political potential of musical representation, albeit within the realm of the poietic. Some recent examples of political contestation over musical meaning might give us a glimpse of where esthesic ground might yet be broken.

A new book by Eric Drott, which I recently had the pleasure of editing for my University of California Press series, *California Studies in Twentieth-Century Music*, gives a really tantalizing glimpse of where such studies may go.[22] It concerns the interaction of a wide variety of musics with politics in France after May 1968, and the myriad ways in which musical genres mediated political expression, in part by solidifying or disrupting group identities. One chapter, on free jazz, describes the efforts of certain critics to tie free jazz to Third World politics and African-American political activism – that is, to turn free jazz into a representation of a particular, politically volatile ideology or faction. Another, on street politics, concerns appropriations of musical artefacts (chiefly *La Marseillaise* and the *Internationale*) as a way both of fashioning political identities and of challenging them. Drott's work shows how the topic of representation in music might be refreshed, and brought into dialogue with some of the most pressing of our recent musicological projects, completely bypassing the bad old questions that have dependably bedevilled discussions of musical representation – questions of immanence, of poetic (or poietic) intent, of mimesis. Rouget de Lisle, Eugène Pottier, and Pierre Degeyter do not figure at all in Drott's discussion, for they, the authors of the hymns in question, let alone their intentions, are of no account in this context.

But if work like this, which delivers musical representation out of the clutches of composers, greatly enlarges the scope and weight of the concept, there remains an even broader, more encompassing sense in which we can speak of musical representation. Many have expressed an intuition that, even if we allow that music is a product of culture not nature, and add for good measure that music is alone among the arts in having no obvious natural model, nevertheless music *has* a nature in that there are things that music always accomplishes, irrespective of anyone's intention, whether composer, performer, listener, or mediator. Roger Sessions enunciated my favourite version of this insight. 'What music conveys to us', he wrote

> – and let it be emphasized, this is *the nature of the medium itself*, not the consciously formulated purpose of the composer – is the nature of our existence, as embodied in the movement that constitutes our innermost life: those inner gestures that lie behind not only our emotions, but our every impulse and action, which are in turn set in motion by these, and which in turn determine the ultimate character of life itself.[23]

Those are beautiful words, and I cannot tell you exactly what they mean, any more than I can tell you exactly what Mozart's Symphony in G minor means, but from the moment I first read them, my whole musical being responded with a great 'Yea' (a response the consciously formulated purpose of Sessions the composer has never evoked in me) – and a great 'Yea', I suppose, is what we mean by an intuition. But one thing I *can* say about this intuition is that it casts music as inherently representational. By nature it is a conveyance. And if we agree that Sessions is saying something similar to what W.H. Auden said when he called music 'a virtual image of our experience of living as temporal, with its double aspect of recurrence and becoming', then Auden, too, sees music as inherently representational – or rather, and even stronger, sees music as being by nature a representation.[24]

Another writer whose intuitions have inspired me is Wye Allanbrook, whose interest in topical analysis was prompted by her realization that 'most music I know can't help but imitate some form of human motion – breath length, gesture, dance, as do the symphonies [of Haydn and Mozart] in a graceful mimeticism removed from all actual occasions but still bearing the marks of their social and affective provenance'.[25] Here Allanbrook recalls the primary insight from her book *Rhythmic Gesture in Mozart*, which chiefly concerned the operas. For Mozart, she contended there, the purpose of music was 'to move an audience through representations of its own humanity', representations drawn from the repertoire of ritualized movement called social dance.[26] As we see, she extended the purview of this insight to cover the sort of textless instrumental music it is still conventional to call abstract.[27] In her late work she extended the purview still further, seeing social representation also in harmonically articulated musical form, whose closures are a virtual image (as Auden would say) of life's consummations as embodied in comic plots. But we all know this. While no one would call *Tristan und Isolde* a comedy, it is surely no tragedy either. What tells us that it is a drama of redemption is the world's most colossal harmonic close.

This aspect of musical representation – its standing as inherent in the musical experience – has another side that is right now commanding a great deal of attention. That is the school of thought that sees the representation not in the music, which can itself have no agency, but in our minds as we listen. According to this idea, music is intelligible to us – a condition that must precede all other effects – because we can represent it mentally in a way that mediates its sounds and makes them meaningful. That intuition is obviously related to Chomskian theories of linguistic competence. Its most extensive elaboration as yet is Fred Lerdahl and Ray Jackendoff's *Generative Theory of Tonal Music*, which is directly beholden to Chomsky, as well as to gestalt psychology.[28] But it is also reflected in the work of cognitive theorists such as Lawrence Zbikowski, and that of some psychologists, some philosophers and anthropologists, and a few evolutionary biologists as well.[29]

And now add one more ingredient. Roger Sessions's and Wye Allanbrook's compelling suggestions about music's *raison d'être* both rely on metaphors of movement. Such metaphors are common; indeed they are customary, accounting for much of our ordinary musical vocabulary. Symphonies have movements. (Yes, in Italian *movimento*, the originating word, means tempo; but that merely restates the definition of time, going back to Aristotle, as the measure of motion.) There are walking basses and running sixteenths. The tempo of the former is *andante*, and we will often find the latter in a *corrente*.[30]

But we all experience music as motion in yet another way that is intimately tied up with the behaviour of symphonic movements. When listening to what we call tonal music, by which we mean music in which form is articulated by harmony, we hear that harmonic articulation in terms of movement: specifically, in terms of departure and return. My vocabulary for describing this effect, as now inscribed in my *Oxford History*, was transformed by a conversation I had many years ago with a then-new colleague at Columbia University, the composer Dennis Riley (1943–99), when we were fellow assistant professors. Dennis had earned his PhD in composition at the University of Iowa, where one of his principal teachers was Donald Jenni (1937–2006). He told me about some of the teaching strategies he intended to take over from Jenni's teaching, and one of these was the term 'far out point' to denote the point from which the harmonic vagaries of the development section begin their turn towards the retransition. Jenni having studied at Stanford, the term was probably a variation on 'point of furthest remove', a favourite expression of Leonard Ratner, whose contribution to the reconceptualization of eighteenth-century music has been sorely underacknowledged (so I take pleasure in acknowledging it here). But Jenni's variant, 'far out point', which in the Oxford History is turned into an acronym, FOP, has a terrific ring, and it has never left me since that casual conversation more than thirty years ago. I have striven ever since to get my students to conceptualize musical form in terms of a harmonic trajectory – that is, a virtual movement that coincides with what we actually call a movement.

Of course thinking about harmony virtually moving over actual time invokes a concept of virtual space as well, and just as many writers resort to metaphors of space as to motion when discussing musical concepts. Fred Lerdahl recently published a treatise titled *Tonal Pitch Space*,[31] but he certainly did not originate the concept his titular phrase so neatly encapsulates. In an article published thirty years ago, Robert P. Morgan wrote, 'Not only do listeners perceive changes in density and volume, they are conscious of different "locations" within the available tonal range', and now recall that in the terminology of medieval music theory, particular pitches – for example, *C sol fa ut* – were called *loci*, locations. Morgan goes on to observe that the available tonal range, 'understood as an abstract indication of the range of humanly perceptible pitches, is in fact commonly referred to by musicians as "tonal space", a designation that corresponds to our perception of music as moving through something – for example from a higher position to a lower one'.[32] Later he describes musical space as 'a space of relationships' of a sort that exists 'in all musical cultures', being 'an accepted set of possible, or "allowable", musical relationships that exists prior to any given composition'. That is precisely what Lerdahl sets out to describe in his book.

Morgan claims that the space of relationships is purely conventional, but among the conventions he enumerates are a few that come close to being universals. 'The concept of the octave, for example', he writes, 'one of tonality's most basic assumptions, provides for the division of the total pitch range into a series of "compartments", each covering an equal segment of tonal space and defined by the appearance of the "same" pitch in different registers.'[33] But octave equivalency is not the exclusive assumption of 'tonality'. There is no form of formally theorized music, to my knowledge, that does not assume it; and one team of researchers claimed to have observed or elicited recognition of octave equivalency in rhesus monkeys.[34] Morgan goes on to describe some features of tonal space that do correlate with tonality, such as a sense of relative distance from what he calls 'a central pitch', involving such additional distinctions as that between diatonic and chromatic members of the total field. Summing up, he writes that 'the uniqueness of any given composition is ... primarily a function of the particular "route" along which it moves temporally through this prescribed space', and hence, that 'any meaningful concept of musical space must incorporate, at some level, the factor of musical time; and equally, a meaningful concept of musical time must include that of musical space'.[35]

Thus it is really a time/space continuum that Morgan describes. Both the temporal and spatial aspects of Morgan's concept, and the specific way in which they are necessarily interrelated as he stipulates, depend once again on the metaphor of motion, as he implies when he imagines a musical composition moving through his postulated space according to its own particular route. Schenker naturally appears in the vicinity of this remark, since Morgan is making music the agent, 'mov[ing] through, and thereby defin[ing], its own musical space'[36] according to the dictates of the tones – *der Tonwille*, if you please, ranging through *der Tonraum*.

IV

But what if we were to think of musical space somewhat differently: not as something through which music moves, but something through which we move as we listen? In his first book of conversations with Robert Craft, Stravinsky makes a really striking comment along these lines: 'We are located in time constantly in a tonal system work, but we may only "go through" a polyphonic work, whether Josquin's *Duke Hercules Mass* or a serially composed non-tonal-system work.'[37] The two things that strike me most forcefully in this remark are, first, that Stravinsky is so comfortable with the assumption of a time/space continuum that he uses a space-word, 'located', to describe our perception of the temporal unfolding of music without any inkling that this usage could be seen as anomalous, or even as metaphorical. Second, as Stravinsky reports his experience, the music does not move; rather he moves (or we move) through the music. Musical space is registered, as it were, somatically, by our imagined physical location, and it affords our virtual bodies a field through which to move.

Add this intuition to those of Sessions and Allanbrook, Ratner and Jenni, and you have a very close approximation of my own sense of involvement in music – or, what I really wish to say, my own inner representation of it. The verbal formulation that comes closest to my own is that of Charles O. Nussbaum, a philosopher with a strong musical past (having started his career as a professional bassoonist), whose recent book, *The Musical Representation*, has given me some new and useful concepts to think with.[38]

The main one, paradoxically enough, is *affordance*. I borrowed it a moment ago in saying that conceptualized or internally represented musical space *affords* our virtual bodies a field through which to move. What is paradoxical is that the term was coined by James Gibson, an ecological psychologist who made a career of disputing the necessity for internal representation. And yet Nussbaum makes a strong case for appropriating the term, despite that irony. Gibsonian affordances are defined as 'properties of objects in the environment that offer action possibilities to the observer'.[39] A chair, for example, has, according to Gibson, a 'sit upon' affordance; a table has an 'eat at' or a 'write at' affordance depending on whether we are hungry or need to work on a conference paper.

Nussbaum's application of affordance theory conceives of music as implicating our haptic and motor responses, but without actually initiating action. He calls this 'off-line' response. 'To run commands off-line', he writes, 'is to simulate actions imaginatively without engaging the relevant motor systems.' And yet, he maintains, our internal representations of music 'effect appropriate motor commands that [do] proceed outward to muscle effectors'.[40] Our actual motor commands are both initiated and inhibited by our musical responses. They are not entirely killed, for many of us – perhaps all of us – do indeed respond to music by moving our bodies while listening, even if we manage to inhibit our impulse to march or dance.

Talk of inhibition will bring the work of Leonard Meyer to a musicologist's mind, and Nussbaum classifies his theory of musical representation as being, like Meyer's, a 'weak arousal theory'. But the theories have significant differences, and one of the most convincing passages in Nussbaum's treatise invokes affordance theory to answer a question that gave Meyer trouble. 'To a fleet quadruped', he writes, 'a flat expanse appears runnable; to a hydrodynamic fish, a body of water appears swimmable.' And to us music-minded humans, listening to music confronts us imaginatively with a similar 'actionable' environment. This is the source not only of motor responses but also affective responses, which arise, Nussbaum claims, 'out of an ongoing attempt to negotiate a musical virtual terrain, to act in accordance with its musical affordances, dealing with surprises, impediments, failures, and successes on the way, and requiring the constant reevaluation of strategy to which emotional response is keyed'.[41]

This negotiation can be enjoyably – or at least effectively – replayed, and this is the way in which it differs from the familiar Meyerian 'implication-realization' model of mental musical representation. Meyer's model was based on information theory. Meyer viewed musical expectations and their pleasurable fulfilment or affect-laden frustration as occurring in actual rather than virtual circumstances; and that is why pleasurable rehearing could be an effectual counterexample to his theory.[42] As Nussbaum observes, 'we are not put into significant *informational* suspense with each subsequent hearing concerning what will happen next, even if we countenance musical "nuance properties" [as Meyer proposed] that are registered in peripheral modular input systems but not centrally represented or retained in long-term memory'. Like any reasonable person, Nussbaum agrees that 'acquiring the same piece of information over and over again quickly palls. Indeed, any reaction, short of genuine reflex, to a novel event will be extinguished through repetition.' Since our pleasure in rehearing music is not extinguished, it cannot derive from information acquisition. And yet, he reminds us,

> *Doing* the same over and over again, even something as mundane as a challenging and varied daily exercise set, can maintain interest, because the interest lies in the doing. The powerful affective feelings that continue to attend the experience even of well-known recorded performances where nuances, even if some of them cannot be held in long-term memory in all their detail, remain exactly the same between hearings, far more plausibly derive from simulated action *undertaken* and experience *undergone* … They derive from *doing*, not from *discovering*.[43]

As I grasped Nussbaum's theory of actionable environments and affordances, my memory furnished a steady supply of corroborations, both from my own experience and from remarks and accounts I have read of other musicians. I was reminded of Scriabin's remark that his exploration of symmetrical tonal pitch space (to use Fred Lerdahl's term) was sparked by his wish to be able 'to walk around a chord' (to use his term).[44] I was reminded of Wagner's conceptualization of harmony as a sea, which is nothing if not a Gibsonian affordance, it being to Wagner a navigable expanse. I even thought of Hanslick. What else could 'tönend bewegte Formen' mean? Why else speak of *Bewegen*? Indeed, Hanslick identifies himself as a Gibsonian in the second chapter of his treatise, where he writes: 'The concept of motion has up to now been conspicuously neglected in investigations of the nature and effects of music. It seems to us the most important and fruitful concept.'[45]

But most spectacularly of all, I remembered Edgard Varèse, who was still a charismatic presence on the new music scene when I was a student. One saw him at concerts from afar, radiating a kind of electricity, not least by virtue of his electrified hair – thin kinky wires that seemed to be standing up or even taking a walk around his head in reaction to some sort of internal ionization. Once I saw him up close, the evening of 19 April 1965, less than seven months before his death, when he came up to Columbia to hear a concert at which his *Intégrales* was played by Charles Wuorinen and Harvey Sollberger's Group for Contemporary Music. He plunked himself down right in front of me, and I spent the whole concert staring at his broad round shoulders and magic hair from behind. He was already very ill and had to be helped in and out of his seat and supported when he walked. He sat slumped and motionless throughout the programme, including the intermission. But when the last piece on the programme, namely his, began to sound, he jolted – or was jolted – into an erect posture and began twitching in response to the music as if a current were passing through him. How I wished at that moment I could have joined him on his inner journey, but then I realized that I could do that and was in fact doing it, responding along with him to the wonderful music he had written and, though I would not learn the word for another forty-five years, its affordances.

The night I was privileged to observe him Varèse was eighty-one. To me (I had just turned twenty), he was unimaginably old, though my perspective on that has undergone some change as I have racked up years. So let me end by recalling an even older lion in winter, Carl Ruggles. In 1970 when Ruggles was ninety-four, Michael Tilson Thomas (then twenty-six) performed and recorded Ruggles's largest work, *Sun-Treader*, with the Boston Symphony Orchestra, and then sought the composer out at the nursing home where he was living in obscurity. 'I had been told that Mr. Ruggles was inclined to be suspicious of new people and retreat behind the curtain of his infirmities', Maestro Thomas recalled,

So … I just walked into his room, said 'Hello', set up a tape recorder, put some light earphones on his old and shriveled head, cranked the volume up as high as possible and started to play an air check of the performance of *Sun-Treader*. The first timpani stroke of the work hit the old man like a hammer. Suddenly he was sitting bolt upright, his eyes wild and open, like an eagle, his breath coming in fast, hoarse grunts and growls and guttural noise: 'Fine'. 'Great!' 'Damn, DAMN FINE WORK!' He kept it up right through the whole piece, sometimes singing or moaning along with the music until the end.

As the conductor left, he asked Ruggles whether he still thought about music:

'Think about it every day – always. I'm composing, you know, right now – all the time. But my body, do you see? It is totally diseased, there's not a part of it that works right. So I'm sorry that I can't write anymore, can't finish what I've started – or start new. But in my spirit I am unvanquished. I can't write but I'm composing. Every day.'

I asked him if he could sing some of what he was composing.

'First there are horns ...' He began to sing, rasp, scream musical lines, all with his distinctive shapes, interjecting. 'Here flutes! And strings – molto rubato, rubato!' And as we turned to go, he said:

'Now don't go feeling sorry. I don't hang around *this* place, you know. Hell, each day I go out and make the universe anew – all over!'[46]

Runnable fields, swimmable water, a rangeable universe – that is music. Ruggles was out there with Wagner navigating the sea of harmony. We also negotiate that inner terrain and can at least tag along with the great navigators. Do we need a representation of the music to avail ourselves of its affordances? I can agree with Gibsonians that we do not need the kind of representation that Jonathan Bernard (uniquely denying octave equivalency) has provided of Varèse's space, or Allen Forte of Stravinsky's.[47] These static images are indeed redundant reproductions of our intuitions, because they try to capture an abstracted image devoid of space and movement. But, as Sessions first disclosed to me, there is an inner space which composers and listeners do inhabit, where they can move and meet; and that music, in representing it, provides the meeting place. What else could be its purpose?

Notes

1 Igor Stravinsky, *An Autobiography* (1936; New York: W.W. Norton, 1962), 53. The original French: 'la musique, par son essence, est impuissante à *exprimer* quoi que ce soit.' The ghostwriter was Walter Nouvel.
2 Walter Pater, *The Renaissance: Studies in Art and Poetry* (1873; London: Macmillan, 1922), 134–5.
3 Susan Sontag, *Against Interpretation* (New York: Delta, 1967), 12.
4 Cf. James Hepokoski, 'Beethoven Reception: The Symphonic Tradition' in Jim Samson (ed.), *The Cambridge History of Nineteenth-Century Music* (Cambridge University Press, 2001), 430; or, Sok-Hoon Tan, 'The "Gypsy" Style as Extramusical Reference: A Historical and Stylistic Reassessment of Liszt's Book I "Swiss" of "Années de pèlerinage"' (Master's thesis, University of North Texas, 2008), http://digital.library.unt.edu/ark:/67531/metadc6046/, accessed 3 March 2010.
5 www.merriam-webster.com/dictionary/extramusical, accessed 3 March 2010.
6 Richard Taruskin, Review of *The Corded Shell*, by Peter Kivy, *Musical Quarterly*, 68.2 (1982), 287–93.

7 Peter Kivy, *The Corded Shell: Reflections on Musical Expression* (Princeton University Press, 1980), 16.
8 Robert Schumann, *On Music and Musicians*, ed. Konrad Wolff, trans. Paul Rosenfeld (New York: W.W. Norton, 1969), 60.
9 Sigmund Spaeth, *Great Symphonies: How to Recognize and Remember Them* (Garden City, NY: Garden City Publishing Co., 1936), 39.
10 Peter Kivy, *Sound Sentiment: An Essay on the Musical Emotions, Including the Complete Text of* The Corded Shell (Philadelphia: Temple University Press, 1989), 204. 'What we would do, what we *do* do when confronted with an expressive characterization of a piece of music, is to go back to the music itself with that interpretation in mind, to see if we, too, can hear what the interpreter claims to hear. And if no consensus develops, surely we are arguing to the best explanation here, as in the case of the aberrant judgment about wine, when we argue that that characterization is "merely subjective." What else, for example, could we say, or need we say, to Sigmund Spaeth?'
11 Kivy, *The Corded Shell*, 148.
12 The most sustained discussion I know is Raymond Monelle, *The Sense of Music: Semiotic Essays* (Princeton University Press, 2000), 17 and 66–73; see also Robert Hatten, *Interpreting Musical Gestures, Topics, and Tropes* (Bloomington: Indiana University Press, 2004), 140–2. (Hatten reminds us that the two-note descending slur, while remaining an iconic sign, can also connote otherwise; for example, 'as the musical analogue to such ritualized social gestures as bows, nods, inflections of the wrist and hand, and other aristocratic social graces'.)
13 V. Kofi Agawu, *Playing with Signs: A Semiotic Interpretation of Classic Music* (Princeton University Press, 1991), 20.
14 Wye J. Allanbrook, 'Two Threads Through the Labyrinth' in Wye J. Allanbrook, Janet Levy, and William Mahrt (eds.), *Convention in Eighteenth- and Nineteenth-Century Music: Essays in Honor of Leonard G. Ratner* (Stuyvesant, NY: Pendragon Press, 1992), 170.
15 Peter Kivy, *Sound and Semblance: Reflections on Musical Representation* (Princeton University Press, 1984), 19 and 216.
16 Carolyn Abbate, 'Music – Drastic or Gnostic?', *Critical Inquiry*, 30.3 (Spring 2004), 516.
17 Susan McClary, *Conventional Wisdom: The Content of Musical Form* (Berkeley and Los Angeles: University of California Press, 2000), 102; further citations will be made in the main text.
18 Hector Berlioz, 'De l'Imitation musicale', trans. Jacques Barzun; quoted in Berlioz, *Fantastic Symphony*, ed. Edward T. Cone (Norton Critical Scores; New York: W.W. Norton, 1971), 39.
19 Jean-Jacques Rousseau, *Dictionnaire de musique* (Paris, 1768), 452; trans. Richard Taruskin in Piero Weiss and Richard Taruskin (eds.), *Music in the Western World: A History in Documents*, 2nd edn (Belmont, CA: Thomson/Schirmer, 2007), 244.

20 Richard Taruskin, Review of *Sound and Sentiment*, by Peter Kivy, *Journal of Music Theory*, 29 (1985), 349.
21 Berlioz, 'De l'Imitation musicale', 39.
22 Eric Drott, *Music and the Elusive Revolution: Cultural Politics and Political Culture in France, 1968–1981* (Berkeley and Los Angeles: University of California Press, 2011).
23 Roger Sessions, *Questions About Music* (New York: W.W. Norton, 1971), 45.
24 W.H. Auden, 'The Dyer's Hand', *The Listener* (30 June 1955).
25 Wye J. Allanbrook, 'The Conundrum of the Magic Flute', paper read at the conference 'After The Magic Flute', University of California at Berkeley (6 March 2010); typescript, 7.
26 Wye J. Allanbrook, *Rhythmic Gesture in Mozart* (University of Chicago Press, 1983), 16.
27 The remark quoted in n.25 was made in direct retort to Karol Berger's characterization of Tamino's magical flute music as the birth of 'modern abstract music' in *Bach's Cycle, Mozart's Arrow* (Berkeley and Los Angeles: University of California Press, 2007), 286.
28 Fred Lerdahl and Ray Jackendoff, *A Generative Theory of Tonal Music* (Cambridge, MA: MIT Press, 1983).
29 See, *inter alia*, Lawrence Zbikowski, *Conceptualizing Music: Cognitive Structure, Theory, and Analysis* (Oxford University Press, 2002).
30 Not every language calls the large divisions of an extended musical work 'movements', and that can create problems of translation. In German, they are *Sätze*, an ambiguous term adapted from grammar (where it usually means 'sentence'), and applicable not only to what we call movements, but also to lower divisions such as expositions and developments, or even phrases. In Russian, the movements of a symphony are simply called *chasti*, 'parts'. I recall an argument I once had with the late Simon Karlinsky, who was a trained composer before he became a literary scholar, and who wrote extensively about Stravinsky. He complained about the Russian edition of Stravinsky's Symphony in Three Movements that translated the title using the Russian word *dvizheniye*, which means, literally and generally, any sort of movement. Simon wrote that the proper Russian should have been 'Symphony in Three Parts', rather than 'Symphony', as he put it, 'in Three Motions'. I agreed, but I had to disagree when he made a similar complaint about the Russian title of Stravinsky's Movements for Piano and Orchestra, which was also *Dvizheniya*. It seemed utterly senseless to call that piece 'Parts for Piano and Orchestra', as actual movement seemed an integral part of its concept (just ask George Balanchine). I am glad that English translates *movimento* with a cognate, for that preserves an intuition about music that I would hate giving up.
31 Fred Lerdahl, *Tonal Pitch Space* (Oxford University Press, 2001).
32 Robert P. Morgan, 'Musical Time/Musical Space', *Critical Inquiry*, 6 (1980), 527–38 (538).

33 *Ibid.*, 530.
34 Anthony A. Wright, Jacquelyne J. Rivera, Stewart H. Hulse, Melissa Shyan, and Julie J. Neiworth, 'Music Perception and Octave Generalization in Rhesus Monkeys', *Journal of Experimental Psychology: General*, 129 (2000), 291–307.
35 Morgan, 'Musical Time/Musical Space', 530.
36 *Ibid.*, 532.
37 Igor Stravinsky and Robert Craft, *Conversations with Igor Stravinsky* (Garden City, NY: Doubleday and Co., 1959), 23.
38 Charles O. Nussbaum, *The Musical Representation* (Cambridge, MA: MIT Press, 2007).
39 Clint Heinze, *Modelling Intention Recognition for Intelligent Agent Systems* (Edinburgh, South Australia: DSTO Systems Sciences Laboratory, 2004), 31.
40 Nussbaum, *The Musical Representation*, 35.
41 *Ibid.*, 214.
42 For his not very convincing rejoinder, see Leonard B. Meyer, 'On Rehearing Music', *Journal of the American Musicological Society*, 14.2 (Summer 1961), 257–67; reprinted in Leonard B. Meyer, *Music, the Arts, and Ideas*, 2nd edn (University of Chicago Press, 1994), 42–53.
43 Nussbaum, *The Musical Representation*, 216–17.
44 Remark communicated to Georgiy Mikhailovich Rimsky-Korsakov, then communicated to Varvara Dernova, who recorded it in *Garmoniya Skryabina* (Leningrad: Muzïka, 1968), 352.
45 Eduard Hanslick, *On the Musically Beautiful*, trans. Geoffrey Payzant (Indianapolis: Hackett Publishing Co., 1986), 11.
46 Liner note to *The Complete Music of Carl Ruggles*, Buffalo Philharmonic, etc., conducted by Michael Tilson Thomas (CBS Masterworks M2 34591, 1980).
47 Jonathan Bernard, *The Music of Edgard Varèse* (New Haven and London: Yale University Press, 1987); Allen Forte, *The Harmonic Organization of* The Rite of Spring (New Haven and London: Yale University Press, 1978).

Index

Abbate, Carolyn, 23, 292, 294
absolute music, 107
Adam of Fulda, 225
Adams, John, 270–83
   Death of Klinghoffer, The, 272, 277–8
   Doctor Atomic, 272, 278–80
   Flowering Tree, A, 272, 276–7, 282
   Harmonielehre, 277
   Hoodoo Zephyr, 271
   Nixon in China, 272–6, 280–1
Adorno, Theodor W., 203
affordance, 303–6
Agawu, Kofi, 220, 291–2
Aiken, George, 115–16
Alberti, Leon Battista, 128
All About Eve, 205, 210–13
Allan, Maud, 145
Allanbrook, Wye, 208, 291–2, 299–300, 302
allusion, 168–79
Al-Rusafi, Marouf, 262–3
American Idol, 80
anime, 90
Apollinaire, Guillaume, 158
Aristotle, 128
Arlen, Harold, 64–76
   'Accentuate the Positive', 64
   'Blues in the Night', 64
   'Come Rain or Come Shine', 64
   'Get Happy', 64–5
   'Man That Got Away, The', 64, 67–71, 73, 75
   'Over the Rainbow', 64, 67, 75
   'Sleepin' Bee, A', 64, 67, 72–6
   'Stormy Weather', 64
Astruc, Gabriel, 150
Atkins, Cholly, 275
Auden, W.H., 299
Augustine, 184, 199
Avedon, Richard, 135

Bach, Carl Philipp Emanuel, 127, 129, 134
   'L'Aly Rupalich', 134
Bach, Johann Sebastian, 19, 167, 271, 291–2, 294–6
   Brandenburg Concerto no. 6, BWV 1051, 167
   Cantata BWV 21, 291
   Cantata BWV 67, 295
   cantatas, 271
   St Matthew Passion, 294–5
   Well-Tempered Clavier, 291
Bacon, Francis, 129, 136
Bailey, Pearl, 71
Balanchivadze, Andria, 54
Balanchine, George, 71, 308
Baldo, Gino, 155–6
Balfour, Arthur James, 261
Barbare, Kevin, 89
Bartók, Béla, 127, 276
Baudelaire, Charles, 110–11, 147, 157
Beatles, 80
Beethoven, Ludwig van, 16, 23, 25, 35, 37–40, 45, 51, 88, 108–9, 111, 118–20, 122–3, 133, 146–7, 150, 167, 294, 296
   An die Ferne Geliebte, 23, 108–9
   Fidelio, 294, 296
   Piano Sonata Op. 27, no. 2, 'Moonlight', 133, 150
   Symphony No. 5, 51, 167
Bellman, Jonathan, 20
Benjamin, Walter, 33
Berger, Karol, 20, 223, 308
Berigan, Bunny, 221
Berlin, Irving, 64–5
Berlioz, Hector, 51, 294, 296
   Symphonie fantastique, 289
Bernard, Jonathan, 306
Bernini, Gian Lorenzo, 241
Bhabha, Homi, 249, 257, 261
Bhagavad Gita, 278
Bicycle Thieves, 220
Birth of Tragedy, The, 112
Bizet, Georges, 52
Body Heat, 221
Bolger, Ray, 65
Bonynge, Richard, 115
Booth, Michael, 115
Bosch, Hieronymus, 138
Bourgeois gentilhomme, Le, 231
Brahms, Johannes, 13–26

Ballade Op. 10, no. 1, 16, 23, 25
Ballade Op. 10, no. 2, 32
Ballade Op. 10, no. 3, 32
Ballade Op. 10, no. 4, 26
Ballade Op. 118, no. 3, 26
Ballade Op. 118, no. 5, 32
Ballade Op. 118, no. 6, 32
Handel Variations, Op. 24, 19
Piano Sonata in F# minor, Op. 2, 21
Piano Sonata Op. 5, 23
Scherzo, Op. 4, 19
'Song of Destiny', Op. 54, 31
'Song of the Fates', Op. 89, 31
Braque, Georges, 158
Bredekamp, Horst, 241
Britten, Benjamin, 134, 276
'Portrait No. 2 (E.B.B.)', 134
Brook, Peter, 71
Brueghel the Elder, Pieter, 138
Buggles, The, 92
'Video Killed the Radio Star', 92
Buhler, James, 220
Bülow, Hans von, 19
bunraku, 271
Burgess, Jean, 91, 94, 96
Butler, David, 221

Cahill, Sarah, 277
Canudo, Ricciotto, 157–8, 160
Capote, Truman, 71–3, 76
Carré, Michel, 114
Carrière, Eugène, 152
Carroll, Diahann, 71
Cassirer, Ernst, 227
Cellini, Benvenuto, 241
Cézanne, Paul, 152, 157
Chaplin, Charlie, 137
Charles V, 241
Chennevière, Daniel, 158
Childs, Lucinda, 280
Chinatown, 203–5, 208–9, 214–18
Chion, Michel, 221
Chirico, Andrea de. *See* Savinio, Alberto
Chirico, Giorgio de, 164
Chomsky, Noam, 300
Chopin, Frédéric, 16, 20, 22, 26, 45, 129, 134, 136, 138–9, 150–1
Piano Sonata in B flat minor, Op. 35, 136
Citizen Kane, 212
Clarétie, Jules, 149
Clarétie, Léo, 149–50
Clark, T.J., 139, 141, 160
Clement VII, 241

Clendinning, Jane Piper, 137
Cler, Albert, 36–7, 39
Close, Chuck, 129–34
Cohan, George M., 64
computer music, 227
Cook, Nicholas, 209
Corbin, Alain, 34
Corigliano, John, 270, 272, 279
Ghosts of Versailles, The, 272, 279
Couperin, François, 127, 129, 134
'La Couperin', 134
Cozanet, Albert. *See* D'Udine, Jean
Craft, Robert, 302
Crary, Jonathan, 44
Crommelynck, Aldo, 136
Cubism, 158
Cultural Revolution, 272, 275–6

d'Annunzio, Gabriele, 157
Dahlhaus, Carl, 15, 182–3, 210–11, 220, 222, 226
Daines, Matthew, 281
Dalman, Gustaf, 254–5
dance, 144–61, 207–8, 276, 279–80, 282, 299, 303
Danuser, Hermann, 17
Darwin, Charles, 148, 195, 197
David, Jacques-Louis, 135
Deathridge, John, 169
Debussy, Claude, 149–51, 158, 203
Degas, Edgar, 152
Degeyter, Pierre, 298
Delacroix, Eugène, 117
Demuth, Charles, 129
Descartes, René, 128
description, 226
Diaghilev, Sergey, 145, 147
Dies Irae, 289
Doempke, Gustav, 20–1
Döhler, Theodor, 45
Doisneau, Robert, 136
Doktor Faustus, 226
Dostoevsky, Fyodor, 199
Dreier, Katherine, 129
Droeghmans, Maurice, 158
Drott, Eric, 298
Dryden, John, 116–17
D'Udine, Jean, 146–50, 152, 154, 159–60
Dunaway, Faye, 203
Duncan, Isadora, 145–6, 149, 155

Eisler, Hanns, 203
Elgar, Edward, 33, 127

emotion, 14–15, 54, 58, 68, 75, 86, 91, 103, 128, 130–2, 148–9, 168, 184, 210, 243, 251–2, 263, 267, 299, 303
Escher, M.C., 138
Evans, Robert, 221
exoticism, 268–9, 272, 274–8, 283

Faust, 114–15
Feinstein, Michael, 72
Fields, Dorothy, 221
film noir, 209
Finnegan, Ruth, 95
Forkel, Johann Nikolaus, 14
Forte, Allen, 306
Foucault, Michel, 251
France, Anatole, 149
Fräulein von Scuderi, Das, 228
Freud, Lucian, 135
Fuchs, Hanns, 169, 172
Fuller, Loie, 145, 149–55, 159–60

G4, 87
Gagaku, 271
Garland, Judy, 64–5, 68–70, 75
Gauguin, Paul, 157
genre, 13–26, 40–1, 48, 53, 58, 80, 87, 89–92, 96, 127, 229, 267–8, 298
George of Hanover, 44–5
Gershwin, George, 64–5
Gershwin, Ira, 67–8
Gibson, James, 303–4, 306
Gilbert and Sullivan, 83
    Mikado, The, 270–1, 281
Gilbert, William Schwenk. *See* Gilbert and Sullivan
Glasenapp, Carl Friedrich, 185
Glass, Philip, 127, 129–34, 140–1, 270, 278
    Einstein on the Beach, 130
    'Music in Similar Motion', 131
    Music in Twelve Parts, 131
    'Musical Portrait of Chuck Close, A', 129–34, 141
    Satyagraha, 278
    'Two Pages', 130
Gleizes, Albert, 158
Glukh, Mikhail, 59
Goethe, Johann Wolfgang von, 25, 114, 279
Goldberg, Isaac, 66, 70
Goldsmith, Jerry, 203, 208–9, 215–18
Goodman, Alice, 272
Goodman, Nelson, 224
Gorbman, Claudia, 210
Gounod, Charles, 114–15

Gowers, Bruce, 80, 87, 95
Graf, Raimund, 254–7
Gramit, David, 251
Graves, Nancy, 130
Green, Joshua, 91, 94, 96
Gumbrecht, Hans Ulrich, 224

Haeckel, Ernst, 148
Hall, Juanita, 71
Hamilton, Richard, 136
Handel, George Frideric, 39–41, 272, 296–8
    Israel in Egypt, 296–8
    Messiah, 39–40
Hanslick, Eduard, 287–9, 304
Harburg, E.Y., 67
Hard Day's Night, A, 80
Harrison, George, 271
Harry Potter, 92
Hatten, Robert S., 220
Haydn, Joseph, 146–7, 214, 299
    Creation, The, 214
Heatley, Michael, 81
Heine, Heinrich, 107–8
Henselt, Adolph von, 45
Herbert, Victor, 64
Herder, Johann Gottfried, 19, 22
Hilden, Joy Totah, 263–4
Hindemith, Paul, 225, 227–34, 239–40, 242–3
    Cardillac, 225, 227–43
    Das Marienleben, Op. 27, 228
Hirschkind, Charles, 251
Hitler, Adolf, 55, 113, 239
Hockney, David, 135–6
Hoffmann, E.T.A., 38, 110, 120, 228, 240–1
Hofmannsthal, Hugo von, 231
Hogarth, George, 41–2
Homer, 257
homoerotics, 168–79
House of Flowers, 67, 71–3, 76
Hullah, John, 41
Husserl, Edmund, 184
Hyginus, Gaius Julius, 118

iconography, 86, 89, 107, 226
identity, 13–15, 20, 65–6, 86, 127–9, 132, 134–7, 139–41, 144
intention, 15, 128, 147, 152, 168, 216, 269–70, 291, 295–6, 298
Irving, Henry, 114–15
Ives, Charles, 127, 208, 289
    Unanswered Question, The, 208

Jablonski, Edward, 64–5, 67
Jackendoff, Ray, 300
Jaques-Dalcroze, Émile, 147, 149
Jaws, 213–15
jazz, 55, 65, 83, 215, 221, 298
Jeitteles, Alois, 108
Jenkins, Henry, 92, 94
Jenni, Donald, 300–2
Johnson, Buffie, 129, 139–41
Jordan, Armin, 182
Josquin des Prez, 302
Joukowsky, Paul von, 176, 178
Julius II, 241

Kabalevsky, Dmitry, 50, 57–8
kabuki, 271
Kalbeck, Max, 22–3, 25
Karmén, Elena, 52
Karolsfeld, Schnorr von, 175, 178
Kater Murr, 120
Keller, Gottfried, 169
Kern, Jerome, 64–5, 221
ketjak, 276–7
Khachaturian, Aram, 53, 57
    Symphony No. 2, 57
    Violin Concerto, 53
Khrennikov, Tikhon, 58–9
Khubov, Georgy, 51
Kirchhoff, Markus, 255
Kivy, Peter, 289–90, 292, 295, 297
Koch, Heinrich Christoph, 13
Koehler, Ted, 65, 67
Kosmodemyanskaya, Zoya, 55
Koval, Marian, 48–9, 59
Kremlyov, Yu., 58
Kripke, Saul, 205–7, 210, 218
Krudy, Gyula, 137
Kullak, Theodor, 31

Lamartine, Alphonse, 154
Lambro, Phillip, 219
Lange, Patricia, 94
Le Dantec, Félix, 148–9
Leib-Monsohn, Avraham, 257
leitmotif, 169, 172, 176, 182–4, 203–18
Leoni, Leone, 241
Lerdahl, Fred, 300–1, 304
Lessig, Lawrence, 93–5
Levingston, Bruce, 130, 133
Lewis, David, 222
Lieberson, Goddard, 72
Ligeti, György, 127, 129, 134–41
    'Continuum', 137

Drei Stücke für zwei Klaviere, 134
    'Selbstportrait', 134–9, 141
    String Quartet No. 2, 137
    'Volumina', 137
Lindbergh, Charles, 240
Lindenberger, Herbert, 269, 278
Lindgren, Ernest, 86
Lion, Ferdinand, 228, 242
Lisle, Rouget de, 298
Liszt, Franz, 45, 51, 111, 113, 117–18, 289
Little Red Book, 276
Livanova, Tamara, 60
Locke, John, 128
Locke, Ralph, 269
London, Justin, 205–7, 210, 212–13
Long, Michael, 208–9
Lorimer, Hayden, 250
Lorrain, Jean, 151
Ludwig II of Bavaria, 173, 176, 178–9, 197
Lully, Jean-Baptiste, 227–32, 234–6
    Phaëton, 227–8, 234–6

Magritte, René, 138
Mahler, Gustav, 75, 167
    Symphony No. 4, 167
Malevich, Kasimir, 135
Mallarmé, Stéphane, 150–2, 157
Mangeot, André, 146–7
Mann, Thomas, 226
Mantell, A.M., 252
Marchand, Suzanne L., 254
Marinetti, Filippo Tommaso, 160
Marston, Nicholas, 120, 122
Martin, John, 43
Mason, James, 68
Matheson, Johann, 13
Matz, Peter, 66
Mauclair, Camille, 159
McClary, Susan, 292–4
McPhee, Colin, 276
Mendelssohn, Felix, 25, 107–8, 289
    'Auf Flügeln des Gesanges', 107–8
    Lieder ohne Worte, 25
    Symphony No. 3, 'Scottish', 289
    Symphony No. 4, 'Italian', 289
mental representation, 104, 304
Mercer, Johnny, 67
Mercury, Freddie, 79–82, 87, 89, 92
Messel, Oliver, 71
Messiaen, Olivier, 276
Metamorphoses, 118
metaphor, 87, 144, 152, 154, 168, 176–9, 300
Metastasio, Pietro, 294

Metzinger, Jean, 158
Meyer, Leonard, 303–4
Michelangelo Buonarroti, 241
Mies, Paul, 21–2
Mildred Pierce, 205
Miller, Kiri, 96
mimesis, 19, 23, 103, 127, 129, 135, 152, 158, 295–8
mise en abyme, 228–9, 232, 234, 236
Mitchell, Timothy, 250
Molière, 231
Monelle, Raymond, 207–9
Monet, Claude, 130, 152
Monk, Meredith, 270–1
Monty Python, 83
Moore, Thomas, 108
Mordvinov, Arkady, 56–8
Moreau, Gustave, 152
Morgan, Robert P., 301–2
Morris, Mark, 272, 275
Moskvin, Ivan, 57
Motown, 275
Moymoy Palaboy, 90–1, 95
Mozart, Wolfgang Amadeus, 16, 19, 37, 208, 242, 272, 276, 289–94, 299
   Don Giovanni, 229
   Il Re Pastore, 294
   Piano Sonata in F major, K. 533, 19
   Schauspieldirektor, Der, 229
   Symphony No. 38, 'Prague', 291, 294
   Symphony No. 40 in G minor, 289–90, 299
   Symphony No. 41 in C major, K. 551, 'Jupiter', 208
   viola quintets, 291
   Zauberflöte, Die, 275
Müllner, Adolph, 111
Muppets, The, 88–9, 91, 94–5
Muradeli, Vano, 57
'Music Fays, The', 110, 115
Mussorgsky, Modest, 81, 84
   Pictures at an Exhibition, 81, 84
Myaskovsky, Nikolai, 48–51, 54, 57
   String Quartet No. 9, 54
   Symphony No. 12, 49–51
   Symphony No. 22, 57
   Symphony No. 24, 57
Myers, Mike, 84

Nägeli, Hans Georg, 251
nationalism, 297–8
Nazi Party, 56
Nestyev, Izrail, 55, 60
Nicholson, Jack, 203

Nietzsche, Friedrich, 110, 112
Nijinsky, Vaslav, 280
Noh, 271
notation, 104, 225–7, 259
Nussbaum, Charles O., 303–4

Opera and Drama, 168
Orff, Carl, 276
Orientalism, 146, 249, 253–5, 267–83
Orlov, Genrich, 52
Orpheus, 104, 107, 117–18, 122–3
Ostretsov, Alexander, 50

painting, 56, 93, 104, 114, 117, 127–33, 135, 157, 295
Parakilas, James, 16, 22
Pater, Walter, 288–9
Paul III, 241
Peacocke, Christopher, 179
performance, 38, 65–71, 73–5, 81–3, 93, 104–5, 140, 144–5, 156, 158, 194, 225, 231–2, 256, 267–8, 273, 275–6, 279–81, 295
Peters, Kathrin, 88, 92
Philip II, 241
piano, 37
Picasso, Pablo, 129, 135–6, 158
Pokrovsky, Mikhail, 49
Pople, Anthony, 287
Popov, Gavriil, 50, 57
Porter, Cole, 64
portraiture, 127–41
Pottier, Eugène, 298
Powers, Harold S., 208
presence, 224
Prior, Nick, 94
programme, 19–21, 26, 47–61, 117, 271
Prokofiev, Sergei, 54–5, 57, 59–60, 214
   Alexander Nevsky, 54
   Peter and the Wolf, 214
   Piano Sonata No. 6, 55
   Piano Sonata No. 7, 55
   Piano Sonata No. 8, 55
   Symphony No. 5, 57
Puccini, Giacomo
   Madama Butterfly, 270, 282
   Turandot, 270, 275, 285

Queen, 79–83, 85–6, 90–1
   'Bohemian Rhapsody', 79–97
Quinault, Philippe, 229

Racy, A.J., 251
Raff, Joachim, 19

Rancière, Jacques, 44
Raphael, 116, 161
Ratner, Leonard, 301–2
Ravel, Maurice, 81, 84
Red Detachment of Women, The, 275
Redon, Odilon, 152
Reform Act of 1832, 34
Reich, Steve, 129, 134, 136, 138–9
   'It's gonna rain', 134, 138
   'Piano Phase', 138
   'Violin Phase', 134, 138
Rembrandt van Rijn, 135
rhetoric, 208, 220
Richards, I.A., 176
Richter, Svyatoslav, 54
Rihm, Wolfgang, 270
Riley, Dennis, 300
Riley, Terry, 129, 134, 136, 138–9
   'In C', 134, 138
Rilke, Rainer Maria, 228
Rimbaud, Arthur, 147, 157
Rink, John, 23
Rizhkin, Iosif, 50
Rock, Mick, 79
Rocky Horror Picture Show, The, 285
Rodgers, Richard, 64, 73
Rodin, Auguste, 152
Roland-Manuel, Alexis, 158
Ross, Herbert, 71
Rousseau, Jean-Jacques, 295
Ruggles, Carl, 305–6
   Sun Treader, 306
Ruhlmann, Franz, 162
Rukeyser, Muriel, 279
Russian Association of Proletarian
   Musicians, 48–9

Said, Edward, 249–50, 253, 255
Saint Subber, Arnold, 71
Saint-Point, Valentine de, 145, 154–60
Saint-Saëns, Camille, 277–8
   Samson et Dalila, 270, 278
Sanders, George, 212
Sarup, Madan, 128
Satie, Erik, 158
Saussure, Ferdinand de, 167
Savinio, Alberto, 158
Schenker, Heinrich, 302
Schlegel, Dorothea von, 111
Schlegel, Friedrich, 75
Schopenhauer, Arthur, 104, 184, 195, 197–200, 224
Schubart, Christian Friedrich Daniel, 290

Schubert, Franz, 16
Schubert, Giselher, 230
Schuld, Die, 111
Schumann, Robert, 16, 18, 21, 23, 25–6, 103, 118–23, 127, 290–1
   Dichterliebe, 23
   Fantasy, Op. 17, 103, 118–23
   Frauenliebe und Leben, 23
Scriabin, Alexander, 304
Scruton, Roger, 217
Seier, Andrea, 88, 92
Seigel, Jerrold, 128
self-portraiture, 134–9, 141
Sellars, Peter, 270–83
semantics, 205, 207, 209
semiotics, 167, 287
Sennett, Richard, 34
Serra, Richard, 130
Sessions, Roger, 299–300, 302, 306
Shaw, George Bernard, 13–14, 18, 26
Shawn, Ted, 280
Sheng, Bright, 270
Shneyerson, Grigory, 54
Shostakovich, Dmitri, 47, 50–2, 55–7, 59–61, 292
   Piano Trio No. 2, 56–7
   String Quartet No. 2, 56–7
   String Quartet No. 8, 60–1
   Symphony No. 2, 50
   Symphony No. 3, 50
   Symphony No. 5, 51–2
   Symphony No. 7, 'Leningrad', 47, 55–7, 59
   Symphony No. 8, 57–9
   Symphony No. 9, 58
Siedentopf, Henning, 137
Simonov, Konstantin, 55
Sinyavsky, Andrey, 60
Smith, John Thomas, 41
Socialist Realism, 47, 50, 55–6, 272
Sollberger, Harvey, 305
Sondheim, Stephen, 66–7
Sontag, Susan, 288–9
Spaeth, Sigmund, 290
Spheeris, Penelope, 79, 87
St Cecilia, 104, 107, 116–17
St Denis, Ruth, 145, 149, 280
Stalin Prize, 54–7
Star is Born, A, 67–8, 71
Star Trek, 89–90
Star Wars, 89, 92, 96, 220
Stein, Gertrude, 139
Steiner, George, 224
Stoker, Bram, 115

Stowe, Harriet Beecher, 116
Strangelove, Michael, 88, 92
Strauss, Richard, 231, 242, 276
   Ariadne auf Naxos, 231
   Capriccio, 229
Stravinsky, Igor, 55, 275–6, 280, 287, 302, 306
   Piano-Rag-Music, 55
   Rite of Spring, The, 275, 280
Strecker, Ludwig, 228
Streisand, Barbra, 66, 73–5
Sullivan, Arthur. *See* Gilbert and Sullivan
Sumac, Yma, 279
Sutherland, Joan, 115
Sutherland, Kev F., 88
Swayne, Steve, 66–7
Syberberg, Hans Jürgen, 182
synaesthesia, 138, 147, 149–50

Tan Dun, 270–1
   Peony Pavilion, The, 271
Taruskin, Richard, 52, 277–8
Taxi Driver, 221
Taylor, Roger, 80–1
Thalberg, Sigismund, 45
Thomas, Michael Tilson, 305–6
Thomson, Virgil, 127–8, 139–41
   'Buffie Johnson: Drawing Virgil Thomson in Charcoal', 139–41
   Nineteen Portraits for Piano, 139
Tiepolo, Giambattista, 117
Tinctoris, Johannes, 13
Titian, 114
Tobler, Titus, 252–4
Tolstoy, Alexei, 51–2
topics, 47–8, 206–10, 212, 217, 287, 291–2, 299
topoi. *See* topics
Totah, Khalil, 257–63
turntablism, 227

Uncle Tom's Cabin, 115–16
Urban VIII, 241

Van Gogh, Vincent, 157
Varèse, Edgard, 304–6
   Intégrales, 305
Vaughan Williams, Ralph, 33
Velázquez, Diego, 135
ventriloquism, 107, 294
Verdi, Giuseppe, 111–12, 268, 280
   Aida, 280, 285

Nabucco, 112
Traviata, La, 268
Trovatore, Il, 280
Villoteau, Guillaume André, 251
Virgil, 118, 122

Wagner, Cosima, 176, 180, 192, 194–5, 197–8
Wagner, Richard, 18, 110–14, 116, 123, 151, 168–79, 182–200, 203, 210–11, 220, 276, 291, 297, 304, 306
   fliegende Holländer, Der, 112
   Götterdämmerung, 177
   Lohengrin, 110–11, 197
   Meistersinger, Die, 114, 181
   Parsifal, 176, 182, 185–200, 222
   Rheingold, Das, 177, 211, 274
   Siegfried, 169–71, 180
   Tannhäuser, 199, 211
   Tristan und Isolde, 52, 113–14, 116, 123, 168–79, 195–200, 300
   Wieland der Schmied, 112–13
Wasilewska, Wanda, 57
Wayne's World, 79–80, 84–7, 89–90, 95
Weber, Carl Maria von, 297
   Freischütz, Der, 297
Weber, William, 19
Weill, Kurt, 239
Weir, Judith, 270
'Weird Al' Yankovic, 89
Welin, Karl-Erik, 137
Wesendonck, Mathilde, 171, 196, 198–9
Wieck, Clara, 32, 118
Wilde, Oscar, 157
Wilder, Alec, 65, 70
Williams, John, 214, 220
Wills, William Gorman, 115
Wizard of Oz, The, 64–5
Wolzogen, Hans von, 203
Wuorinen, Charles, 305

Youmans, Vincent, 65
Young, Robert C., 249–50
YouTube, 87–8, 90–6

Zbikowski, Lawrence, 300
Zhdanov, Andrei, 58
Ziadeh, Nicola, 263–4
Ziporyn, Evan, 270
Zuccalmaglio, Anton Wilhelm von, 21

CPSIA information can be obtained at www.ICGtesting.com
Printed in the USA
LVOW02*0606180614

390404LV00003B/3/P

9 781107 021570